The game,
As she was writ
funny

The Lost Art of Baseball Humor (1860-1900)

In 19th Century Baseball Writing:
The Golden Era
An Annotated Anthology of
wickedly witty baseball journalism

"Sockdolagers, Lallycoolers, and Fanning the Redolent Air"

Vintage baseball cartoon art, too!

Gerard S. Petrone

Pocol Press
Clifton, VA

POCOL PRESS
Published in the United States of America
by Pocol Press
6023 Pocol Drive
Clifton, VA 20124
www.pocolpress.com

© 2018 by Gerard S. Petrone

All rights reserved. No part of this book may be reproduced in any form whatsoever without the express written consent of Pocol Press. Exceptions are made for brief quotations for criticism and reviews.

Publisher's Cataloguing-in-Publication
Names: Petrone, Gerard S., author.
Title: The Lost art of baseball humor (1860-1900) / Gerard S. Petrone.
Description: Includes bibliographical references. | Clifton, VA: Pocol Press, 2018.
Identifiers: ISBN 978-1-929763-81-8 | LCCN 2018943530
Subjects: LCSH Baseball stories. | Humor. | Baseball--United States--Anecdotes. | Baseball--United States--Humor. | Baseball--United States--History. | BISAC SPORTS & RECREATION / Baseball / Essays & Writings | HUMOR / Topic / Sports
Classification: LCC GV873 .P48 2018 | DDC 796.357688--dc23

Library of Congress Control Number: 2018943530

TABLE OF CONTENTS

1	Opening Pitch	1
2	The Baseball Writer is Born	3
3	The Rise of Baseball Slang	12
4	Purveyors of Wit	27
5	Humor in Winning	49
6	Humor in Losing	69
7	Humor in Errors	130
8	Humor in Bad Weather	140
9	Humor in Baseball Maidens	169
10	Humor in Coaching	177
11	Humor in Pitching	193
12	Game Account Formats	228
13	Humor in Off-the-Wall Writing	258
14	Humor in Being Hit by a Pitch	280
15	Humor in Baseball Etiquette	285
16	Humor in Umpires	289
17	Humor in Uniforms	317
18	Humor in Fans	327
19	Humor in Making a Hit	357
20	Humor in a Baseball Writer's "Confession"	377
21	Recap	379

Dedication

I dedicate this book to the memory of my
late brother, Ed, erstwhile American Legion pitcher
and co-founder of corkball,
—and—
lifelong friend and personal baseball muse, Dave Hendry.

Disclaimer

This book consists of a compendium of humorous baseball writing, as it was published in pre-1900 newspapers. As the bulk consists of quoted material, please note the following:

1. Notations in parentheses following a word or phrase clarify its meaning. The same goes for specific baseball personages mentioned in quotations. Many of the latter were well-known in their day, be it player, umpire, manager, team owner or whatever. Similarly, outmoded words or phrases are starred for definition.

2. To aid in comprehension, reproduced copy has been edited to correct spelling errors, misprints, omission of punctuation and other grammatical oversights. Some writers, for example, were notoriously stingy with commas, which are inserted to prevent confusion in reading long sentences. Hyphens likewise suffered the same fate, which, too, has been emended.

3. The Latin notation, *sic*, appears from time to time to denote an odd or erroneous word that has been quoted verbatim.

4. The baseball cartoons ornamenting the text are original and true to the era. Most were the handiwork of amateur artists, presumably on newspaper staffs; others, such as those created by the aforementioned Robert Edgren, developed into a popular graphic art form that embellished sports pages in major newspapers well into the Twentieth Century.

5. Lastly, an apology: Mischievous gremlins messed with a few newspaper sources, which explains the annotation: "Source misplaced." Sorry; stuff happens.

1. Opening Pitch

Reader, kindly sample the literary flavor of these passages lifted from professional baseball game accounts of long ago:

Ganzel soaked a roaster to Doyle, who had Ganzel out like a bird, and then threw to Murphy, doubling Nash in a jiffy. The play was a real rainbow act.

Langford came up with a wild, ravenous look in his eyes. But wild, ravenous looks don't amount to shucks. I never saw a wild, ravenous look make a hit in my life.

Shugart variously fumbled, muffed or threw away as luncheon for the dickey birds five golden opportunities that the song writers say will never come again.

A tad over-the-top, you say? Of course, but the words surely forced a smile, maybe even a snicker. Now then, sink your teeth into these tasty morsels:

In two innings it was a gone game. The bright sunshine had become a hollow mockery of blasted hopes, and the gentle zephyrs, which ever and anon floated across the field, bore to the ears of the affrighted umpire curses loud and deep. But it wasn't the umpire, nor the absence of mascots, for Manager Phillips had a full supply of the article on hand, nor even the superior playing of the big, ugly, black Giants. It was the listless playing of the home club more than anything else that seemed responsible for the defeat.

In the soft enchantment of eventide, when the rose-leaf clouds were burning at the zenith, the west was filled with crimson banners, and the darkening shadows were creeping over the purple world, the Omahas scraped the dust off their backs with an old piece of weatherboarding, and slowly and solemnly wended their way up Charles, and out across Seventeenth street, down into Missouri's broad bottoms to mourn and lament the evils of the day.

The final appearance of the Minneapolitans was characterized by Letcher, waving his bat ever and anon at a streak of light as it passed over the home plate, until eventually the umpire ordered him to go away, and then the visitors packed their bats and left town.

Wacky, but funny—right?

Now, when do you think such literary burlesque appeared in print? Thirty, forty years ago? Wrong; but here's a hint: Try your great-grandfather when he was in knickers, around 1890. Now you're in the ballpark.

The point of the above illustrations are this: Modern-day baseball writing lacks humor. Sure, you <u>hear</u> plenty on cable television's sports talk shows or on game broadcasts, but you rarely <u>read</u> it in game reports.

As proof, open tomorrow's newspaper/website, turn to the sports page and scan the account of the game your team played yesterday. Does it ever make you chuckle, even in defeat? Does it hit you with catchy lines, as: "*Gordon romped down to second like a singed cat*" or "*Arrieta had a drop of a professional lyncher*"? Or, better yet, "*Joe West escaped from the New York Asylum for the Blind and became an umpire,*" or "*Errors are as common to Villar as pig tracks in an Arkansas swamp.*"

Don't you wish.

2. The Baseball Writer is Born

Up in the press stand sits the baseball writer; at his side a telegraph operator, sending play after play to the newspaper office, and, towards the last, snapping off the details fast as lightning. As the last play is called, the forms are closed, the paper flies to press, and is cascaded into the street with a speed that is bewildering for fair. Naturally, each sheet tries to beat his rivals in the open air, and the writer who can send a play the soonest, aided by a fast telegrapher, is the boy who is believed by his managing editor.
[El Paso Herald, April 2, 1913]

They were there at the very dawn of baseball—the writers. They haunted ball grounds customarily utilized by amateur clubs, such as the Boston Common; the Fashion Course, Long Island; the posher accommodations of the Union and Capitoline grounds, in Brooklyn; and, frankly, any urban lot or rural field relatively large, level and obstacle-free enough to accommodate a game of ball. There they recorded history.

One playing ground in particular, favored by clubs in the greater New York City area, was the Elysian Fields, of Hoboken, New Jersey, a cricket ground and public park cleared from surrounding woodlands. It was there, one day in 1856, that Henry Chadwick, sports reporter of the *New York Times,* stopped to watch a game of baseball between the Eagles and Gothams, amateur clubs of New York City. He later remarked:

"The game was being sharply played on both sides, and I watched it with deeper interest that any previous ball match between clubs I had seen. It was not long before I was struck with the idea that base ball was just the game for a national sport for Americans."
[Chadwick's "Game of Base Ball," 1868]

Prophetic words, indeed. Baseball, within a few years, would be declared America's national pastime.

The impact of the Civil War, from 1861 to 1865, slowed its growth as volunteers thinned the ranks of baseball clubs. Soon after war's end, however, the regional variations of baseball, such as "the Massachusetts game," "the New York game," "two-old-cat," "barn ball," etc., morphed into a unified form that now defines the sport. Amateur ball clubs sprang into existence, matches were scheduled (complete with playing rules), and the popularity of the sport quickly spread from the big cities to rural communities in many parts of the country.

Baseball officially became professional in 1869 with the first openly-salaried team, the Cincinnati Red Stockings. The National League was established in 1876, followed in 1881 by the American Association, the pair constituting what would be eventually called "the major leagues." The sport narrowly escaped demise due to rampant, unrestrained betting on games and particularly the infamous "Louisville Four" scandal of 1877, when players were caught conspiring with gamblers to throw games.

Driving the fervor of baseball was the first generation of writers, who achieved this title almost by default. General sports writers originally, they were assigned by editors to cover this new passion in outdoor sports, where men played primarily for recreation and bragging rights. However, as baseball grew in popularity, many of them became specialized in this area, acquiring the coveted job title of "baseball writer."

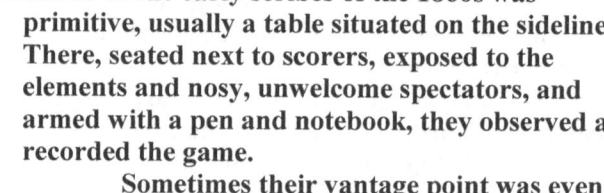

The work station of the early scribes of the 1860s was primitive, usually a table situated on the sideline. There, seated next to scorers, exposed to the elements and nosy, unwelcome spectators, and armed with a pen and notebook, they observed and recorded the game.

Sometimes their vantage point was even more spartan—a reporter, covering a match in Detroit, in 1868, for instance, facetiously described his stand as "lofty," being a broad wooden platform about half way up a large tree situated behind the catcher!

Working conditions for writers were slow to improve, as those in Cincinnati would loudly complain in 1876:

The Cincinnati Enquirer says they have erected a wire screen before the reporters' stand on the Indianapolis base ball ground for the purpose of keeping foul balls from the reporters' noses, and foul expressions from their lips...In St. Louis, the management furnishes the reporters with lemonade and lunch. Here in Cincinnati the reporters have no lemonade, no lunch, no screens, no nothing.
[Brooklyn Eagle, August 15, 1876]

By the 1880s, writers were finally provided with small but permanent and private quarters at the ball park, up high and usually on the roof: the press box. Space was often at a premium, however, and they had to rub elbows with colleagues (both in- and out-of-town), official scorers, visitors (legitimate and otherwise) and the indispensable telegraph operators with their crews.

The cramped compartment then resembled a sardine tin, as described in this comment of 1888:

> *The scene in the recently enlarged reporters' box at the Recreation park grounds (Pittsburgh) yesterday was an animated one. Facing the wall on a high shelf were some five or six telegraphic instruments which were reporting the incidents of the game almost simultaneously with their occurrence in as many distant cities.*
>
> *Then there were the attendant operators, probably half a dozen linemen, and last but not least Manager Clark, of the Western Union. The 20-odd observers were wedged in pretty closely, yet the utmost good humor prevailed. At times 40 feet commenced a lively tattoo on the floor, which to the people in the grand stand below must have resembled distant thunder.* [Pittsburgh Press, April 21, 1888]

Drumming the National Pastime

Baseball writing expanded in the 1890s with the formation of full-time sports staffs on big-city newspapers. Editors hired skilled reporters who understood and cared about the game and their duties at the ball park followed a familiar routine. After finalizing the game writeup, they either dispatched it to the newspaper office by messenger, or telegraphed it, where it was transcribed into press-ready copy for late-night or morning editions.

The sport was also covered by professional writers-for-hire called "correspondents," who could be found in most cities fielding a professional ball club. Since the 1860s, newspapers, sporting magazines and related periodicals utilized their services to provide the latest dope on baseball teams, matches and other related matters. In particular, the *New York Clipper,* a weekly founded in 1853 and devoted to outdoor sports and the theater, relied solely upon this source to report the ongoing glut of amateur games played across the eastern and southern United States and, later, major league action as well. By 1878, the *Boston Herald,* with a circulation exceeding 90,000, was devoting two columns daily to the national game.

Correspondents also sold their copy to newspapers to allow local readers to keep current with the latest scoop on their respective hometown teams. The *Baltimore American*, in the early 1880s, for example, devoted nearly a full page of baseball gossip in their Sunday editions from correspondents in Chicago, Philadelphia, Louisville, New York, St. Louis, and Cincinnati. Likewise, Harry Palmer, of Chicago, in

1888, was one of the first to write a nationally syndicated column that circulated in many smaller-city newspapers.

The dissemination of news by the newspaper industry, was, in turn, indispensably reliant upon telegraphy for the transmission of news matter to the press. Since 1860, long-distance communication among amateur clubs, such as scheduling matches, forwarding travel itineraries and other business matters—even game scores—was handled routinely through telegrams, and the combined efforts of the two mass media services fueled the rage for the sport.

An historic event occurred in 1865 when Western Union leased wires linking ball parks to newspaper offices. This allowed telegraphers at out-of-town ball grounds to flash reports of a game to sports desks at speed approaching that of light.

Seizing a golden opportunity, enterprising businesses frequented by ball-crazy loungers also tapped into this convenience by 1869, as noted:

The interest taken in the games of the "Red Stockings" in Porkopolis (Cincinnati) has been prodigious. At several hotels, cigar stores and newspaper offices, arrangements were made to have the games reported by telegraph by innings, and each afternoon dense crowds would assemble and wait patiently for the news. On the day of the match with the Athletics, the crowd around the Gibson House blocked up the street and looked like a political gathering.
[New York Clipper, July 3, 1869]

The adaptability of telegraphy to baseball did not end here. Later, all major league ball grounds were interconnected with a common wire, allowing the latest scores of all games to be transmitted league-wide, where they were chalked up by hand on an outfield blackboard.

As a convenience to hometown fans, many major daily newspapers installed bulletin boards on the exterior of their buildings as early as the mid-1860s.

On November 7, 1865, for example, the *Brooklyn Eagle* announced:

The readers of the Eagle were apprised last evening of the game (Atlantic vs. Athletic), as far as it had progressed up to time of going to press, and our bulletin board proclaimed the result, at conclusion. The game in detail is given below.

By 1887, outdoor bulletin boards of big-city dailies, such as New York City's *Sun*, *Tribune*, and *World*, for instance, played to immense audiences. On important game days, such as the Temple Cup series between St. Louis and New York in 1888, thousands of fans thronged their buildings, so thickly that it brought street and sidewalk traffic to a halt.

Improvements quickly followed. Some boards featured simulated diamonds where color-coded wooden pegs representing players were moved from base to base, as well as the posting of inning-by-inning scores of other league games.

In 1889, the bulletin board concept was taken indoors by an enterprising businessman in Boston, where a manually-operated production was set up on the stage of the Boston Music Hall.

Ball Games by Proxy

> CONVENTION HALL.
> **Baseball by Electricity.**
> The Compton Electric System.
> TO-DAY at 4:30 P. M.,
> WASHINGTON VS. CHICAGO.
> Admission, 10c and 25c.

The highest level of mechanization was reached in 1894, when the indoor model of game re-enactment became electrically powered. Advertised as "Baseball by Electricity," each production differed in its details according to the patented scheme that governed its operation; the Compton Electrical System, patented in 1890, was the most widely used.

These shows, intricate and surprisingly realistic, variously featured announcers, wooden puppets dressed as players, sound effects (bells and gongs), music, flashing colored lights and other assorted frills. Venues were typically rented opera houses, music halls, auditoriums and theaters in cities as New York, Boston, Washington, D. C., Indianapolis, and Baltimore. Admission for adults was a quarter; kids forked over a dime.

Basic to all productions was a special telegraphic wire connecting a distant ball park to the site. Every pitch, every play, was faithfully reproduced to the delight of the patrons, who experienced the suspense and emotional highs and lows of a real game.

So, what was it like to attend one of these dog-and-pony extravaganzas? Let's take a look:

Kernan's Theater, Washington, D. C., 1894:

> *A new feature in the amusement line was introduced yesterday at Kernan's theater. The patrons of that resort and a great many baseball enthusiasts were eye and ear witnesses of every detail of the two ball games*

played between the Washington and St. Louis teams in Sportsman's Park, St. Louis, Mo., without the trouble, expense, and loss of time necessary to go there.

The games were played upon the stage of the theater, and to those conversant with baseball, every movement was as plainly visible as though they had been present in Sportsman's Park. That the games were thoroughly enjoyed by the audience in the theater was attested to by the frequent outbursts of applause when a good play would be made or when the Senators scored a point.

...The enterprising management of Kernan's had direct wires from the park at St. Louis to a telegraphic instrument on the stage, at which an expert operator sat, taking a full description of the game from another operator at St. Louis, beside whom stood a baseball expert, giving a graphic description and all the details of the game.
[Washington (D. C.) Times, July 5, 1894]

Ford's Theater, Baltimore, 1895; this management offered a unique twist—puppets:

The game was reported by marionettes, and was at once indescribably funny and interesting. A miniature ball diamond about three feet square, represented for the time, the ball park in the City of Brotherly Love...The players of the two teams were represented by dummies about eight inches tall. The Birds were dressed in white, and the Quakers in red uniforms. The only thing absent from the game was the ball and the kicking against the umpire. Every move made on the ball field was reproduced by the marionettes, and done with a dash of fun that made the gallery saints hug themselves with delight, and so far forget themselves as to shout to McGraw to, "Slide, Mac, slide."
[Baltimore American, June 20, 1895]

Palmer's Theatre, New York City, 1895; their main gimmick was the ingenious use of lights:

The actors in the region of Thirtieth street and Broadway yesterday afternoon must have felt that their profession was slighted when they saw the crowds that poured into Palmer's Theatre, where a new automatic baseball scheme was shown for the first time. Before the doors opened at 4 o'clock, there was a throng on the sidewalk, and when the game was called in Washington at 4:30 and commenced here by electricity, there was not a vacant seat in the house.

The stage was set with a scene representing the interior of a baseball field. The diamond is laid out on a raised platform, and small dummy figures stand at the points occupied by the players. The plays are telegraphed directly from the grounds in the city where the teams are playing and called off from the wings.

Some of the figures are movable and run to the bases, but the progress of the game is indicated by an electric light which, passing from the hands of one player to another, shows the movement of the ball. When the pitcher has the ball, the light appears in his hand. Then it appears in the hands of the catcher, and, whether it is thrown to the bases or batted into the field, its position can be seen from the movement of the light. In the same way fouls are indicated, and when the player at the bat makes a first or second base hit, one of the figures runs around the diamond.
[The Sun (New York), July 31, 1895]

Another article details the show at Palmer's:

The stage is set out as a baseball field, with "diamond" and green baize turf, abounding in vampire traps, through which the players disappear when put out, instead of returning to the bench with more or less dust on their clothes and language on their lips. The path to the diamond from base to base is grooved for travel, and the ground covered by the catcher is also grooved in order that he may close in after "two strikes."

All the outs have their proper position in the field, and are represented by dummy marionettes, in the uniform of their side and between two and three feet high. Besides these and the men of the in team are seen on a bench waiting their turn; two coaches gesticulate wildly on right and left field, and back of the pitcher is an umpire who calls the game and waves his arms with professional energy. The sound of the dropping bat, which the batter at the home plate flings down as he makes for first base, arouses all the sporting instincts of the audience, who are thus brought into close touch with the game from the start.

The field is sloped gently upward, so that everything is in full view. Along the footlights runs a scoring-board, which gives the figures not only of the game in progress but of the other league contests. The difficulty of enabling the audience to follow the course of the ball is ingeniously solved. Each fielder, as well as the pitcher and the catcher, has a white incandescent lamp in his hand, which lights up only when he has the ball, so that one always sees and knows where the ball is. When it leaves the pitcher's hand, his white light goes out, and the white light is seen in the catcher's hand. If the catcher's hands are above his head, it is "one ball." If the light shows with his hands at his waist, it is a strike. If the batsman hits the ball foul, it is shown within the foul line by a green light at the spot. If the batsman gets a solid hit, the track of the ball across the sward is shown by a series of white lights flashing instantaneously one after the other across the baize. If the ball is a "fly," its course through the air is marked by a series of white lights strung from the flies. If the "fly" drops safely in the hands of a fielder, his white light at once shines out. If he fumbles, the light flickers, and if the ball drops, a red light at his feet indicates the error. In running to base, if the ball gets there first, the white light is seen and batsman drops out of sight through a trap; but if otherwise, the light goes out.

The actual movements seen on the field are supplemented by the work of an elocutionist, who repeats the messages coming directly from the original game and received by an ordinary sounder set. The lights are flashed and all the movements are indicated by means of a switching and controlling board, not three feet square, and, all told, fifty incandescent lamps are used.

[San Francisco Call, November 1, 1895]

Sporting Tickers

Baseball fans' obsession with the need for speed of ball scores was further advanced by telegraphy in 1896 through a novel means: sporting tickers.

These small, dome-shaped, glass-encased machines, familiar fixtures in stock brokerage houses, printed out game results on thin strips of paper, after the fashion of stock quotations. It was the brainchild of Charles A. O'Rourke, of the New York Press Association. The devices allowed the simultaneous, across-the-country announcement of the results of sporting events the moment they were available, be it ball games, horse races, prize fights, or boating regattas.

This specialized service proved extremely popular. Tickers soon found welcome homes in hotel and bank lobbies, newspaper offices and especially "pool rooms" (betting parlors). The iconic Wall Street symbols also added an elitist touch to those familiar establishments catering to the all-male, working-class clientele—saloons, billiard rooms, and cigar stores, whose proprietors considered the modest installation fee of $200 a prudent investment.

What of the Future?

To baseball fans of the 1890s, the technological achievements to date were staggering. One can only imagine their thoughts as they left, for instance, a "Baseball by Electricity" performance.

They knew one thing for certain: The most image-provoking prose in a newspaper could never match the reality of a ball game reproduced by the spectacle they had just witnessed. Many surely believed that the future did not hold hope for more such miracles. Who in their wildest imagination could have predicted, within a few decades, the coming of radio, then television, to serve and promote the national pastime?

3. The Rise of Baseball Slang

Humor first appeared in baseball journalism during the 1860-70 period through the medium of game accounts and in the form of slang, witty discourse, or a combination of the two. Its use, however, was hampered by conventions governing how games were initially reported in newspapers of the day.

Since most contests were not personally witnessed by writers, inning-by-inning dialogue was fashioned from telegraphic dispatches transmitted from faraway ball parks to the newspaper's sports desks, a setup demanding short descriptive phrases that carried the full story for the newspaper's evening editions.

In this manner was born the "baseball sentence," a journalistic device that lasted well into the 1870s. Reporters simply slapped a bit of literary dressing on the bare-boned, one-line statements and assembled them into a finished piece. Being expressed in leaden, cookie-cutter language, though, game reports made for understandably bland, tedious reading; most accounts, in fact, seemed to flow from a single pen.

"Sliding home."

See for yourself:

> Pearce made his first on safe hit to right-field. Smith caught out by Sensenderfer. Pearce made second on passed ball. Start out on fly by Bechtel in left field. Chapman made his first on safe hit to right field, sending Pearce home. Ferguson out on fly by Radcliffe.
> [Evening Telegraph (Philadelphia), May 30, 1870]

Constant repetition was the bugbear, lest baseball fiends lapse into a trance. Noticeably missing, however, was passion, giving the impression that a troupe of robots had performed in front of a mute, paralytic audience. These obstacles posed major challenges for writers itching to break free of the stifling hackwork. They didn't have long to wait. Salvation in a most unusual form came to infuse life into baseball journalism—slang.

Language of the Ball Park

The basic terminology laid out in the official rules of baseball play as early as the 1850s gave rise over time to an informal language of words and phrases adopted by those who played or watched the game; this defines "baseball slang." No other sport in America ever amassed the amount of technical and non-technical terminology as exists in the national pastime, and its incorporation into baseball writing constituted the first appearance of humor in this specialized field of journalism.

Baseball slang proved to be both bane and boon to the sport, denounced by language purists as needless, unintelligible gibberish, but embraced by many writers as a new and refreshing means of expression as well as diehard cranks who were drawn to its exclusivity and mystery.

No ground rules existed when it came to creating ball park slang. Anything and everything connected with the sport, both on and off the field, were subject to a new name, especially if it was catchy. As time passed and the sport grew in popularity, the dialect of the ball park expanded with each passing season, fed by an endless spate of newly-coined words and expressions arising from the three basic sources: players, fans, and journalists.

Idle comments or expressions uttered by players on the field, for example, were echoed by occupants of the stands and worked into everyday baseball discussions. Similarly, a funny remark made by a fan could end up the same way. Reporters also played key roles as inventors and chroniclers. They either made up slang of their own or repeated in their columns the current *patois de jour* that had reached their ears, transforming what originally was a spoken language into a written one as well.

Kahoe Stole Home.

Baseball slang quickly caught the fancy of writers. Its unconventional, yet highly entertaining style proved novel and novelty in this case bred an avid following. It wasn't Shakespeare, cranks knew, but it was sure fun to read.

How Slang was Writ

Slang entered baseball literature in the 1860s and was as scarce as triple plays, dropped here and there by reporters who had yet to recognize its magic. Scanning game reports during this decade, for instance, reveals such rare finds as:

Wright led with a corker to the left field; the Mutuals were now obliged to accept a duck egg from their opponents; Hurley went to second on a hot 'un through Goldie's fists; Chapman twirled the willow as saucily as possible; Wright sent a bee-liner to Meagher in left field; Flanly mowed the timothy near third base.

    A few snippets of slang, designed to color the narrative, were unobtrusively worked into the main text by some writers, as evidenced below in 1867. Aware, however, that they were straying from orthodox talk, they highlighted the word or phrase with parentheses, a habit, helpful to modern-day researchers, that ran into the 1890s:

    It was exciting when Ferguson took the bat. By a fine hit to right field he sent "all hands round," he "nestling" on the third. McDonald brought Ferguson home, gaining his second on an overthrown ball from Martin to Goldie. Kenny, by a clear hit over the railroad track, made his first home run for the Atlantics.
[New York Clipper, August 10, 1867]

    By the 1870s, concomitant with the explosive surge of interest in the national pastime, game accounts grew in length and detail, and, with it, diamond jargon, such as:

    Berthrong struck a daisy-cutter to left; Devlin made a pretty pick-up of Clapp's grass-mower; the little fly was pocketed by Dehlman; Cummings couldn't hit Leary and took a squat on the bench; Gaffney tallied on Mason's screamer over Smiley's head; he welted the atmosphere three times; Chicago tendered them the whitewash bucket.

    Writers expended enormous amounts of creative energy, for instance, in describing the most fundamental event in a ball game: striking the ball. In fulfilling this simple need, no action verb known to English-speaking peoples was overlooked.
    Take the example: "Jones flied out to Smith." Normally, this concise, but coma-inducing sentence ended up on an 1860s sports page in an untouched or slightly altered form. However, in the hands of an inventive writer fluent in slang, it was instantly riffed into one of rare beauty, such as: "Smith raced across the left pasture like a hunted deer and hauled in Jones's cloud-kisser with his sticky maulers."
    To illustrate additionally, a take-your-pick schematic of sentence parts, extracted from game accounts of long ago, shows how the system worked:

Van Haltren wielded the ash and:

banged, basted, biffed, boomed, bowled, carolled, chipped, chopped, clipped, coaxed, corked, cracked, dribbled, drove, hammered, hoopsnaked, hustled, jabbed, kangarooed, laced, lambasted, lammed, larruped, lashed, lathered, nailed, pasted, pelted, peppered, pinged, planked, planted, plunked, poked, pounded, pummeled, punched, pushed, rapped, rattled, riffed, ripped, sandbagged, sandwiched, scooped, scratched, scorched, shied, shot, shoveled, shuffled, slambanged, slammed, slapped, slashed, smashed, smote, snaked, sneakabooed, soaked, socked, spanked, stung, swatted, swiped, thumped, tomahawked, twisted, welted, whacked, whanged, whangdoodled, whipped, whisked, whizzed...

a/an:

blazing, corking, cracking, crooked, incandescent, jumping, lamb-like, lazy, leaping, lightning, jumping, rakish, rattling, red-hot, saucy, scorching, shin-breaking, slab-sided, slashing, sozzling, stinging, ugly, vicious, wicked...

banger, beaut, beauty, bingo, blazer, blisterer, bounder, clipper, cloud-trimmer, cooler, cracker, crackerjack, dandy, dart of lightning, dewdrop, dust-disturber, fire-eater, grass-scorcher, honey-cooler, hummer, hurricane, Jim Dandy, man-eater, Oklahoma fly, paralyzer, peach, popper, ripper, sailer, scorcher, screecher, sky-scraper, sod-pounder, star-finder, steeplechaser, stem-winder, stinger, twister...

over the left field fence, to the right field wall, into the carriages parked in center field.

See? Easy.
The life expectancy of colloquial terms was unpredictable. Some were interred early, such as those choice, but long-forgotten equivalents of today's "hard-hit ball": "lallycooler," "sozzler," "whangdoodle" and "sockdolager." Some, born during the 1870s, were blessed with eternal life and still find use today. Remember that, readers, the next time you hear "skyscraper," "in the box," "southpaw," "whitewash," or "struck out."
This article of 1894 pretty much summarized the basics of slang reporting, poking fun at it at the same time:

The first man who came to bat did not make a base hit. He "walloped out a single." The next did not do anything so tame and antique as to send a fly to center field or fly out. He got real demonic and "fungoed to center." The center fielder wasn't a bit terrified either, for he "hugged the musty fly." What the innocent lover of baseball had taken for a three-base hit was nothing of the kind. Such conventional things are not allowed on the grounds. It was worse than crying twins. It was a "whistling triplet."

   A fielder did not catch a high fly. He "connected with a balloon fly," *and the young man who was rash enough to follow up this phenomenon was not put out at first base. He arranged his own funeral and* "died an easy death at first." *Catching has gone out of fashion entirely. When a player catches a ball, he is fined by the umpire for insulting the intelligence of the spectators. He* "clasps a high one," *or* "hauls in a fly," *or* "pulls a throw down."
   It seems that at this game an active player had "wings on his heels" and "tabasco sauce in his arms." *Yet he was perfectly tame and tractable when not* "larruping singles," *or* "lacing an easy one," *or* "slashing out a peach." *There was a nice-appearing young man on one of the teams who did not look as if he would harm a fly, but he was really a fiend incarnate for he deliberately and in cold blood* "unchained a cyclone with his willow and tore out the ground back of center field."
   One player seemed to jog along to first when given a base on balls. But the baseball Shakespeare denies this malicious charge. He says that he "ambled to the bag." *This same man did not steal second base. He* "pilfered" *it. Altogether he was a pretty disreputable fellow, for he also* "robbed the visitors of third." *His career of crime was checked, however, for when he tried to* "embezzle the plate," *he was* "nailed," *though to what is not on record.*
   The players all had peculiar gaits. Some of them galloped, others romped. cantered, scampered, some "piked it to second," *or* "trotted a heat." *One man even got so mixed-up in his seasons that he* "tobogganed to third." *But not a soul of them ever walked or ran. One man, evidently jealous of the forms of locomotion,* "kangarooed to second."
   A batsman can do lots of things that the unsophisticated person would never dream of. On this day one man, who had three strikes called on him, "cut the plate with three called balls." *Another* "flied softly," *and* "Denny froze it sweetly." *So in spite of the stabbing and cutting and slashing, there is sometimes rural gentleness. A man who was excited sent a* "sizzling grounder rattling through the legs" *of somebody, and another, who was politeness itself,* "fanned the warm air." *One player* "sent a biffer past second," *and a rival* "popped a mushy one abaft first." *Nothing happened, though, the lee scuppers. Speaking of batsmen none of them used a bat. These men* "wielded the ash and willow handles" *and* "toyed with the sphere."
   Players never get put out in these days. The methods of their disposal vary. Some are put to sleep, some are allowed to languish in solitude and some are tortured to death...one man "groped vainly for the elusive" *and* "played dead on the bench." *One was* "coppered at first," *and another was* "cinched at the plate." *Still another* "expired in anguish" *at first and an unoffending but popular youth was* "smothered to death at second."
[New York Tribune, reprinted in the Wichita Daily Eagle, July 20, 1894]

To enjoy the best examples of slang, you need only turn to one of its most prolific and accomplished composers, and as-yet-identified writer for the (New York) *Evening World.* His creative mind was a bottomless pit of new terminology, which was churned out to jazz up the paper's evening baseball editions from 1888 to 1894. Samples of his eye-opening art appear forthwith:

August 14, 1891

First inning.—The sometimes petted darlings of Gotham went to the bat first, as usual, and Whistler allowed the famous Tony, of Porkville, to fool him into three strikes and out.

Tiernan joined Whistler on the New York bench a few minutes later, for all he could do was to chase a rippler without weights to McPhee, who kiboshed it and the batter at first.

Richardson punched the pellet on the nose and nearly cut a tendon out of Mullane's arm when the latter tried to stop it. McPhee managed to jump like a bull frog a few feet skyward and hug the ball close to his chest, but Danny was safe at Reilly's base.

O'Rourke lost sight of the fact that the very animated human splinter, Pete Browning, was in left field, but Pete let 'em all know he was on deck as he sailed like a sculpin on land after James' ricocheting fly. He got it. No runs.

A rank error on Bassett's part, letting McPhee's bouncer cuddle through his spindles into left field, put Mac on first in elegantly easy shape. Arlie "Circus" Latham repressed his volatile spirits and tried to be serious in his effects to bunt. Carmencita was out for scalps, though, and the seductive smile of Latham availed him naught.

Arlie cut three apertures in the ambient and showed his teeth in a murky grin. But Halligan got the same dose, and that ameliorated the feelings of the chagrined comedian. Browning out, Bassett to Connor. No runs.

Second inning.—The people are with Roger Connor to the last. He got an encouraging hand today from the grand stand and acknowledged it by hoisting up a sky disturber to Smith, which the latter clung to most affectionately. Glasscock's hit nearly punched a hole in a cloud bank over between second and right, but McPhee pulled it in like a little major.

Bassett stung Tony's prettiest for three bags into deep left, where Pietro Browning was bothered by a spectator who calmly walked in front of him and made him lose the ball. The three bases cut no figure at all, though, for Burrill flied to Halligan. No runs.

Didst thou ever seen Reilly at the bat? He is a sight. Not over six feet seven inches tall, he is shaped much like a sweet pickle as anything else. Imagine that kind of chap twisting himself into many kinks and uncertain shapes, and you can see what fun Reilly has at the bat. He grotesquely hit a honey-cooler to Glasscock, and was out for a dead moral certainty to Connor.

...J. Ewing flied to McPhee, and the hit was nothing compared to the liner with a tail of blue fire hanging to it which Whistler soaked into Smith's hands. The fielder shook his seared palms for a full half inning after his catch.

Tiernan gulped three big hunks of air through big holes in his bat. No runs.

(Connor) slammed the pellet in the face and it never stopped until it rolled beyond the ropes at left. It was a silky three-bagger...

Browning carved out a trio of slashes in the ether, each just about as long as himself, and it wasn't any wonder he never saw first. But it was an awfully hot one that Reilly sifted to Glasscock, and it caromed way off Jack's shinbones into left.

...Mullane's birdie-loo of a fly fell snugly into Tiernan's cornucopia.

Burrill trimmed the ragged edges of the grass with his foot-high hit to Smith, but the latter didn't think it too hot and salted it down to Reilly, nipping the little catcher. J. Ewing slashed one to McPhee, and he, too, was a batting memory of this inning.

...It was a treat to see Richardson watch Latham's fly sail ether ward, ever so far up, and then look at it quizzingly as it began to drop, drop, drop into Richardson's mucilaginous mittens. There is grace is every action when a fellow catches a fly in this Richardsonian fashion.

May 30, 1894

...The "Tot" got his mawleys on to Mr. Burkett's rasping bounder, and Burkett was a corpse at Doyle's corner.

...Mac dashed like a mad March hare to the middle hillock before the Albino found agility enough to soak the pellet back to the infield. Ewing tried to work the mossy bluff that he was hit by the ball, but they gave Buck the merry ha ha.

Zimmer has the appearance of an Arapahoe who would rather eat drop curves and inshoots than cut a fat watermelon. The way he swatted at a beauty of Rusie's was a caution. The pellet rollicked down to short, and this time Davis nabbed it like a sailor, slung it to Doyle so hard that it nearly knocked Jocko off his pins, but Zimmer was no more.

McGarr dribbled up a feeble fly, which has just wings enough to carry it back of short...A turf-eating grounder from the tip of Childs' bat sizzled along the ground, doing a veritable serpentine danse du venture, but Murphy, like a poised hawk, swooped relentlessly upon it, and then he slashed it to J. Montgomery at second, putting Cuppy in a trance at that base.

    Burkett gave the rooters ossification of the cardiac when he belted a hit which had designs on the flag pole at the foot of the field...

    Murphy ripped one off the reel to short and McKean pulled it down and had the fragment (i. e., the diminutive player, Tot Murphy) coppered at first...Doyle sent one on the romp to McGarr, who fielded it grandly, but when he threw it to Childs, the chubby cherub muffed it as if it was a blazing tamale.

    Rusie snapped out a crackajack past short, good for a base...

New York vs. Louisville: June 13, 1894

    First inning.—Big Tom Brown made a hopeful beginning when he larruped a safe hit behind third. Larry Twitchell helped things along amazingly on his clean single into short right, which shoved Brown up to third. O'Rourke plunged the Colonels into the doldrums when he popped up a mushy fly to short, which Murphy hauled in. On a poor throw by Farrell to Murphy, to nip Twitchell at second, Brown romped across the plate, while Twitchell kangarooed over to third. Weaver appeased the wrath of the Coxey Army in Burkeville's bleachers by flying softly to Ward. Pfeffer couldn't send the ball beyond Ward, who nailed the captain cleanly at first. One run.

    Murphy was the softest of things on his easy, straight-up fly, to which Denny froze sweetly. O'Rourke wasn't accustomed to playing short, and the just let a sizzling grounder from the end of Burke's bat rattle right through his legs. Eddie got to first easily on the error, and when Davis slapped out a dandy single past second, Burke rushed on to third. He scored on Doyle's timely sacrifice, Pfeffer to Weaver. Davis all the while piking for dear life to second. Georgie, however, in his anxiety to land at third, was thrown out trying to steal the bag from Denny. One run.

    Second Inning.—Stratton couldn't do a thing against Rusie's elusives, and he fanned three times, and "played dead" on the bench. Jerry Denny found himself in precisely the same fix. Then Hemming came up to do or die, and he died on an easy bounder to Murphy, who had him coppered at first. No runs...

The War on Slang

    By the mid-1880s, slang had become well incorporated in baseball writing, and was often referred to as "baseballese" or "baseball English."

But its use was always contentious. Backlash arose from English purists, the fair sex who enjoyed the sport and the odd newspaper editor or fellow writer. While much of the disapproval was well-earned, there were a few critics who believed that all slang-slinging writers should be plowing fields in Kansas.

It is hard to assess the extent of slang used in game reporting during this era, owing to the limited number of newspaper archives available for research today. Judging by its relative paucity, though, the art was probably limited in scope, but, because of its shocking nature, was undoubtedly blown far out of proportion by detractors with very loud voices. Needless to say, slang was not for all writers; most continued to churn out daily game reports in the traditional manner.

For starters, here is an early rebuke of slang:

There is something good, however, in the multitudinous palaver of commencements. It affords the newspapers a refreshing and perennial grist of news in pleasant contrast to the hybrid, half-alphabetical, half-numerical statistics of the base-ball reports and swaggering slang of the diamond field, which the base-ball reporter hurls with reckless unintelligibility at the dazed heads of the uninitiated.

Ordinary people can understand that Miss B's charmingly written essay on "Adversity, like Night, Reveals the Stars," was mellifluously rendered by the Rev. Verisophot Gusher in his most gurgling, cooing, tear-compelling style.

But neither Webster's Dictionary, nor the Encyclopaedia Britannica, nor any other creature can clear the eternal mist that clouds the announcement that "A's two-bagger carried B to the third, where he died on an error of C's, caused by D's foul hit to first, who muffed the sphere and spoiled the nest of goose-eggs of the opponents, despite a whitewash and two hot grounder jumbled by the short stop," or words to that effect. [South Carolina Advocate, reprinted in Watchman and Southron (Sumter, S. C.), July 13, 1886]

Edgar Wilson "Bill" Nye (1850-1896), a popular humorist whose sketches of American life and social institutions made him a household name, weighed in at length on the silliness of baseball slang in 1887:

I am extremely sorry that Matthew Arnold (English poet/literary critic) did not live to hear more of our American base ball literature. I think he would have liked us better if he had done so. In saying that we are a vulgar people and that the American humorist was a national misfortune, I think he criticized us hastily, for he was only in this country a little while and judged our humor largely by the supply he read while here and which he brought with him in his trunk; but if he could have seen the base ball word painting of our glorious country, he would have loved us.

If he could have read that Richardson went out, Irwin to Farrar, that Foster hit safely and stole second, that Welch flied out to Wood, and all about Tiernan's scratch hit and Ewing's failure to sacrifice and Ward's miss of a grounder that went through him, Mr. Arnold would have said that he had done us an injustice.

We do not claim much for our long line of ancestry, and those of us who came over in the Mayflower try to conceal it as quietly as possible, but here in this wild and savage land we are trying to build up a classic style of writing up our national game that will make the mother country tired.

I admit that I cannot understand it all yet, but I am striving to do so and I am willing to work hard.

I sometimes wish that Lord Tennyson could come here for one summer and sit with me on a bleaching-board, with his numerous hairs hanging over his topcoat, while I explained to him "that it looked rather squally for the Giants, for instance, till Slattery jolted merry thunder out of the horsehide, tore the tar out of the willow, smashed the leather, and then, while the Phillie fumblers were pulling dandelion greens behind the Harlem, the Metropolitan infielder lit out like future punishment beating tan-bark-accumulated (sic) a one-bagger, a two-bagger and a three-bagger, straightened himself out like a long-waisted jack rabbit across the plate and made his royal red home run just as the New York Central got in with the ball and the band played "Tommy Make Room for Your Auntie."

Daniels, was presented with one base as a mark of esteem, and with a blister as big as a hornet's nest where he had tried to bisect the orbit of a hot ball with the bosom of his knickerbockers, he bungled a second and while Hallman was muffing the orb, catching invisible crabs, fluking everything in sight and corking himself generally. O'Rourke hit out like a scared-to-death bobtail hornet, fell horizontally, and with his ear full of hot ball, a blister across his meridian, a fractured thing and his mouth full of sand, hoarsely ejaculated: 'Judgment!'"

I think Tennyson would like that. If me Bard likes a vivid and searching still, he would find it here.

I am only beginning to write in this way and it is new to me, but I think I can ultimately give a description of a ball game that will appeal to every heart. When I begin, I would have said, for instance, that O'Rourke swatted at the ball and missed it, 'till the pitcher hit O'Rourke's person with it, and then he went to first and gradually got to third base, but now I would say that O'Rourke, the Gothic extended catcher of the Giants, strove to belt the blooming ball to windward, mauled the atmosphere two times, and concussed the life preserver on the leg of the umpire.

There is a description that appeals to every heart. There is a literary moss agate that ought to tickle a man like Tennyson, unless he has a foolish prejudice against American writers.

My ambition is some day to write the lurid description of a baseball game which will go snorting down the corridors of time, along with Balaklava, Marco Bozzaris and the stubborn youth who stood on the burning deck. I want to write it so it will be bright and jaunty in style, and yet I would like to sock a little sadness in it, a description that should be rich in coloring, and yet free from information, a carefully and professional prepared gem of literature that would contain about a column and nothing else whatever.

The London Saturday Review says that "what American wants is a literature that shall smack of the soil." Here is the opportunity. Let the umpire take down the remarks of a Giant who has tried to reach nine feet and catch hold of the third base with his front teeth, and then demand judgment before spitting out the north end of the Polo ground.
[Bill Nye, in New York World, reprinted in the Philipsburg Mail (Mont.), May 17, 1888]

It is hard to tell if this lengthy, yet smile-inducing complaint against slang filed by Mr. Lampton, a baseball fan, in 1896, was on the level, but he made his point. Judge for yourself:

To the Editor:

Admitting without argument that elegance of diction is not one of the prerequisites of a successful baseball player, I desire to inquire if it is no more a prerequisite of the successful baseball reporter? I am prompted to make this inquiry by some samples of baseball English I read in the Washington Post descriptive of the second game of the season between the New York and Washington clubs.

I confess to an imperfect knowledge of the national game, and, wishing to learn something of it, I resolved to read reports of games this season, and as far as possible witness a few games for my instruction, and later, my amusement. I began my reading with this report of the second game between the "Giants" and the "Senators," which, I have learned, are the technical titles of the two great organizations emanating from the metropolis and the Capital, but already I am thirsty in my understanding, and I come to The Sun, that "well of English undefyled."

For instance, I read that "Doheny was removed from the slab by Irwin during the seventh inning," and I would like to know if that means that Mr. Doheny was dead and Mr. Irwin was a friend of the deceased who had come to remove the body. Again, I find that "Charley Farrell clapped his hand over his bread receptacle," and I am at a loss to know whether Mr. Farrell had brought his lunch basket with him to the game, or what is meant. A little further along in the report I find that: "As Doheny had a larboard paddle, he was a Nemesis for Brown, Joyce, and Abbey"; and again, I fail to grasp the necessities in a game of ball, played in a dry place, on a dry day, of a larboard paddle; and why was he a Nemesis? Wasn't Nemesis a lady? Is Mr. Doheny a lady-like person?

The report continues: "They were deuces for Doheny, whose south side wing brushed them out in the first inning." Has the game changed to poker? If not, why "deuces"? And has Mr. Doheny developed into an angel with a south side wing and a north side wing? And has he wings on the east and west sides? In the next paragraph is this: "In fact, these Senatorial left-handed swatters couldn't flirt with Doheny." Doheny must be a lady, or how could they flirt with him? And what is a left-handed swatter?

Continuing, the report says: "Joyce was the only one of the three who saw the first cushion until German began to twirl." Is there a cushion in a baseball game, and is it to sit on? And what was the matter with German that he should begin to twirl? Was he inebriated or just dizzy?

Then I observe, in a play between Gleason and McJames, that "the twirler of the anarchistic frizzes tarried over the groundling." Possibly those who understand this understand it, but why don't they let us, who do not understand it, have a baseball glossary? Immediately following this, I read that: "Scrappy executed a St. Vitus dandie over George's lawn mower." What do they use a lawn mower for? To cut the grass on the ball field? And why should they execute a St. Vitus dandie over it? What is a St. Vitus dandie?

Again I find a reference to eating, though this time it is not bread, but pudding. The report says: "Big Mike Tiernan presented McJames with a plate of tapioca, which he and Ed Cartwright demolished between them." Why did they eat the tapioca pudding? Were they so hungry after their violent exercise? Possibly they hadn't enough to eat at their hotel. I should think that oatmeal would be a better diet on the field than tapioca pudding, but as I know so little about baseball, I shall not insist on that point.

Immediately after serving the tapioca pudding, I read that "Frank Connaughton, the Titian blonde, plunked on McJames for two stings, a clean double 'twixt Jimmy Rodgers and the second divan, and Gleason and Davis scored." I can readily understand what scoring is, and I now see that the cushion before referred to is for use on the divan here referred to, but what is it to plunk on McJames, and what stung him twice?

In the next paragraph, I reads of "the obsequies of Davis, with Cartwright as undertaker." Was Mr. Davis killed? Again I find a reference to Mr. Doheny's wings, this time it being: "Doheny's sinister wing developed such an attack of rattles as to fly wild," and I wish to inquire if a reference to the south wing as a sinister wing is now an evidence of sectional prejudice? Neither did I ever hear of wings having rattles. I thought rattles were in the tail.

Going on deeper into the game, I notice that "the Senators were staked to three horse collars in the third." Do they wear horse collars in the game? If so, why do they wear them? Soon after this, I read of "the south winged Nemesis compelling Joyce and Abbey to take three swipes at General Humidity, who was registered at .88 down on the diamond." In the name of the shades of the athletes of ancient Greece and Rome, what does that mean? Why did they take three swipes at General Humidity? If General Humidity means the hot weather, why didn't they take a dozen swipes at it? Why didn't they swipe it off the face of the earth? Three swipes, indeed! In the fourth inning the report says: "Kid Gleason strung Jimmy McJames to the tune of three strings, a clean push-down toward Charley Abbey." Is Mr. McJames a musical instrument that Mr. Gleason could thus string him? A clean push-down I fancy is one that is not soiled. That's easy enough. In the fifth inning I notice that "Al Selbach became a deadhead for the third time," from which I imagine that Mr. Selbach must have influence with somebody. However, a little further on, I notice that he "pendulumed to third." Does Mr. Selbach run like a clock?

A lot of other odd things happened in this inning which I fail to comprehend, but I go on to the seventh inning. Here I find that "Joyce waited Doheny's pleasure, and by Tim Hurst's leave, helped himself to H. Davis's upholstery. It was the first time Billy had seen this furniture during the game."

What kind of furniture was it, and how was it upholstered? Do baseball players carry a cabinetmaker's kit around with them? They either do that or carry a stock of ready-made furniture with them, for right after this, I see that Joyce purloined Kid Gleason's "ottoman."

This is a degree of moral turpitude which does not speak well for our national game players. In the eighth inning, I note that Tiernan "got his mitt on the ball and let it filter through his mitt." Now, how could a hard ball, solid and well-made, filter through a mitt? And is a filtered ball any purer than an unfiltered one?

But I cannot call your attention to all the baseball English in this remarkable report. What I want to know is what is meant by all this queer language, and if it is the only language in which baseball games are to be reported, would it not be simple justice to us who want to read about the game, for the Association, or League, or whoever it is at the head of affairs, to issue a glossary, so that we can tell what we are reading about?
[The Sun (New York), April 20, 1896]

From Whence Slang Arose

The role played in the origin of slang by that iconic figure, the boy at the ball park, was defined by this writer in 1889. To facilitate

reader comprehension, the quoted juvenile conversation was encoded in Brooklynese:

Some very amusing things frequently occur in connection with the game of ball, but nothing more so than the slang phrases indulged in by the occupants of the bleachers and the ubiquitous small boy, who views the game through a knot-hole or from the elevated branches of an adjacent telegraph pole.

Returning from a game recently, the reporter overheard two newsboys discussing the features of the day's play. They kept up a steady flow of comments on the game, which might have been taken for Greek or Hebrew by those uninitiated into the language peculiarly the property of the national pastime. The conversation ran something in this style. The boys will be called Dick and Jack for the sake of convenience:

Dick—"Say, but Gaffney was yellow today. He trew de soup into de Browns every chance he got. He gave dat bloke what twirled for de Brooklyns both corners while he made King split de oyster every time. He was dead rank on de bases, too."

Jack—"Dat fellow Caruthers is a cute mug anyhow. He's got a good nut on him, and he knows where de Browns are weak. He was shooting a snake up dere at dem, and dey couldn't get widin a mile of it."

Dick—"I didn't see no snake. I thought dey came up dere as big as a balloon. Tip O'Neil and McCarthy had rotten eyes, and when de bases was full, instead of lining it out, just popped up baby flies, which Smithy nabbed."

Jack—"Lath was very old gold, too. Say, but dat's a fresh mug. But den he keeps de boys full of ginger, and so de gang don't mind his guff."

Dick—"Lath's all right. He gives de gang on de other side the razzle dazzle, and when dey get to trowing de ball, de jig is up. Once dey get the razz-me-tazz, dey's done up."

Jack—"Dat feller Fuller's a cuckoo. He eats 'em up down dere at short and dey can't come too hot for him. Did you see him squeeze dat liner today? Dere was one went down here dat left a streak of fire after it, but he just smothered it."

Dick—"Dat feller is a bird, but Robby's de boy for me. Did you see him give Darby O'Brien the leg? Dey talks about dirty ball, but dat's what wins the rag. Den, too, he's dead foxy at the bat. He's a dandy waiter, and when dey comes up nice, he just touches 'em off. You can bet Robby's the stuff."

Thus the conversation ran until the two urchins tired of the subject and turned the seat into a crap board.

[Baltimore American, June 24, 1889]

In 1894, the New York *Tribune*, a notorious slang-censuring newspaper, fired off this editorial broadside (or was it a put-on?) at those writers who would stoop so low as to express themselves in such rot:

...For these and other reasons, therefore, we offer a benignant salutation to the opening season, but not without a word of remonstrance and of caution to the ardent young gentlemen who will record its progress.

The main drawback to the game of baseball is the manner in which it is too frequently reported. In the lapse of time and through the exercise of a perverse ingenuity, it has been invested with an artificial terminology which may possibly in years gone by have produced that pleasant sense of surprise, which is said to be the essential test of wit, but which in its persistence iteration, has become a weariness to body, mind and spirit.

We are pained to observe that all these jaded vocables have been promptly mustered into service once more to disfigure the chronicle and exasperate the reader. As of old, the batsman "fans the air," the runner "purloins second" or "perishes at the plate," and "the planet-searcher is pulled down in left"; while again the record grows tiresome and shabby with outworn nicknames and epithets.

It is a mistake. So far from needing these amiable attempts at the picturesque and sprightly, baseball owes to them perhaps in some degree its recent decline, and assuredly can recover its prestige more readily without than with them.
[New York Tribune, April 29, 1894]

HUGHES KNOCKED OUT OF THE BOX.

4. Purveyors of Wit

Reader, it is time to put baseball slang in its rightful place. As edgy and provocative that it was, it remained a low-class, primitive street language, trash-talk, if you will, that never qualified as refined humor. Writers with a command of slang found it easy to meet the  plebeian needs of its devotees because they never had to tax their imaginations. The fad, however, failed on many points of meaningful comparison to its more cultured and better-educated cousin: wit.

By the 1880s, the true baseball humorist had emerged to satisfy a discriminating readership that preferred more intelligent reporting. Thus, clever writers with a twinkle in their eyes blended the basic elements of humor—sarcasm, parody, cajolery, mockery and the well-crafted *bon mot*—into traditional ball park dialogue that literally bounced off the pages with energy and excitement. Fresh and sassy, rich in punny similes and metaphors, this lyrical prose, constrained for years by rigid custom, suddenly rained down upon apathetic readers as a welcome relief. It was word candy, long overdue.

Hometown fans could now taste the same emotions as those who attended the game; the excitement of a crowd's roar, the suspense of "Casey-at-the-Bat" moments, and joy accompanying a successful bottom-of-the-ninth rally—or sorrow at its failure—all through the power of the printed word.

The purpose was to raise a smile on the baseball fan's face, for laughter was the balm that softened the sting of defeat and heightened the thrill of victory. Humor also tweaked that dark place within us where childish spite dwells, allowing readers to revel in the gratification that accompanies the well-aimed sarcastic thrust.

First, some history:

Wit Fit to Print

As with slang, witty narrative was shy in making an appearance in early baseball journalism. During the 1860s and 1870s, serious-minded reporters were more preoccupied with employing technically correct language in game write-ups; humorous asides never seemed to enter their minds.

Memorable exceptions existed, however. Baseball was only a few years old as a roughly organized sport when this extraordinary article was published, and, in terms of wit, decades ahead of its time. The writer tells the story of two New York City amateur clubs doing battle in 1857 in a light, breezy and amusing way, with a few slang terms thrown in.

Peruse and delight in its telling:

Eagles vs. Gotham

On Friday, the 10th inst., another exciting contest between these spirited base ball clubs came off at the Elysian Fields in Hoboken. The weather was all that could be desired, although the sun's rays had been somewhat powerful in the early part of the afternoon.

...A very large assemblage of hilarious and fashionable spectators graced the scene. The smiles of the fair imparted a tone of chivalry to the manhood so nobly and yet harmlessly displayed. A tent for the female friends of the players had been prepared by the Eagle Club with their usual gallantry. The most cordial kind of decorum seemed to actuate every person present. The fine old trees, sparkling in the brilliant sunshine, seemed to nod a gratified assent to the entire proceedings; and at a quarter past three o'clock "play" was called.

With Mr. Bixley for pitcher and Mr. Gelston for catcher, the striking remarks commenced in the skyrocket style, and Mr. Yates (at the first base) soon got notice to quit, when the quadrangular dodges began. All hands in the field were evidently wide awake, and seemed to be saying—

"From base to base they hurry me,
And think that I forgot"—

but the ball was well looked after, and throughout the match the catches on the field were really wonderful by both sides of players. After some very spirited runs, the first innings closed (by the discomfiture of Messrs. Houseman, Armfield and Williams) with nix, otherwise nil, for the Eagles.

The Gothamites now rubbed the palms of their hands as if something nice was coming along with "that ball." With Mr. T. B. Van Cott for pitcher and Mr. Vail for catcher, some splendid balls were offered for the consideration of the fielders, but Messrs. Wadsworth, Vail, and Van Cott, having been caught napping in various ways, the first innings closed with only one run to the credit of the Gothamites.

On the commencement of the second innings, the Eagles seemed bound to do their prettiest, but sundry slips of misfortune on the part of Messrs. Smith, Yates, and Bixley, put their pipes out without a single whiff of comfort yet in the shape of scoring a run.

The Gothamites then stepped in with a kind of take-it-easy air which gave their styles of both batting and fielding almost a mathematical certainty at all points. This was maintained with such successful effect as to score them ten more runs by the time the second innings closed with a trip-up or two between Messrs. Winslow and Vail.

The third innings brought up the Eagles like men who had enlisted for a forlorn hope, but manly fortitude sustained them into some remarkably fine play which elicited rounds of applause from the bystanders, who had now become quite enthusiastic as to the merits of the match, while many of the uninitiated uttered exclamations of delight at the mathematical beauty and manly features of this exhilarating game. Eight runs were scored, the only discounts of misfortune being on the well-intended dashes of Messrs. Houseman and Gelston, when the innings closed.

The Gothamites again assumed their usual posts, otherwise bases, with a nonchalant manner, but in reality did their very best, and managed to score four more runs by the time that defalcations on the part of Messrs. Johnson, Van Cott and Commerford, closed the third.

As for the Eagles, they had now regained their usual confidence, and seemed to think that "a sicker child than that might be cured." They went in "accordin'," and soon ran up seven more in their fourth innings, thus making a tie (in runs, at least) with their opponents. The only drawbacks fell to the lot of Messrs. Armfield and Williams.

...17 to 18 was considered "not so very bad," but the Gothamites had yet to take their six essays in searching after the ball of health, which they did with a perfect looseness in the way of running thirty-yards' sprints; for, although there was a stick-and-bang with Messrs. Vail, Wadsworth, and Turner, eight more runs were scientifically added to the new triumphant score of the Gothamites.

The Eagles now had to face a run of bad luck quite as trying as the sunshine in the eyes of the gentlemen who had to stand at the first base and face the departing glories of the sun then sinking in the West. They rallied their powers, and did all that play could do, but circumstances were against them. Three hands were lost, a very inconvenient "foul ball" was declared, and the innings closed with another nix. Seven was not a lucky number for the Eagles. After this, their chances were slim indeed.

The seventh essay of the Gothamites was commenced with a gentlemanly mixture of artistic circumspection and fraternal generosity. Their play was superb indeed, and merited all its success. Besides, fortune made them "bound to win," almost as if "wedder or no." Messrs. Turner and Johnson made what the French might call a "fox pass," but yet six more runs were added to the run of luck already attained, making the figures 32 to 17 on the even innings. It required eagle eyes to face such disasters, and Mr. Yates, as he stood smiling at the first base, seemed to be just one of those men who know that "all is not lost while honor remains."

Our report need not enlarge further, although the interest of the match was kept up wonderfully to the last by the undoubted abilities of the respective players.

> *The eighth innings added more runs for the Eagles, and seven more for the Gothamites, making the disparity still greater.*
>
> *The ninth innings for the Eagles ended in another nix and added four more to the score of the Gothamites, leaving the figures 43 to 20.*
>
> *"Three cheers of the Eagle Club!" cordially proclaimed by a member of the winning club, told the story of defeat, and "Three cheers for the Gotham Club!" attested the grace of manly acknowledgment as these cheers were harmonized on the air by all the members on either side.*
>
> *The following is the score of hands lost and runs made...*
>
> [New York Clipper, July 18, 1857]

More instances of wit slowly surfaced in the early years. Imagine the shock experienced by baseball fans when, in 1870, their eyes fell upon these two companion pieces.

To explain: In June of that year, the Atlantics, a scrappy amateur team of Brooklyn, took on the powerhouse Cincinnati Red Stockings, baseball's first professional team, which, a year earlier, had toured the country and won 56 games without sustaining a single loss. The upstart Atlantics won.

Humor entered the picture when a Chicago sportswriter, obviously bearing a grudge against the losers, imagined how the sad news was received in Cincinnati in classic witty prose:

> *The news of the defeat of the Red Stockings by the Atlantics fell upon the inhabitants of this town like a thunderclap out of a sunny day. The death of Dickens did not create anything like as profound a sensation, because Dickens was known only to a few newspaper men and others, while the boys with the red hose were known and beloved everywhere from the Ohio to the railroad depot, and from that depot back again to the Ohio.*
>
> *Every man, woman and child in Cincinnati felt a family interest in that club which they sent forth in all their pride and glory to conquer. They were regarded as invincible. But, alas for human greatness, strong men were seen to drop tears on the sidewalk, women rushed frantically into mourning stores to procure sombre apparel, and little boys and girls went home sobbing, and at the moment they are sitting in sackcloth and ashes.*
>
> *It was a terrible blow to Cincinnati. The bells tolled the death-knell of her departed braggadocia, and a band of music marched slowly and sadly through the streets, playing the Dead March in Saul.*
>
> *Midnight—Nobody in bed yet. Several babies cut their teeth prematurely, owing to the excitement, two have been suddenly attacked by measles, and seven two-year-olds have been sent to the Insane Asylum. The saloons are in full blast, everybody getting drunk to drown his misery, and everything is going to smash. At the prayer-meetings thanks were offered for the defeat of the Club, because even the church members were going to*

Satan on base ball. Resolutions of condolence from Chicago were received...
[Chicago Tribune, reprinted in the Brooklyn Eagle, June 17, 1870]

Then the fickle hand of fate turned. A few weeks later, the selfsame Atlantics dealt a humiliating loss to the Chicago writer's hometown team, the White Stockings, at which time a Cincinnati writer exacted full revenge upon his obnoxious counterpart with an equally witty piece:

The announcement of the defeat of the White Stockings today at Brooklyn by the d___d Atlantics is a heavy blow to the enterprise of our great city. Potter Palmer is inconsolable, and, and it is reported, proposed to transfer his magnificent hotel project (Palmer Hotel) to the home of the Red Stockings.

A rumor gained credence this evening that (manager) Tom Foley not only fainted, but while in a comatose state, seized a knife and madly plunged it into the tender bosom of a reporter of the (Chicago) Tribune. In justification Tom says the great State of Illinois and the wonderfully enterprising city of Chicago are both comatosely played. The most poignant grief prevails in our great city, and the streets are filled with weeping virgins of both sexes.

The shrill voices of urchins in lamentation frequently commingle with the base boo-hoos of the more matured residents of the greatest city in the world, and, I may add, most enterprising. We are fully desperate in our bereavement; and if, like Kilkenny cats, we fight among ourselves, believe me if it is only because we are citizens of the most enterprising city in the universe; and I may add the fight will be long, for we are the liveliest citizens of the greatest known city.

It is not the $18,000 that grieves us, for we are wealthy, yes, very wealthy; but it's the future that portends so much disgrace; it's the Red Stockings. Ah! woe is Chicago, the most enterprising city of the New World. Our grief is too heavy for the wires to bear a greater load at one time than the foregoing.
[Cincinnati Times, reprinted in the Brooklyn Eagle, July 9, 1870]

More examples of ancient baseball humor exist. This article, composed by a different Chicago writer, appeared in 1870:

The last game played by the Troy nine in Chicago was that with the Baltimores on July 4th, of which the Chicago Times gives the following "sarcastic" account:

"Discomfiture at the hands of the Mutuals did not shake our bright anticipation, nor did Athletic victory weaken it, for the old veteran patrons

of the played-out Chicago Club turned out in thousands yesterday to see Mr. Wood, assisted by McAtee, Zettlein and King, annihilate the presumptuous Lord Baltimores, who, minus their regular pitcher, were defeated at Guelph, and still cheekily sought for victory here.

"It seemed like old times again to see the thousands streaming in at the gates, accompanied by well-filled pocketbooks ready to 'go $5 that McAtee would ultimately make his base,' and then to see them stream back again when the game was over—hot, dusty, euchred, dejected, spit upon, their pocketbooks depleted, but still confident as ever that McAtee would ultimately make that base, and that the old relics of the twice-tried and found-wanting Chicagoans would finally win the championship.

"And yet there was a prevailing sentiment in Chicago on last evening that the Haymakers could not consistently remain in Chicago longer—that they were wanted in the east. It would be tedious to give the innings in detail. Suffice it to say that the Troy boys were out-batted and out-played in every position of the field.

"Of the Troys, Wood is the only person who did anything particularly creditable. In the field he was the same conscientious, watchful and vigorous player as of yore, while he did good execution at the bat is shown by the score.

"Bellan and Godney batted well; but the former muffed at short in a manner that rivaled Hodes and Pinkham in their palmy days. King muffed three flies; Force was useless at third; McAtee popped nice, easy little flies for Radcliffe and Pike, while Allison caught as lazily and, at times, threw as stupidly as any player ever caught or threw before.

In all this carnival of muffinism, the double play of Zettlein and McAtee in the 3d innings should not be forgotten. It was on Carey's fly which Zettlein put to 1st in time to catch Fisher getting back. Still it is popularly believed that both these gentlemen have friends waiting for them at Troy.

"On the part of the Baltimores, Radcliffe's fielding cannot be too highly commended. Nothing that it was possible for skill to stop escaped him. The other basemen did well what fell to their lot to do, and luckily Carey had but little to attend to. Higham had but few passed balls; while the fielders gathered in all the flies that came their way. At the bat, York and Radcliffe excelled, but the others made commendable records with the ash, and, indeed, on their part, it was a batting display equal to any that this season has permitted Chicago to gaze upon.

"But enough has been said to show that the Trojans are no longer needed in Chicago. Chicago is not mean and niggardly. We have enjoyed nearly a month of Trojan muffinism, of McAtee's 'pop ups' and 'out at first,' of Bellan's jugglery, of Force's sand clawing, of Zettlein's agile ponderosity, of Martin's easy tosses, of Allison's chronic sluggishness, and we cannot reasonably wish them to remain longer in the west. But it is

barely possible that Jimmy Wood may return next season to be captain of a real Chicago champion nine. Who knows?"
[New York Clipper, July 13, 1872]

Writers with a Wry Eye

O. P. Caylor (1850-1897)

The earliest baseball humorist of note was Oliver Perry Caylor (nicknamed "Opie," after his initials), who was born in 1850, in Dayton, Ohio. He spent less time as a lawyer, baseball team manager, (Cincinnati, 1886; Metropolitans, 1887) and newspaper owner (1888, Carthage, Missouri) than he did writing baseball for the *Cincinnati Enquirer* (1874-1881), the *Cincinnati Commercial Gazette* (1883-86), the *New York Sporting Times* (1889-92) and the *New York Herald* (1892-96). The career journalist also authored a nationally syndicated newspaper column entitled "Caylor's Ball Gossip," which ran from 1891 to 1896. With his health wracked by lifelong consumption, he finally succumbed to the disease in 1897 at the age of 47.

Caylor was a fervent champion of fair play in baseball. His writing style, variously described as "distinctive and entertaining" and "pungent," was a perfect blend of straightforward honesty (at times too much) and subtle humor, which, in the late 1870s, caught the eye of veteran baseball historian and colleague, Henry Chadwick, who remarked:

That Caylor, of the Cincinnati Enquirer, is a funny fellow and he does get off some nice little bits of sarcastic humor in the best style of his art. Here is his latest. It is in reference to the exceptional order of the Cincinnati nine over the Providence team. O. P. regards it from a medical standpoint, as follows, yellow fever paragraphs being the order of the day out Cincinnati way. He says:

"After the defeat of the Providence team yesterday by the Cincinnatis—9 to 0—the Board of Directors held a called meeting for the purpose of inquiring whether there was danger of the disease spreading or gaining a foothold. Several old experts who had passed through the epidemic of 1870 unscathed were called in and induced to carefully examine the victory.

"After mature deliberation, they pronounced it a well defined case, but expressed the opinion that it was sporadic, and fears not to be entertained of an epidemic. It was the general belief that a few more cases of yaller* victory might break out among the Cincinnati Club, but if proper

sanitary precautions were taken, no danger of a fearful visitation need be feared.

"Our base ball physician, however, who has studied the disease for five years and attended the few scattering cases which prevailed here in '76 and '77, is inclined to believe that we have not seen the worst. The case of yesterday was such a vigorous one that others of probably a less violent character may be expected. It looks as if the disease of victory had sown its seeds in the Cincinnati souls and the end is afar off."
[Brooklyn Eagle, July 20, 1879]

*The word "yellow," as used by contemporary writers, denoted "bad, or sloppy."

Good pitchers this year are scarcer than angels' visits.

For keen good-humored sarcasm, Caylor of the Enquirer, takes the palm in base ball writing. He is a specimen. He is writing of Will White's batting, Will not being as successful with the ash as he is with the ball.

Caylor, in commenting on a base hit that Will had made, says:

"When he realized that he actually was on first and no mistake, he called for a map of the route, and, after studying it intently for a moment, stole second. There is no telling what that wild young man might have done if Kelly and White had not been put out almost directly afterward. It was truly wonderful. On arrival at first, he had to be introduced to O'Rourke, who said he had met all the other Cincinnati players except him. William is really getting very giddy, and it would be well for the deacon to keep his optic on him."
[Brooklyn Eagle, July 27, 1879]

Caylor of the *Herald*, in describing the scene, says:
"Comiskey threw down his bat so hard on the rubber plate that it bounded a foot. Then Commy jumped up three feet into the air and came down on the ground with hands and feet at the same time. The action was too profane to be further described. Arlie Latham laid down in the dust and let loose a war whoop that would shame a Comanche.

"Finally everybody got around (umpire) Lynch, and he, poor, dear man, carried on for all the world like a stump orator putting the finishing touches to a very exciting political campaign. There nine ball players who differed with him, and some spectators, as was evidenced by a little hissing, but what he said went. See? The decision, right or wrong, lost the game to the Cincinnatis. It made Comiskey so blear-eyed that he struck out."
[Brooklyn Eagle, September 10, 1892]

In 1883, the *New York Clipper* reprinted a typical example of Caylor's pithy sarcasm:

Caylor, of the (Cincinnati) Commercial Gazette, when Detroit's team had a lead in the race for the championship, observed:

"Detroit's enthusiasm knows no bounds. The city will be bonded to raise $2,000,000. Each member of the nine will be presented with a brownstone front, a drag and blooded team, a bulldog, two clean shirts, a pair of socks never before worn, a toothbrush and instructions on how to use it, a box of soap and towels, a Greek lexicon and a first reader.

"Men have offered themselves as tutors, and Derby, who can already spell, will be run for Congress. Mayor Thompson has issued an order requiring the citizens to raise their hats when passing the honorable aggregation; school children will sing 'The Conquering Hero' when one of them approaches; Bennett will be sainted, and McGeary (his name used to be Mike, it is now Michael) will have a colored gentleman to wait on him. Later.—They will pay no bills whatever. Anything they see is theirs."

(Caylor, leading off a column on a Brooklyn-Boston game):

"There is no balm in Gilead. Also in Brooklyn. Had not the eccentric Bridegrooms checked the rush of the champions yesterday, many rooters would have kept to their beds all day today with ice applications at intervals, for the news which came over the wire in large gobs and thickness from Baltimore (the Giants lost, 20 to 1) yesterday afternoon was distressive to the metropolitan minds which pulsate in the interest of championships. But, thanks awfully to the hired hands who labor at Eastern Park (Brooklyn), our Giants, disfigured as they be, are no further from the van* on this beautiful Sabbath than they were when the sun came up yesterday."
[New York Sunday Herald, August 12, 1894]

*League lead

O. P. Caylor takes a fall out of "The Kicking Duke of Marlboro" so:

"Catcher Farrell has a grievance. The New York club offers him only $400 a month. Grinding poverty, just think of it! And yet the world expects a ball player to eat meat and wear white shirts! Truly times are hard—very hard—harder than hard-boiled eggs, when a ball player has to drag through the hot summer on a beggarly $16.66 a day, including Sunday."
[Omaha Daily Bee, April 1, 1894]

Once Caylor famously summarized a New York Giants' ball game in two words: "Rusie pitched," followed by the box score. To

draw a modern comparison, it was like saying: "Nolan Ryan pitched." No further explanation was necessary; the odds-on victory was inferred solely by the pitcher's name.

Even near death, Caylor's wit remained irrepressible:

O. P. Caylor, who has for many moons written the baseball stuff for the New York Herald, is off on a vacation. He is now in Minnesota, down with consumption, and weighs but seventy-three pounds. Billy Norr, the New York World's baseball man, who died a few weeks ago, had made a ($5) bet with Caylor every New Year's Day for seven years that he (Caylor) would die in twelve months, and Caylor chuckles between hemorrhages, tickled with the idea that he has outlived Norr and is $35 ahead of the game.
[Evening Times (Washington, D. C.), September 28, 1897]

Outstanding Talent

Leonard Dane Washburne (1867-1891)

A train accident in Illinois on October 18, 1891 tragically took the life of this promising and talented writer on the *Inter Ocean* (Chicago) sporting staff at the age of 24, a rising star in this specialized genre of baseball journalism.

His biography is summarized here by a former employer, Victor Murdock, editor of the *Wichita Eagle*, which illustrates the often strange and circuitous routes taken by those who later become baseball scribes, including, in Washburne's case, no experience in the sport at all!:

Leonard Washburne was born in 1867 in Terre Haute, Ind. His father was a Union soldier and his mother a woman of superior mind. He was sent to the Cincinnati Art School, and later worked in the Vandalia Railroad office at Terre Haute. Disgusted with office routine he ran away, went to St. Louis, went through the red tape of the 'Frisco offices and succeeded in securing a pass for Oswego, Kan. He tried to be a hotel clerk at Oswego with ludicrous results. He then came to Wichita and worked as abstracter and reporter on the Eagle. During his last days here he met with Alex. Butts, editor of the Kansas City Star who was impressed with Washburne. Chas. Gleed, a leading lawyer of Kansas, having his attention drawn to him, secured young Washburne the position of librarian of the Santa Fe system of railroads.

> *Then he went to Chicago and worked for a short time on the Tribune. Leaving there he was given the superintendency of some compilation in Minneapolis by Rand, McNally & Co. Then he went to The Inter Ocean. That is all. Washburne was reticent about his history. He was athletic, literary and artistic. I have a thousand reminiscent anecdotes of his career in memory which he told me and are characteristic of his fine and delicate fiber of heart.*
> [Inter Ocean (Chicago), October 16, 1891]

Washburne first secured employment at the *Inter Ocean* in the winter of 1889 as a general writer, but his transition into baseball literally came about by accident, as detailed here:

> *One day, in the absence of the regular man, he was detailed to "do" a baseball game, and his report was so novel and original that he was kept at this kind of work, on which he achieved a great reputation. (Indianapolis News, reprinted in the Inter Ocean (Chicago), October 19, 1891)*

Finding his niche, Washburne launched his career by writing up game accounts of Chicago's Players' League team in 1890. Possessing an outrageous imagination and skill in literary expression, sometimes bordering on the surreal, he amused readers with his renditions of action on the field. The meat of Washburne's journalistic shtick was the liberal use of similes, pitchers being his favorite target. He always traveled with the team when it played out of town, or "abroad," as it was called, thus assuring fans of a daily diet of comical sketches instead of a correspondent's bland impressions.

The next year, 1891, Washburne continued to report Chicago games with characteristic flamboyance and *eclat*. Defying a trade tradition, he proclaimed authorship by scandalously signing his columns. For future historians, however, it aided in its identification.

Revel in these savory samples of his handiwork:

> *Rusie!*
> *He is not a handsome man. His legs lack repose, his fists are too large for their age, his face is a clam-chowder dream, and his neck is so inextensive that he can not wear a collar without embarrassing his ears.*
> *But how long that big, lopsided man can pitch ball! The sturdy Adrian C. Anson, of this place, has had enough of Mr. Rusie to last him until the heavens are rolled together as a scroll. When Colonel Anson*

goes to bed, Rusie, a hideous and ghastly shape, sits on the foot-board with flaming eyes. All the long day, Rusie, an invisible presence, grim and terrible, is at his shoulder. He gives Mr. Anson an iciness, a sickening of the heart, an unredeemed dreariness which no goading of the mind can remove. Through the dark nights Mr. Anson hears but the ceaseless swish of a ball that shoots by him into eternity with the frightful speed of a flaming meteor across the inky sky. He hears the cracked voice of a low, brutal umpire remarking that he is out, and then he sees a parboiled face grinning at him through the gloom. It is Rusie
[Inter Ocean (Chicago), July 14, 1891]

The one act of the afternoon which stands out like a wart on a man's nose was a catch by Colonel Browning in the fifth inning. Mr. Duffy, a distinguished townsman with whom it is a genuine pleasure to deal, tripped to the bat with his teeth set so hard that his jaw bones stuck out like handles on an Etruscan vase. He reached for the first ball which Mr. Bakely was good enough to land over the rubber. The sound that followed was the same as when the slats fall down in an old-fashioned bed.

The ball mounted toward the town of Jefferson until it was lost to sight. It came into view again in a few moments in the extreme left field, and then it was observed that Mr. Browning was only a few rods away. He rattled his lengthy legs toward his heart's desire as long as possible, and then jumped in a northwesterly direction, turning four times in the air and stretching one arm for the ball in the manner of a boy after his second piece of pie. He got it.

Then applause went up from the grand stand like an insane man experimenting with a French horn. Peter had to doff his cap a dozen times.
[Inter Ocean (Chicago), June 5, 1890]

About this time the lower gate swung open and a cavalcade entered. At the head marched one of the likeliest drum majors ever seen on the West Side. He strode haughtily in with a big band blaring at his back, tossing his be-jeweled baton like a man in a fit. A moment later President James Hart, with a blood-red rose in his coat and a silk tile that pained the eye, rolled in on a barge with violet wheels. With him were a number of timid reporters trying to hide in the bottom of the vehicle. The vast crowd held its breath.

The band then escorted the players to their benches—first the grays and then the colts. As the first body neared the grand-stand the cheering was tremendous. Pretty girls waved their kerchiefs and big men, who have been cooped up by the steam heater with colds in their heads all the weary months, arose and blew their voices out into the air until the grand-stand was a sheet of purple flame.

When quite near the amphitheater Peter Browning who was marching at the right of the column, unhinged his face and smiled. The cheering ceased and a whisper of superstitious awe ran through the crowd.

But when the second installment of talent came down, the crowd let go all holds and sent up a wild roar that withered the grass. The band struggled bravely, but only the artist with the tuba, who bent himself double and blew until his spinal column was twisted like a plate of spaghetti, could be heard above the tumult. Captain Anson bowed like a man dodging a rotten apple. Every one of the crew were picked out by squads of admirers and cheered lustily by name. It was a gorgeous spectacle.
[Inter Ocean (Chicago), May 2, 1891]

Mr. Staley, who pitches for the strangers, did not have speed enough to pass a street car going in an opposite direction. His balls wandered down toward the plate like a boy on his way to school.
[Inter Ocean (Chicago), May 5, 1891]

Mr. (Cy) Young would be an attractive man on a ball field if it were not for his appearance. He is large and broad and allows his legs to dictate to him too much. But when he pitches the ball, what grace! At the moment when he says farewell to the ball he looks like a corkscrew with an ecru handle. His arrangement of himself at such times was so taking to the eye that four men struck out before they could control themselves.
[Inter Ocean (Chicago), May 9, 1891]

It is probable that Pittsburgh would have won the game had it not been for a party named Miller, who played short for the wanderers. He covered about as much ground as a woodshed, and threw to first like a drunken man with a cork leg. By close attention to details, Mr. Miller rolled up four errors, and three of them cost three runs...Ryan hit an easy one to Miller as soon as the procession started. Mr. Miller picked up the ball with great agility and hurled it with wonderful speed at an elderly gentlemen in the top row of the bleachers. Then Reilly threw Cooney's effort so that Beckley could easily have handled it had he been eighteen feet tall.
[Inter Ocean (Chicago), May 5, 1891]

Other Washburnesque similes applied to errors:

> *the throw was as high as strawberries in Siberia*
> *every error cost like a pair of boots in war time*
> *Wilmot could stop a greased pig easier than a ground ball*
> *Clarkson, in throwing to first, carelessly hit an inoffensive man in the bleachers*
> *errors were as plenty during the game as men in neighboring saloons*
> *Here were the bases full. This man Fields came to the bat again. The very first thing he did after getting the proper amount of dirt on his hands was to hammer out another home run! And he did it with the easy grace of a man ordering a champagne cocktail when somebody else pays for it. Four red pair of legs trotted across the rubber, and a man from the Stock Yards, who had $1.80 on the game, was so mad that he went out to the front gate and tried to lick a lemonade peddler.*
> *[Inter Ocean (Chicago), June 6, 1890]*

> *The day was dismal; the clouds hung in shreds on the tips of the flag poles, and the sky was so overcast that the ball could not always be followed with the eye from the grand stand. There was a floating bluff overhead that it would rain in two minutes, all afternoon, but Mr. Charles Weidenfeller, who bet a bag of peanuts with everybody in sight that it would rain before the fifth inning, had to draw a check on his banker to satisfy the refreshment vendor. It didn't rain, and when Baldwin threw the last man out with his fat right arm, every one was glad it didn't.*
> *[Inter Ocean (Chicago), August 14, 1890)*

> *Thomas Jefferson Lovett pitched for the Brooklyns. Mr. Lovett, who has a good deal of reputation as a wind splitter, is a man with considerable meat on him. His ears jut out violently from his head, and he apparently lost the back of his head in early life. He wore a look-out-or-I'll-eat-you expression as he strode to his toil, and a shiver of terror ran round the amphitheater. The first ball pitched did not bury its head in the catcher's glove as Mr. Lovett had previously contemplated it should do. James Ryan threw in his bat, there was as rattling crash like a furniture wagon running over a hand organ, and the ball was gone from the sight of men.*
> *[Inter Ocean (Chicago), May 16, 1891)*

Ren Mulford, Jr. (1859-1932)

Another accomplished baseball humorist of this era was Lorenzo J. ("Ren") Mulford, Jr., who was born in Cincinnati in 1859. He served as sportswriter on the *Cincinnati Times-Star* from 1890-95, then relocated to the *Cincinnati Post* in 1895 as editor, where he remained until 1900. In that year, Mulford replaced Harry Weldon as sporting editor of the *Cincinnati Enquirer* upon the latter's death. He died in 1932.

Mulford's wit was freer and more expressive than Caylor's:

(Former pitcher) Larry Twitchell has been a king bee in the field at Omaha and Captain Shannon whispered: "Prithee, try thy arm in thy box once more." He tried it and Lincoln ordered up a furniture car to carry off their earned runs. Sixteen of the eighteen scored were made on nice, clean, everyday sock-dologers.
[Omaha Daily Bee, June 14, 1891]

Ren Mulford philosophizes as follows:
"If Alamazoo Jennings was as sure of finding a million as the Baltimores are of dragging down the pennant, the erstwhile popcorn king could afford to give away enough roachicide to kill all the bugs in Rat Row, Little Bucktown and every ten-cent lodging house in the city. The Chicagos and Clevelands drove the iron of defeat deep into the Bostonians and killed the last fond hope they had nursed that possibly 'on the road' they could overtake their sprightly rivals from Maryland.

"New York, too, found trouble in ambush in Cleveland, and the disaster there was followed by another at St. Louis yesterday. Without an error on the books against them, the Giants fell before Arthur Clarkson, who was as great a puzzle to them as his brother, 'King John,' was to the whole tribe of horse hide swatters during his long and successful reign. That defeat was a sad blow to New York's ambition."
[Baltimore American, September 18, 1894]

Ren Mulford says: *"Bert Inks came. He saw. He conquered once by a scratch. He lost twice. He has drawn his release, and thus endeth the umpteenth chapter of the tale, 'Capt. Ewing's Search for a Southpaw.'"*
[Pittsburg Press, June 26, 1896]

What, oh, what is fame? Six weeks ago, all Louisville was tossing laurel branches at the spiked feet of a new hero. Col. Rogers—Manager

Jim—was in clover up to his knees, and all the new babies and horses in the Falls City were named "Jamesy" or "Jeems," in his honor.

For the first time in years, the Colonels were cutting a figure in baseball society. To Manager Rogers, who assumed the doubtful role of management after William W. McGunnigle's betrayal, was accorded full meed of praise for the work of the rejuvenated.

Then one of the infield cogs slipped. Shortstop Dolan became as valuable as an armless man, and with green subs and understudies at that post, victory linked arms with the other fellows and slipped through that hole like a small boy wriggling by the watchman in a game of "vineyard." Manager Rogers is not much of a second baseman, but his release outright was a sort of paralyzer for the whole of fandom.

"Only a few weeks ago," mused Frank Bancroft, "he was a little tin god on wheels. Now, they don't even let him figure in a trade."

Managerial life in Louisville is not the most pleasant existence in the world, for baseball's sarcophagus is full of the skulls of ambitious mortals who were beheaded in Kentucky's metropolis. Gus Schmelz was the first victim of there season of '97 at Washington; Jimmy Rogers ran second at Louisville. Who will be next?
[Cincinnati Post, reprinted in the Evening Times (Washington, D. C.), June 21, 1897]

Ren Mulford philosophizes in the *Cincinnati Post*:

"Baseball is built on a foundation of inconsistencies. Managers search far and wide for batsmen who can hit the other fellow's pitchers, and look for pitchers who can prevent the other batsmen from getting hits."
[The Times (Washington, D. C.), June 20, 1898]

A stolen base is frequently of greater value than a base hit. Three or four fellows on a team who are at any time liable to swish through the air from one base to another, taking advantage of a momentary attack of paralysis of a throwing arm, or a congestion of the gray matter, will give the most sanguine and astute manager on earth an attack of incipient insomnia. Many a base is stolen successfully because the runner takes advantage of cobwebs getting stationed before the optics of an opposing player.

These plays count, and likewise general victories, where the standstill and expectant base runner, like Micawber, looking for something to turn up and waiting for a succeeding sticker to plug the ball and curtail his sojourn at one of the bags, accomplishes little else than that of permitting himself to be tagged by a waiting infielder, or finds himself screwed to a base on a fly-out. And when the finale of the inning ensues, he sheepishly walks to his allotted place on the field, bewailing the hard luck visitation to him from the failure of the batsman to accomplish anything whereby he might roll in to the plate.

The faithful weep tears of anguish at the way Trouble barnacled their favorites and turned them down. The wrinkled brow of the discriminative manager or the remark of the shrewd and observing player in a forceful, though polite manner is a comment denoting disgust at the chance thrown away.

It's beyond the understanding of the chap who had found himself anchored to the base when, in talking of the "hard luck" that kept him from getting over the plate, his manager or captain says something about "cab drivers" or "ice wagons"; and I guess it is sort o' like sprinkling ice water on a a chap's back while he is taking a hot water bath.

And then the effort is straightway put forth to change the conversation. Some of these hard-luck bluffs are occasionally exploded and a deep research will discover a release attached to a part of the wreck.

Base running is unquestionably an art, and in these days of mighty wings that do rapid firing and brilliant execution successful work of this character is, withal, valuable for the team fortunate in having men who may succeed, while a sensational feature s provided for the spectators. Primarily, base running is a play that ought to be encouraged, as, next to the long hit that come at irregular periods, it is the spectacular of the sport. The game has not witnessed the improvement in this department that it has in other lines, and I firmly believe that legislation calculated to increase its volume would be of great value and meet with universal approval.

[Mulford, St. Louis Republic, August 12, 1900]

Charles B. Dryden (1860-1931)

The most highly acclaimed baseball humorist of this era was Charles Dryden. Born in Monmouth, Illinois, in 1860, he spent a restless youth engaged in various occupations and nomadic travels, much of it at sea. Blessed with a natural gift for writing, he was nonetheless a relative late-comer in baseball circles.

Dryden's early journalistic endeavors of the late 1880s and early 1890s remain blurred, allowing only that he "wrote for newspapers in Tacoma and San Francisco." Newspaper reports confirm that Dryden wrote for the *San Francisco Call* from 1891 to 1893 (but not baseball), and later moved across town to the rival *Examiner*, William Randolph Hearst's flagship newspaper, from 1893 to 1895. The journalist's efforts brought him much local celebrity, a fact noted in September, 1893 when the *Call* proudly described him as "the well-known humorous writer of this city."

In October, 1895, Hearst bought the *New York Journal*, and relocated Dryden and several others on the *Examiner's* staff to New York. The big-city exposure and his boundless wit vaulted Dryden into almost instant fame. He continued at the *Journal* until 1900, when he was lured away by the Philadelphia *North American* (1900-1905). Dryden finished his career in Chicago, first with the *Chicago Tribune* and later the *Chicago Herald Examiner* (1912-19). He died in 1931, and, with his passing, this glorious era of the baseball humorist vanished into history.

In 1965, his distinguished writing career was posthumously recognized with the J. G. Spink award, the highest honor bestowed by the Baseball Writers' Association of America.

The most remarkable feature of Dryden's writing was his ability to come up with fresh and truly funny material, year after year for decades, without resorting to deadly cliches, repetition, or baseball slang.

Dryden was a consummate storyteller with a free-wheeling imagination. Nothing during a ball game escaped his curious eye and, if deemed suitable, waggish comment. The most unlikeliest of sights—a pitcher's handkerchief, a player blowing his nose, an overweight runner struggling to circle the bases, or an overzealous bleacher denizen at work—became instant fodder for his columns. Dryden exploited the full range of the idiomatic English language and was a prolific inventor of campy phraseology; this was the essence of his journalistic genius.

The following quotations, all extracted from his time at the *New York Journal*, are but an infinitesimal fraction of his extensive work:

An inspection of the list of casualties (box score) below conveys but a faint idea of the horrors attending the earthquake that struck the Giants in the closing game of the series with Nash's men (Philadelphia) yesterday afternoon. It shook the overalls off (Giants' pitcher) Dad Clarke with its two tremblers, Connie Flynn lasted through one convulsion, and Mr. Doheny almost collapsed waiting for the shock which did not come.

An element of luck enters into every game. So do bases on balls and hits by the pitcher in some games, associated with errors which, like wedding presents described in the society column, are both numerous and costly. These little issues are all very lucky—for the other side.

Thus far the most pathetic spectacle encountered on the circuit was at Youngstown, Ohio...The sight that wrung men's souls was (New York catcher) Parke Wilson staring madly through the window of a pie and sandwich morgue at the depot. It had only been one hour and twenty minutes since dinner, yet Parke was on the verge of famine. But the catcher had no money, not even the price of a hard-boiled egg. The fellow behind the counter was about to send for the police when the train pulled out.

While there's times at bat, there's hope in baseball.

Then appeared (New York pitcher) Amos Rusie, large of girth but scant of wind, who shoved an easy grounder at Collins. The bagman handled the ball cleanly, and, with plenty of time to spare, threw low to Tenney. The ball rolled under the ropes back of first base, with Tenney in frantic pursuit, while Amos winged his canal boat flight to second base. For a time it was thought that Tenney was hiding behind the feet of a policeman in the crowd, whither he had chased the ball, so Rusie, having nothing else to do, waddled on to third.

There he stopped, and had just emitted a cloud of steam when Tenney reappeared and slammed the ball over to the bleachers. Again Mr. Rusie resumed his frenzied career and thundered across the plate with protruding eyeballs and a bosom that throbbed and undulated like a bag of cats.

Had the Quakers been working for $1 per day, with 50 per cent off for cash at the end of the month, they could not ground out a more lifeless, listless exhibition than the opening game of the series with the home team yesterday.

There seems to be a dull, dead pain gnawing at the vitals of these young men who started the season with so much éclat a few short months ago. At that time the wire-tipped battlements of (Philadelphia team owner) Colonel Rogers's ball park echoed with their battle cry, and the yellow dust rose in clouds as they slid from bag to bag.

But now, alas! a change has come. The Quakers perform with the reckless abandon of white rabbits, and the Colonel may yet find it profitable to shut his athletes up in the enclosure and feed them on raw cabbage.

It's the same thing all over again, with variations. This day the Giants outbatted their opponents, and twice had the game as good as won. But an unkind fate in the shape of base hits, bungles and bases on balls, and, as a fitting climax, the balloon went up and the Giants dropped with one of those old-time sickening thuds which are now nearly obsolete.

While many of those points of recognized and imperative parlor etiquette cannot be introduced in baseball, yet the sport offers a vast field for improvement. We all have noticed that fact, or will when your attention is called to it.

J. Nops, one of the very few foppish ball players who employ a handkerchief during business hours, furnished much entertainment for the Giants. In two rounds only did they locate him with any degree of satisfaction, and his clever fielding headed off at least three efforts that might have gone safe.

The handkerchief employed by Mr. Nops was a dainty bit of linen fabric. In the eighth inning, he hypnotized Gleason with the wipe, and turned the laugh on the ex-skipper. The Kid made a hit, and was standing eight feet away from the bag, watching Nops groom his nose with the pretty white handkerchief.

Nops held the ball in his left hand, but Gleason was so fascinated by the other unusual operation that he stood still when the pitcher threw suddenly to Doyle. The combination caught Gleason in his trance, and yet he kicked when Carpenter called him out.

A bilious moon, made so by the saffron-tinted exploits of the Giants, shone dismally into the arena when Bill Clark, looking a shade or two darker than usual, waddled to the plate in the last half of the seventh.

Two terror-stricken Giants huddled on the bags, two runs were needed to win the game and the Pirates had disposed of two men after a vast amount of agony.

Here was a chance for Big Bill to make a little ephemeral hero of himself, and ward off a curtain lecture at the same time. With a mute prayer on his tobacco-tarnished lips, Bill grunted and swung his bludgeon simultaneously. Whether the grunt or the prayer did it will probably never be known, but a base hit stands in the table of contents opposite the immortal (pro tem) name of Clark. It was the only one Bill pinched during the whole ghastly spectacle, but it was enough. The game was won and Umpire O'Day called time.

The Pirates immediately lifted up their voices in protest. They said it was not yet dark, and that, too, in the face of the man in the moon. Pittsburg should have been glad of darkness or bags or something in which to hide their freckled faces. The game had once been handed over on a platter, so to speak. A fragrant galaxy of bungles in the fifth turned out four tallies, and two more appeared in the seventh...

There were not many rooters present, for which favor Joyce and his men should be devoutly thankful. The Hot Roasted Peanuts or any other sand lot team of amateurs would blush at the kind of ball the Giants played in spots. However, the small crowd and Old Well Well shrieked, yelled and whistled until the din jarred the cotton from the ears of the timid Mr. Killen.

This eminent southpaw is of a highly nervous temperament. The deep-lunged baying of the baseball cranks annoys him dreadfully, so much so that he upholsters each ear with a couple pounds of cotton before the game. Being aware of this weakness, the loyal rooters turned loose on Mr. Killen. He lost his grip; also his cotton. A batting rally followed and the game came back to those who had thrown it away.

The Unknown Others

No baseball writer before or since matched the sustainability and sheer volume of Dryden's printed humor. Despite the master's greatness, however, there were scores of contemporary writers who were his equal when it came to wit in game reports.

National recognition unfortunately eluded them, for they never enjoyed public exposure beyond the newspaper's readership in the small- and mid-sized cities where they wrote. Their work, once published, remained unsung and unread until brought to light by chance discovery.

Today, these erstwhile prodigies suffer from added indignation—their names remain unknown. They were ghost writers in a way, victimized by the trade custom of the times: their work was never signed.

Dryden was fortunate. In 1897, by the time he joined the *Journal*, Hearst had initiated a policy of giving publishing credit to its writers. With the newspaper reaching well over 300,000 subscribers, it was easy to understand how Dryden achieved such astounding success.

The daunting task of identifying Dryden's contemporaries is left to future researchers. It won't be easy. Try to find the name, for instance, of the writer who composed a delightful piece (you'll read it later) that appeared in the Quincy (Ill.) *Herald*, in 1895.

But much old-time baseball writing was fortunately left for future generations to read, thanks to the technology of electronic digitalization of long out-of-date newspapers never thrown out with the trash.

Any historian sifting through countless pages of online newspaper archives will find much of this highly unique style of baseball writing. The focus then of this book is to show appreciation for—and pay homage to—the Mark Twains who once wrote baseball, those wordsmiths who injected amusement into prose to make points with a smile, who recapitulated diamond action in unforgettable baseball language that had never been printed before—and very little since.

5. Humor in Winning

Victory Celebrates

Nothing succeeds like success. This old saw, despite its silly redundancy, has been timeless in its application to all fields of human endeavor, and, also, not so strangely, to a baseball nine and the rooters who support the team.

It is a well-known fact, you see, that most baseball fans can weather any major adversity that befalls them, just as long as their local ball club won the game that day.

For baseball writers backing a constantly struggling team, a victory afforded them a welcome breather. They now had good news to report for a change: the pitching was unhittable, the fielding beyond praise, and timely hits the order of the day. And it gave them pause to once again reaffirm the team's worth and, for one day at least, paper over the club's glaring weaknesses.

Lastly, the welcome break allowed them to ask a familiar, oft-repeated question that was more reminiscent of a dying man's last words: Could this be the turning point?

In Other Words

Baseball writers used a number of expressions to denote victory, most of them now long lost to time. One, dating to the 1860s, found its origin in ancient history and was centered on the palm branch, the symbol of, among other desirable things, triumph. Thus, to *carry, take or bear off the palm* worked out just dandy. A team leading in a game, or perched atop the league listing, was said to be *in the van*.

A thrilling, come-from-behind win often acquired descriptive adjectives of a hirsute nature, such as *hair-bleaching*, *hair-raising* or *won-by-a-whisker*, or were cardiac in origin, such as a *heart-disease finish*.

A curious variation in this category was a *Garrison finish*, as in *"the Colts made a Garrison finish and won by a nose."* The surname simply begs for explanation, though, which, once known, makes perfect sense.

It was coined in recognition of Edward R. "Snapper"

Garrison, a contemporaneous jockey who had a habit of hanging back during most of the race before finishing first with a sudden burst of speed, thereby earning his well-deserved reputation. Ipso facto.

Dangling Golden Carrots

Instilling a winning spirit on a team and encouraging players to perform beyond their natural abilities, has been—and still is—the ultimate goal of every baseball club owner and manager since the game began. Bearing directly on this point was another maxim of life, one generally true, but decidedly crass: Cash talks.

To answer the question, how, you must first return to those early days of baseball when players became spoiled by the pampering of an overly indulgent audience.

It was a familiar scene on baseball diamonds by 1881, for example, when play was unexpectedly halted and popular Detroit catcher, Charley Bennett, was presented with a gold watch and chain by "some of his friends."

This, and countless other instances of public largess and coddling, gave club owners the idea of making similar inducements to enhance player performance, but this time in legal tender. Now, this was in addition to salaries generally running to $2,500 or more for six-month's work, which were deemed obscenely generous in the first place. Any stove molder or hod carrier in America at the time would have agreed, the irony being that these were often the same menial jobs engaged in by those men lucky enough to spend some time in the bigs. Simply put, the carrot-and-stick plan was a bribe.

Theory was put to a test in 1886, when members of the Metropolitan club of New York were each promised $200 by management if they won the American Association pennant. It didn't pan out, though, but it caught the fancy of other magnates, who employed the same tactic with minor modifications.

Soon the system was expanded to awarding cash prizes for lesser, but just as important accomplishments, such as leading the team in home runs, stolen bases, batting average and the like. In 1887, President Sterns of the Cincinnati club made local headlines by handing out a $10 gold piece to a player if he made a key hit.

The pecuniary habit of player stimulation went on for years.

In addition to greenbacks, outstanding performances on the field were rewarded with all sorts of prizes, including silver bats, bicycles, diamond pins, cigars, clothing apparel, chewing tobacco and gold-headed canes.

Other institutions involved with the sport also caught the fever. Newspapers, such as the Boston *Globe*, promised $5,000 to the Red Stockings' team if they won the pennant in 1887. The next year, the Cincinnati *Times-Star* presented a gold medal to the member of the team making the greatest number of runs during the season. In 1891, the New York *World* awarded $100 to any player hitting a red bulls'-eye, six feet in diameter, on an outfield fence.

Local merchants also joined the action by placing advertisements on outfield fences, which, when hit by a batted ball, were good for any number of premiums. It developed into an extremely popular means of advertisement that lasted forever.

A Western exchange says:
"Veach of the Des Moines sent the ball over the fence at a critical moment the other day. This is what he got for doing so: A gold watch, a gold-headed cane, a suit of clothes, a shave and a hair cut for a year, a box of cigars, and numerous other trifles, such as neckties, etc. Finally he got the 'big head' and was suspended.
[The Sun (New York), September 4, 1887]

The minor leagues invented customs uniquely their own. In Denver and Kansas City, for example, spectators showed their appreciation to a player who made a winning hit by throwing coins at him, appropriately called a "silver shower."

...Then Andrews concluded to hit the ball, and he lined out a home run, which brought down upon his head a perfect shower of silver from the grand stand. But that didn't end it.

Tom Nagle, although in a crippled condition, concluded that he would make enough money to get his washing out of soak, and the home run hit he smashed over into the carriages was beautiful to behold.

Money! Why, he got enough to buy a laundry with. It rained dollars, quarters and halves, and the amount of greenbacks thrown out would have made a mattress.

[Omaha Republican, July 5, 1889]

    Owners of hapless ball clubs sometimes resorted to lucrative come-ons that represented, at best, wishful thinking, and at the worst, outright folly.
    To illustrate: In 1897, the Louisville management established cash prizes to be distributed among its players for finishing the season at various league positions, the highest amount, $9,000, being allocated for first place. The magnates' money was safe, though, as the inept team had as much chance of crawling out of the cellar as witnessing a western sunrise.

Championship Series: Where The Real Gold Lay

    Best at motivating a ball player's desire to win, however, more so than dumb things like league pennants and silver trophies, was a chance to participate in post-season championship play. While the pride and prestige that came with being a league winner were nice and all, they weren't bankable.
    But divvying up game receipts of a full slate of games comprising a championship series? Well, now, that was really worth fighting for, as distributed profits could put the equivalent of another two months of regular pay into the pocket of every player.
    The foundation for what would become the present-day World Series was laid in the late 1860s, when top-rated amateur teams held periodic, late-season tournaments, where the winner was declared a regional "champion."
    The term "world series" first appeared in print in 1887, when it was applied to post-season competition between the winners of the National League and American Association.

Phrasing a Win

    Baseball reporters wrote up a victory in different ways. Some, low-key by nature, described play in muted, impassive tones, as if to convey the notion that winning was a completely normal thing to expect. This was usually the case with strong teams.
    Those writers representing weak teams, however, were quick to transfer the celebratory mood of a win directly into that of the game account. Doing less, in the eyes of hometown fanatics, would be seen as traitorous.
    Even in these cases, though, temperance ruled. They were

not so unwise as to be too boastful or cocky, lest the morrow bring them a reversal of fortune with a heap of crow for dinner and humble pie for dessert.

The ecstasy of winning was never better expressed than this delicately nuanced metaphorical masterpiece composed by a Cleveland writer. Celebrated was the occasion when, for the first time in nine years, Cleveland led the National League, albeit for two weeks, before finishing fourth by the end of the season in 1892:

The Cleveland Leader, flushed with the novelty of having a team at the head of the league, gets off this highly dilatory but excusable outburst:

"Perhaps the remainder of the league will pardon Cleveland today if the dear, sweet girl puts on her best gown, crimps her hair in beautiful undulating waves, dabs a little violet powder on her lily-white nose, a speck of rouge on her cheeks, and sails up and down before the pier glass in the front parlor a few times. For today Cleveland is queen of the May. In other words, the local team for the first time in base ball ages holds undisputed sway at the head of the big league.

"Saturday the Forest city deigned to let Philadelphia and Brooklyn swing in the same hammock and say sweet things. Today, however, these smaller towns have been given the mitten, and we never speak to them as we pass by. It is a new sensation, this being at the head of the league. It is like a long, wearisome climb up infinitesimal steps to be overwhelmed upon reaching the top by the magnificence of the landscape.

"The small boy who 'skins the cat' on a turning pole until his head swims like a black bass in Lake Erie can realize how Cleveland feels with its new base ball honors. Likewise the man who goes abroad early in the morning seeking what he may devour and is trundled home in the heat of the day, overcome by studious application to the seductive but unconquerable Manhattan cocktail.
[Brooklyn Eagle, August 7, 1892]

Other representative writings follow, where happiness and joy simply bubbled over:

There was more fun than at a Coney Island cake walk in yesterday's ball game—for the Giants (who beat Brooklyn, 19-4). Scrappy Joyce and his men had a huge picnic and they made the most of it.

They ran around the bases as if they were enjoying a practice session, talked politics on the bases until compelled to move on by the succeeding batsman and sauntered across the plate with as much unconcern as a small boy who has just helped himself to the family preserves. As for the Brooklyns, had there been any cyclone retreats of the grounds, it is doubtful if any of them would have appeared after the seventh inning.

No excuse can be found for the miserable work of Barnie's men, especially after their showing of the last three games. They have played poor ball in the past, but nothing so disgracefully bad as yesterday. Everybody seemed to have a mortal terror for making a clean play and a less easy-going manager than Billie Barnie would have read the riot act in several languages, most of them unprintable, after the contest was over. It is probably that he had something today, but he avoided many opportunities to talk seriously with the players while the slaughter was in progress

...The only feature of the remaining inning was Joyce's* kick on a decision on first, with the score at 19-4 in his favor. (Umpire) Hurst looked at Scrappy quizzically for a moment, and remarked:

"Don't you see the crowd suffering. Give them a chance to get home before bedtime."
[Brooklyn Eagle, September 16, 1897]

* New York player/manager

Well! well! well! The Tigers' claws have been cut.

The manicure who did it was Tony Mullane, although he was assisted by eight young men who wore St. Paul uniforms and cordial smiles. The striped terrors of the Eastern jungle (Detroit) have been tamed by the mild magnetism of Mullane and the softening civilization of St. Paul, as exemplified in the work of its base ball club. By the time they have been on the Western circuit a week, they will be docile enough for ladies to drive or children to play with, and all their wildness will be in the pitcher's box.

"Music hath charms to soothe the savage breast," the poet said, and the music which mellowed the warlike Detroits was the merry rat-tat-tat of singles and two-base hits against the side fences of Aurora park. When St. Paul was at bat, the game was like musketry practice on the Fort Snelling range; when Detroit was at bat, it resembled commencement exercises in a graveyard.
[Saint Paul Globe, May 14, 1896]

The happiest man in Baltimore last night was Manager John

Kelly (of Louisville, after trouncing the Orioles, 14-2)). His face was full of smiles and so jubilant was he that ten-cent cigars were not markers to what he treated himself with. Only Perfectos were his limit, and a number of quarter dollars fell in the coffers of the tobacconists around headquarters.
[The Baltimore American, June 2, 1888]

    The erstwhile Giants wore a crippled and saddened look as they departed from Recreation park yesterday, crushed to the aspect of dwarfs after their third defeat at the hands of our own Allies (Alleghenys).
[Pittsburgh Press, August 18, 1889]

    Scrappy Bill and his band had a rollicking good time with the Done Browns (St. Louis) yesterday and nearly exhausted themselves in the hilarity of chasing one another around the bases.
    ...The victory belonged to Washington from the beginning to the end. The Senatorial committee simply murdered Pitcher Donahue, who officiated in the box. They hammered his curves with humiliating freedom and luxurious ease.
[Morning Times (Washington, D. C., July 13, 1896]

    Beneath a clear sky and in the presence of 4,000 enthusiastic fans, the Blues yesterday took a gracious and timely fall out of Charley Comiskey's oochie-coochie aggregation of sun dancers from the staked plains of the Minnesota reservation (Minneapolis).
    Flushed by a brace of successive victories, arrogant in a deep-rooted belief in their own prowess, and cheered up by the thought that the Blues were weak in the pitcher's box, the blanket tribe warriors frisked out on the field and prepared to make merry while they dallied with the olla podrida of curves as they were emitted from Louis' Johnson's left wing.
    The Blues were still staring under the lashing received on the previous day, and they went into the fray with the true Grecian spirit of do or die.
[Kansas City Journal, April 26, 1897]

    A target for the jeers of the multitude, (Pittsburg pitcher) "Pretty Pink" Hawley didn't stick to the earth long after he entered the box yesterday against the Champions. Ever since a memorable Saturday afternoon early last season, Hawley has begged off from twirling against the Orioles in this city.

Yesterday Manager Donovan's heart was adamantine to his pleadings, and so "Pretty Pink" had to face his bete noir—the bleachers at Union Park. The expected dose came through without delay, and there was no sugar coating about it. Hawley was lambasted by the batters and raked fore and aft by the bleacher wits. He stood it manfully, showing that he has plenty of heart, and toward the end, pitched in good enough form to have won out, had he begun that way.

...As soon as Hawley made his appearance on the rubber, the crowd went at him tooth and nail. In moments of weakness he has shown himself thin-skinned enough to be impressed with the wise sayings that come from the hot boards. That is meat and drink to the dwellers in bleacher land, and confusion to Pink. He began with a sheep-to-slaughter air, and it was only after the worst had happened that he seemed to able to pitch.
[Baltimore American, June 19, 1897]

Queer, isn't it, how popular sentiment goes up and down? Now, just before yesterday's game there played on Omaha's grounds three as fine contests as ever delighted the heart of man, and yet the crowds went away kicking. Why, forsooth? Because Omaha lost!

May be. Well, yesterday's game was as full of blunders as a dog is of fleas, some of the blunders aforesaid being vile beyond description. Yet the voice of the crank was raised in gladness, and his joyous yelp rent the warm air in many places. Why? Omaha won.

Thus do you see how ready even the gentle, guileless base ball fanatic is to make merry at his fellowman's fall.

It is perfectly plain to Omaha now. Some people had wondered why Indianapolis couldn't win a game. Nobody who saw yesterday's game will do so any longer. There is no use, however, in wasting space explaining this. Go out this afternoon and see for yourself.
[Omaha Daily Bee, May 1, 1892]

"Cy" Seymour has captured Cooganville (bleacher seats at Polo Grounds). He laid siege to that metropolis yesterday afternoon at 2 o'clock. Training his in-shoots, speedy out-curves and slow-drop ball on the fortifications erected by the Louisville Colonels at half-past six in the afternoon, he had reduced the battlements to dust and rubbish and had won the day.
[John Foster, New York Journal, June 4, 1897]

Well, well, well!
We have gone and done it at last, and, in addition to the game

acquired and the hoodoo abashed, "Bumpus" Jones was reduced to utter imbecility in three innings and long "Rube" Waddell, who was put in the box, was handled in pretty much the same way.

A small, but select, congregation of pessimists attended the services, and opened up proceedings by yelling "play ball" ahead of time, causing (Umpire) Sheridan to be a couple of minutes late in opening the pot.

Columbus was first at bat, and the melancholy croakers huddled on the benches near the ends of the grand stand gave them kindly advice as to the location of various old women alleged to be drawing salaries in the outfield. A settled air of gloomy resignation, interspersed with dismal forebodings, brooded over the assembled mourners even as a hen over a couple of door knobs.

Kahoe's three-bagger in the second was not enough to illuminate the tenebrosity to any perceptible extent, and not until Fleming made a step in the third round toward redeeming himself by a hit for two of them and Ace Stewart followed with a grand, sweet soak of the spheroid away down yonder in deep center field that carried him all the way around did the vast assemblage of five or eight hundred enthusiasts get into the game.

Once around and one over was the batting record from Buffalo's easy marks in this inning, while McFarland, Kahoe, Flynn and Newton also made the circuit of the diamond by easy stages and the crowd waked up. This was the end of "Bumpus." By the time it was over, he was so far in the empyrean that reports may be expected from Millersville, Southport and adjoining towns of a strange object whizzing through the heavens at lightning speed and emitting sulphurous flashes intermittently.

Waddell, who succeeded the departed Jones, is remarkably agile for so long a man. In the eighth inning he turned a somersault over a little bit of an infield hit by Stewart and a cleverer piece of acrobatic work has not been seen on the local vaudeville stage this season.
[Indianapolis Journal, May 2, 1899]

Whoever said that you learn more from losing than winning is an idiot. And that place in the Bible, where it says, "It is more blessed to give than to receive"? Clearly a misquote.

The sole object of competing is to win. Losing is for losers, who seek, and often find, solace in psychobabble drivel pandered by poets and sentimental fools. After all, nothing satisfies more than a game of ball won; all else is folly. It is always thus in baseball

This harsh, cynical attitude was sometimes seen in writers

who represented powerhouse clubs unaccustomed to losing. A good case in point was a writer for the Baltimore *American*. His team, the Orioles, had won the National League championship three years running, from 1894 to 1896, and would have "four-peated" had they not lost a crucial and dramatic showdown series with Boston at season's end of the next year.

During the remarkable run, this particular writer adopted the arrogance, swagger, and fighting spirit of the team he represented, which shows through clearly in his write-ups:

> *Nearly ten thousand people saw the Champions (Baltimore) take sweet revenge on the Philadelphians for all the suffering they had been made to endure last Thursday. The unlooked-for defeat then sustained had worked them up to such a pitch that, with one accord, they determined at the next meeting to rub it into the would-be champions even more thoroughly than the latter had rubbed it into them. Those who spent two hours at Union Park yesterday afternoon must admit that this determination was adhered to.*
>
> *Such a crushing defeat as was administered to the Philadelphians has not been sustained by any other club this season. From the time the Champions went to bat until they tired of running about the bases, it was biff-bip-bang. They began feasting on singles, but, as their appetite increased, nothing less than a double or a triple would satisfy, until finally Billy Keeler rounded off with a home run.*
>
> *It was a genuine slugging banquet all the way through, which everybody enjoyed, except the Philadelphians, who had to furnish the service. When finally the capacious maw of the average Oriole had been accomplished, the count showed that they had rolled in twenty-three runs, while their opponents were lucky in getting as many as four. [Baltimore American, April 21, 1895]*

> *Hanlon's (Baltimore manager) hard hitters gave an exhibition of beautiful, scientific ball playing in the game with New York yesterday, such as has rarely been seen on any ball field. The mighty men from Gotham, flushed with their former victories, came over here on Friday to show Baltimore how they proposed to win the pennant.*
>
> *The Birds, however, wanted revenge, and they got it—they fairly glutted their ire in base hits and runs galore and wiped up the earth with the unfortunate Gothamites. Not satisfied with outplaying them at all points Friday, they fell upon the poor things yesterday and made schoolboys out of them—laughed at them—played all around and about them—toyed with them as a cat with a mouse, and finally defeated them,*

20 to 1, to the unbounded delight and hilarious enjoyment of 7,800 howling, happy enthusiasts.

McMahon, though his arm still pained him, went into the box. He had blood in his eye for this arrogant aggregation from New York, and they were as infants in his hands. He pitched superbly, and was superbly supported...The New York club were never in the game for an instant. They were so clearly outclassed that it was almost ludicrous. It was one-sided from beginning to end.

...Thus it will be seen how much at the mercy of the Orioles their would-be rivals were, and what a superb exhibition of pitching was given by McMahon. But for Burke's single and Davis' triple coming together in the sixth, the poor sojourners from the banks of the Harlem would have been shut out without a run. But what energy they saved in base running was needed in chasing the ball in the field. During all this, while that "Mac" had been toying with the Gotham batsmen, the Orioles had been rapping gout singles and doubles and triples, and piling run upon run until it seemed they would never stop.

...Hanlon's hard hitters have completely recovered from their "batting slump," and, oh, how they did bat! They were in the feathers yesterday, batting like fiends.
[Baltimore American, August 12, 1894]

    Murderous to the hopes of the (Brooklyn) Bridegrooms was that sixth inning. The cup of victory, truly touching their lips, was ruthlessly dashed aside and a vigorous drubbing administered.

Bright visions of winning again from the Champions gave the visitors a jaunty air, when the home team pounced on Stein and batted him so mercilessly all over the lot that he lost his head. Stein's condition was contagious, for his field got ragged right at this critical time—all the worse for them. When that mighty inning was over, the Orioles had scored eight runs, and the whole complexion of the game was changed. It was a hard pill for President Byrne's aggregation to swallow, and they made a wry face over it, doing quite some kicking over new balls being used in place of old ones.
[Baltimore American, April 27, 1895]

    It will not take long to tell the story of today's game at Sportsman's Park. The Baltimores used up three St. Louis pitchers, broke five bats, swatted out twenty-three hits, with doubles, triples and homers, till you couldn't rest, and took a ludicrously played game from Von der Ahe's rejuvenated Browns by a score of 22 to 4.
[Baltimore American, July 12, 1897]

The Birds made it three straight from the Colonels today. It was a case of the Champs vs. the Chumps, judging from the playing of the tail-enders in the first two innings.
[Baltimore American, July 15, 1896]

There were indications of trouble right from the start. Those haughty young men from Oyster Bay (Baltimore) swaggered around with the easy confidence of a private detective at a society ball when they indulged in their preliminary practice, and when they hammered out two runs in the very first inning, the 15,896 people who filled the stands, terraces and bleachers and overflowed in generous proportion on the field, had a sort of foreboding that if the Reds won at all, they would have a hard struggle. Three policemen were kept busy restraining the crowd of coatless patriots in the right-field bleachers from jumping on the lawn.

Long before the clubs started to practice, standing room was at a premium, and several loads of chairs had been distributed in rows in front of the grand stand. It was by all odds the largest crowd at the park this season. Pretty nearly every one of these 15,896 spectators went to the game prepared to cheer for the Cincinnatis, and in the sixth inning they fancied that the time had come. At this juncture the Reds bunched a few singles on Mr. Hemming, and three runs came in before the visitors realized what was happening. The multitude tooted horns, rang cowbells and filled the air with a volley of shouts and cheers.

But joy was short-lived. Even the three runs failed to tie the score, and before the Cincinnati's had another chance to go to bat, a succession of happenings got in their work on "Red" Ehret. Out of the chaos of hits, the Orioles snatched a half dozen fat runs, and, hope for success being abandoned, the audience put in the balance of the afternoon in inviting Umpire Sheridan to get off the earth, telling him that he was a rank incompetent, and insinuating that he was directly responsible for the defeat which finally came after eleven successive victories had marked the home series of Ewing's men with the indelible stamp of good team work.

Either the Baltimore batsmen were at their best or else "Red" Ehret was thinking that he was pitching for the St. Louis Browns. At all events, the Orioles had little trouble boarding his curves as they whisked around the corner, and doubles and triples were as thick and as cheap as men who can tell you all about "this currency question."
[Baltimore American, July 19, 1896]

This Baltimore writer held no patent on vindictive humor. More sore losers were around who viewed a loss as cause for a day of national mourning. Here are more snotty commentaries:

Billy Barnie (manager, Fort Wayne), the Bald-headed Eagle of the Chesapeake, at the close of the game yesterday afternoon, looked very much as the parrot did after the monkey got through with him.

It was his first appearance in base ball in the wild and woolly west, and the slap, bang fashion of Uncle's hired hands (Omaha) was too much for his delicate nerves. Billy has been accustomed to the hare and the tortoise style of ball as played back in Baltimore, for lo! these scores and scores of years, and yesterday's get up and hurrah contest almost started a second growth of hair on his devout head.

...There was but little ceremony about opening up the battle, and before Manager Barnie could comfortably settle himself on the bench, Uncle's slaves were fondling and caressing young Mr. Keefe (Fort Wayne pitcher) with an abandon that amounted to simple recklessness. (Omaha won, 17-7)
[Omaha Daily Bee, June 12, 1892]

The veil of voodooism has been lifted, and for the first time since the Allies (Pittsburg) made their jump into the (National) league, they have been able to win the majority of games from the citizens representing the village on the banks of the Delaware (Philadelphia.).

There is no question but that Manager Hanlon knew what he was talking about when he asked the inhabitants of the most progressive city in the state, good old reliable Pittsburg, to suspend judgment until the team demonstrated what they were able to do in the last two weeks of the season.

Who, in their wildest flights of fancy, would have ever had the temerity to say that, after the exhibitions that have been given us, Our Own would turn in and take 10 out of 11 games played? The general impression seems to have been that the gentlemen representing this city had fallen into such a frightful state of innocuous desuetude that nothing could happen to arouse them to a realizing sense of their duty. That this idea was erroneous in the past two weeks, and now they can, beyond question, own the town if they continue on at the same pace and finish the season ahead of Cleveland (fifth place!).
[Pittsburg Press, September 29, 1889]

The Weary Williams, of St. Louis, departed hence for Philadelphia last night with nothing but bitter recollections and a bad

taste in their mouths. No birds ever were snared easier than the St. Louis team which was brought into New York's net during its brief stay in this city. Three games were won hands down, and the worst that happened to New York was a scare for a cent in the second contest.
[John Foster, New York Journal, June 16, 1896]

Here is Charles Dryden's caustic take on the St. Louis chumps:

Mr. Von der Ahe's cellar champions battling for a hopeless cause are not a stellar attraction at the Polo Grounds these days. Sad-eyed and dejected, the Browns threw a few despairing stunts yesterday afternoon in the presence of a small but select assemblage.

Tail-enders do not draw multitudes with the Giants in third place, and with their gaze turned ever onward and upward. There was little demonstration on the part of the cranks and none of the noise that attended the series with Cincinnati. About the only sound in the grand stand was the plaintive wail of the young man who peddles "cigarettes, pipsin gum and fresh-roasted pinits," whatever they may be. Also "cushions to set on."

Not more than 4,000 people nerved themselves to witness the Browns. The rabid fanatics seemed to take it as a foregone conclusion that the visitors couldn't win, and so remained away. This is not right. Patrons should turn out and see just what the esteemed Mr. Von der Ahe has to offer in the way of baseball remnants.

About the only remarkable feature noticeable in the team is the number of athletes whose names begin with H. There were no less than five in the cast presented yesterday. No wonder the outfit is hoodooed with H's. The genial Chris has given us a Hart, a Harley, one Hallman, one Houseman and a Hartman. He should sign an Iceman and let him put the rest in cold storage.

However, the wretched young men from St. Louis did not do so badly. They behaved the best they knew how, but it isn't in the combination to win, particularly against a team that aspires to Temple Cup greatness and renown.
[New York Journal, September 5, 1897]

When Victory Occasions

"A blind hog will pick up an acorn once in a while. [Anon.]

The sweetest win of all belonged to the team stuck in a long

losing streak or muck of the league cellar, which was made doubly sweet when a pennant-contender was knocked off. Writers, in a sudden state of giddiness, saved their choicest words for these rapturous moments:

Let the trumpets blow. Put more pitch on the bonfires. Bring out the tin pans. Stop the street car. Muffle the bells of the bicycles. Go out in the fields and gather the wild flowers and with the jasmine vine wreathe garlands of beauty. Fill up the glasses again and paint the town red. Cincinnati had won a game!
[Cincinnati Tribune, reprinted in the Brooklyn Eagle, April 30, 1896]

There is a homily among woodmen that you can't keep a squirrel on the ground; neither can one club or any combination of clubs defeat the Senators three times in succession.
The Senators had tasted the bitter dregs of defeat for two days until yesterday when the chalice was passed from their lips and the Boston's made to quaff copious draughts of the mixture that leaves a dark brown taste in the mouths of the vanquished club and the partisans thereof.
Scrappy and his band were a little late in getting at 'em, but when they did they made a slaughterhouse of the premises.
[Morning Times (Washington, D. C.), July 2, 1896]

Word was received at nightfall in this town yesterday that the Kansas City Blues had won a game of baseball. The information spread like wildfire, and immediately there was intense excitement. Crowds congregated about the bulletin boards and discussed the report in all its phases. The people were unprepared for the shock attendant upon the announcement of the strange intelligence, and many refused to give it credence.
It was such an improbable story that much corroborative evidence was needed before it would pass current for fact. All night long the newspaper office telephones were besieged by excited people who asked for particulars of the accident.
About midnight, a man, with a voice husky with emotion, called upon The Journal to ask where he could purchase a large, serviceable telescope. He said he wanted to use it in looking for the millennium.
Here is the story of the eighth wonder of the world:
Detroit, Mich., June 11.—And it came to pass that, after wandering in the wilderness for thirteen days, the Blues from Kansas City, which is at the mouth of the Kaw, captured their first game. And

they lifted up their voices in rejoicing.

Prior to today they had engaged in twelve battles, and sustained grievous defeat in each. Today's victory came as balm in Gilead, and Manager Manning was as pleased as a society belle with her debut on the stage.
[Kansas City Journal, June 12, 1898]

>*If you happen to meet*
>*A fan in the street*
>*He'll declare that he thinks it will snow,*
>*With a wink of the eye,*
>*He'll say, if you ask why,*
>*The Statesmen (Washington) won two in a row.*
>*[Brooklyn Eagle, July 17, 1897]*

Shut out by St. Louis. Greater calamities have befallen our city and its base ball team, but to be blanked, Chicagoed,* goose-egged by an aggregation that has been the football for nearly every other club in the league is a disaster from which it will take a long string of victories to recover. It came, too, just when the cranks were in a supercilious state of mind; they were puffed up with pride over recent victories and apparent superiority of their team over anything that could come this way. The fall was terrific and the injury to feelings was greater than the effects the defeat may have on the standing of the team in the pennant race.

It was a sad blow in its sudden unexpectedness, sadder because there was no chance to charge it to the umpire or luck.
[Brooklyn Eagle, June 4, 1897]

* Shut out.

>The Dawn of Hope

>*The shades of night were falling fast*
>*As through an uptown street there passed*
>*A newsboy who did loudly roar,*
>*'D' base ball extree! Get d'score!*

>*And there he met a baseball crank,*
>*Whose leaden heart within him sank,*
>*Lest, when he'd bought the fateful sheet,*
>*He'd learn of yet one more defeat.*

With trembling hands and feverish zest
He found a tuppence to invest,
And with emotion, putty pale,
Purchased the telegraphic tale.

So shook the sheet he scarce could see
The glorious news of victor-ee,
But, when, at last, it met his eye,
Both loud and joyous was his cry.

Oh, rapturous bliss so sweet and keen
Washington 5; New York, 14;
The Giants now have won a game,
Hope humps herself and dreams of fame.
[Evening Star (Washington, D. C.), April 28, 1894]

A widely known baseball critic, who is distressed over the way Louisville has of downing visiting clubs at times, says:
"Almost any team that imagines it is a team thinks that the Louisvilles have no right to win a game. Occasionally, the Colonels get together and give these swell-headed gentlemen a trouncing which hurts. So the visitors on the slightest provocation try to intimidate umpire and Colonels. The latter refuse to be intimidated, and there is your scrap, for which puffed-up visitors, and not the home team, are responsible."
[Evening Times (Washington, D. C.), August 11, 1897]

At last! Who said the St. Paul club would never win another game? Let him hide his head in every shame. Of all the crimes charged to erring men, next to high treason, comes disloyalty to the home baseball organization, when they are doing what the angels do—the best they can.
Let the knockers retire to oblivion and the rooters rear their proud crests again. The happiest individual in town yesterday was the small boy with a cowbell who tested the acoustic properties of Aurora park between 3:40 and 6 p. m.
[Saint Paul Globe, June 21, 1896]

We stop the press to note the fact that the Washington Baseball Club has won a game.
[Morning Times (Washington, D. C.), July 28, 1895]

A Garrison Finish Told in Words

Biff! That was Larry's tree meeting one of Billy's straights. Then a phosphorescent streak was descried in the air as the ball soared out in the west. A gray-clad man was seen tearing frantically toward the fence. He reaches it, holds up his hands imploringly, but it is too high to scale. Then he lingered and gazed and dreamed—the scene was so soothing, the tranquility too holy.

Larry had knocked the ball over the fence! And all three runners came home.

Say, that was sweeping Sioux City's hopes into the tomb, like the leaf of May is wafted by the breath of October.

The tumult that followed was scandalous. Everybody took on so. They howled like a giant in agony; their unearthly, mocking voices sounded like the jabberings of a legion of maniacs. But that is what it is to win a game of ball on a hit over the fence in the twelfth inning.
[Omaha Daily Bee, July 3, 1891]

Winning Bigger

Baseball writers skilled at the art of lurid hyperbole were able to turn an ordinary victory into a super duper one. The language undoubtedly horrified English professors, but fans had to love it. What do you think?

Precisely at that moment, the members of the Milwaukee team commenced to sarcophogate the remains of the squad of visitors from Siouxdom (Sioux City). Tenderly and lovingly, they wound the cold gray folds of the winding sheet around the manly but mummified forms of the dear deceased, leaving with friendly consideration one little eye-hole, through which with staring orb they could watch for the change in time and events, and keep tab on the lay of the land as the hour approached for Gaby (Gabriel) to toot his horn. For two innings yesterday, the locals sulked in the well-known order of one, two, three. Then a chance came o'er the spirit of their dream, and they pulverized Mr. De Wald with a persistency that was appalling.
[Milwaukee Journal, June 2, 1891]

(Buffalo 7, Toronto 3):

No matter how hard Chapman's convict-coated Canuck crowd plays ball, no matter how much encouragement they receive from the many scores of Canadian rooters who reside in this city, the poor over-

the-river ball players are always doomed to disappointment when they face Morton's merry men in this city. Yesterday these two teams came together once more in mortal combat on the green field and once more the local papers announce in exultant tones that the foreigners were bested, lammed, jammed, smashed, jumped on, upper-cut, punched—-in fact, summed up in one word, they were defeated!
[Buffalo Enquirer, July 1, 1895]

(Rochester 8, New Haven 5)

>There is no doubt about it.
>The New Haven hoodoo is a hoodoo no longer. Three separate, distinct and successive times has it had its tail twisted and three separate, distinct and successive times has it been driven off the Rochester premises with no more ceremony than a man displayed when in the calm and stilly watches of the night he rises from his downy couch and throws his boot jack at a Tom cat on the back fence. The hoodoo was pretty thoroughly demoralized on Saturday, but yesterday it was done for entirely and three thousand people saw the operation and laughed thereat three thousand gurgling laughs.
>But Burnham, he of the ruddy cheeks and seductive smile, laughed not, save when he reached out his chubby hand for his share of the shining simpletons that the crowd gave up to see the game. It wasn't Burnham's day for smiling, and to think of it he's not had a very jolly time in Rochester this trip but then he can't expect to win against such ball playing as is all the ragged in the Rochester camp these days.
[Rochester Democrat and Chronicle, July 25, 1891]

>The Flour-snufters (Minneapolis), whose census-stuffing proclivities have led them to believe that they know it all, have left Milwaukee with a full-sized flea in their ear. When in their native hencoop, they managed, and the Lord only knows how, to wrest a game away from the coming champions. Then they swelled themselves out like so many poisoned toads, and with little Tommy Hurst, ex-slugger and whilom umpire, at their head, came boldly forth to conquer. The story was soon told; they came, they saw, and they are "our'n." Their best endeavors were about as effective as a straw before a whirlwind.
[Milwaukee Journal, July 8, 1890]

>The Kansas City contingent went to the ball ground yesterday afternoon with the fixed determination of winning the game. Not only did they believe themselves to be the people, but they bet money on it and

got left. So enthusiastic had this contingent become that they enthused everybody who wanted to think the same way that they did, the result being that even Second-baseman Manning was foolish enough to place $100 on the success of his team and lost it.

"Toll for the brave, the brave that are no more."

Saddened at heart, silent-mouthed, sunken-eyed, loose-jointed and with lower jaws hanging upon their manly bosoms, the flower of Cowboydom chivalry passed out from yesterday's game into the gloaming. The world exhibited for them as roseate a hue as it does for the man whose wife has recently become a widow. Their well-intentioned efforts only went to prove, more conclusively than ever, that while a good-natured, good-looking, gentlemanly lot of fellows, they fell far short of the requirements of the occasion; in the language of the old soldier, "they were h__l on dress parade, but not worth a d__n in action."

They couldn't keep up with the procession. They weren't in it at all, and it was palpable, even to themselves, after the third inning that the corpse they had started out to bury was the livest one that they had seen in many moons. Why, it was as full of bristles as a porcupine. [Milwaukee Journal, July 11, 1890]

CANNOT BE BEATEN

6. Humor in Losing

Bad ball playing is the parent of bad luck.
[J. Earle Wagner, co-owner, Washington Senators, 1896]

Loss Mourns

If ever there was a need for humor in baseball writing, it was to console the dejected rooters whose team had lost a game, and especially so when the home team was caught in a death spiral of losing. In response to these dreadful crises, writers naturally turned their attention to the usual and rightful source of the problem—the players.

Since time began, critiquing the home club's play was one of the baseball writer's chief responsibilities. Those associated with a winning club had it easy in this regard because, as success never breeds fault, their columns fairly well glowed with words of high praise and good cheer.

However, when luck soured, losses mounted, and the local pets plummeted in the standings, writers' reactions varied. Some continued to write up games with the same indifferent manner that preceded it, refusing to acknowledge the elephant on the playing field.

Most, however, got angry. Like lawyers preparing for court, they laid out their arguments in strong language and demanded immediate change in language heavily laced with sarcasm.

Of all the noise generated by the press under these frightful circumstances, the most inventive and provocative, yet most refreshing, arose from writers who viewed life through warped lenses that allowed them to see something droll in any of life's ghastliest moments, be it a public hanging, a deadly cholera outbreak, or a twelve-game losing streak.

When disaster struck, they unleashed their sarcastic wit. It ranged from one-line zingers to paragraphs of blistering type, at times bordering on absolute contempt. Vitriol could actually be wrung from the newspaper columns. No one in the organization was immune from their libelous roasts and the pressure was applied as long as necessary, whether a few weeks or the entire season.

The aim of employing mockery was to spur the local dubs into playing better ball. While the intention was well-meaning, its effectiveness generally proved futile. While powerful words on the sports page might change readers' views, they could not transform defeat into victory. That trick required a magic wand. Games were won—and losing streaks stopped—through good pitching, tight fielding, and three-run homers, not parody.

The venting was not all in vain, however. Both writers and fans alike enjoyed a good laugh at the expense of the locals, and, in so doing, released pent-up anger and resentment. This catharsis softened the sting of defeat, dispelled suicidal thoughts, and assured their allegiance for yet another day. And in the process, these writers, almost by accident, discovered that humor possessed magical restorative powers as an antidote to apathy and heartbreak. Or maybe it was just a case of misery loves company.

Whatever the case, the outpouring of satire by these resourceful writers produced a glory hole of priceless humor, which zested up otherwise staid and business-like baseball columns at the time.

A Loss by Any Other Name

Baseball writers spawned a multitude of terms that described the simple loss of a game; the same went for teams demonstrating a facile propensity to do so.

Easy-to-beat clubs were referred to as *tail-enders, footpads, marks,* and *soft snaps.* The verb phrase, *to have a picnic,* also sufficed in this category, as in *St. Louis had a regular picnic with the Brooklyns yesterday.*

More evocative equivalents of defeat assumed a confectionary air, such as *easy fruit, pudding, tapioca,* and particularly *pie (*peach or cherry being favored), which gave rise to statements as: *Nichols always was tapioca for Baltimore,* or, *the Bridegrooms were not at all easy fruit.*

Other suitable descriptors included: *taken into camp, fall into the tureen, eat humble pie, throw in the sponge, reduced to straits, colors dragged in the dust,* and *get frescoed.*

The phrase, *to get whitewashed,* or *shut out,* was as good then as it is today; so was *skunked,* which has been around since 1870.

Kalsomine, used as a noun or verb, was also used in the same context, as the old-timey word meant the same as whitewash. *To get Chicagoed* was also used for the same purpose. This term was invented by a writer when, on July 23, 1870, the amateur Chicago team was shut out by the Mutuals of New York, 9-0. It stuck.

Finding slangy phrases for losing streaks presented no challenge. The most common expressions employed were built around the key word, *toboggan,* an apt choice as it implied movement in a downward direction. So it was thus writ: *the Indianapolis team is tobogganing,* or *the Pittsburgs have started down the toboggan. Gliding the gutter* and *shooting the chutes* were acceptable substitutes, as they, too, painted the same painful picture.

Toboggans sure are fearful things,
And yet they're restful, rather
For though the team is falling fast,
They soon can fall no farther!

[Philadelphia Times, reprinted in the Evening Star (Washington, D. C.), July 1, 1896]

Feeling the Media Heat

Singling out players for ridicule started early in the history of baseball, a dubious honor that poor Leggett would never know of. This catcher for the Excelsiors, an amateur team of Brooklyn, had an off day in 1863 and was set upon in a most hurtful way:

Though Leggett made five fly catches on foul balls, he also missed five catches. He must remember that he is not, nor ever will be again, the Leggett of 1860, when he touched the highest point of the ladder. He has been descending since then, and though still a good player, he is not A-No. 1 now, his inability to throw weakening his play exceedingly.
[New York Clipper, June 27, 1863]

With precedence set, writers followed suit by indicting

individuals—or the entire team, if necessary—for basic ineptitude:

Wansley was lazy, McMahon indifferent, Hunt rather afraid of swift balls, and Harris not in a condition to pitch.
[New York Clipper, June 3, 1865]

As the crowd betook itself from the grounds, there could be heard remarks on all sides to the effect that the Chicago Club is a dismal, hopeless failure, and that it is a base swindle on the public to put them forward as anything like first-class exponents of base ball.
[Chicago Daily Tribune, June 27, 1875]

The attempts of Capt. Miller to play right field are ludicrous in the extreme. The dumpy catcher was never built for an outfielder. If a fly ball comes where he can reach it, he easily nails it. But if he has to sprint for it, it's a cinch that it will get away from him. The reason seems to be that Miller runs in a jerky, unsteady sort of way, that makes it very difficult for him to capture a ball while in locomotion.
[Baltimore American, May 11, 1895]

If, as charged, Pitcher Hawley sulked yesterday when Manager Mack called on him to replace Hugney in the box, he well deserved the call-down that the usually too considerate manager gave him. Most men, with the knowledge Hawley has of his poor work this season, would have been glad to respond to such a call.
The trouble with the Beaver Dam boy is that he has been petted too much, both by those owning the club and the patrons of the game. A man with Hawley's ability to play ball should endeavor to get out of his baby period, and occasionally realize that he is full-grown and a man. The vanity born of previous success and a handsome face have worked more to Hawley's injury than anything else.
[Pittsburg Daily News, reprinted in the Baltimore American, July 14, 1896]

A St. Louis writer, who is not wildly infatuated with Roger Connor, says: "The actions of Roger Connor on the field are indicative of a diet confined to cracked ice and mush melons. If (manager) Mr. Buckenberger would dissolve about two pounds of red pepper in a gallon of liquid ginger and inject the entire solution into the capacious system of the great first baseman, it would do him a whole world of

good."
[Baltimore American, April 30, 1895]

This is (pitcher) Winnie Scott Mercer's fourth year in creme de la creme base ball society. During his scintillating career, this velvet-orbed dealer in diplomatic schools and kinks, has, in the diction of Steve Brodie, "turned down" many a promising team of pennant-bidders and gathered divers laurels.

But it has always befallen Mercer to flop and to thud when confronted by the Hanlon flock of Orioles. In the past four years, Mercer has dealt the choicest number in his repertoire to the Orioles. But the birds feed fat off his fare. Tuesday he was as consistent a performer as ever against the champions.
[Washington (D. C.) Star, reprinted in the Saint Paul Globe, May 20, 1897]

It looked as if the (Boston) Beaneaters were trying to outdo the (Brooklyn) Grooms' infield in the matter of blundering. Shindle was hypnotized. Daly had axle grease all over his fingers, losing a chance for a double (play) and fondling the ball when an easy chance was offered to shut off Lowe at the plate.
[Source misplaced]

Last night, a cold, clammy silence pervaded the general atmosphere around the cranks' headquarters. Like the Egyptian darkness, it was dense enough to feel, and once in a while a fellow would reach out and grab a handful of it as much to say, "We can't have much of you tonight, and you know it."

"What of the game, oh, my father?" would invariably bring the unhesitating reply, "I've nothing to say, my child; nothing to say."

The game was in fact so one-sided that a snap shot picture taken of it by an amateur camera fiend revealed that nothing but (Omaha pitcher) Clark's mouth as it ground out a string of anathemas that looked and smelt like a pound of early summer dog sausage.

The game throughout was a poor excuse, failing to either amuse or interest. The O'Hogs (Omaha) put their big bare feet upon the local team, squashing it fairly out of sight, until it looked like a defunct road.
[Milwaukee Journal, May 20, 1891]

Off-days and fishing excursions would seem to be bad medicine for the Birds, judging from today's exhibition. The game the Orioles put up this afternoon was of the opera bouffe character, and made the team look as cheap as the tail-enders in the Gas Belt League.

The fact is, two-thirds of the men acted like they were asleep. They could not get out of their own way at the bat and in the field, and they did seem to care who knew it, either. Such a lifeless, careless and headless game has not been played by the boys in many moons, and it is to be hoped will not be seen again in the near future.

The trouble began in the box. Big Bill Hill pitched, or rather made a bluff at it. He was about as lively and spirited on the slab as a mammoth lobster. His delivery was pie for the Pittsburg sluggers, and they hit him just about as they pleased.
[Morning Herald (Baltimore), August 1, 1899]

And pre-eminently the most putrid exponent of the application of decay to original atoms of base ball playing sense was an Irishman named Dowling, who, in his youth, became infatuated with the rhythmic poetry of Sir Walter Scott, and when he became a ball player, assumed the nom de diamonde of "Glenalvin."

There was nothing so easy that this man could not make a holy show of himself. He muffed flies, fumbled grounders and fell over his toes with a deprecatory abandon that might have signified that base ball was only a pastime for him, however it might torture the spectators who had paid their cash to see it. Mr. Dowling had able assistants. But their sins paled into dimness beside the egregious inefficiency of this Dowling.
[Saint Paul Globe, June 10, 1898]

George Brooklyn Smith, the sensational short stop of the Reds, is not himself by a great deal. He is just as capable as he ever was, but his nerves need strengthening. He became panicky at critical stages. On two occasions yesterday, he had chances to cut off runs at the plate, but he lost them both. George will make a meal on nerve food this morning and be ready for business this afternoon.
[Cincinnati Enquirer, reprinted in the Pittsburgh Press, April 15, 1892]

Ward has only himself to blame for the defeat. His muffs and fumbles were gall and wormwood for the New York rooters. He handled the ball as if it were spikes with quills like a porcupine, dropping everything that came his way.
[Brooklyn Eagle, May 11, 1893]

The Rochester Base Ball Club has a tendency to give one large and thick-necked dose of "that tired feeling" that the vendors of the various brands of sarsaparilla talk about so much in the spring time. Its members act like a lot of men who have no excuse for living save that there are two salary days in each month and there would be more life in a lot of wooden-legged men than they display while on the diamond. They walk up to the bat with an "Oh, I'm dead out" air that gives the opposing club all the confidence in the world and that is rapidly driving the base ball lovers of the city to drunkenness and crime. They play with about as much spirit and life as nine mummies from the pyramid of Cheops, and that is the principal reason why they go on day after day and lose game after game in the way that they are doing now-a-days.

If there is any possible way by which they can be pulled, or hauled, or worried, or frightened, or coaxed out of their trance, it would be numbers of large and shining and valuable simpletons in the pockets of the owners of the club to find that way out and apply the remedy with a good deal more force than politeness.

The person who was directly responsible for yesterday's defeat was that convivial Kentuckian, Colonel Lafayette Lumbago Shreve. The Colonel pitched like a man suffering from Saint Vitus dance. The wildest hawk that ever stole a chicken out of a farm yard was not in it for purposes of comparison when that pitching is taken into consideration. The Colonel gave no evidence yesterday of being able to pitch a basket of hen's eggs off a railroad bridge, to say nothing of getting a Spalding ball over the home plate. He gave nine bases on balls, hit one man and made a wild pitch with three men on bases. But he was not alone to blame, for the rest of the nine could not hit a barn door with a hatchet, and they they went into the tureen again.

...Their base running was not remarkable for its intelligence. Right here it is not out of order to inquire where Joe Visner got the idea that he could steal a base! Joseph is a couple of stacks of red chips shy on that particular branch of the game and his efforts are getting to be a little painful.
[Rochester Democrat and Chronicle, July 1, 1891]

(Brooklyn pitcher) Knell pitches left handed and bats right handed, and excels at neither pastime.
[Brooklyn Eagle, June 5, 1894]

Pie! Puddin'! Purification! Any of these terms is applicable to the Phillies. Come on, you Colonels, get a good thing while it lasts. St. Louis was in hard luck not to have been here this week. We can hear (manager) Irwin gnashing his teeth over in New York that his moss-covered lobby was not scheduled to get a bit of it. Blue Monday came and we took defeat good-naturedly. Tomat (sic) Tuesday followed, and

again we got it where pappy wears his Christmas present.
And what shall we call Ash Wednesday? Ash Wednesday would be a little out of season, but the ashes are ours all the same, dear friends. As a rule, we have shown during the middle and latter stages of the week that we know at least something about the game, but this week we are making a new record. It must be awful strong dope the boys are smoking this weather. Manager Shettsline ought to take Professor Scanlan to the races and familiarize him with the injection process. It could not do any harm.
[Philadelphia Inquirer, reprinted in the Pittsburg Press, June 12, 1896]

(Following a 41-8 loss to St. Paul the previous day):
The Minneapolis papers are sad over Sunday's results. The Tribune advised the team to spend the holiday in solitude and prayer.
The Journal said: "The police are working on the theory that the Minneapolis players were kidnapped on their way to the ball park, and are still confined in some beer vault, and that a number of small boys were induced by liberal promises of candy and cigarettes to go out in the field and pose as the Minneapolis team."
[Saint Paul Globe, July 7, 1896]

This game postmortem, slow and grueling in their telling, showed how hope could be made to die by a thousand cuts:

To heaven, it was a crying shame that the second game was not won. Golden opportunities galore knocked at the door of the Champions (Baltimore) but to be turned down. Time and again did the flood tide of prosperity invite the home team, but they were never wise enough to launch their bark, until it had passed by, never to return.
The first game was simply a nightmare effect, with Hoffer as the chief devil. There was but one thing in that grotesque exhibition to stir anything but lamentation. That one thing was the great box work of "Brother Joe," and on that this tale will dwell later. It is of the second game that historians will delight to talk. Invitations to win never ceased through the contest. Fortune wooed the Birds as the Old Dame seldom woos. With every door of opportunity held open by the master hand of Dr. Pond, the home team was dazzled by the brightness of the prospect, and stumbled and fell down. Even to the last, fortune never abandoned them, and, as a final caress, let them off with a tied score.
There was never a time in the game that there was not a dramatic situation. The ending of it was with a grand flourish of trumpets, and a climax that sent local hopes a-glimmering. Of "ifs"

there is an oversupply. If Clarke, Kelley, Jennings and Brodie had or had not done certain things at certain times, the game would have been easy enough. (Cleveland pitcher) Sir Cuppy was again at the point for the Spiders, and the little man is convinced within himself that he never can win two games in the same series from the Birds. If it is a false presentiment, it was not the fault of Cuppy. Though he did as well as he had stock in the shop, yet he acted as though he was beaten, and simply wanted to make the thing close.

Though climax trod on the heels of climax, the chief climax of all came in the very last of the game. One little hit or a fly would have won; one little bit of hustle by Bill Clarke on the bases would have won, and so would have some other things won, as was patent to the searching glances of the nearly twelve thousand spectators. Irish fashion, the best part of the telling is the ending of it. When the ninth inning opened, the proposition for the Champions was to keep the Spiders from scoring. That was their part of a winning contract.

In a moment of mental aberration, Joe Kelley fancied himself the chief orator in a debating society, instead of the left fielder of a ball team that was trying hard to win something which it needed in its business. Instead of watching the batter, Joe had his mind fixed on making reply to some witty sally from the crowd of bleacherites who stood on the field nearby, having crowded off the seats. Tebeau himself opened the argument in that inning.

In the two games Pat had made but one lone hit, and he was watching a chance for some break in the Champions' line of defense. His quick eye caught the fact that Kelley was having a tete-a-tete down in the left garden, and his quick mind settled upon the plan to drop one down there just to break up Joe's earnest little speech. So Pat lifted the ball to left. It was an instant before Kelley could wrench his mind from the abstract of a juicy piece of witty logic to the everyday fact that a fly ball was journeying his way. When he did accomplish the psychologic feat, it was too late for him to capture the ball, sprint though he did, and what would have been an easy fly got through a two-base hit...
[Baltimore American, August 26, 1896]

    Peck Sharp was fined twenty large round dollars for absenting himself from the morning game, and should have been fined about twice as many for appearing in the afternoon.

He succeeded in getting his feet in the way of a ground ball or two, but that is about all, and there are several thousand unemployed men in San Francisco with feet just as large as Mr. Sharp's who could be hired to block ground hits at a much less salary than Mr. Sharp is

getting.
[Morning Call (San Francisco), July 5, 1893]

"Jocko" Fields, saucy little Jocko, who is rarely out of one scrape until in another, was unconditionally released by the Pittsburg club last evening. Fields came to Pittsburg from Buffalo in 1886 and has always been considered a promising young man kept in the background.

The truth of the matter is that Fields was never reliable and had no ambition above having a good time, as he understood it. While a fair batter, he was the poorest base runner in the league, and whether at the bat, in the field or on base, at a critical period, he was almost sure to do the wrong thing.

The wonder is rather that he was not released long ago, as he was continually bringing the club into disrepute through his low associates.
[Pittsburgh Press, July 14, 1891]

Roat left Grand Rapids without a murmur, leaving in his wake a vague suspicion that his stupid playing of late had been all that it seemed.
[Saint Paul Globe, June 26, 1897]

This is the way the World deals out the New York team:
"The fact is that they are giants no longer. They are very small potatoes, and in an advanced state of decomposition, too. They have been treated too well, and are spoiled. What is now needed is a general toning up all around. One or two men have been allowed plenty of string, and rove at will like a choice Alderney in a clover pasture. They should be brought to their senses, and made to know that their first mortgage on the affection of the people is past due and about to be foreclosed. They must be made to recognize the fact that a lien on the Polo Grounds does not permit them to look upon the entire city as really belonging to them."
[Baltimore American, May 12, 1887]

It does seem as if somebody must lose two games of ball in this part of the country every Sunday. A week ago it was Oakland, but little or no comment was excited by the fact. People looked upon defeat as a matter of course and would have surprised at the reverse.

Yesterday, Henry Harris' combination submitted to a couple of terrible drubbings, one before and one after taking dinner, and both administered by the royal adherents of the Duke of Santa Clara, otherwise Mike Finn. Harris does not know exactly how to account for it. He was present in the morning and saw his handsome young men crushed by a score of 12 to 4. A few hours later, he endured the excruciating torture of seeing the San Joses staggering off beneath another load, consisting of 11 bloated tallies, while his own men had but 5 shriveled runs with sun cracks in them.

It may interest some to know that Sharp has sold his grizzly bear mascot. McGucken, however, retains his white rat. The bear was disposed of late Saturday night, but his evil influence is still felt. If Sharp would only invest the proceeds of the sale in a tomcat mascot, and introduce him to the rat while McGucken was not looking, the luck of the Frisco team might change.

The primary cause of the defeat was the absence of runs. Errors also entered largely into the result, which is disheartening to say the least. Then those San Jose fellows have realized that there is a tide in the affairs of batsmen, which, if taken at its flood, leads on to base hits, and sometimes doubles. It is true that Harris' men whack the ball, and whack it hard; but it is mostly at a time when there is no one in a position to profit by the hit. With the Gardeners, it is different, and that is where the horseshoe business comes in.

Otto Young, a gnarled and knotty-legged Dutch boy, with a rugged, sun-burned grin of seraphic sweetness, was responsible for four of Frisco's five runs in the afternoon game. He was born with the smile, but his legs became bowed from carrying heavy lunches to school when but a lad, so he says. Otto hit the ball twice, each time for a three-bagger.

The first time he did this, the bags were empty, but the hit was well received on its merits alone. In the seventh, with two men out and two runners watching for chances, O. Young pulled himself together and jammed the ball down toward the clubhouse. He would have stopped at third had not Everett thrown wild to Ebright. Mr. Everett was unduly excited and thought Mr. Ebright was taller than he really was by at least thirty feet. So Otto took advantage of this natural mistake and came loping gaily home.

Those who have made a study of the national game, either from the grand stand or bleachers, have doubtless noticed that at times the players are afflicted with hallucinations. They think they see a player where he isn't, and when the ball is thrown to where the player isn't, but the other fellow thinks he is, why, runs come in. That is how San Jose got some of its runs. The others were produced in various ways, but there are so many of them that it would take too long to give even a brief sketch of each one.

An awkward squad of four tallies came marching across the plate for San Jose in the seventh. Two errors, which, like misfortunes, never come singly but in pairs, and one single filled the bases. Then a grounder to Hassamer forced McVey out at the plate. Big Bill had a hallucination at the time he threw the ball, but Clark unhooked a couple of links in his vertebra and got the ball. Harper's single scored Dooley, and Sweeney's fumble of McGucken's drive let in two more runs. Then Hanley popped up a fly to Hassamer, who caught it, and, forgetting that Harper was on third, rolled the ball along the ground to Young. Before it could be recovered, the runner scored.
[Morning Call (San Francisco), June 8, 1891]

There is a certain individual on the Buffalo nine named Samuel Wise. If the records don't lie, this nimble young colt began playing ball about the time the pyramids in Egypt were finished and he has managed by a Svengali-like trick to hypnotize baseball managers ever since into the belief that he is a ball player, and that when an opposing pitcher gazes on his measly form, as bat in hand he faces the twirler, the box-artist immediately has a bad attack of rattles or heart-failure and Mr. S. Wise is the man who wins games.

But this same Mr. S. Wise reckoned without his host yesterday, for "Pompadour" Rudderham put curves in and around Sammy's neck until that person thought he was hitting at a sky-rocket. Not only did Sammy strike out twice, but he succeeded in playing, or rather attempting to play, second base yesterday ranker than it has ever been played in Buffalo this season. Every one of his errors was inexcusable, and he evidently stands in with the official scorer, for if he didn't make four errors yesterday, he didn't make one, but this official has him down for only two.

Then there is another mountain of flesh who is paid to make a showing at playing third base. His name is Drauby, surname Jacob, more familiarly known as Jake and the laziest man who is in the Eastern League. He can't, or at least doesn't, stop one out of ten liners that come his way, and his silly bluffs in running after fly balls are laughable. He could be dispensed with and very few of the rooters would shed tears—except of joy.

Last, but by no means least, is a certain individual named Field. He is slim and lengthy and last year, when he was playing against the Bisons, he apparently had some nerve and was known as a kicker and he was a terror at the bat. But he is none of these this year. His voice sounds like the moan of a dying man, his coaching consists of two or three utterances of the words "Zing, zing," and a 10-year-old kid could hit the ball better than he does.

And then people wonder why Buffalo loses games?
[Buffalo (N. Y.) Enquirer, July 22, 1895]

Won't somebody please go and buy your (Chicago player/manager) Uncle Anson a ball team?

A public as patient as a spring lamb in a snowstorm, and as long-suffering as a man standing on his head with a boil where his hair parts, will forgive an occasional beating, but when to the crushing burden of two defeats from the despised men from Gotham is added another by the Senators, patience becomes a felony.

Washington won, but they were hardly to blame. They made as many errors as the Colts, but there were of the harmless, funny sort, which are applauded by laughter instead of groans. The Chicago errors were made with the deliberate malevolence of a small boy who has been whipped by his father. They occurred at the critical points of the game as though they had been carefully picked out beforehand.

Dahlen played the worst game within the memory of (Chicago owner) Jim Hart's dog, and the dog is older than Arlie Latham's jokes. Pug juice was the most charitable reason assigned for his interference with the game. The play which passed within reach of him without being spoiled was as lucky as the man who dodged the avenging wrath of a disappointed brickbat.

Truby is still in the hospital, but the game Reilly put up at second was as superior to his attempt of the day before as a ten-case note is better than a promise to pay from a deceased fruit peddler.

The funniest error of the game was Mercer's muff of a pop-up in the seventh inning. It was as easy as sleep in a millionaire's bed, and Winnie dropped it so neatly that the ball never knew how near it had been to death as well deserved as the man who tells the story about the balky mule and kicks his interested auditor in the same way the mule was kicked.
[Morning Times (Washington, D. C.), May 22, 1896]

This is what the Baltimore *Herald* says of the game the Orioles lost at Washington on Friday:

"Whether prosperity was too much for them, or whether it was the rough and tempestuous voyage around Point Judith and up the sound that affected the boys, no feller can find out, but the fact remains that from an aggregation of pennant-winning ball players they were transformed in the short space of 24 hours into as heterogeneous a lot of butterfingers as ever contended for the championship of Skowhegan

Crossroads."
[Pittsburg Press, August 4, 1895]

(Chicago player/captain) Anson's pet horse, "High Ball" (Chicago pitcher Friend), broke onto the field and refused to be downed, but even this luck-bringer failed, and the slaughter went on. Baltimore started the run-getting early in the third inning. It was then that they persuaded Friend to retire to some peaceful valley.
[Baltimore American, July 18, 1897]

Here's how the Phillies get it from the baseball writers in that city when they lose:
"The Phillies need to take a brace. Their work on Wednesday was not only the poorest they have done this season, but absolutely the worst that has been seen at Philadelphia Park this season by any team. They cannot, of course, play championship ball in every game, but their lazy, devil-may-care style of playing on Memorial Day will never succeed in bringing a pennant to this city."
[Evening World (New York), April 28, 1894]

The town of Sioux City is in sackcloth and ashes, the sounds of mirth that once arose from the corporate limits are hushed, and the corn palace no longer has any attractions for the citizens.
Their team was beat in Omaha yesterday (22-0). And it was a scathing defeat, too, one of those wallopings that are remembered for days, aye weeks, months, even years.
But it was their own fault. They put Webber in the box—the man with the slow but deadly curve—and expected to win from the greatest slugging team in the league. It was sheer folly on their part, and bitterly do they repent it.
[Omaha Republican, July 5, 1889]

The Minneapolis Journal says their pitchers cannot locate the plate, their batters cannot locate the ball, and the only thing they can locate is their boarding house. How about the last position in the league standing?
[Saint Paul Globe, date misplaced]

Back to the barn has been sent the blanket that once adorned the hack horses that drew the "hard-hitting Apostles" through the streets. If the St. Paul club could bat as hard as they find it to bat, the fence at Lexington park would have to be repainted daily, and (manager/captain)

Comiskey's fortune would be spent in re-upholstering horsehide balls ruined in practice.
[Saint Paul Globe, June 8, 1898]

If anything in the base ball line was ever more graceless than the first game played between St. Paul and Minneapolis yesterday, it must have been the combination in one day of such a contest with the second game played between the same clubs, at the same place, and, generally speaking, in the same haphazard style.

The recurrence of two such games in a day, either in the past or the future, might be esteemed as an epoch marker, for republics have risen and empires fallen, darkness vanished and light appeared, ignorance fled and wisdom advanced, since such a combination was ever before produced.

King Ahasuerus' golden robes, moldering for ages in the spice-laden atmosphere of the tomb, would give forth an odor fresh as that of new-mown hay when compared with the musty, moldy, rotten exhibition of alleged base ball produced by the St. Paul team on its last appearance here for an interval but too short.

Compared with the first game, the second is tolerable for its sins of omission; compared with anything on earth, the first game of yesterday must look black, black, black as the cross section of a Cedar street sewer tunnel at 12:05 a. m.

Ten fielding errors by St. Paul in one game prepared the humiliated rooters for the presentation of five more in the second. The fact that the Minneapolitans made five in each of the games is consolation perhaps, but not palliation.

Do you want the hideous details? Then listen...
[Saint Paul Globe, September 8, 1898]

The championship season opened here yesterday in a blaze of glory that shed its brightness over Baltimore for just one hour and a half. Then there was a grand transformation. The flame suddenly died out, and all was darkness. The Baltimore Orioles had been ruthlessly slaughtered by the Philadelphia Quakers. For seven innings the gay bird had it all his own way, then his left wing began to tire and he fluttered helplessly to Mother Earth.
[Baltimore American, April 19, 1895]

The 450 people who went out to the Messer street grounds Tuesday afternoon to witness a good ball game, came away deeply disgusted with the perfidy and treachery of Sweeney, who with malicious *deliberation placed the home club in such a dilemma that they were forced to drop the game. Sweeney had apparently caught Radbourn's complaint, and was kicking over the traces.*

The first evidence of this was in his conduct at Woonsocket on Monday, when he showed up with a woman whose he seated on the grand stand. On that day he refused to come home and report with the rest of the team, willfully remaining until a late train. He went in to pitch in yesterday's game with young Miller in right field. He knew that this was done to save him if his lame arm gave out, or pained him too severely. The game progressed slowly. It was a comedy of errors from the start.

...Sweeney went into the dressing-room, and when it came time for Providence to take the field in the eighth inning, he could not be found. Manager Bancroft went after him and found that he was discarding his uniform. He ordered him on to the field, when Sweeney called him a son of a ___. Director Allen was called, and he also ordered Sweeney to play, but he refused to do so. When threatened with being laid off without pay, Sweeney laughed and said that he could get more money by not playing for Providence,

...The game went into the air, eight unearned runs being gained, Sweeney looking on and laughing at the ill luck of the Grays. At the conclusion of the game, Sweeney sauntered out of the grounds, in company with two women. He was subject to hisses and all sorts of talk, but seemed to glory in his dishonorable action. After the game Sweeney was formally expelled from the club.
[Providence (R. I.) Evening Press, July 23, 1884]

And here is what the *Boston News*...says of the crooked work that robbed Chicago of the pennant:

"They called them ball games because there nine men on a side, and bats and balls were used. Outside of that, there was no more resemblance in the exhibitions at the South End yesterday than there is between the moon and a pair of shears.

"The New York Giants were the individuals that pretended to give Boston a tussle for victory, and if they can't play better ball than they did yesterday, it is time they were driving horse cars for a living or learning the precarious but lucrative trade of pearl divers. They put up a game that would have disgraced a picked nine from the fatally injured ward of the City hospital, and would have driven a female ball team to eating hasheesh.

"It was something never to be forgotten, the way they played, and if they are not ashamed of themselves, it is because they are reckless

and careless of public opinion. Boston wants to see that pennant dallying with the autumn zephyrs, but it doesn't want to get it too easily. The Giants (heaven save the mark!) will please roll this fact up with their cigarettes. Selah!"
[Pittsburgh Press, October 7, 1891]

    It had been a sweet, gentle, idyllic sort of a game. It was like the upper Oise, as Stevenson described it—so easy, so placid, so dreamy!
    Anson, the Ancient, had a grip on the game that could not been dislodged with an ax, it seemed. Dear old Hutch had stood before the enemy like Horatius at the Bridge. Twice only had they hammered the ball into safe pastures, and one of those was a scratch.
    It was a palpable shut out, and that fine old gentleman James Hart was so happy that his eyes shone like twin candles through the cold, crisp air. The Chicago men had four runs; they had been giving perfect support to a grand exhibition of pitching; they were nine runts who had vanquished nine fat-headed Goliaths. They were happy, the crowd was happy; roses bloomed on the furniture and around each player in white gleamed a nimbus that was to shine down through the years.
    Bang! The spectators sat erect and rubbed their eyes. Buckley had made a hit.
    Biff! Rusie had made another.
    George Gore hit down a long, low, loping ball to Cooney. Cooney went at it earnest, grasped it confidently, juggled it wildly, spread his legs, and looked around dejectedly. The bases were full and nobody out. Richardson hit a high fly to Wilmot. The fielder got under it after a beautiful run, and wrapped it in his horny hand.
    So far, so good. But now the real trouble began. A few cases of wild, weird, panic terror began to unfold. Wilmot threw the ball home. He could easily have made a double play unassisted, for Rusie was further away from second base than he, but he threw home. Kittridge got the ball and threw it back to second. There was still time to blow out Mr. Rusie. But Kittridge, in his haste, threw high. Three men scored.
    There was still hope. But two minutes later there was not enough to wad a gun. Tiernan hit safely into right field and Connor followed with a crack at the ball that sounded like the explosion of a box of prunes. The leather mounted high in the air and Carroll dashed back after it. It was a long, hard run, and Carroll only combed the ball with his finger tips. He grabbed it from the ground and threw to second. Then Pfeffer threw to third.

If Pfeffer hadn't thrown to third!

The throw was as high as strawberries in Siberia. Dahlen made a mighty jump, but the ball sped on like a demon. Tiernan and Connor rattled over the plate with fierce joy wrinkling their faces like a corduroy road.

That was all. This whole sad history of the cold, eerie afternoon was compressed into three minutes of actual time.
[Washburne, Inter Ocean (Chicago), May 27, 1891]

Tips on the Quiet

Let Sharp catch Friend, and when not behind the bat, let him hold down the bench.

Don't play the Fall Rivers any more. They are not in our class as the team is today. If you do, have over the fence out. This will keep their score down.

Don't hit the ball too hard with the bat; you might do harm.

Don't charge any admission to the grounds until all of the team commences to play baseball. It is robbery.

When going after a fly ball, remember it must be caught in the air. It used to be out on the first bound, but that does not go now.

Don't go out west for more ball players. There is an army of them in New England whom you can have cheap.

Don't imagine that you heard thunder last evening. It was the noise of cannons being fired off in the state of Maine. They are having praise meetings in the logging camps.
[New Bedford (Mass.) Evening Journal, July 26, 1895]

Here's the Saint Paul *Globe* writer again with another humdinger:

In checkers, there is a losing game. It is scientific and played by well-defined rules. In baseball, there is also a losing game, but it is unscientific and has no limitations.

However, the St. Paul club is a master of it, for thrice in the space of three short hours yesterday did the aggregation variously known as the Saints or the Apostles give the game away. Nay, even worse than that, they literally tried to choke it down the throats of their courteous guests from Missouri (Kansas City), who, with the courtliness of true Southern gentlemen, gave them every opportunity in the world to win the initial game of the home series.

Every ball player has made errors, and any man has his off days, but it is rarely, indeed, that a baseball-loving public is treated to such a yellow and fantastic burlesque of the national game as that which took place at Aurora park yesterday. (St. Paul lost 16-15)

The phrase "took place" is used advisedly, even although it may be strictly correct. It is possible that those rare combinations of chump fielding, butter-finger muffs, and wooden-headed base running that cost the locals the game were really supervised by some all-powerful force whose ways are beyond the comprehension of the ordinary "fan." But it had every appearance of being the happy result of mischance multiplied into circumstantial hard luck and increased by the inherent proneness of man to err when he has half a chance. So let's say that it occurred, and blame anyone for anything except just what he did himself.

Well, there's Johnston. Aside from the fact that he gave seven men bases on balls, and hit Menefee three times besides, and was slugged all round the lot for eighteen safe ones, Johnston pitched a pretty steady game. That is to say, it was not much worse anywhere than at any other given point. For general excellence it probably would not have taken better than third place in the Connemara patch sweepstakes, but it was a fair, reliable game. You could rely each inning on about so many bases on balls and so many hits. Occasionally, he created a diversion by a wild throw, and twice, if recollection serves aright, he perpetrated that artistic triumph of baseball known as a strike out, but as a matter of cold hard fact, (New York pitcher) Amos Rusie is winning nearly as many games as Johnson, and Amos hasn't warmed his arm up this season.

Then there's Jack Pickett. You all know Jack. Been playing a great game on the trip. Taking all kinds of chances and occasionally hitting the ball. Yesterday was Jack's off day. He couldn't have stopped a policeman with a box of cigars. Jack had his mustache shaved off while he was away, and the shorn Samson act which he did yesterday as a sort of entr'acte specialty was anything but delightful to the assembled multitude—about 346 of whom had paid to get in. Let's draw the mantle of charity about his trembling form and pass on.

Billy George and Jack Glasscock were seized with locomotor ataxia or some other terrible trouble when they were both away from the bases to which, under the rules, they should have been immediately contiguous. Instead of making a double steal, they were victims of a double play, and that is a good deal of difference. They retrieved themselves somewhat by their work at the stick, but if there is anything which will make varicose veins in the throbbing forehead of the average fan, it is to see a dumb play on the bases, especially by old hands who are past the kindergarten period and ought to be able to go outdoors unaccompanied by their parents or guardian.

They were not the only ones, but these, perhaps, were the most

flagrant. The game was exciting. So is getting a tooth pulled, perhaps. But it is not the kind of excitement that people go into the suburbs on a hot day to enjoy. There are other ways of whiling away the humdrum existence that is called life on this terrestrial sphere these days.
[Saint Paul Globe, June 20, 1896]

George Davis says that the only signals the New Yorks used last season were signals of distress along about the latter part.
[Evening Times (Washington, D.C.), January 30, 1896]

One-Two Punch

This is only part of the "roast" served out to the Columbus team by the *Dispatch* of that city:
"There is no disguising the fact—we now have the poorest, cheapest lot of ball players that ever graced our festal board. For a time I rather expected to see them make a spurt and reel off some of the soft games that happened to pass their way, but yesterday's exhibition entirely removes the starch from our fondest anticipations.

"With everything coming their way, the entire team let opportunity after opportunity glide idly by—then quit—ignominiously quit. First Daniels was soft picking for the visitors from northern wilds (Detroit). Sharpe let one get away from him when there were two men on the bases. Genins—the only outfielder ever discovered—according to the oracle—pied the form out in center and Carney's high fly slipped through his digits."
[Indianapolis Journal, August 14, 1896]

Here is another "roast" from the *Columbus Dispatch*:
"Thus far the management has succeeded admirably in promises. In any other country but ours, the entire aggregation would be imprisoned for obtaining money under false pretenses.

"In Russia they would be banished to the lead mines; in China, toasted upon the gridiron and served with boiling oil. If Mr. Loftus cannot give to this city what he had time and again agreed to do, why on earth doesn't he spike the gates and get out of the game. Day after day the gullible public stack up against the dollbaby racket, and it's high time to make a strenuous kick. It is nothing short of a shame and a disgrace that a city of this size should be the laughing stock of the baseball world, after it has turned out players of national celebrity in the past."
[Indianapolis Journal, August 15, 1896]

Winning two games and making a hard fight for a third seems to have fatigued the Oaklands to an alarming degree. They are either suffering from that tired feeling or else looming up in their old 1891 form. The game they played yesterday was not only giddy, it was simply awful. Before the first inning was fairly underway, the tail-enders knew that they were beaten, but they went ahead and played the game out anyhow, just to verify their suspicions. Score, 12 to 6.

In addition to these figures, Oakland stacked up eleven heartbreaking errors, besides committing a few indiscretions that do not appear in the table of contents, such as stupid base-running and other wasted opportunities; also some subdued cuss words.

Poor Lester P. German was not feeling well and suffered accordingly. Not only was Lester freely lambasted, but played a disastrous part in other ways. He was unusually liberal in his distribution of bases-on-balls favors, made a very dinky-dink throw, and, at a critical juncture, Lester went into a trance, which enabled Carl McVey to make the shortest two-base hit on record.
[Morning Call (San Francisco), June 26, 1892]

Our neighbors would, no doubt, rather lose to any club in the League than Patsy's Spiders, and that they were beaten so ingloriously by the Cleveland aggregation last Saturday renders the candor of the following from the Baltimore Herald positively refreshing:

"(Player/manager) Patsy Tebeau and his Hannaites came to town yesterday and in the afternoon took a game from Baltimore. Nemesis never haunted a guilty wretch with more untiring pertinacity than the Cleveland hoodoo displays in its relentless pursuit of the champions. The Spiders have been comparatively easy of late, but no sooner do they shy their castor into the ring with the Orioles than at once they brace up and play like fiends.

"It was the old, old story. Cuppy was in the box and the champions were hypnotized from the start. Cuppy has always been Baltimore's Jonah, and is, without doubt, the most effective twirler in the League against the Orioles. The boys seemed to be paralyzed when they faced him and handled the stick like old women. They made by seven hits off his delivery and Brodie made three of these.

Four innings in succession they went out in one, two, three order without getting a man on first. It looked a bit as if the boys had made up their minds that they could not hit Cuppy before they stepped up to the plate. On the other hand the Spiders had on their batting clothes, and uncorked an entirely new vintage of base hits. They hit the

ball early and often, and got in their full vote before the polls closed."
[Morning Times (Washington, D. C.), August 24, 1896]

    The afternoon game will be long remembered by those who witnessed it (Baltimore 12, Philadelphia 11). It is doubtful if ever there was such a game played anywhere on the League circuit. There were stages of the game when the players gave unmistakable evidence of having smoked green pills; there were stages when they gave signs of having been surcharged with mental alertness.
    Some of the misplays were of the kind that Shakespeare had in his mind's eye when he spoke of something "stinking to heaven." Some of the good plays were of the kind that will be recalled during the long winter evenings around the stoves in the back rooms of the barber and cigar shops.
[Baltimore American, September 6, 1898]

    Yesterday's performance at the ball park, which was recognized as a ball game by several men who used to play that very sort of stuff themselves on the back lots Sunday afternoon with a woolen ball and a bunch of fence pickets, was more noted for the monotony with which a voice in the grand stand yelled various unmeaning syllables, than for anything else. Even above the constant rattle of the bats of the Cowboys against the easy things sent in by Kellum and Newton and the constant thump, thump of Kansas City feet slapping themselves down in endless procession around the bases, could that raucous roar be heard.
    As for the game itself, it was such that one man in the right bleachers went to sleep just as a Kcaesar (play on term, Kansas City-er) started for first base, and took a half-hour nap, only to wake up and find the same old crowd still running bases the same old way in the same old inning. Those tail-end dubs from the banks of the Kaw, especially in the fourth inning, when they secured seven runs and six hits, were so busy running bases and such that long after it was all over, you could still hear the echoes of their whizzing resounding through the neighborhood like the song of an old-fashioned horse-motor threshing machine athwart the dewy lea in midsummer.
    ...Quenching the burning indignation of the patriot for the moment, and viewing the massacre from a cold-blooded, technical standpoint, there was nothing in the game worth recording, and not even an "if" to offer saving grace in explaining the ridiculous result. Post mortem:...
[Indianapolis Journal, June 6, 1899]

    "If" Walter Wilmot had not made two errors yesterday, the

(Columbus) Senators would have had but one run. "If" Umpire Ebright had done justice to the visitors and Wilmot had not erred, the Senators would have had two runs, and the score therefore would have been a tie at the end of the ninth inning. But, "if" Kid Hulen had not erred in the fourth inning, the (Minneapolis) Millers would have one less run and the Senators would have been victorious "if" Umpire Ebright had given them the run they really deserved.

There, you have all the "ifs," unless you wish to add that "if" it had rained yesterday, the game wouldn't have been played and there would have been no occasion for the "ifs" used above, or "if" no one had made an error and Ebright's eyes had been good—but then, who knows, any old thing might have happened, and the game might have broken up in a row, but it didn't. The only sure thing to bank on is that the Senators won, and they won because—well, principally because they secured more runs than their opponents.
[Saint Paul Globe, May 26, 1897]

A whipped cur, despised at home, imposed on abroad, may at least crawl under his master's barn until his disgrace is forgotten; the Minneapolis base ball club, less fortunate, must turn out in its own home, crippled and disheartened, and suffer the jeers and taunts of its whilom ardent admirers. Consul Goodnow's young men behaved yesterday like a canine who is captured by a lot of small boys. They could not tell whether it would be a kettle or a bunch of fire crackers, but they felt that they were sure to get the worst of it anyway. They went into the game beaten; they came out of it unconverted. It was not a bad game to look at either—for St. Paul fans.
[Saint Paul Globe, June 30, 1897]

When the Buffalo Bisons defied pre-season predictions by falling dangerously near last place during the 1882 National League race, the local press reacted with righteous indignation:

The Buffalo Courier spends the season by claiming that the Bisons were the creme de la creme of base ballists. Now ye Courier says: "Wanted—A ball club to represent the city of Buffalo. Apply at Room 11, White building. Tonawanda, East Buffalo and Hamburg clubs please take notice.
...Disgusted Buffalonians are now beginning to take interest in the lacrosse game."
[Providence (R. I.) Sunday Star, June 11, 1882]

(Pitcher) Hahn did not get a fair show yesterday. He was surrounded in an open field by a number of young men, eight to be exact, half of whom played as though they had lost all their hands in some terrible wreck, and were handicapped by the stumps being shoulder-bound.

They could not catch a fly with a sheet of fly paper, nor hit the ball with a cricket bat. They threw like the unknown angle traps at a gun club field day, and if they had ever been so fortunate as to get on the bases, there is no telling what troubles they would have found there.
[Saint Paul Globe, May 29, 1897]

Perhaps the tide has turned again. It is to be hoped that such is the case. Providence has won a game at last, and in a way that speaks well for the future. The Greys batted with old-time vigor, fielded well, and were not dead on the bases. Has the riot act been read? If so, read it again, Manager Wright; make the men paste a copy of it in their hats.
[Providence(R. I.) Evening Press, August 16, 1883]

Many unkind things are always said of a lot tail-enders, but the most cruel shot the Cincinnati Reds ever received was from (sportswriter) Leonard Dane Washburne when they were in Chicago. He said:

"That Cincinnati team shows up mightily in the pictures, but it won't do. It needs filtering. A man with a good eye and a shotgun loaded with slugs could crawl upon the club, when it was well bunched, and do a great deal of good.

Now, there is John Reilly. He has been known to give a performance at first base that was apples of gold in pictures of silver—perhaps he can now in the proper environment—but Long John playing center field is a sight to drive women into hysterics and strong men to tears. John has a figure like a fire escape, with not enough meat on him to feed a dog, but he chases around the middle pasture like a one-legged man running a lawn mower. Then there is Keenan on first. Before most of us were wearing suspenders, Mr. Keenan was a swift ball player. Now he covers first base in the manner of a blind woman in an egg race."
[Pittsburgh Press, July 6, 1891]

"How It Feels to Be in Seventh Place," published by Cant, Play, Ball & Co., and on sale at all news stands, is the latest work from the pen of (Minneapolis manager) Walter Wilmot. It describes in detail the manner in which warfare is carried on in the Western states, and gives a graphic description of several skirmishes in which Captain Wilmot and

his men narrowly escaped with their lives.
[Minneapolis Tribune, reprinted in the Kansas City Journal, June 27, 1897]

About 500 people sat in the amphitheater at Lexington park yesterday, bought popcorn and soft drinks and passed sarcastic comments on some form of sporting diversion that was being enacted on the grass plat between the hours of 4 and 6 p. m. Some who had seen the programme as announced in the morning papers said it was intended and advertised to be a ball game, but it was lacking a number of eminent requisites. About the only ray of light that illuminated the barren waste of dismal woes was the fact that the boy that marks the blackboard put on more accumulative figures for St. Paul than he did for Kansas City.
[Saint Paul Globe, September 1, 1898]

The man who calls up the newspaper office to ask "What's the score?" has changed the query to, "How much did they beat us?"
[Kansas City Journal, June 11, 1897]

Poems were common space fillers in old-time newspapers; some ended up on the sports page. Here are a few dedicated to the subject of winning and losing at baseball:

The Saintly aggregation ain't worth a single—
When it comes to lining out the ball with good and healthy slam;
Their saintliness o'ercomes them, and they hit toward the sky,
Or their meekness is asserted as with infield hits they die.

So thus 'tis their speedy runners who a base or two could steal,
Adorn the players' bench a while and of the umpire squeal;
Then out into the field they trot, a losing game to play—
For, though their fielding were the best, it would not win the day.

And if, perchance, one hits the ball, it gives the rest a scare,
So they start to fill a poultry yard or pound the empty air,
Or sometimes make a dinky bunt—a sacrifice it's called—
And get the runner round to third, and then, alas, he's stalled.

But when they neither field nor bat, for any team they're pie,
And like the sacrificial lamb they walk up just to die;
And give the rooters such a pain about the diaphragm

>   That they cannot cuss the um-pi-er or swear a single ___.
>
>   Then, Commy*, take your outfit out to some small prairie town,
>   Where you may chance to find a gang your Saintly crew may down;
>   We'll take for representatives some amateur kid team;
>   Their game will not be much—but then, they'll be just what they seem.
>
> *[Saint Paul Globe, June 10, 1898]*

[*Manager Charles Comiskey]

>   No enemy is at the gates;
>   No plague with fatal hand
>   Has swung its deadly scythe and reaped
>   The noblest in the land.
>   Then why these crowds with gloomy brows,
>   These eyes so sorrow-tossed?
>   There's been a game of base ball, and
>   The local club has lost.
>
> *[Morning Star (Wilmington, Del.), May 4, 1890]*

>   Hark! hark! The dogs do bark!
>   The Phillies are out of town.
>   If some good soul will keep them there,
>   We promise not to frown.
>
>   Hey, diddle-diddle, the cat and the fiddle;
>   The Phillies play ball--they do.
>   The little dog laughs to see such sport,
>   And every one else laughs, too.
>
> *[Evening Star (Washington, D.C.), July 7, 1896]*

The New Orleans *Picayune* base ball fiend writes:

>   "Our pitcher is sick and our catcher is lame;
>   Our shortstop is playing a very poor game.
>   Our men on third base, and the second and the first,
>   Are trying to see who can play ball the worst.
>   Our left fielder has a big corn on his toe;
>   Our middle field man suffers greatly, we know.
>   What ails our right fielder no person can tell,

But in other respects, we are doing quite well."
[Pittsburgh Press, June 9, 1888]

   Oh, the day seems sad and somber,
     And like a dismal pall
  Are the spirits of the rooters
    When the team plays losing ball;
 Life, itself, is not worth living,
    And everything seems tame
When "Scrappy's" aggregation*
     Plays a
      down
       hill
        game.

   Oh, the sting of disappointment
    Oh, the woe and wounded pride,
  When down the steep toboggan
    The home team takes a slide;
Then the world seems cold and dreary,
    And friends are not the same
  When our boasted combination
     Plays a
      down
       hill
        game.

  When the fan the morning paper
    Takes and opens to the page
  Where the daily base ball record
    Tells him how the battles rage,
When he finds the home team beaten
    He slinks away in shame,
 For there's nothing kills a rooter
     Like a
      down
       hill
        game.

   When we view the field of battle
    Where past victories were won;
  View the grand stand and the bleachers

Soaking idly in the sun,
Then our souls are filled with ruing,
Life is lacking in its aim,
While our absent team is playing
In a
down
hill
game.

Time there was when every statesman
Scorned to shoot the base ball chute,
Then we daily found the bleachers
Filled with rooters born to root.
Bring those times again, O "Scrappy,"
Play past glories to reclaim,
And save the team from stigma
In a
down
hill
game.

[* Nickname of William Joyce, Washington's player/captain]
[New York Times, reprinted in the Saint Paul Globe, July 28, 1896]

With a hideous yell
He reeled and fell,
As he clutched at the atmosphere,
And he writhed and screamed
Till it surely seemed
That death was hovering near.

Then the doctors came,
With a Latin name
For the cause of his frantic fit,
Which was all from joy,
For his favorite boy
He batted a three-base hit.
[Scranton (Pa.) Tribune, May 19, 1894]

How pleasing is the playing when the home club wins;
How everybody laughs and chaffs, and everybody grins,
And the umpire is forgiven for all his heinous sins;

So pleasing is the playing when the home club wins.
The boy upon the bleachers is as happy as a king;
The maiden in the grand stand is as sweet as anything;
The crank is all in clover and the butcher is on top;
He sells a peck of peanuts and a half a gross of pop.
The fellow from the country widens out his mouth and eyes,
The manager is smiling and assigning happy sighs,
The mascot is a-bounding and a-sighing as if he were on pins,
So pleasing is the playing when the
                    Home
                            Club
                                    Wins.

But what a sad sensation when the home club slumps,
The umpire is a villain and a dastard chump of chumps,
We're on the road to ruin, and we're deeply in the dumps,
For the sad sensation when the home club slumps.
The manager and mascot are a very worthy pair;
One has a yellow liver and the other yellow hair.
Our captain is a quitter and the other is a thief,
There's not a word in Webster which can give a man relief.
No, not the wine; they've had too much already—my belief.
Why don't they let the blockheads go and sign a nine of stumps?
For oh! the sad sensation when the
                    Home
                            Club
                                   Slumps.

[*The Sun (New York)*, reprinted in the *Baltimore American*, May 16, 1895]

In Search of Elusive Lady Luck

This Pittsburg writer artfully equated fate with a missing person in classic metaphoric form:

During the continuance of the last Washington-Allegheny game, (Pittsburgh) Manager Phillips congratulated himself that the locals' luck had come home to roost again, but the fickle goddess, evidently disgusted at the demands made upon her resources, took wings in search of some more deserving community. For some time, Mr. Phillips wondered and the club lost two consecutive games with New York.

Since then, search parties have been organized and the whole country is being scoured for the hiding place of Fickle Fortune. Horace

(Phillips) threatens to chain her to the flagstaff at Recreation park unless she promises to remain at home in the future. He will first have to find and then secure this evanescent little jade.
[Pittsburg Press, July 11, 1888]

Snatching Defeat From the Jaws of Victory

Much ironic humor made its way into print when writers described the game that got away:

Just fancy this, ye cranks! The last inning was started with the Bostons none and the home players two. Two of the visitors were easily put out and two strikes on the third. Then, by remarkable mistakes, the Bostons were enabled to score four runs and win the game. The history of Tantalus has nothing more disheartening than that.
[Pittsburg Dispatch, August 19, 1892]

Yesterday the poor Raws (Rochester) experienced another slap in the face from the hard, horny hand of Fate. Ability to safely locate Jack Barnett's curves and brilliant fielding by Sweeney's Pets had the game 9 to 4 in the first half of the eighth innings and everything looked lovely for a great two-column head of eulogy in the morning Rochester papers when, as said before, Fate got in his fine work and hit Duryea a swat in the spinal column which nearly dislocated his vertebrae.
In the last of the ninth the Rochester twirler hit Moss twice and after two doubles, three singles and a couple of errors were extracted from the chaos, it was found that Kuntsch's crowd had won the game by piling up six runs. Then there was wailing and gnashing of teeth, but the rattle of incisors didn't cut any frozen water, and the (Syracuse) Stars got the victory.
[Buffalo Enquirer, July 3, 1895]

There is lots of fun in baseball, and a deal more uncertainty. The unexpected is just about as likely to turn up in an argument in the national game as on Gottenburg race track (near Pittsburg). Had anybody ventured to remark yesterday afternoon at Exposition Park at the end of the seventh inning that the champion baseball players from Boston were going to defeat our sluggers, they would have been told to go to bed.
Oh, how nice everything looked for the home representatives at that stage. Baldwin had only been touched up for two little single hits; Nichols had been thumped lively at an opportune stage, and the score

stood 4 to 1 in favor of the home sluggers. Everybody was feeling at peace with himself, except (Boston) Manager Selee and his team. Matters were going along as smooth and pleasant for the locals as a new ship going to sea.

But that eighth inning came, and what a disastrous change it brought with it. Those terrors from the locality of beans, beauty and intellect let loose, and before a fellow could take his hat off, they had taken the lead, and the day was theirs. What a surprise it was!

...To be sure the majority of people had fully expected the champions to win before the contest started, but when it had commenced and had proceeded so far as to make everybody believe that the home team could not lose, the unexpected result just about paralyzed everybody. And victory was so very, very near to the home players. Just think of it. Two men were out in that terrible inning, and no less than five hits were banged out and a base on balls donated. This piece of business just managed to score the Bostons four awfully big runs; they looked as big as pyramids, and that was just sufficient to win. They generously stopped at that number. Had an earthquake swallowed up the diamond, the little crowd could not have been more astounded...
[Pittsburg Dispatch, August 19, 1892]

After blowing a 3-0 lead in bottom of the ninth, Indianapolis lost to the Buffalo Bisons, 7-3, thus inviting this writer's retribution.

Now, who would have expected a herd of raging bisons to exhibit the malicious cruelty of the feline tribe? Yet that is what they did to the innocent and lamblike young gentlemen whom Manager Allen led to the sacrifice before four thousand earnest well-wishers who overflowed four deep from the bleachers on either side of the field. A meaner trick was never played than the way in which the "new boys" of the league let the Hoosiers gambol along in merry confidence, occasionally picking up a nice warm run, until the time came for all friendship to cease.

Like a cat with a mouse, the Buffalo three-shell outfit let its victims get away almost within escaping distance again and again until it was time for the feast to be served. And then—there came a crash of thunder sound, and Scott, oh, where was he? They batted him all over the place and behaved in general after the manner of a Georgia assemblage of leading citizens with a colored brother in hand. The fickle populace, of course, immediately transferred their affection to the visitors and each black-suited Bison was welcomed home with cries of fiendish delight.

Fleming, away down in left, with no company but his thoughts, was responsible for part of it, though there were enough run-getters left and to spare without counting Pickering, whose fly to left, "Flem" did not deem worth preserving.
[Indianapolis Journal, May 1, 1899]

Over the years, some baseball clubs hit rough patches of losing that made for memories best forgotten. Here's a look at a few:

Pittsburg

The Pittsburgh Alleghenys, or more familiarly "Allies" (later Pirates), fielded some truly forgettable teams during this era, which provoked an endless stream of pithy digs by the local press:

Beaten, yes, beaten fairly and honestly for the third time and by clubs that are rated below the locals. This, too, after winning a majority of games from New York and breaking even with Chicago and Boston. Does the coming of the Hoosiers presage another such period of calamity as ensued when the home team paid its first visit to Detroit?

Then seven straight games were lost and Allegheny stock was just taking a header below the financial horizon when hope was again renewed. If such another time of disaster threatens local pride, is there not among the best, the noblest, and the richest in all the Iron City, one who will make a martyr of himself, that the self-respect or the balance, might be retained?

Perhaps the fates might be propitiated by such a sacrifice and indulge the Pittsburg boys with another victory ere they start on their eastern pilgrimage. Another contest won at home would ease the present unsatisfied longing after something apparently unattainable more than a dozen promised triumphs abroad.

Is your present company too fast, boys? If so, your shortcomings may be forgotten and forgiven. If not, what excuse can you offer for dropping three consecutive games to such clubs as Indianapolis and Washington? Is it that you underrate your opponents and would use them up on the strength of laurels you have gained against more formidable adversaries, or maybe you imagine your mission in life, like that of the knight errant, is to stand betwixt the strong and the weak, occasionally smiting the former lustily and then turning your other cheek to the pygmies who are now not only doing you up, but rubbing it in on you at the same time.

Such sentiments sound very beautiful on paper, but they will not

earn your salaries. If you would carry the public with you, there must be some reciprocal evidence on your part that you appreciate its generosity and are willing to deserve it. Brace up, boys, be yourselves, else it may be written against you that ingratitude, the worst of all crimes, is your besetting sin.
[Pittsburgh Press, May 25, 1888]

Rain prevented another slaughter of the Pittsburg team.
[Pittsburg Dispatch, July 20, 1889]

"I feel just as though I had awakened from a dream," remarked a Pittsburg club official this morning. "It was a horrible nightmare, just such an experience as would satisfy an ordinary man for a lifetime. I thought my hair must have turned white through the night, so horrid was the unreality of the thing. I thought at first (player/manager) Ned Hanlon was in the saddle and had unhorsed his most dangerous rival. I dreamed we had a new third baseman who could give cards and spades to young Dahlen, of Chicago. The fact that each Pittsburg player had made a base hit in the last two or three games also passed in front of my disturbed mental vision, and the shock was so great that I have not yet recovered from it.

"In my dream I beheld the ideal base ball official, and while I contemplated, he commenced to speak, while a half dozen reporters hung upon his inspired utterances. They wept with him when he was compelled to tell the truth, and rejoiced with great joy when he commenced to draw upon his imagination, which he did frequently. He did not abuse his board of directors oftener than once in a while. While I dwelt upon his many excellences, my spirit was troubled within me at my lack of experience and sense of my own unworthiness.

"The more I contemplated this wonderful individual, the firmer I became convinced I was not in his class and could never hope to equal him. So I decided to remain what I was and tell the truth now and then. As soon as I reached this conclusion, the vision vanished and I awoke to hard realities. Having viewed the ideal official at his best, I am now more than ever satisfied I did not lose my head and follow his example, and so I shall continue to pray."
[Pittsburgh Press, July 8, 1891]

Everyone sympathizes with the directors of the Pittsburg club in their efforts to place a winning team in Pittsburg, but the results are at variance with their efforts, laudable as has been their ambition. The team was selected with good judgment and the prospects for a successful

season two months since were never brighter, but since then the team has been steadily losing ground. A number of changes have been suggested to the board, but beyond the release of Staley, Browning, Stratton and Fields, and the signing of Shortstop Shugart, the board has pursued a very conservative course. It may be the part of wisdom, but the people ask for results. In the meantime, we all commiserate together.
[Pittsburgh Press, July 15, 1891]

Pittsburg's aggregation of weaklings and quitters needs a guardian badly, in spite of President O'Neill's efforts to bolster them up.
[Pittsburg Press, June 12, 1891]

The Pittsburgs won two games last week, and the base ball world was turned upside down.
[Pittsburg Press, June 29, 1891]

Jim Galvin is said to have made a convert of Manager McGunnigle to the art of hoodooism and the two hold nightly seances at which other members of the team allege strange things take place. Baldwin and King have been taken into the secret and they are betting money Pittsburg will finish the season in fifth place. Charley Reilly is said to have procured a charm from a Philadelphia professor of the black art and is playing ball with more confidence than ever.
[Pittsburgh Press, September 17, 1891]

Mr. Browning, remotely of Louisville, has not a very handsome pair of legs. They wouldn't draw a salary in the front row of a ballet, and the pants—hiss pants since the Minnesota ballet died—with which he covers a portion of the aforesaid legs are painful things to look at. They are apt to cause nervousness on the part of sensitive people. They appear to be constantly on the point of dropping off, but they and the alleged legs inside them get over a great swath of grass, and Cincinnati ball players both hate and fear those legs of Browning's. They cut off several runs today, they reduced a home run to a three-bagger, and several doubles to plain singles. Browning played ball today, and his two-by-three legs were in it—very much in it.

Now, Miller's pants are much on the order of Browning's, but (Pittsburg player) Miller wasn't in it today. If any ball player who has appeared on these grounds this year has put up a choicer, more widely diversified, energetic, whoop-in set of errors than did Miller today, his name has been forgotten. If it had been his one ambition to make brilliant sweepstakes errors, he couldn't possibly have done better. Once

Mr. Hanlon walked in from the field and had the game stopped while he remonstrated with his shortstop. With a load off his mind, Mr. Hanlon walked dignifiedly back into the field and put a morocco-bound, gold-clasped error himself. Mr. Miller didn't say a word; the spectators did that for him, and Hanlon got the laugh.
[Pittsburg Press, May 10, 1891]

    As a spectator remarked yesterday: "What can you expect from a glass arm outfield, a half-ragged infield and nine men who can't hit the ball a little bit. If the Pittsburg club cannot bat out its games, an error was made in the calculations of the builders." ...The cranks have waited and waited for the sluggers to commence to slug, but they seem very slow to strike their gait. We are all willing to enthuse good Manager Hanlon and jolly your gang to the end of the chapter, but now and then we would like to see something like results.
[Pittsburg Press, 1891]

    It is often said when things get to their worst, they mend, and if there is any truth in that old statement, we may expect the local baseball club to improve daily from this on. It can hardly be imagined that the team can get any worse than it is; that is, taking the last two or three games as a sample.
    The two games put up at Recreation Park yesterday by the home players against Indianapolis were such as to make the 1,200 spectators regret the day they first took an interest in baseball. Very frequently defeats cannot reasonably be grumbled at, but yesterday's pair hadn't a redeeming feature about them. Downright bad playing, particularly the pitching, caused both of them.
[Pittsburg Dispatch, August 3, 1889]

    The people who witnessed the National league game at Recreation park yesterday went away much disgusted and many of them promising not to return until the colts commenced to play ball. The heroic surgery of Director O'Neill (Pittsburg manager) has had no effect on the playing strength of the club up to date. Indeed, none of the players have a sure thing on remaining at present. Lawson, one of the new crop pitchers, was in the box, but he might just as well have been somewhere else. Indeed, there are several amateur clubs about the city that may be relied upon to play better ball with little or preliminary practice.
[Pittsburg Press, June 3, 1890]

After Monday's game in Pittsburg the Daily News said: "Ring out, wild bells. The Pittsburgs actually won a game yesterday. As a result two men died of heart failure, an iron dog went mad, and a pair of timber wheels shrunk until a handkerchief could cover them."
[Saint Paul Globe, September 7, 1896]

None of the wise men of the world have ever evolved a plan that will make winners out of every club in a base ball circuit. All the millennium ideas grouped in Utopian splendor cannot do that. When those wonderful Colonels captured for Louisville the booby prize in 1889, losing 111 games and winning but twenty-eight, enthusiasts thought a record had been made that would survive the ravages of time and be as everlasting as the hills. The idea of a club that could lose more games than that seemed incredible—a figment of a shattered mind. Still, within the next twelve months, that celebrated regiment of nomads known as (team owner) Jay Palmer O'Neill's Folly company of Pittsburg, had succeeded in dropping just 114 games, while but twenty-three victories were credited to them.
[Omaha Daily Bee, June 12, 1892]

END OF THE NINTH.

Few losses were more humbling to a good team than losing to a cellar dweller.

Sour Grapes

The year of 1898 was a bitter pill for Baltimore writers to swallow. After the Orioles had won the National League pennant three years running, from 1894 to 1896, expectations of "four-peating" soured as the team struggled. This bothered some Baltimore writers who could not hide their disappointment:

Won't somebody please stop 'em? Turn 'em around and send them back to the paths they were wont to tread. Whoever stops those runaway Orioles before they land at the bottom of the heap will be rewarded with a season pass and a plush red cushion aside the red water cooler in the press box at Union Park. Only stop 'em before they get so far gone that there will be no recovery, at least for this year.

Local rooters accustomed to the rush to the top of Hanlon's men stand amazed when they contemplate their turning tail and running madly to keep company with the second division clubs.

While baseball memories are short, and the joys of repeated victories are easily doused in the sadness of defeat, yet the fans should be wise enough to know how often have the spirits of the Birds drooped but to make more dramatic their final spurt, which landed a pennant.

Very prone are the patrons of the national game to forget the pleasant paths of winners when they are struggling along near a crowd of hitherto tail-enders. From long range it is hard to imagine the ex-Champions going down day after day in defeat. Pitchers have done fairly well, and yet the tale has been the same. It was one of the worst weeks in recent years for the Baltimore players, and on every hand is heard the familiar question. Why?
[Baltimore American, May 29, 1898]

More bitter sentiments were spilled before the fateful season-ending series with Boston, which the Orioles lost and, along with it, the pennant.

Nothing but a catastrophe can now rob Boston of the pennant, and local rooters of a sanguine temperament needs must think of the chances of next season for comfort. Again the flag was lost by apparent trifles. It's impossible to turn the mill with water that has passed, and yet the disappointed fan cannot refrain from reflecting on what might have been.

The pathway of the season was strewn with the losses consequent upon little mites of carelessness, or, the Oriole arch-enemy, over-confidence. Yet, after all, the season's work has not been altogether discreditable. There were many times when to finish a strong second seemed impossible. While Hanlon's men did lose a number of games in a most aggravating style, there were other times when they retrieved apparently hopeless defeats by the use of exquisite science and tenacity of purpose.
[Baltimore American, October 9, 1898]

Humor in Losing by One Run

It wasn't classy journalism, but it sure caught your eye and put a smile on your face:

Pittsburg, September 3.—The Birds did not make a clean sweep of the bargain day affair they played in Pittsburg today. They fully expected to walk away with both games. In this they failed, though by the closest margin. A base hit or two more and better treatment from one of Nick Young's minion would have turned the trick. It was one of those grand 1 to 0 games which have been more than plentiful this season. Magnificent fielding and pitching was presented, and when the game was over, Pop Hanlon said, "Sure, the people got value received today."

(Baltimore pitcher) Dr. McJames was on hand with splendid work, but it was his fate to be classed a loser and all the honor given to the veteran Hart, whose team was judged by results. McJames was invincible after the first inning. It was in this round that the Pittsburgs made the tally which won the game.

It was the lot of an ex-Oriole to accomplish the work. Tom O'Brien was the lucky lad, and the glory came in good stead, for O'Brien has not been in good standing lately. The Birds took the first try at the ball and failed to place a man. Donovan, the first Pirate, struck out. Then came O'Brien. He drove a beautiful triple far over Holmes' head. McCarthy pulled a single to right, scoring O'Brien. A wild pitch put McCarthy on second, but the next two men were easy.

This was but one run and the game was young, So the Orioles didn't worry. They felt sure Hart would be easy picking; but he wasn't, and the battle waged to the finish. It was marked by sharp fielding on both sides. Base hit killing was the order of the day. Joe Kelley began the display by making a fine running catch of Gray's long drive in the third. An inning later, McGraw was applauded for a display of pluck. After being hit on the eye by a would from his own bat, McGraw lined a single to center. In the fifth Robby aroused the patrons by chasing to the grand stand for a foul.

The Birds felt their time had come in the sixth. Keeler strained himself in beating out a slow one. Jennings flied to Donovan, whose throw to first for a double play passed Clarke. Keeler went to second on the error. Ely stopped Kelley's single too late to throw. Then came a play which ruined the Birds' chances. McGann hit to Ely, who tried for a double play, Ely assisting at second. McGann struck first base ahead of the ball, but Connolly said the ball beat him, and gave a double play. All the Birds flew at Connolly. He stood their chirps for a few moments, then ordered McGraw out of the game. Ball took his place.

The Orioles were disgusted. They couldn't do anything after that deal. The seventh was marked by a grand catch. McCarthy pulled down Demont's liner after a hard run. The fireworks fielding kept up to the last. In the ninth Dick Padden robbed Kelley of a base hit on one of the most remarkable stops ever seen on the ball field. After two hands were out, McGann hit safe, but Holmes ended the game by a fly out.
[Baltimore American, September 4, 1898]

The pathetic poem which relates the catastrophe that overtook the celebrated Casey when he went to bat exactly describes the situation in New York baseball circles today. There may be joy somewhere on earth, possibly in Beantown, but there is none in Gotham. Our baseball idols have been pushed down upon the damp earth at the Polo grounds and had their nice white flannel suits soiled by the mischievous young men from the Hub. Once again has the benefit of association with the classical Bostonese shown itself on the ball field.

Ward and his men struggled with might and main to overcome the rarefied intellectual qualities that distinguished the work of the Bostonians, but it was in vain. The New York entered the game with high hopes and emerged with crushed feelings. The most exasperating feature of the game is the fact that it is impossible to lambast anybody for the defeat. The umpire was all right. The decisions that were loudly hissed were correct and impartial. There were no flagrant fielding errors and no glaring errors in judgment. Therefore the crank who is looking around for something on which to vent his pent-up rage is perfectly helpless, and will be compelled to gnash his teeth in silent wrath.

...the game, while close and interesting for five innings, degenerated into a slaughter thereafter. The Bostons were not at the Polo grounds to be beaten if they could help it, and they have great success in avoiding anything they dislike. The game is simply added proof of the honest of the national pastime. A victory for New York would have meant thousands of dollars in the treasury today. The Bostons shut their eyes to all financial questions, and proceeded to administer a disheartening beating to the New Yorks.
[The Sun (New York), April 29, 1893]

The Brooklyns hardly deserved to win; they put up such a miserable fielding game. The way they erred in the matter of dropped fly balls was enough to make the Jamaica Bay wind whistle a dead march. Even Griffin was at fault in this respect, and Dailey and Kennedy also showed evidence of having what the boys term "butter fingers."
[The Sun (New York), May 7, 1893]

Brooklyn has a tale of woe, and sturdy Tom Lovett is the central figure in the tragedy. Thomas, all smiles over the fact that he had been selected to pitch for the Brooklyns at a ladies' day at Eastern Park, was confident of making the Baltimoreans waft themselves away on a Jamaica Bay wind, sadder in spirit but wiser in their opinion of T. Lovett.

Thomas, however, was doomed to disappointment. The Baltimores, encouraged by Clark, the catcher with the turkey gobbler

voice, lit on to Lovett's curves and sent the ball in as many different directions as goes the corn scattered by the farmer feeding his poultry.
[The Sun (New York), May 18, 1893]

> The team hailing from this city with a hospital corps of six men went up against nine robust Beaneaters at Boston yesterday and was routed horse, foot and dragoons. The slaughter did not cease until sundown, when the remnants of the club that was to finish the season in fourth place or better, were quietly removed to the Quincy house for protection.
> The poor little innocents away from their mammas and the sheltering influence of home are billed for one more struggle this afternoon with Michael J. Kelly's Boston savages. It is to be hoped that they will be allowed to leave the "Hub" alive. The people of that city bear them no particular ill will, but it grieves that exceedingly every tim your Poor Boys are barbarously treated. Still, they should either come home or change their name. SEP It would be tedious to follow the Allies through nine innings, and relate in detail how they were humiliated, how they played for full nine innings with one hit off such pitchers as Clarkson and Sowders, and how Jim Galvinn was knocked out of the box and had to give way to young Garfield. The score tells the story, and no other comment is necessary.

[Pittsburgh Press, July 13, 1889]

Kansas City

The Kansas City Blues of the Western League posted a miserable year in 1897. Sinking to the cellar in late May, they managed to claw their way up to finish next-to-last, taking well-deserved heat from the local media along the way.
Read away:

> When Manager Manning went into the baseball markets of the world early this spring and expended hundreds of dollars getting together a team that would give Kansas City a fair representation in the race for the pennant, every indication pointed to the conclusion that he had selected a strong aggregation.
> The players who comprise the Blues came here with established reputations. There seemed no room for doubt but that the team would be in the first division all the time, crowding the leaders for first or second place honors. Individually, there are some strong men on the team, but there is a flaw somewhere; the work is not being gotten out of the men of

which they are capable.

The work of the team in the games of the past two days has been so surprisingly bad that even their best friends have marveled at it. When it is all that Kansas City can do to break even with the tail-enders on home grounds, and by the barest of chances escape a brace of shutouts, there must be something radically wrong.

In baseball, as in everything else, there enters an element usually ascribed as "luck," good or bad. When the Blues lost game after game in the early part of the season, all their ills were ascribed to ill luck; but when it figured that they have won but eleven out of thirty-one games, another element enters into consideration, and it is called bad ball playing.

A critical scrutiny of the work of any individual on the team leaves room for doubt as to demerit; closely watching the team from day to day shows that the losses of game have largely come from the most unexpected sources. Up to the last two games every loss, nearly, could be traced to a misplay by an individual at some crisis of the game; but the last two games showed the team up in a lamentable light.

Of course, it must be taken into consideration that the men are playing against the adverse criticism of disgruntled fans; they are openly roasted on the field, and their misplayed are loudly and boisterously berated from the bleachers.

But baseball playing is a business, and the milk of human kindness has never been quaffed by the average fan so that he can daily "root" for and "jolly" a losing team. It is a difficult thing to do, of course, to pay no heed to the jeers of the bleachers, but the consoling thought should ever be uppermost that the jeers can be metamorphosed into paeans of praise by a few successive victories.

Many excuses have been advanced for the showing of the team. Some say it is over anxiety; if it is, let's have some careless ball playing. Others declare that all is not harmonious on the team; if this is true, there should be some "weeding."
[Kansas City Journal, May 29, 1897]

The day Kansas City ignominiously displaced the Grand Rapid Bob-o-Links in last place caused this local writer to look introspectively as he tried to answer the nagging question: How in the world did this happen?

End of the Line

The team has lit. After weeks of weary travail, and tears, and sorrow, and heartaches, the Blues at last have touched bottom. They are now in a class by themselves, and there is none to do them reverence. When the season opened—aye, weeks before—hope beat high in the breasts of the expectant fans. They chuckled as they in fancy saw the boys in blue walloping all comers and their voices were attuned to the inspiring command: "Bring on your old pitcher and see us swat him out of the lot."

The advance notices recorded wonderful feats by the various players. There were the Bannons—phenoms from down East, b'gosh. Manager Manning had the left field fence torn down so visiting teams would have less ground for complaint because of so many home runs being made off their pitchers. There was Reilly—who had kissed the Blarney stone before he joined the big show. There, too, was McFarland—alas, there, also, was Johnson and Truby.

And now echo questions, "Where are they all at?"

The Blues opened the season by losing to St. Paul. But the fans were not discouraged. They said one unto the other: "A bad beginning taketh a good ending," and they journeyed out to the park to root the team to victory. As the season advanced and the team continued to lose, the fans thrashed an umpire or two and threatened others—but the team kept losing.

Then the fans said: "There is a hoodoo on." The captain of the team bought rabbits' feet. As the scores showed that the Blues had outbatted and outfielded their opponents and yet lost the games, this list of stock phrases came into use:

"The umpire robbed us."

"Hard luck."

"We outplayed 'em, anyway."

"We've got a team of good players. Wait till they strike their gait."

*"___ ___ ___ __! ! ? ? ? * * *: :___ : : ! !"*

Why doesn't Manning get into the game?"

There isn't a team in the league that hasn't beaten us; whipped us out of our boots. From present indications they will continue to wallop us; rub it in; make merry with our pitchers; gloat over our fielding errors; puzzle our batsmen with their inshoots and their outshoots; whitewash us; beat us by a run; by a dozen; by as many as they please.

Yesterday Grand Rapids (former tail-ender) beat us 11 to 4.
[Kansas City Journal, June 5, 1897]

A great many baseball patrons left Exposition park yesterday in a disgruntled frame of mind, when, as a matter of fact, they should have gone away with light hearts and rejoicing. The fans seemed to be cut up because the Blues had lost two games of baseball. Apparently they lost sight of the wisdom and almost prophetic foresight of the schedule-makers of last winter's snows.

Suppose, instead of two game scheduled for yesterday, there had been three? That would have been something like a bitter pill to swallow. Three losses in one day! Three long strides deeper into the gradually narrowing bottomless pit! It would have been an occasion to try out the heroic soul of a Mark Tapley.

As it was, the Blues had only lost two games when, at 5:10 o'clock yesterday afternoon, long strings of people began to ooze from the park gates. It was only a fair day's work for the Kansas City Blues at that. They could have lost more if they had been given an opportunity.

...The Blues are graceful losers. They appear to take an interest in the science of artistically scattering their losses around the circuit, playing no favorites—first come, first served. Once or twice yesterday forenoon, it looked as though the Blues would inadvertently win the game. There two or more men on bases at critical stages and a hit meant an unexpected victory.

But the batsmen knew what they were there for, and relieved the anxiety which fluttered in the hearts of the other members by striking out, or sending a ridiculously easy bounder across the diamond.

"Brownie" Foreman was on the firing end of the battery in the forenoon game, and when he realized that the opposing batsmen were unable to solve a victory in his twisters, he conveniently landed several body blows that sent Milwaukee feet pattering down the line to first. On two other occasions, he located the plate several feet from where it was originally imbedded in the earth, and, in the technique of the game, allowed the men to "walk on balls." In this way he strewed the visitors' path with roses, and caused them to understand that life after all isn't six inches of foam and one inch of beer.

After the first inning, he admitted of but one hit. The Blues scored their lonesome run on two errors by Taylor, who fumbled a grounder, and then threw it to the club house in an apoplectic attempt to head the runner.

There was less fuss and feathers to the second. It was forked right over to the visitors in the first inning. In return for which the men from Milwaukee touched off some Fourth of July day fireworks that quite eclipsed anything presented at any of the local parks in meteoric splendor.

Mr. Albert Abbey, who struggles along on the miserly monthly stipend of $225 for exercising his right arm one hour every alternate day of the week, Sunday excepted, was the predominating factor in the presentation of the game, inflating the balls that he passed up until they sailed down to the plate as big as life preservers.

On the other hand, the visitors used a ball that grew smaller and smaller as it neared the plate and finally shrunk away to the meager proportions of a BB shot. Handicapped in this manner, it is little wonder the visitors ran right away with the second game. It was like matching a ten-second sprinter against a wooden-legged citizen.

The scores...
[Kansas City Journal, July 7, 1897]

Softly and silently, the Kansas City Blues yesterday settled down into last place. The arrival of the team at the bottom has been expected for some time and the event caused little excitement among the members, although a majority of the players seemed relieved to know that they had at last reached their proper level.

The mental strain of clinging to the eyebrows to seventh place is thus happily averted, and, with a continuance of the remarkable pluck and endurance evinced by the Blues during the past two weeks, there is no reason under heaven why they ever should be dislodged from their present resting place. The unsatisfying taste of tail-end life given the team three weeks ago aroused an uncontrollable desire for more.

When the (Minneapolis) Millers dislodged the Blues, they clung to the place with a pertinacity worthy of a better cause, but the indomitable endurance and rock-ribbed tenacity of the Blues finally told and yesterday the Millers were routed bag and baggage. The Blues are now at home.

Excitement distresses the Blues. They fret and chafe under the suspense of doubt, and it tickles them immensely to be in a position to occasionally, by design or accident, injure the standing of some one of the other teams without being in a position to be injured themselves. The report that the Blues were going to organize a croquet club is erroneous.
[Kansas City Journal, July 4, 1897]

The Kansas City *Times* had this wail about the two games the Blues lost to Columbus:

"If there is any particular point in the national game in which the Senators from Ohio did not outplay Mr. Manning's some-time marvels yesterday afternoon, it would be interesting to know just where that point is concealed. The Blues fielded like a lot of peroxide soubrettes; they batted like the last nine rows in the primary class, and

as for their pitchers—a bloomer girl club would have made them look like four checks on a wrecked and ruined bank.

"It was a delirium of jumbled rainbows, in which there was something of every color except that of the rose. It resolved itself into a case of twenty men wandering through two games in a way which suggested that each of them had slept in a dry goods box with the faucet on the gas pipe turned the wrong way. It was the perfection of dope dreams."
[Saint Paul Globe, September 17, 1898]

A corpse-like pallor of indifference frustrated the Blues in their blundering attempt yesterday to wrest the second game of the present series from the aged gents from Ohio. Baseball of the paresis-stricken order, with but one visible ray of lingering semblance to the national pastime, was served up to the handful of fans who journeyed out to Exposition park yesterday afternoon. Columbus won—5 to 3.
[Kansas City Journal, August 25, 1897]

The season is as a tale that is told. The hopes—the fears—the expectations of the fans have been nipped as by a frost—a killing frost—and in this pathetic hour of their extremity they cannot turn a deaf ear to the ever-recurring siren song of managerial origin: "We'll win the pennant next season."

Out of the turbulent sea of professional baseball, the wild, wild waves washed to Kansas City shore the flotsam and jetsam that was cast overboard by nearly every wind-driven hulk that cruised the main. Never in the pea-green history of baseball in this city have the changes of players been wrought with such dexterous rapidity. Without the illusive lime light effect, men came, played their part, heard the applause—or the jeers—of the multitude, and then disappeared. The stock phrase, "Who's playing first base for the Blues today?" came into general use.

Sweeter music, when echoed, rose and fell and swelled into a grand diapason of harmonic sound, never was heard by Kansas City fans than the orchestral accompaniment which marked the prelude to the season. Did we not have the Bannons—Jim and Tom—"little, chunky fellows, you know, full of life and activity; natural born baseball players!" filled the East with sorrow to see them leave. Their advertisement set forth their accomplishments in colors of light. Could run like startled deers! Hit! Didn't we take down the left field fence to quiet the probable storm of protests from visiting managers because of balls that would be lost outside the grounds?

And there was Truby—aggressive, not afraid of the umpire; a guaranteed timely hitter! Just the man to come to bat when three men were on bases, with two out and four runs needed to win the game! We often needed the runs—but that's another story.

Then there was Josh Reilly—"wait for the big parade." He liked to mix acrobatic feats—ground and lofty tumbling—with his work. Many's the time he has delighted the bleacherite by his unexpected and rapid contortions on the gory field of battle, where our part in the plot was simply to furnish the gore.

Jack Carney guarded the initial sack and kept his suit clean, while Fred Lake and a quid of tobacco stood behind the plate. Carney turned his ankle, and Mr. Manning turned him loose. Lake is chewing tobacco down in the Eastern League.

Pitchers? We had 'em galore. It seemed that none escaped us. We tried 'em all, and the bleachers declared them guilty—every mother's son of them. There was McFarland, Barnett, Reust, Brunner, Johnson—the list is a long one. There were ins-and-outers, southpaws, men expected to set the baseball world aflame. But the season ended and no ruddy glow suffused the heavens, unless the low, deep flow of profanity of an earnest-looking paleontologist out at Fifteenth and Prospect could be mistaken for a conflagration.

Now that the melancholy days have come, when the swat of the bat is no longer heard in the land, when the stands are deserted and the well-intentioned young person with the loud voice who always insisted that the batsman should "Hit it out, old man; you can do it," is training his vocal organs on a hob-nailed diet of sound for the opening of the "Rah! rah! ree! Who are we!" season—now that all this, and more, has come to pass, it may be just as well to delve down into the score books and bring to the light of day the names of the scattered army of men who at various and sundry times, comprised the wonderful and fearful 1897 Kansas City Blues.

The roster is as follows:...
[Kansas City Journal, September 20, 1897]

The same grief-stricken author also summed up the team's entire season in a mere three sentences:

The Blues lost the opening and closing games of the season, to say nothing of ninety-seven other games which they neglected to win. St. Paul took the first and the rival town of Minneapolis took the last. Probably the most wretched season in baseball in Kansas City came to an inglorious close at 4:40 o'clock yesterday afternoon, when a Miller brought in the winning run on a passed ball that did not roll fifteen feet

from the plate.
[John Foster, New York Journal, June 3, 1897]

More Sad Songs

This is the St. Louis Republic's way of announcing that the Browns will play a game:
"Brooklyn and St. Louis will play a game of baseball at Sportsman's park this afternoon. The Browns will make the usual tremendous effort and boldly bid you read about it in the advance notices of the games, and which never seem to materialize on the field. But, as said before, the Browns might win a game, and then you would be sorry if you missed it. You would as soon have missed seeing the airship."
[Kansas City Journal, May 29, 1897]

President Vanderbeck (Detroit team owner) was profoundly grateful to the Brewers yesterday for permitting his gang of cripples to take a game. The contrast between Milwaukee's playing the article the nine put up against the Indianapolis team was so great that a man in the grand stand bought three score cards in succession, doubting that it was the Glenalvin crew (Milwaukee) at all.
It required two pitchers to give away the game gracefully. Nonnamaker started in to do the trick and withheld his generosity for three innings. In the fourth he became a trifle liberal and the visitors got a run. In the sixth, however, he hung out the latch-string and allowed the men from the City of the Straits to make five runs on two doubles, four singles and a base on balls.
This was "going it" too strong and Barnes was put in in the seventh. For a while Barnes was a trifle miserly, but in the ninth, he opened his heart by giving four bases on balls and forcing in the run that won the game.
[Milwaukee Journal, July 16, 1896]

When Mr. Shakespeare wrote his lines about the tide in the affairs of men which taken at the flood led on to fortune, he anticipated with marvelous accuracy a large element in the success of an exceedingly intricate game invented since his time, that of base ball.
And the St. Paul base ball club seems to have caught it yesterday when it was distinctly on the ebb.
Pitted against a motley company of despised, and hardly self-respecting colts, hardly worthy of their steel, but raised to the pinnacle

of bliss by some early hypodermic injections of bull-headed luck, the Minneapolis youngsters yesterday led the veterans of Comiskey's team a busy, but fruitless nine innings' chase, and all because the Apostolic batsmen, the peer of any team of hitters in the league, made two base hits when they were as useless as a vermiform appendix, and struck out when good hits were as necessary as sunlight to the world it blesses.
[Saint Paul Globe, May 15, 1898]

    When old Charlie Getzein*, with a black jersey and blue trousers, a goodly bulk of adipose tissue and the same old German smile, took the ball in hand and stepped to the slab at the ball park in Chicago on Sunday last, there were men in the crowd who thought the days of 1886 had come again.
    "Pretzel! Pretzel!" was the cry which ran round the park. "Where's Ganzell?" shouted the old-time ball crank from the bleachers. "Where's Brothers, White, Rowe, Richardson and Thompson?" demanded another. And the Pretzel, hearing these calls out of the long dead past, humped up his back, tried to remember the skill he had ten years ago, and for a few hot innings, threw them over the plate like bullets.
    The Younger Generation was before him—the little boys that used to bring in balls that went over the fence and who used to get up on the bleachers and tell him that he was a wonder, but he wouldn't do. Now, in uniforms, and bats in hand, these same little boys were arrayed against one who was pitching ball when they were in short dresses, and for quite a while their reverence for him seemed to keep them from hitting the curves he threw.
    For five innings, Getz was strong. Then the strain began to tell upon the stout old German. He puffed like a grampus. The perspiration came in great beads upon his visage. Somebody—some disrespectful youth who had been playing only ten or twelve years—made a three-bagger. "Ich habe geplassen geplatz," said Getz. "Dis vill do me vell, nit!"
    And they thumped him for all there was in it the last three innings.
[Evening Times (Washington, D.C.), September 2, 1896]

    * Getzein was part of the one-time famous "pretzel" battery, with catcher Ganzel, when Detroit won the League championship in 1886.

    Yesterday's performance closed a most uninteresting series with

the St. Pauls. This, of course, is neither the fault of the Milwaukee team or management, but it is awful hard work to sit around and watch a lot of fellows play who haven't the animation of the most ordinary lot of bones you could scare up out of a country graveyard. The St. Paul management should diet their young men on ginger before starting them out on another starring tour.
[Milwaukee Journal, August 22, 1890]

The Cleveland Leader is not enthusiastic over its own nine, and it evidently does not like Detroit, vide an item concerning one game, which the latter won:

"Yesterday the home nine was again given a severe trouncing at the hand of 'those duffers from Michigan,' otherwise known as the Detroits. There was much weeping and gnashing of teeth in the Forest City last night, and in Detroit the inhabitants were well nigh crazed with delight."
[Providence (R. I.) Sunday Star, May 7, 1882]

No Joy at the Bottom: The Last-Place Blues

The stigma of a team being a loser followed it into the next season, and nothing mitigated the stench of defeat until it was replaced by that emitted by another, even more hapless team:

The admirers of the Baltimore Club have given up all hope of the club winning a respectable position in the championship race, and the only request they make of the manager and players is to keep away from that tail-end. The city has had a representation for so many seasons in that position that it has become monotonous, and if the Metropolitans would only lose a few games while the home team is winning, there would be a possibility of the Baltimore team getting seventh place.
[Baltimore American, August 29, 1886]

The vaunted Wabash club, proud member of the Indiana-Illinois League, got off to a miserable 0-14 start in 1899, which prompted this letter from a local supporter, who generously offered his "services":

To the Baseball Editor:
I hear a great deal about the Wabash team of "cripples," and

would like to know if there really is such a team. I am a hunchback, with one crooked leg, and walk with a crutch. This ought to make me eligible. My right leg is sound, and with my crutch I can bat a rubber ball farther than any of the "crips" at this institute. I can hop to first, and beat out a bunt nearly every time, and sometimes can steal second. My arms are long and strong, and I am a good pitcher. I would like to have a chance to pitch for the Wabash Cripples. The Institute Cripples have an open date for Decoration day, and would like to meet some good team.

WALLY BOWLEGS, Pitcher and Captain, Indianapolis Surgical Institute.
[Indianapolis Journal, May 25, 1899]

There's one thing very commendable about the St. Pauls, and that's their determined effort to remain at the rear end of the procession. Such persistency is truly refreshing, for next to doing a good thing brilliantly, there's nothing like doing a bad one with a vehement and unflinching abandon.

Do not be alarmed, gentle reader, this is not heresy on our part, but a simple expression of what may be termed the acknowledged qualities of commercial value. Hence the fellow who steals a million is dubbed emperor of finance—a devilish clever fellow, don't cher know—while the man who pilfers a loaf for his starving little ones is accredited with being a d___d scoundrel.

Therefore, we say unto you, do whatever you undertake with all your might. Should your desires tend toward a life in commerce, barter and trade even up to the doors of the sanctuary; are you inclined to be a dude, don't make an ass of yourself, but be such a one that the caricaturist would find his occupation gone; would you be an acknowledged philanthropist, give with both hands, and don't make any fuss about it, either; and if a thief, be so true to the "profesh" that you would sooner rob yourself than remain idle.

Such being our dogma, we reiterate that it pleaseth us that the Apostles have concluded to be recognized as the tin-can brigade in the onward and victorious march of that anatomical monstrosity known as the Western association. Do what thou doest with all they might, my Christian friends, and people will not only appropriately recognize your effort, but will have the satisfaction, like the world-renowned Eli, of getting there.
[Milwaukee Journal, June 5, 1891]

Oh, tempora! Oh, mores! Oh, Giants!
Was it not enough that you should have been "swiped" twice out

of three times at Boston without returning to New York, and there be "swiped" again twice in succession in the presence of 15,000 of your best and most enthusiastic friends?

Why this sudden loss of that skill in picking up and throwing the ball that has characterized your brilliant performances hitherto? Are your fingers all thumbs, your arms but the revolving sails of a windmill that blow with every passing gale?

Where are those eyes that once could search the furthermost bending of a curved ball and, catching git at the full, could straighten it until it was flatter than beanery pancake? Are your optics eclipse or your optical nerves paralyzed? Tell us.

Four times in succession to be defeated by Boston. And what is Boston? Why, in seasons gone, Giants, you were accustomed to walk over Boston until that suburb's place on the baseball map looked like a banana trod upon by an elephant.

Giants, you need a brace. It is not too late. Nothing or nobody is ever too late in this world until after the last train has departed for home. And there are trains the next day. Bestir yourselves; shake the cobwebs off your eyes and the knots out of your arms. It is still six weeks to the end of the season and Temple Cup money.

Fifteen thousand citizens in a delirium, gasped, rooted, howled, struggled for breath, perspired and collapsed after five hours of heartbreaking baseball yesterday afternoon. (lost twice to Boston)
[John Foster, New York Journal, August 13, 1897]

The Cincinnati fans and rooters are struggling in gloom and sorrow, which, like Mill Creek miasma, has poisoned the atmosphere of their enthusiasm and blasted their fondest hopes and expectations. Their baseball team, which, a short time ago, occupied a proud place in the League race and promised the realization of hopes long deferred, have not justified the confidence that was reposed in them.

Harry Weldon, the Apollo Belvedere of the sporting scribes of that metropolis, is entirely cast down. There is pathos and tears in his obituaries that clearly indicate the poignant anguish of his soul. Ren Mulford, classically and reverently assails the fate that so cruelly disrupted the serenity of a mind usually at peace with all the world. Charlie Zuber seeks the solace of his closet, where, in the undisturbed stillness of night, he can make up a tabulated list of games lost by bad umpiring. Buck Ewing, who yesterday was a prince in baseball, today is a peasant, and his cons and jollies are regarded with scorn and derision. Too bad! Too bad!
[Evening Times (Washington, D.C.), August 26, 1898]

Editorial:

The "Senators," as a facetious country has dubbed our baseball players, are engaged usually in a desperate struggle to keep from taking a place near the tail end of the league at the tail end of the season, and if the Goddess of Liberty on the dome of the Capitol has any local pride, she must weep at what she has seen happen in the park a few blocks north of her. She has observed the home club walloped all over the grounds, and has been humiliated beyond endurance.

Long ago, Washington had a club which went abroad all over the land and mowed a mighty swath, but since the time of the old Nationals, our glory has departed and that hope deferred which makes the heart sick has been the portion of local enthusiasts. Still, hope has been maintained and exists today.
[Washington (D. C.) Critic, April 24, 1889]

Colonel Shannon evidently had that special session of his corps d'armee yesterday, as advocated in this paper. He must have labored with them ardently and impressed upon their receptive minds the horrors of the path which they were treading. They must have sworn a steel-clad, copper-riveted, moonlight-skull-and-crossbones sort of an oath to reform, for they all took beautiful braces and sent Providence, apparently invincible, in precipitate retreat, carrying the wounded Willie Friel, who was extensively shattered.

And all this shows what an uncertain object a base ball team can be when it feels that way. Rochester started out with an unprecedented string of victories and attained the head of the procession. This unique and awesome performance took the faithful by storm. They yelled themselves hoarse with delirious joy; they shook their heads wisely, agreed that Rochester had a winning team, and took the home end of the game every time they went in on a "pool."

Then came the smash. Hope took a tumble, bolted and disappeared in a cloud of dust, when Providence struck town. Strong men grew white and wan. Hearty voices sunk to childish treble. There was no joy among the band of the faithful. Yesterday, after a protracted siege of the blues, the talent took another lease of life and were once more happy.
[Post Express (Rochester, N. Y.), May 19, 1896]

The tail enders made it three straight yesterday and the Omaha fans left the grounds with the biggest crop of disgust they have harvested this season. And it was enough to make any loyal friend of the national game rise up in wrath to see how our alleged ball team burlesqued it and held it up to he ridicule of the rabble.

Why, those yellow-backed Suckers simply laid down along the base lines and laughed to see how poorly Papa's hired men could play when they wanted to, and at times the spectator was led to doubt whether some of the those players had ever really played the game before, or had served their time playing mumblety-peg in their grandmother's back yard.
[Omaha Daily Bee, August 20, 1894]

Often it has been said of a ball game that Tom Brown, Bill Smith or perhaps the whole nine "threw it away." Not because the game wasn't a good thing and worth keeping, but because Brown, Smith and the aggregation weren't good ball players. In fact, they were of that quality unfit for trading assets against the contents of a junk cart.

...By way of parentheses it is well to insert here that what the New York team didn't do prior to this ninth inning would fill one of these big grain elevators on the other side of the North River. What it did do would look better inserted in brackets and expressed by dashes and exclamation points, to interpret faithfully and fitly what the bunch of Harlem rooters thought and said.
[John Foster, New York Journal, August 1, 1897]

New Bedford was massacred yesterday. If you want to know how, just look at the shattered fence surrounding Olympic field, glance at the mown grass that bedecks the outfield, examine the wilted daisies, size up the lop-sided balls and cracked bats, and then examine the base hit column below and the story will be told simply, briefly and conclusively.

Hardly had the triumphant yell of victory been sounded when a defeat that will immortalize the local records of the game came as unexpected as the refreshing shower follows the brightest gleams of midday sun.

The Cuban Giants were the aggressor, and in accomplishing the signal victory, they build up a new record for themselves that will live long in the memory of those who saw the game.
[New Bedford (Mass.) Evening Journal, July 14, 1894]

Wanted—For the season of 1892, a cheap ball team. Players with established reputations for "being out for the stuff" and high-priced, unless contract jumpers, not wanted. Salaries low, but sure. For obvious reasons, apply not later than Oct. 15, to (owner) Jay P. O'Neill,

Pittsburg base ball club.
[Ohio State Journal, reprinted in the Pittsburgh Press, August 20, 1891]

That wonderfully constituted Hoosier aggregation of base ball tossers, of which it was said by (Indianapolis) Manager Spence that better ball could be played away from home on account of the evil effect of Indiana's balsamic atmosphere when here, has dropped from sixth place to eighth since starting on the present trip. Bring them back as soon as possible, Spence, so that they may again become infected with malaria.
[Indianapolis Sun, reprinted in the Pittsburgh Press, August 17, 1888]

Perhaps it was boredom, acting on a dare or seeking acclaim as an author beyond the confines of the local baseball stadium that caused this writer to use an everyday Pittsburgh loss as a theme for a sketch on pathos:

There was a halo of sunshine around the blond ringlets of little Eddie Morris as he pranced into the pitcher's box, Recreation park, in the afternoon; there were 4,000 smiling and expectant faces in the grand stand and on the bleaching boards which half enclosed the diamond; the players of the home club seemed as active as crickets, and altogether a more auspicious opening for a ball game was never seen on well-kept grounds of the Allegheny club.

The ladies, God bless them, almost filled their allotted space in the grand stand and shared in the general hopefulness of the occasion. Their costumes were the brightest of the season, and it was enough to put the most unsentimental leather chaser on his mettle to see them unbutton their gloves when the umpire called time, in order that they might the more freely applaud with their dainty little palms when stalwart Fred Carroll knocked the ball over the fence and dear little Mr. Sunday stole a base, but Mr. Carroll wasn't making home runs that afternoon, and blue-ribbon Sunday seemed to have some qualms of conscience on the subject of base-stealing. Besides, the naughty Giants were on their muscle, and the way they slugged the bounding pig skin whenever Mr. Morris put it within their reach was a sight to behold. Mr. Keefe, on the other hand, was aggravatingly cool, collected and effective, and he kept the Alleghenys knocking flies and easy grounders to the infield until they were covered with perspiration and red in the face in their frantic but unavailing efforts to beat the ball to first base.

In two innings it was a gone game. The bright sunshine had become a hollow mockery of blasted hopes, and the gentle zephyrs, which ever and anon floated across the field, bore to the ears of the affrighted umpire curses loud and deep. But it wasn't the umpire, nor the absence of mascots, for Manager Phillips had a full supply of the article on hand, nor even the superior playing of the big, ugly, black Giants. It was the listless playing of the home club more than anything else that seemed responsible for the defeat and brought an unpleasant recollection of the way things were "evened up" in that famous Allegheny-Indianapolis-Syracuse tournament in 1877.

"You see," said a disgruntled crank, "the New Yorks open their new grounds with the Alleghenys on Monday afternoon and the latter get 25 per cent of the receipts which are expected to be very large. The winning of two games apiece during the present series will materially increase the attendance at the forthcoming contest in New York."

The crank's insinuations may have resulted from an extra allowance of spleen, but his suspicions certainly took deep root in the grand stand before the end of the game. It was evident that Mr. Gore was out for his namesake when he stepped up to the plate with that easy stride of his in the first inning. It wasn't half a minute until a base hit was traveling through the grass of the outfield. Then Mr. Tiernan made himself equally obnoxious by a safe one to left, and Connors long two-bagger brought both men in.

The Allies couldn't do anything with Keefe, and although they blanked their opponents in the second inning and had two men sent to base on balls, it was a succession of blanks up to the sixth inning, when the solitary run scored by the home team during the game was brought in as the result of Dunlap's life, Kuehne's base hit and Tiernan's fumble in right field.

The cloud of disaster which gathered over the devoted heads of the home nine in the first inning grew bigger and blacker as the game progressed. The loose fielding of the Allies added to its density. Morris got a little wild in the second inning and banged batsman Hatfield with the ball. This encouraged Dunlap to fumble a grounder in the succeeding inning. Morris contributed his mite in the shape of Tiernan's three-base hit, Richardson's single and Connor's base on balls and two more runs were added to the score.

In the fourth inning, after two men were out, the visitors scored their fifth and sixth runs. Single hits by Gore, Ewing and Connor did the mischief, aided and abetted by Dunlap's wild throw. The seventh inning capped the climax, the Gothamites scoring their seventh run on inexcusable misplays by Kuehne and Miller. The "little Dutchman" seemed to be badly rattled from some cause. Probably the report that he was to be relegated to the outfield to make place for Deacon White had

reached his ears. Altogether it was a most unsatisfactory game, and the dispirited crowd which poured out of the grounds after the game seemed relieved when the last man was out.
[Pittsburgh Press, July 7, 1889]

Really, this is getting monotonous! Something should be done about it. Colonel Shannon should call a special meeting of his corps d'armee, open the convention with song—a dirge would be highly appropriate—wrestle with their spirits and tell them where they are off, and show them the error of their ways.

Where is that former greatness; where that victorious mien which was erstwhile the joy of the faithful, and the pride of the talent? It has taken a spring vacation, gone away, scooted, vamoosed. Perhaps Uncle Dan has been hoodooed, perhaps—oh, well, perhaps lots of things. After all the perhapses and ifs and interjections and conjunctions, the sad, funereal fact remains that Rochester has taken a large slide downward.
If Colonel Shannon would stop to consider the fact that Rochester may suffer the frightful fate of a percentage tied with Toronto, he will get a couple of kegs of spring tonic, and give it in large tablespoons before meals. Think of having the same percentage as a club to which belongs Chauncey O'Stuart! It's enough to make the wooden statue of the Goddess of Liberty that used to be on the court house turn green and drop her last remaining balance.
[Post Express (Rochester, N. Y.), May 18, 1896]

(Team owner) Louis Ost, when he read the score from Lincoln (Quincy lost, 23-6), locked the front door of his butcher shop, blew out the gas, laid his head upon an old ram's hide with his feet next to the ice chest and a chunk of artificial ice at his head. He has not been seen since.
[Quincy (Ill.) Daily Herald, May 10, 1895]

This doleful obituary, including a strong whiff of imminent scandal, summed up the tragic passing of an ill-fated losing team, the first sentence doubling as an epitaph for its headstone:

The Aurora (Ill.) News has the following to say of their defunct ball club:
"Conceived in error, born by mistake, nurtured in misfortune and productive of nothing but a disappointed feeling and a big lot of

unpaid bills, the Aurora base ball team and the Western Inter-State League has passed in its checks and gone to the wall.

No tears have been shed up to date. Manager McDowell, of the so-called Aurora aggregation, packed his grip yesterday while the team was being defeated for the last time, and at night, while the players were dreaming fondly of a payday when they could see the color of 'mon,' the protege of Onion Bill McCaull waded out into the dark and disappeared forever from the ken of Aurora creditors."
[Quincy (Ill.) Daily Herald, May 25, 1895]

When Loss Was Not a Loss—or, It's All in the Telling

Honestly, after reading the following game accounts, one wonders how baseball fans back then could ever have become upset over their teams' loss when the story of it was presented in such a cunningly refreshing way that it tickled the funny bone? It was as if the writing transported their minds into a nepenthe-like state, where pain and recall did not dwell. In truth, though, it was nothing more than journalistic sleight of hand, but pulled off masterfully.

In the first part of the game the Rockfords played ball like dudes carrying a hod and they handled the ball like a one-armed man carving turkey.
[Quincy (Ill.) Daily Journal, June 26, 1891]

The series between the Brewers and the "Indians" (Sioux City) wound up yesterday with the defeat of the former. It was like the last and most emphatic kick a mule would give before starting out on his own hood, or the manner in which one would expect to see a tramp who had been denied pie, shake the dust of a locality off his feet.

It was, in fact, an exposition of sumptuous nonchalance, with a good deal of the "only-been-monkeying-with-you-boys" kind of an emphasis thrown in. This untoward and unexpected action on part of the aborigines tore another length off the tail of our kite, and while we still hold the second position on the list, as well as in the hearts of our fellow citizens, it will take but one more swipe of the kind given yesterday.
[Milwaukee, Journal, July 6, 1891]

The alleged Aurora base ball club made a great record at Sportsman's park yesterday afternoon! Here it is. Gaze on it.

Runs, 0.
Errors, 11.
Base hits, 1.
Stolen bases, 0.
Bases given on balls, passed balls, 5.
Wild pitches, 2.

How is that for a record? The Aurora directors made a ten-story mistake Tuesday. Instead of firing their manager, they ought to have boxed up about six of their players and shipped them to "Darkest Africa" C. O. D. My! but they did some bummy ball playing yesterday.
[Quincy (Ill.) Daily Journal, May 7, 1891]

"Ad" Gumbert (Chicago pitcher) was the Phillies' victim. "Ad" has not been at his best this season, and the cunning which generally lingers in his right shoulder seems dormant just now. At any rate his curve ball does not twist and shoot with that depth of purpose necessary to deceive the practiced eye of the wily batsman. It curves, of course, but it has a tendency to remain within the batter's reach.

That was the trouble today. The ball was kept busy knocking paint off the fence at the park, and Wilmot, Carroll, and Ryan ran around until their tongues protruded and their eyes stuck out. Uncle Anson was kept busy dodging cannon-ball hits, and the infielder who would have had the temerity to face some of the line balls hit today would have deserved the same rank of honor as the soldier who throws an unexploded shell out of the trenches.

Thus it went. The Phillies thumped the ball and the Chicagos thumped the circumambient atmosphere. The result was inevitable. Eight red-hosed, red-faced sons of toil labeled Philadelphia ran, slid, and walked across the plate, and nine black-hosed, red-faced ball-tossers labeled Chicago stood and envied them from the depths of Western souls.
[Chicago Tribune, June 3, 1891]

Quincy is rock-rooted in sixth place. No accident that is known in base-ball casualties can send her down another peg. She has staked her claim, and no band of left-handed, waddling, big-paunched boomers from Oklahoma, or elsewhere, is going to plant profane feet on her native heath.

Peory (Peoria) be—blessed! Her whilom conquerors come too late. We have slid until there is not enough of us left to make a bar of soap, but we are still waggling where the tail is wont to be.

We are proud. We cannot tolerate familiarity. In the list of 1890 we desire to be at peace on one side, the under side. We do not choose to be squeezed in between other cities. We like the calm joy that comes to one who is let alone. The ambitious may expect to have their entrails continually gnawed at by the envious. We are not ambitious.

Let cultured Content stalk arm in arm with meek-eyed Humility. We are not of the world. We aren't in it. Let worldliness chew the cud of disappointment; our duty is to put some sugar in a square piece of cloth, give it to our callow management and do penance for ever permitting ourselves to yearn.
[Quincy (Ill.) Daily Journal, May 7, 1890]

If the Buffalo aggregation ever knew how to play ball, they certainly don't want to show it these days. Defeat after defeat isn't a very pleasant task to chronicle, but it must be done, my masters. To be beaten by Providence or Springfield is bad enough; to be walloped by that Saltville crowd of Anarchists (Rochester) is worse, but when a gang of misfits, cast-offs, has-beens and putty fingers whose baseball days have been over many moons ago and whose knowledge of the national game consists of visions after hitting the pipe, then it is time to rise up in our anger, oh, brother rooters, and lynch these traducers of Buffalo sport and Buffalo reputation of being first in everything. The Queen City people always lead; never follow, but if we don't use a galvanic battery on these rheumatic giants of the present Bisonic outfit, we'll be leading from the other end of the list.
[Buffalo Enquirer, July 10, 1895]

"See saw, see saw,
Now we go up and down,"

not in the direction of London town, but from gloom to delight and then down again to gloom with a thud that unfortunately made us see more stars than runs. We're in the soup up to our necks, and while the band played "Annie Rooney," the gentlemen from Burlington knocked us down, rolled us over two or three times, then sat on us and yelled to the man on the ladder with a whitewash brush to mark up another run.
[Quincy (Ill.) Daily Whig, May 2, 1890]

The sable shades of night, about which poets love to write, were never in their palmiest days more than half as black as the gloom that overhang Harlem yesterday evening after the bat's last crack.

With a lead of two runs and the idols of 2,500 spectators at the beginning of the ninth inning, the Giants at its finish had lost all but their uniforms and bats, and stood for a swift trip to the junk shop.

Fifteen minutes of heartache sent a grief-stricken crowd home with the headache.

It happened in this wise and the tale will make your heart both sad and weary.
[John Foster, New York Journal, June 3, 1897]

Beaten by Baltimore and by a score which would drive a Chicago prairie nine to disbandment.

You could have toasted muffins on Anson's neck at any stage of today's game. The old man was so hot that he couldn't see, and the day must have made a year's decrease on his lease of life. Aside from (Chicago pitcher) Ignatius Ingo Luby, the crabbed old man contributed more to the afternoon's disgraceful defeat than any one else, and that Chicago's weak spot is first base was made apparent by Anson's doddering work. He played the first game with about as much skill and baseball sense as a coal passer on a lake freight boat would exhibit.

Three errors, each of them as costly as they were inexcusable, were made by Anson and had the effect of completely upsetting the team. And then the Old Man had the bold and daring effrontery to turn about and roast his men for falling in line with his own stupidity.

Never in the history of modern baseball was such a frightful exhibition of the National game put up. There was absolutely nothing about the Colts but the word "Chicago" across the breast of their suits to indicate that they were ball players.

Luby was hit for twenty-three base hits, doubles, triples, and home runs being plenteously mixed up with them. The people are so accustomed to seeing the Orioles done up that the games are always entered in the "lost" column before they are called. A third-rate club would be stoned out of town here if it failed to win a game. And so it is not to be wondered at that Anson, after meeting defeat by a score of 23 to 1, was afraid to enter the carriage after this evening and ride home with his team.

The people here hooted and yelled at the Old Man this afternoon on the grounds until he frothed at the mouth with rage.

"Take him off the field," yelled a man, shying a big wad of dampened paper at Uncle.

"Yes, and off the earth," supplemented another.

"What did Hanlon give you to throw the game?" lustily inquired a third.

"Go jump into the Patapsco and weight yourself with Luby," put in a bleacherite.

Anson could do nothing but swallow his wrath and let it take vent in perspiration through the pores of his face until that expansive picture looked a central figure in one of Dante's hot air chambers. This is how the blot on the escutcheon was daubed:

...That was all, but, as the guillotinist said when asked why he didn't have an extra blade to his machine—enough.

The score:
[Inter Ocean (Chicago), June 7, 1892]

7. Humor in Errors

Uneasy rests the man who's made an error.
[Anon.]

Once, in describing a ball game, a writer remarked that *errors, like the description of wedding presents in the society column, were numerous and costly*. It was spot on.

Blunders during play were committed inordinately often during this era, largely because old-guard fielders were slow to adopt the use of gloves. By the mid-1890s, however, gloves came into pretty much universal use, pitchers being the last holdout. Dropped balls was, by far, the most frequent misplay.

One of the earliest terms of baseball slang, dating to the 1850s, was *muff*, which meant to drop a ball. The noun form, *muffin*, naturally followed, which was soon applied to the error-prone player, or, much less often, a good player doing poor work.

Over the years, numerous words and phrases were coined by writers to replace the word *error*, such as *fumble, juggle, make a mess of, drop the ball, blundering play, dropping a safe one, lunkhead play, make a miss of a grounder, piece of negligence*, etc. The more apt and expressive term, *buttered fingers* (later *butter fingers*), first appeared in 1893.

This is how an error was described in 1872:

He popped up a high ball to left field which McMullen got under to take. It was a sight to see the crowd and all the players just at this critical turn. All eyes were bent on McMullen as the high ball was seen falling towards him. Apparently Mack tried to mesmerize it, for as it fell, he waved his hands aloft as if sure of the catch; but when it was gripped and the innings ended, the crowd, forgetting the Mutuals had to go to the bat, flocked in the field, cheering and tossing their hats in the air like mad folks.
[New York Clipper, July 20, 1872]

Generally speaking, writers were forgiving of players and their miscues, often couching them in a humorous light. After all, it was bad enough for guilty parties to be hooted down by spectators at the game without being savaged by the press the next morning. Some reporters, though, remained sore about the act and flavored their comments with a good bit of vitriol.

Unfolded here is a full spread of remarks:

the ball went through Glasscock like a Rice street pickpocket through a river excursion

Freeman did not stop many balls, but the many that got away from him he chased in a way that cautioned snakes

the ball slipped through his fingers as though it was money sent from home

he pawed around after the ball like a kitten with a spool of thread

Urquhart's fly fell between a couple of hams Tommy Poorman carries around and calls hands

Moran, who played right in a pair of eighty-ton gloves, made a murderous muff of Devlin's easy fly

he dropped an easy pop fly as neatly as an agricultural ever dropped his money in the wilds of a great city

Smith juggled the easy grounder with as much proficiency as any magician from India you ever saw

Joyce fielded the ball with his slats (legs) instead of his fins (hands)

Hogan went at the ball with the spirit of a dumbwaiter and let it bound away

Joyce's wild throw came to Dahlen like the governor's reprieve to a condemned man

(after losing track of a fly ball) he felt as bad as an organ grinder who had misjudged a nickel thrown from a second-story window

Munyun grabbed up a fistful of the United States instead of the ball

Burke let the ball go through him, following this overt act by an inert statuesqueness that might be construed as an armed neutrality

he let Reilly's grounder skate by him like an Icelandic Nimrod in search of ptarmigan

Glenalvin let Fisher's grounder go through him like the measles through a city school

he let Wolverton's grounder slip through him like an eel through a wicker basket

    Gleason toyed too long with Sullivan's grounder, playing football, golf and handball all in one
    Bud Lally wabbled under Davis's fly like a fox terrier looking for a place to lie down, and then dropped it

    Warner fell ill with lapsus throwus, lapsus memoria, and some other lapsi
    a grounder went through his hands like a greased pig through a policemen's picnic
    then Strauss pushed one to Eddie, and what did Eddie do but pick it up as if it weighed a ton, and, turning to fire Swart out at second, he knocked a panel out of the carriage gate and Swart kept right on to third
    Whitney's liner cut its way through Bastian's hands
    Ben threw with mighty force at Willie Krieg, and, like a fluent pill, the sphere went through Willie's outstretched shovels
    Newell let Darby's dust agitator get through his slender but asymmetrical limbs
    Mannasau dropped down on his prayer bones to head it off, but the ball caromed off his knee-pan and shot over the fence
    Hemming put a little grounder into right. Marr had his front door open, and it got through while Griffin was playing football with Reilly's single
    Rudford's legs made a beautiful hoop for Van Haltren's grounder to bound through
    When Shorty Fuller makes errors, there is no reason to deliberate about them. They are generally of the bungled order and need no explanation.
    Glasscock hit a high fly to center field. Hogan, McCarthy and Shannon were around it like flies around a lump of sugar, but none of them touched it.
    the short stop did the Colossus act as the ball passed between his pedals
    this exciting game was not a fine game; it had errors to build bonfires with
    there were five or six men in the field who couldn't have held a pretty girl without making a misplay somewhere
    Gillen hit toward third. The enemy was hit in the weakest spot. Reilly fumbled.
    Delehanty hit to Nyce, who played with the ball a while and then threw it into the crowd in front of the south bleacher. When order was restored, Del had second base for a resting place.

  DeMontreville was unable to locate first base and made several throws in that direction of a hair-raising description
  there was not a man on the infield who could have stopped a bottle with a cork
  Eustace raised a pop fly back of first base, where enough athletes collected to catch the ball, but none of them touched it
  Keeler went for a fly, but got mixed up with a sparrow, and chased after the latter instead of going for the ball
  the New Yorks made errors until scorers had to work with two hands
  he made errors early and often
  Wilmot, who never could stop a ground ball with a snow shovel, fell all over himself, and let the ball go through him
  a rank error on Bassett's part, letting McPhee's bouncer cuddle through his spindles into left field, put Mac on first in elegantly easy shape
  Fuller let it go through his hands like water through a sieve
  Hogan made a bad fumble and then looked up at the sky to see if it had moved while he was locating the ball
  Glasscock hit a hard one through Hines' skylight
  he made one lunge at the ball, missed it and spun around like a five-cent top
  errors were thicker than blueberries on a Pennsylvania mountain
  Lachance reached for the ball as a blind man groping for a door knob
  Glenalvin threw the ball at empty space
  he allowed the ball to filter through his hands like a small boy playing with Coney Island sand
  Shindle's half-rate grounder ripped its way through Stafford's legs
  Bannon's grounder slipped through him as though it was greased
  Hulen let Campau's grounder go through him like a shell from the Brooklyn through a Spanish fleet
  his error in the bitter sixth was so wretched that it is a wonder the dark clouds did not open up and carry the lad away in a whirlpool of rainfall
  yesterday's game was as full of blunders as a dog is of fleas, some of the aforesaid blunders being vile beyond description
  Crooks had lard on his fingers
  McPhee's bouncer cuddled through Bassett's spindles into left

field, the ball croqueted through his legs

the first ball batted went through Latham's anatomy

Hogan made a bad fumble and then looked up at the sky to see if it had moved while he was locating the ball

Chris' woes at present are as numerous as those of a newly-made widow

Staley made an old-fashioned, butter-fingered, gentlemanly muff of his fly

the razzle-dazzle grounder from the long bat of the longest Brown squirmed its way between Bassett's legs

Whit is not a giant in height, but if he was twenty feet tall, he couldn't have stopped Buck's throw

Errors? Don't mention it. They were thicker than blueberries on a Pennsylvania mountain. (Foster, New York Journal, July 6, 1897)

errors of judgment were as frequent as those of commission, and Washington failed to score oftener through their own dislike of overdoing the thing

out on the field Jim Bannon made a brace of errors that would be ordered fumigated by a sanitary commission

Then the great Burns made a ghastly throw. Gore jammed the ball at him, and "Burnsy" threw it about eight feet, six inches over old man Anse's head.

Longer accounts served to prolong the perpetrator's pain and embarrassment:

With the bags full, Lush got tangled on McPhee's fly, and old Sol's wink puzzled the fielder. The ball dropped safe behind him and the three Reds scampered home.

Every ball player has made errors, and any man has his off days, but it is rarely, indeed, that a baseball-loving people is treated to such a yellow and fantastic burlesque of the national game as that which took place at Aurora park yesterday.

How to Make Two Errors in Four Paragraphs

Sheibeck made an error big enough to walk on its hands—Walsh's easy drive going through him. (Pitcher) Vick, to vary the form of his free distribution, plugged the Bulgarian in the ribs with the ball, then in concert he and Walsh stole a base.

  Vick was plainly perturbed, and he could be seen lecturing himself.
  He kept his visual organs unveiled, however, and by as pretty a trick as was ever seen, he caught Walsh napping at third. Both runners were leading off, and Vick pretended to be laying for Reddy, but instead turned and made a savage bluff at throwing down to second, but kept right on turning, and cut loose to Collopy. Joe had taken the bait and started in home and was fairly caught, that is, he might have been—sad words these are.
  Instead of throwing the ball into Collopy's outstretched palms, he just missed an English sparrow perched on the eaves of the grandstand. Walsh came home and Reddy took his place on third.
[Omaha Daily Bee, April 28, 1892]

  Sharp fielding work characterized the game throughout, though the (Sacramento) Senators were guilty of a few scandalous blunders. It would not be a bad idea for the field hands of the Capital City to get some of those life-nets like the firemen use, with strong rope handles at the corners. They might have three or four of these nets stationed over the field already spread out for action. Then when a high fly came out, the fielders could gather up their net, stand under and keep the ball from coming into violent contact with the cold, cold ground like it did yesterday.
  Two of these distressing accidents took place in the ninth inning. Danny Sweeney sent a high one to short left. Work, Peeples and Huston surrounded the spot where the ball was about to land, and, with a show of politeness seldom seen on a ball field, each waited for the other to take it. A few minutes later, Clark sent up a fly that came down back of the pitcher's box. The entire infield was there, urging the other to go ahead and do something. By the time they arrived at an understanding, it was everlastingly too late.
[Morning Call (San Francisco), May 25, 1891]

  Burkett caught the ball on the nose for a hustler into center field. It came clipping along the ground toward Stenzel, and then it went clipping along the ground through Stenzel, and into deep center. While Jake was gamboling after it, Burkett was wearing out his spikes going to third.
[Baltimore American, August 20, 1897]

  Tom Brown lost a golden opportunity to laurelize himself. McGann hit a terrific swipe into left center, and the Kentucky gold bug

sped away to capture it. He seemed a regular two-year-old on the run, but when he turned to catch the ball, the simile fails.
[Source misplaced]

    Canavan gave Foutz a long fly and a most wretched muff resulted. Foutz has no business playing center. He wanders around in the field like a yearling goat in a barrel factory and gazes at the ball with an impression of pained curiosity that wearies the eyes of the spectators. Once in a great while he catches a ball and then goes down to the newspaper offices and has bulletins hung in the window announcing the event.
[Source misplaced]

    Then Hallman lifted a high fly to right, and the ball, in an obstinate mood, settled directly in the sun's face and compelled Tiernan, blinded by the light, to let it fall to the ground safely.
[Evening World (New York), July 23, 1889]

    A careful and detailed description of the game would not be complete without a few words concerning Chauncey. That's only his first name. He really has another, so he has. It's Stuart, or O'Stuart, or MacStuart, or something.
    He is a lovely young thing, and plays short stop for Toronto. His trained vocal organs were in full play all the time, and he made 5 bad errors, showing that no man can do two things at once and be successful. He seemed to have a far more exaggerated opinion of his own importance than the actual facts in the case demanded. In a word, Chauncey O'MacStuart was objectionably and wearisomely fresh.
[Post Express (Rochester, NY), May 6, 1896]

    Thomas Easterbrook says he can "stop a ball in nine different styles." The reason he has not stopped any this year is probably because he tried all nine styles on the same play.
[New York Tribune, May 15, 1887]

    There were errors with ragged edges and errors with gilded whiskers, and they were costly. It seemed as if the players would sometimes wait until all the possibilities that could attach to an error

were ripe and mellow, and then they lugged in the error at the proper time, and the runs came.
[Morning Call (San Francisco), July 2, 1893]

Kelly lifted one 'way up over Sutcliffe's head. It looked as if it never would come down, and so far as old Cy was concerned, it might as well have stayed up, for when it did descend, he let it slip through his flanges, and the crowd gave him the hoss laugh.
[Omaha Daily Bee, June 14, 1892]

Talk About Guilt: A Catcher Bemuses His Fate

Francis Bacon Boyd, catcher to the massive manager of Rochester's own, did not sleep that soft childlike sleep which characterizes his hours of rest, last night. His slumber was uneasy and far apart. When his troubled eyes closed and his youthful head fell back amid the eiderdown softness of the luxurious couch, he moaned and tossed and kicked the clothes up at the foot and waved his arms about. He acted like one who has attended a banquet in company with chronic dyspepsia.

He was not happy. His dreams disturbed him. He thought he saw a man running to first base; he thought he saw a ball right in front of him, which he threw some eight or ten feet wide of Mr. Dooley's capacious fist; he imagined he saw two runs come in. He heard people say: "The game's lost, and Boyd lost it." He would sit up, clutch wildly in the air and murmur, "Boyd hath murdered sleep."

It must be said. Boyd lost the game. There's no getting around it. Of course, Lovett had been hit pretty hard; of course errors had been made; but Boyd's wild throw to first in the eighth inning lost Rochester the game. It was too bad. Boyd generally is too steady for a thing like that.
[Post Express (Rochester, N, Y.), May 16, 1896]

The making of an error (unabridged version):

Parrott hit the ball, but it went straight for the center field. "Oh, ho! You're out," was heard in exultant rhapsody from one of the sixteen Minneapolis fans, who had purchased seats in the grand stand, the rest being deadheads and St. Paul people; "Wilmot won't do a thing to that, I guess."

The ex-Chicagoan poised himself on tiptoe as if meditating whether he had better play it down the cushion or four times around the table. Then he let his heels down and danced a few bars of an ancient dime museum tune.

He smiled haughtily. The ball was coming right toward the waist. It seemed to be drawn that way. Walter's waist was not checked either, although they say he is great on drawing checks. The ball had reached its highest elevation. Parrott, chasing along toward first, watched it with a look of despair upon his face. In a majestic curve the ball descended.

"Oh, my, Walter'll get it," proudly and confidently exclaimed a fair fan as she waved another fan.

From far across the park could be heard the kerchug of a falling body striking some tangible obstacle; the eye observed a few frantic clutches reminiscent of Ophelia, trying to pick lawn mowers out of her hair, the ball rolled a few feet in the gravel field, and from the parched throats of the Minneapolis fans came a hoarse "Oh!"

It was not the exultant rhapsody of the wedding march; it was the funeral measure of a dirge. Walter had muffed a fly.
[Saint Paul Globe, May 25, 1897]

Eulogy to a Very Bad Throw

This writer, with fatalistic, almost sympathetic understanding, examined the cost of Joe Mulvey's errant behavior, namely, a lost game caused by his wild throw in the bottom of the ninth, allowing Baltimore to overcome a three-run deficit and pull a game out of the fire, defeating Pittsburg:

The luckiest thing about yesterday's game was Mulvey's bad throw, which lost the game to Baltimore. Although twenty-four hours have elapsed since the contest, the cranks—or "enthusiasts"—will all lift their hands at this and gasp: "Wha—wha—what's that? Oh, what'cher saying?"

Nevertheless, it was a lucky thing.

From time immemorial, Joe has been indulging in the custom of making one particularly bad throw each season. No one knows when it is coming. It is just as likely to be in the ninth with two out and bases full of the enemy's men, as in the first with no one on the bags.

It comes when least expected, like the thief in the night. And when it does appear, it is so "yellow" that it casts a shadow on the sun. It takes the breath away from the bleachers, Harry Wright stops pulling his whiskers and the red-capped boys for the moment forget to call "peanuts and cigars." No yell goes up; no one has wind enough in his lungs nor energy in his will to raise a cry. A silent sadness settles a foot deep on the whole gathering.

Now, as Harry Wright, the genial manager of the Phillies, knows, and as every well-posted base ball enthusiast should remember, Mulvey enacts this tragedy once a year. Last year when he did it, Harry Wright's feelings were so wrought upon that "Mul" was laid on the shelf, whereat "Mul" was so cast down in spirit that he refused Washington's offer to come here, not deeming himself good enough for us. That's when genial Harry made a big mistake. He should have kept Mulvey on third. The agony was past. The deed had been done. Thank fortune that it was over with.

It is reflections such as these as cause rejoicing for that terrible throw of yesterday. We all know that it has been made and will not have to live in dread of it for the rest of the season. As the "sports" say, the game is young yet, and a victory or two now doesn't make much difference. Better to have that throw now than along in September, when it may decide our position in the championship race. If any one expects "Mul" to repeat such a play he simply shows his base ball ignorance.

...but in the terse and elegant phraseology of a Baltimore contemporary: "After a spirited uphill fight the Orioles defeated the Washingtons in the last inning. The Baltimores won the game by nerve and persistency and played ball as it should be played, never despairing of victory until the last ray of hope is obliterated."

That's the way it seemed to the visitors. To the Washington people, it looked as though Mulvey was taking pity on the visitors and gave them the game out of charity, for two being out it was an easy matter to throw Kelley out at first, instead of sending the ball ten feet over Larkin's head. But it all depends on the point of view whether a victory is won by nerve and persistency or lost by inexcusable blundering.

The Philadelphia Press heads the account of the game: "One of Mulvey's old-time throws."
[Evening Star (Washington, D.C.), May 13, 1893]

THE LATEST WAY TO CATCH A FLY BALL

8. Humor in Bad Weather

Delay or postponement of baseball play due to adverse weather conditions has forever plagued the national pastime. Rain, mud, wind, dust, cold, fog, hail, mist, thunder and lightning—even cyclones—all took turns contributing to the eternal problem. Of it, no truer assessment existed than that uttered in 1893 by James A. Hart, owner of the Chicago team: "The weather makes or unmakes base ball."

Rain, Bodies of Water, and Ever-Attendant Mud

Rain, by far, topped the list of meteorological nuisances and its negative effects were never underestimated. Rain-cancelled games meant loss of revenue, which could be substantial if the two most profitable business days of the baseball season were affected: the Fourth of July and Decoration Day (now Memorial Day).

For poor-drawing teams, the impact could be crippling, as gate receipts from these two holiday games alone could sustain them through an entire season. Visiting teams were also affected, as they were contractually entitled to a percentage of the revenue. Just as financially threatening were unusually wet seasons, which caused a number of minor league clubs to fold, sometimes the league itself.

Principally for these reasons, umpires were urged by Nick Young, President of the National League and appointer of umpires, to avoid postponing games in order to make the sport pay. As a result, play was allowed under extreme conditions, even when accumulated water turned infields into quagmires and low spots in the corrugated outfield into ankle-deep pools. Players risked injury under these dangerous situations, despite loads of sawdust and sand hastily shoveled into the muddy slurry at strategic points by groundskeepers.

Baseball writers of this era often referred to rain as "Jupiter Pluvius"; variations of it, such as "J. P." or "Pluvial," were also acceptable. This quaint term meant "rain giver," and was formed by joining "Jupiter," the mythological Roman god of sky and thunder, with "pluvius," Latin for "rainy."

Complaints about rain appeared early in the annals of baseball writing. In 1868, a reporter, irked by its capricious and game-killing ways, declared war on it in a comical way. Along the way, in a moment of idle fantasy, he envisioned a covered playing field that, a century later, turned into reality when the Houston Astrodome, baseball's first domed stadium, opened for business in 1965.

Behold:

The continued inclement weather is playing sad havoc with those interested in open-air pastimes. Cricket, base ball and quoits suffer alike in this respect, and the players are at their wits' end how to compress the showery effects of Jupiter Pluvius.

A base ball "rink" is the latest suggestion of an ardent admirer of the National Game. A covered ball field would, indeed, be a novelty; it would protect both players and spectators from the elements, and old Sol, J. P., and even Old Boreas*, might combine their powers, and unless they raised the roof off the "rink," they would be powerless to stop the little game of the ballists (baseball players). But such a thing as a covered ball ground is out of the question, so we must devise other means to circumvent the evils attending the wet season.

Let a convention of all the devotees of outdoor sports be convened at once, and articles of impeachment made out against the Clerk of the Weather. This functionary has undoubted violated some of the provisions of the "Constitution' of the National association of Ball Players. Therefore, let this body act as a High Court of Impeachment, and arraign the offending individual for "high crimes and misdemeanors."

As base ball is the National game, and is played everywhere from the Atlantic to the Pacific, the members of the court should be drawn from all sections of the Union. This would give the accused a fair trial, and would undoubtedly bring J. P. and his clerk to their senses.

Seriously, however, there never was a season in which the elements played the deuce to such an extent as they have this year...
[New York Clipper, May 30, 1868]
* **Greek god of the North Wind.**

Early writers with winsome dispositions turned rain and its predictable consequences into passages of humor:

Eckfords vs Olympics

The grounds were in poor condition for playing...being completely flooded with water on the day previous.
...Miller...made the first bag on a muddigger...Parkham dropped one in the centre field lake for two...Eggler drove one into the duck-pond and made one base...Malone sent one into the pond for a run...Hurley drove a beauty clear into the lake for two bases.
[National Republican (Washington, D.C.), October 6, 1869]

Philadelphia vs Brooklyn

All parties went on the field, and to the regrets of all present, its condition, though far better than as expected after such a storm, was found to be sadly against successful fielding operations.
In the hollow, back of the first base, water sufficient to afford swimming facilities to hundreds of bathers, was found collected; and in various portions of the field itself there were pools of water sufficient to make fielding a difficult task to perform.
Under the circumstances, these drawbacks were considered as mere trifles, and not obstacles sufficient either to adjourn the match indefinitely or even to another ground. Consequently the game was at once proceeded with.
[New York Clipper, June 14, 1862]

Baseball rules stated that games called because of rain before the completion of five full innings had to replayed, usually the next day, for which fans were issued free passes, called "rain checks." If games were called after five full innings had been played, but not completed, the score reverted to that which stood after the last full inning played.

Oddly, the circumstance of rain threatening to shorten a game in progress gave birth to a truly outrageous scheme called "playing for rain," which was implemented by enterprising teams to either preserve a victory or, less often, avoid a defeat. Of all the zany antics that marked these formative years of baseball, nothing matched the farcical scenes on the diamond during their deployments.

To preserve a victory, the plan worked like this:
If, after five innings of play, Team A lost its lead during an

inning in which Team B had rallied, simultaneously with the arrival of a storm very likely to result in the game being called off. Team A would then deliberately forestall completion of the inning until the game <u>was</u> called off, at which time the score reverted to Team A's previous lead, according to the rules, and thereby ensure the win. Timing was crucial, as was the element of luck, for if the umpire did not call the game, the effort went for naught.

This transparent ruse was not illegal. Umpires stood by, exasperated and helpless, as the entire team in the field practiced well-rehearsed roles in grinding down play to a near halt. Pitchers took their time delivering the ball; easy grounders rolled harmlessly into the outfield; pop-ups were muffed; overthrows and wild pitches became the norm, and so on, as the team did their utmost to avoid putting an opponent out.

Conversely—and to complete the absurd tableau—the opponents, in a frenzy to finish the inning before the game was called and thus claim the victory, did everything they could to make an out in equally outlandish fashion by ambling along base paths, swinging at bad pitches, etc.

To prevent a loss, the same tactics were re-employed when rain threatened a postponement before five full innings had been played. If Team A had fallen substantially behind Team B in the first four innings, it stalled play, hoping the rain, once it fell, would induce the umpire to call the game before the fifth inning, which would then have to be replayed. The subterfuge didn't always work, but when it did, Team A was spared an almost certain defeat. Again, timing and luck reigned paramount.

There was yet another use for these staged acts. Teams utilized them to nail down victories when nightfall was the issue, not rain, which was called, naturally enough, "playing for darkness." In all instances, the dodges met with enough success to warrant their use.

Here's how "playing for rain" worked:

Rain has its uses. In the last half of the tenth inning yesterday, when the score was in the favor of the Blues, the Brewers had one man at second and another at third, with nobody out, and Terry at bat. A hit meant a score of 4 to 3 in favor of the visitors. The fans were disturbed in spirit, for it looked very much as though a beautiful contest was going to terminate disastrously.

Dark clouds that had rimmed the horizon the most of the afternoon came scurrying from the southwest on the breast of an energetic breeze. A rain drop splashed in the umpire's face. Other raindrops fell in the field. The ball became as slippery as an eel. Two balls had been called on the batsman, and it looked like a cakewalk.

The breeze stiffened a little, pushing clouds still further zenithward, and the water began to fall in sheets. It soaked the base lines until they became like unbaked bricks. Pools and puddles dotted the field, and the players went scurrying to places of shelter. Umpire Manassau called the game, and the score reverted to the ninth inning— 2 to 2. Next to a timely hit, nothing is more welcome than a timely rain storm.
[Kansas City Journal, July 5, 1897]

The ensuing quotations (and poem) deal with rain, many of which were sprinkled with a dash of humor to make the point.

The first chronicles the far-reaching effects of a rained-out game upon members of the team:

A wet day in a base ball crowd on a date fixed for a game is one of the most miserable sensations the average mortal should be called upon to encounter.

The players, thoroughly miserable, wander about the corridors of the hotel, telling hard luck stories and guessing the weather for the next day. The manager, who has financial interests at heart, mentally calculates what the rain is costing his club, and looks even bluer than the rest of the gang.

The cheery traveling man tries in vain to teach his fellow sufferers some of his own cheerful philosophy. The theatrical manager stopping at the hotel places a box at the disposal of the disgruntled heroes, but nothing will compensate for the loss of the day's game except another one tomorrow.
[Pittsburgh Press, April 9, 1892]

Here is a game account dealing with the game strategy surrounding the approach of darkness, as related by the inimitable Charles Dryden:

Captain Adrian C. Anson.........$25
Bunglesome Bill Everett...........10
Bill Decker................................10
Total.......................................$45

This is what it cost the Chicago team to defeat the Giants in that tie game of Saturday, which was played off yesterday afternoon. Anson and a couple of his talking men wanted the contest called at the end of the eighth inning because of the gloaming, but (umpire) Emslie insisted, and properly, too, that the game should be finished, as the sun was still shining.

"You're afraid to call it. You're a coward," yelled the red-faced veteran of a thousand kicks (Anson).

"So are you," replied the umpire.

"You're a dirty, stinking coward. So there, now!" retorted Miss Anson.

"Get out of the game and off the grounds!" howled Emslie, "and I'll fine you $25, too."

Thereupon Messrs. Everett and Decker dipped in their oars and each caught a ten-dollar crab. Play was then resumed, with the Colts at bat, but the inning was so long drawn out that when the Giants turned to, darkness had fallen. The only object distinctly visible was Anson's face on the bench. So the umpire called the game.

Thus the end of which the windy chief of the Colts had fought and been fined came to pass after all. This incident goes to show that in nine cases out of ten, these ball players don't know what they are kicking about.

Had Anson exhibited good sense, the game would have been played out to the satisfaction of the spectators, with plenty of daylight to spare. There would have been no disgraceful wrangling, bad language and fines, for which Anson is al one to blame. He is one of the players who have been interviewed at length, and who warmly advocated gentlemanly submission to the rulings of the umpire. His men had outdated and outplayed the other side from the beginning, and the game was as good as won. The Giants couldn't hit Griffith, who showed them that he knew how to pitch, and the Colts had hammered Seymour and Sullivan all over the lot. The sun was still shining, but Anson knew that it would probably set in the course of events, so he kicked.
[New York Journal, August 31, 1897]

> No game today. Alas!
> How slowly creep the hours;
> Rain floods the diamond's grass,
> The storm cloud darkly towers.
>
> Hushed is the umpire's voice,
> The coachers, too, are dumb;
> Gone are the bleachers' joys,
> The managers are glum.

> *The bats are laid aside*
> *Which once the zephyrs fanned,*
> *The players sadly slide*
> *Up to the free lunch stand.*
>
> *Nothing but rain! No game!*
> *Life is a dreary blank,*
> *A foul, a contest tame,*
> *A put-out for the crank.*
>
> *[Pittsburgh Press, September 17, 1889]*

It rained all day Saturday (in Chicago) and for a while today the players feared the management would not take in enough money to fill the payrolls. Those who had overdrawn accounts patted themselves on the back for their foresight.

The rain ceased before time to call the first game, but it left behind it a bank of gray clouds that looked like a headache, and a stretch of black mud that made players with reputations as stealers, wonder what color they would be when they escaped—if they ever did.

When a man slid for a base today, he disappeared from view. A shoveling brigade was in readiness to respond to a riot call at any time, but every one slid until they reached the base and climbed out on that. It felt like it does when one goes to sleep in a sewer and a heavy rain comes up during the night. The bases were lost to view early in the day, and the catchers had to use a compass in throwing to them.

[Morning Times (Washington, D.C.), July 20, 1896]

(Umpire) Tim Hurst made Scrappy (William Joyce, Washington captain) and his band play in a hard rain at Pittsburg yesterday, and as the Pirates got a big lead at the start, Joyce diplomatically delayed the game, hoping that the downpour would become so heavy that even the mudlark of an umpire would call time on the "regatta" before five innings had been pulled off. But when Timothy won't, he won't, and as a result of his obstinacy and the rain and other things, the Senators were given the worst beating of the season and sustained their first shutout.

[Morning Times (Washington, D.C.), July 9, 1896]

Cincinnati, April 30.—Your uncle (Chicago player/manager Anson) kicked like a mule before the game today. He was not disturbed by any qualms of conscience about breaking a record of years' standing about playing on the Sabbath, but he did object to taking his colts out on such a field as lay before him.

There were puddles enough in the suburbs to give all the web-footed bipeds of Goosetown a bath, and every time an outfielder started for a fly, he gave an imitation of Paul Boyton (well-known showman and swimmer) walking on the water. It rained all morning, and the sullen clouds occasionally leaked during the afternoon.
[The Sun (New York), May 1, 1893]

The Browns, in their snow-colored uniforms, looked like a section of the white squadron, and large patches of the unsodded outfield contained water enough to sail navy launches in. The infield section also had "swampy" spots in it, and the shoes of the players during practice often sent up young waterspouts as their wearers went slashing about after the ball. At the start of the game, both pitchers, Clausen and Hawke, found it difficult to control the slippery ball, and each forced in a run by filling the bases through wild delivery.
[The Sun (New York), May 1, 1893]

What did pitchers do with a wet ball they couldn't control? Veteran player O'Rourke had a solution:

Hardie Richardson was talking about the old Buffalo Club of 1880 not long ago, and said Purcell, now with the Baltimore Club, is a fine player.

"He is called 'Cut-the-ball Purcell.' The Buffalo Club was playing in Providence. I was in left, O'Rourke in center and Blondie in right. It had been raining, and Galvin, dear old chap, couldn't handle the ball, it had become so slippery.

"In those days we dressed at the club-house instead of at the hotel. O'Rourke captained the Bisons. The game was going against us. Between innings, O'Rourke slipped into the club-house and got his pocket-knife. He gave it to Purcell and told him to cut the ball at the first opportunity. Blondie did so, and was caught in the act. Of course, it made quite a sensation and O'Rourke got out of it by fining Purcell. No wonder O'Rourke has since developed into a lawyer."
[Baltimore American, May 3, 1888]

Rained Out: A Whimsical Reflection

They seem to be extremely timid about the weather, do the Big People and the colonel, and the rest. They think a little water is a dangerous thing. A good many other people do, too. They have co-

religionists in the same belief.

Of course it was disappointing, very disappointing, when it began to rain in streaks along about 2 o'clock yesterday afternoon. Immense crowds collected at the street corners to take "This car to the Ball Grounds," and nearly screwed their necks off, looking at the sky in the west. When they were tired of doing that, they said bad words to themselves, which, as everybody knows, is just exactly as wicked as saying them out loud.

At 3:45 o'clock, the sun was shining as brightly as if there wasn't a cloud in the sky, but when the crowds had arrived at the park, behold, James Buckley, esq., said, "No game; wet grounds."

This made everybody ask foolish questions, until James hastily immured himself in his block house whence tickets are dispensed, and refused to say a blessed word. Most of the crowd went on to Summerville, where they looked at the lake, and told hyperbolical tales of base ball games in which they figured in the misty past, and speculated on the chances of Rochester's holding first place.
[Post Express (Rochester, NY), May 28, 1896]

St. George, Staten Island, June 15.—Two small boys, six men and five umbrellas dauntlessly held their positions on the bleacheries and religiously sat out the intermittent showers, which wet everything in sight, for an hour and a half previous to the time set for this afternoon's ball game.

Early boats bore near upon a thousand cranks to the grounds and, with the above-mentioned exceptions, they put up the ante necessary and stowed themselves away under the protection of the long grand stand.

Jupiter Pluvial was as capricious as a flirtatious schoolgirl; bawling like a baby one minute and then, yielding to Sol's entreaties, permitting the hot sunshine to dry his tears, but all the time the old god allowed his blue-black clouds to threateningly overhang the grounds, and every now and then electrified the crowd with a lightning grimace, and followed those signs of awful mirth by thunderous growlings, which augured, no game today; and all the time the people shucked their peanuts, swore at something called the weather and dwelt with words of admiration upon the pennant-winning work now being done by Mutrie's champions (New York Metropolitans).

James M. himself was here, there and everywhere. Perhaps his recent ducking accustomed him to cold water—on the outside, at any rate. Jim apparently doesn't mind the rain in the least, for he hustled about in the wet like a hen earnestly caring for a brood of chickens.

Hopes that a game would be played were rife until 3:45, when freshly assembled clouds let fall their pent-up water and speedily turned the grounds into a pond of muddy water. The fierceness of the shower didn't last for more than three minutes, but everything looked sick when those same clouds rolled by and, for the time, the rain ceased. The clayey diamond looked more like flats after a recent ebb tide than a spot where championship ball is played. Then "no game" was heard on every side.

Manager Mutrie and Wright were pacing restlessly about the grounds, each bent upon a game if such a thing were possible.

...After a half hour spent in striving to get the grounds in shape, the workmen retired in disgust. Manager Mutrie gave it up, and Umpire Barnum, attired in full regimentals, came out in front of the stand and said that the game was postponed.
[Evening World (N. Y.), June 15, 1889]

Here or thereabouts, it began to rain. It was not a vociferous, talkative rain, but a pleasant drizzle that whispered cheerful things about laying the dust and cooling the atmosphere. It was just the quality of rain most likely to cause William Hart (St. Louis pitcher) to lose his control of the ball. He succeeded in doing so with the utmost grace and abandon in the fourth inning.
[John Foster, New York Journal, June 16, 1897]

From their proud eminence in second place—think of it, good people, second place—the haughty Colonel (Robinson, Oakland owner) looked down upon (San Francisco manager) Hank's doubtful dubs yesterday while those wretched athletes floundered in the cold, cold mud, trying to retain a slippery hold on the tail end of the baseball business.

When they all got through, the diamond looked like a buffalo wallow in the springtime. Great patches of earth were torn up here and there and carried away on the raiment of the young men, while two, long, parallel streaks showed where an agonized athlete had gone skating through the slime, feet first.

Every player engaged made one or more impressions in the soft yellow earth with his person. Their hooves grew heavy with mud, and it is a wonder that some of them didn't break their necks. But luckily the game ended without mishap and the Colonel carried off a mud-stained victory by a score of 11 to 3. Poor Hank! He hasn't won a game for two weeks and his chances for doing so are growing beautifully less every day.

While the mud was flying from the heels of the young men, he sat on the bench and tried to inspire them with a winning gait. But they did not inspire that you could notice it, and waded around with their opponents like a lot of mud hens.

Rain ruined the grand double bill of two games under one canvas for a single price of admission and sadly interfered with the one they did perpetrate. Pools of muddy ooze stood under the benches and along the base lines, making it impossible for a runner to maintain his feet and a high rate speed at the same time.
[Morning Call (San Francisco), October 17, 1892]

A number of stray clouds, which had been loafing about Indianapolis since early morning, put up a job on the baseball cranks yesterday afternoon. The clouds gathered together in a bunch directly over the ball park, just when the game was becoming interesting and emptied themselves of all the rain they had left over from Saturday.

The shower was entirely confined to the ball park, so far as can be ascertained. The game was called and the crowd hastened out of the park with upraised coat collars, only to find a bright sun overhead and dry sidewalks underfoot. One man, who went back after a forgotten umbrella, was overheard to declare as he boarded a street car, that it was still raining hard in the park. At all events, the elements were against Sunday baseball.
[Indianapolis Journal, April 10, 1899]

For several days it has been a question whether the Polo Grounds were not a portion of the bed of the Harlem River. Waves thundered against Burkeville*, and fierce eddies swept and tossed about the club houses. Huge breakers combed over the foundation around the flagstaff, and the undertow was strong enough in (outfielder) Mike Tiernan's garden to carry all the grass out to sea. It is true there never was much more than eighteen inches of water in the grounds at any times, but the description can't suffer on that account.

The New York management, not having a sufficient supply of life preservers to accommodate a crowd of several thousand citizens, desired to play the game in Brooklyn, but it was finally decided to "swim out, O'Grady," and let it go at that, owing to the fact that the transfer of games in the National League is becoming unpopular.

..."Ducky" Holmes marched to the plate with his shoes full of salt brine from the wavelets about Burkeville*.
[John Foster, New York Journal, July 31, 1897]
* Left field bleachers, named after popular fielder Burke

As seen through swirling sheets of snow, the game was fairly interesting, and the crowd departed apparently satisfied. Under existing circumstances, no one expected a finished performance. The talent did well to stay through seven rounds and keep their blood in circulation. With their eyes cleared by the rarified atmosphere, the regulars found the ball often enough to pound in a victory at the outset.

...A sheet of wet mud, with ice floes in it, encircled the diamond, and the grass of Manhattan Field (Polo Grounds) was so moist and slippery that the players could scarcely keep their feet. From the home plate to the backstop, a causeway of boards was laid to enable the catchers to retrieve foul flies, and the pitchers were given a pile of dry sawdust with which to groom the ball. Behind the players' bench stood two pails of drinking water, with their labels "for fire only," partly concealed by icicles, thus heightening the Arctic effect of the exhibition.

The game opened with a flurry of snow...Joe Hornung, who had forgotten his overshoes, consented to umpire, and chanced pneumonia in the interests of baseball....Dad Clarke, in a brand-new store uniform, finished the engagement. Three of the youngsters, who couldn't tell whether they were pitching a Peck & Snyder (brand of baseball) or a snowball, worked the lightning change on the other side.
[Dryden, New York Journal, April 4, 1896]

A pleasing aquatic spectacle, with "Bug" Holliday in the role of amphibian, ushered in the first run. With Sullivan on second in the third round, McCreery launched the ball into the lake on left field. "Bug" pursued it, floundering through the yellow liquid like a blind horse crossing a ford. When Mr. Holliday struck the water, he forgot all about the ball and yelled for help.
[Dryden, New York Journal, September 4, 1897]

Wet as the outfield was, and heavy as the running, the ex-Chicagoan (Algernon) chased around the water-logged garden like a motorcycle on a tar track.
[Source misplaced]

Nothing short of a whirlwind that rushed out of the west when the end was nigh saved the scalps of the Giants in the opening game at home. While the weary crowd sat viewing the last sad rites there came a roar of mighty waters. Darkness that was moist and opaque settled down on the scene.

Then a clap of thunder broke and a gust of wind, bearing the rain, yanked flags and banners from the grand stand and sent them flying over the heads of the players. And before the rain struck the base lines, the wind caught up and carried swirling columns of yellow dust, in which the Giants were glad to hide their stricken heads.

Nor was this all. Ere the pall sank low and obscured the diamond, (New York captain) Scrappy Bill Joyce could be seen shaking his lumpy forefinger ominously to and fro under the nose of Umpire Lynch, but for what reason could not be learned in the grand, spectacular finale presented by the elements.
[Dryden, New York Journal, April 27, 1897]

A downpour of rain accompanied the gale and prevented the practice game scheduled for this afternoon. When some of the boys went out to inspect the grounds at noon, they reported an alligator stranded on third base and flying a signal of distress. As no one went to his assistance, the reptile is probably there yet, waiting for (shortstop) Gleason.
[Dryden, New York Journal, March 12, 1896]

Referring to the 13-11 game of Wednesday, the Kansas City Times says:

"For two hours and thirty-five minutes a yellow mist hung over the Exposition park ball grounds yesterday. In novels, mists are always gray, but this one was not. It was of the yellowest yellow that ever tinted the roof garden end of a Kansas sunflower.

"Then, suddenly, the mist was dispelled and in its place there came a rainbow of every color. In the prismatic flashes of red and green, purple and violet, the yellow sank out of sight. Weeping was turned into joy; wailing was changed into loud hosannas of victory."
[Saint Paul Globe, June 26, 1897]

"Dog gone the rain," conservatively said the recent principal actor in Hoyt's 'A Run Away Colt' (Anson). "I am afraid this sudden downpour will deprive us of a puddin' with your much touted Senators."

Then Anse navigated the diamond and brought his blue eyes to an X-ray-focus on the ominous clouds flitting overhead. "Here, Bridget," he called to (catcher) Donohue, who was chaffing with a newspaper man in the grand stand, " get out here and see if your face won't stop the rain; it oughter stop most anything."
[Source misplaced]

"Bridget" obeyed orders and the water-laden firmament rolled *away toward Anacostia, where shower baths are ever needed.*

It would have been better from a Chicago standpoint had Uncle Adrian not used "Bridget's" classic County Clare countenance as a cork on the lowering skies. When Jupiter Pluvius got a shy at Donohue's face, he packed his hose and quit trying to reign and rain over National Park. "Once was enough for me," ejaculated Jube as he sailed away across the Potomac and rested on the hills of the town of bob-tailed cars.

Though the water quit at 5:45 o'clock, Chicago's "Waterloo" did not cease until 6:30. It required the Senators only one hour and forty-five minutes to go the distance, and on a muddy track at that.

That Anson expected to win the game admits of no question. He was as confident as a shell-worker in a rural fair before the teams lined up. "Why, it is as easy as finding money," said the big blonde from the shores of Lake Michigan as he donned his mitt and walked over to the bag. "We will cinch this one and fasten the next two with copper rivets." About that time McFarland gave Tom Brown a base on balls and Tom scored on Joyce's double. The rest on Anse's troubles are told below...(Washington won, 12-1)
[Morning Times (Washington, D. C.), June 9, 1896]

The national game is a plant that cannot be killed by excessive moisture. No matter how thoroughly soaked it may be, just as soon as Old Sol shows his smiling face, the sport blossoms like a Jack rose in a hothouse. Therefore, when Jupiter Pluvius shut off the faucet of his rain reservoir and sunlight began to break through, the loyal cranks across the bridge prepared for a day of huge enjoyment.
[The Sun (New York), May 6, 1893]

When, after a hard uphill game, the Saints at last got a lead of one run on the Columbians, the clouds which had been overhanging for hours massed right over the diamond, and it was so dark that Umpire Sheridan could not see the fast ball that Denzer was pitching.

The Columbians chafed a little under this manifest dispensation of a benign divinity, and were wont to suggest that the umpire had been hypnotized, but before they could pile their traps into the bus, they were overtaken by a cloudburst, which made the boulevard from the main gate down, resemble their beloved Scioto (river), and drove them into shelter forthwith.
[Saint Paul Globe, June 20, 1898]

Chronicled here are the crafty machinations utilized in "playing for rain":

Ball games have been played under more attractive conditions than those which greeted the Brooklyn and Cincinnati teams and 1,500 spectators at Eastern park yesterday. A chill, damp wind swept across the diamond when play was called and before two innings had been completed, a cold, penetrating rain fell, making things equally disagreeable to players and onlookers. It was more so to the Brooklyn, because the Reds had bunched their hits and secured a lead, which meant victory should five innings be completed.

It was not surprising, therefore, that Captain Griffin should try to get the game called before the deciding point had been reached. He called the attention of Umpire Sheridan to the few scattering drops that were falling during the third inning, but Sherry simply smiled and bade the game "go wan." The drops became numerous in the third, while in the fourth there was a perfect shower. Cincinnati's half of the fifth was played with little rivulets running down the backs of the men, but Sheridan simply turned up his coat collar and seemed to bid defiance to the elements.

Then came Brooklyn's turn and Griffin held an animated conversation with the official, while the players got their bats sadly mixed and seemed to be in trouble. But Sherry again ordered Mike to the bench and told Dwyer to pitch. Two were out when Griffin went to bat and Mike made one more effort to influence the umpire.

It was no use and the next few minutes were spent in as funny a battle of cross purposes as ever occurred on a ball field. Sheridan was anxious to finish five innings and was backed up by Dwyer, while Griffin was just as anxious to delay matters.

First Mike stood on the plate and looked at Sheridan and then at the inky clouds above, while Sherry motioned to Dwyer to deliver the ball. But the Cincinnati pitcher was loath to pitch a ball that might injure an opposing player and waited until Mike got into the batter's box. Then he sent over three wide ones and a couple of strikes, Griffin in the meantime fouling off a number of good ones. He lost one ball, which delayed matters some more while a new one was put into play. Just as Dwyer made another motion to pitch, Mike got another idea and wasted a few more seconds while he ran to the pitcher's box and bathed his hands and bat in saw dust. This about exhausted his ingenuity and he sent up a foul to Irwin.

With a game certain, the methods of the teams changed. The Brooklyns were anxious to finish the nine innings while the Reds tried to

delay matters until the rain, which was falling faster every minute, should come down hard enough to end the game. While the Cincinnatis were at bat in the seventh, Sheridan, to the surprise of everybody, called " Time" and made a bee line for the dressing room. It wasn't raining any faster than in the fifth, and the Brooklyn outfielders could not realize for several minutes what had happened. It was a rough deal, but there was no redress, and after thirty minutes' wait the game was declared at an end with the score 5 to 3 in favor of Cincinnati.
[Brooklyn Eagle, September 6, 1896]

The ground did not dry for some little time, and even at 4 o'clock, when the game was finally begun, the infielders would frequently do the "split" and other concert hall specialties in the slippery earth of the diamond. Between the pitcher's box and the home plate, the soil was of the consistency of mortar; behind the catcher it was like mush; at second base it resembled oyster soup at a church social.
[Saint Paul Globe, July 15, 1896]

Ever hear of a game cancelled due to artificial rain? Well, it happened once—honest. Here's proof:

This story is told of Frank Bancroft:
One day, while he was manager of the Cleveland Club, he had a game on with the Providence nine, but two of his men were sick, and he was at his wit's end to know how to arrange matters so as to get a chance against his formidable opponents.
About noon, a light rain fell, and he saw his opportunity. The rain itself was not sufficient to affect the grounds, but he hurried to its assistance, ordered out the fire hose, and soaked the field thoroughly. When the Providence men arrived, the ground was examined, and it was decided that it was too wet to play on.
[The Sun (New York), August 30, 1884]

It was, to be sure, a tank-drama sort of baseball that he (the pitcher) appeared in, outfielders in Lexington park needing rubber boots more than spikes, and light flannels to save weight. For that reason many hits that would have been out on a dry field were made safe, singles lengthened into doubles, and, to even things up, some that would have rolled out for homers, had it been dry, struck in the mud and became but singles or doubles.
...Nyce, however, hit one pretty high...It rolled through a puddle

or two, and when the fielders found it, their shoes were heavy with St. Paul realty and their hearts with the realization that Nyce had reached third. He, too, suffered some from the slow track, or he would have played the full circuit.
...McBride drove the ball into the middle puddle for two bases, and Hollister splashed into it like a brown dog in a duck pass. When he came up, he had the ball in his webbed paw, paddled out to the shore, and threw in to the park...Shugart drove one out for three bases into Hollister's natatorium...George opened up another batting streak, mowing the raindrops off the grass in the left meadow.
[Saint Paul Globe, date misplaced]

Grand Rapids vs St. Paul:
The drizzle was so strong now that Umpire Snyder called time. The banner that keeps the crowd from seeing the game from St. Albans' street hill was stretched tenderly over the pitcher's box, while the batsman's area was covered with pine boards.

The fans from the bleachers were ushered into the stand, and at 4:37 the stop watches were started for the half hour's run. There was twenty minutes of drizzle, during which the fine drops sifted through the wire netting and turned the frizzes of the fair spectators into shapeless tousles on their chilled foreheads. Little lakes showed the low spots in the diamond, and the grass took a new start.

Ten, fifteen, twenty, twenty-five minutes elapsed, when suddenly the clouds broke in the western sky. The sunlight came through, the precipitation ceased, and Comiskey's men took the field. But Umpire Snyder would not order Grand Rapids into the field, and called the game back to the end of the fifth inning.

A hundred urchins gathered around him, to ask how much Carney (Grand Rapids' captain) paid him, and if they smoked cigars out of the same box, and like impertinent questions, but the most ludicrous thing was to see Jack Carney protecting the umpire, who is twice his size, in their march to the Interurban train.
[Saint Paul Globe, May 15, 1896]

Amidst Storm and Thunder, the Game Sloggeth On:
A Mini-Essay on Perseverance

Willie Keeler stood at the plate. The distant thunder rolled, the air was thick and dark with the gathering forces of nature and the wind savagely whisked dust about his natty form; but, like the boy on the burning deck, Willie was there for keeps, and looked neither to the right nor to the left, but plumb at the doughy little German, who, too, cared not a whit for thunderstorms.

...But now there were two out, and it was not a time for experiments. Just why Willie should have worked so hard it a study. It must have been just because he wanted to. There can be no other reason, as the fast gathering clouds encircled the fired with an ominousness that was unmistakable.

Way off in the direction of the business portion of the city, it could be seen that it was raining in torrents. Great waves of water would alternate with waves of smoky dust to blot out the higher points of the city, while ever and anon the heavens were split with savage flashes of lightning and the clouds boiled with their fury.

Yet Hughey stepped to the plate, and never once thought of all that. Champion Jim Corbett, who had been talking on the players' bench to Manager Hanlon, thought discretion the better part of valor, and took up a place in the grand stand, but Hughey went on with his work. He fouled off a few, and Breit. was working away at him in fine shape. The outfielders first began to show restlessness and shifted their places. Then the infield became affected, while the less devoted of the bleachers began their search for shelter, the grand-standers feeling safe under the big roof that protected them.

Murray looked about nervously and scanned the sky, though it was quite unnecessary to do much scanning, for a blind man could have told what was coming. Just then three men seemed totally unconscious of the impending storm, and if they had been way off in some torrid clime with a typhoon just as ripe, they would have played on. Breit, in the box, Hughey at the bat, and that good and tried catcher, Peitz, never gave a thought to whistling wind or cleaving flashes as they played on.

"Joe" Kelley broke the charm. It was a shame for Joe to do it, as he did when he darted out into the field and began a search for his glove, lest it get wet.

Manifestly, it would not do for Hughey to hit the ball out there when Joe was plodding around, for the force of habit might have compelled both Joe and Cooley to go after it, and then there would have been a collision and more electricity. So Hughey and Breit and Peitz were brought alive from their absorption, and before Joe got out of the field to give them a chance for a relapse, the proverbial flash of lightning, peal of thunder and torrent of rain were on in full blast, and the business of everybody then was to get out of the wet.

And the rain rained as it seldom rains. It came in great waves, and made a lake out of the diamond in general, and rivers out of the base-lines. Ground-Keeper Murphy, a martyr to his job, rushed through *the flying sheets, and was soon tugging on the pennant halyards as though his life depended on it. So proud was the flag that it flaunted its folds in Murphy's face, and refused to budge. The halyards had gotten wrapped about the pole, which swayed and bent like a whip, but Murphy held on in a manner typical of how the team will hold on, and, after persistent efforts, and being wet through, got it down, and, tucking it under his arm, ran for cover. And the crowd of four thousand sheltered themselves as best possible, and watched the rain-storm.*

After it had come down for thirty minutes, Umpire Murray drew a long breath, and, rushing out, shouted the startling news that the game was called, as though anything else could be done. Just as Murray again turned to cover, Jupiter Pluvius turned off his spigot, and the clouds rolled by at the same time, the sun coming out in dazzling brightness. As the several hundred rooters turned back to the seats, they wished Murray had held his little speech for a few minutes, but that would have been of no avail, as the grass was of the consistency of a wet sponge, while the bald places looked like a brick-yard at work.

So tucking their rain-checks snugly in their pockets, and thinking of their potency for the first game Monday, they plowed through the mud towards home.
[Baltimore American, September 1, 1895]

Fifteen minutes before the time set to start yesterday's game (with Cincinnati), a regular Western tornado struck the ball grounds, and for half an hour the rain came down in torrents. It was preceded by a wind storm which blew the dust across the field, encircling the Brooklyn players, who were practicing at the time, in a perfect maze of smoke and dirt. Then the lightning flashed and the entire Brooklyn team ran for cover. Big Dan Brouthers says that a flash of lightning struck dangerously near him and he scampered for his life.
[Brooklyn Eagle, July 8, 1893]

At the hour of the scheduled for the opening of the game, 3:45, the sky was as clear as the melting notes of the nightingale, the sun as bright as a Neapolitan sunset.

But it rained Monday. It also rained last year. In fact, it rained yesterday morning. It may rain again some day.

At 3 o'clock the rival base ball aggregations were seized with the idea that the deluge was going to be encountered, and that, not having any Noah's ark, they must find an Ararat or a Guaranty Loan building. Hence they buttoned themselves into their cute little blouses and hied them back home, while the faithful fans paid their good money

and wasted their good time in the not only unprofitable, but uncomfortable amusement of riding in crowded street cars.
[Saint Paul Globe, May 12, 1897]

The details of this writeup would impress a civil engineer:

Water, water everywhere and not a place to play was the condition that confronted performers and fans at the Polo Grounds yesterday afternoon. That portion of the cloudburst that exploited itself in Harlem inundated the Eastern end of the ball field to the depth of eighteen inches in places.

Two games between the locals and Clevelands were declared off on account of high water. Patsy Tebeau and his employees offered to dig two barrels of clams in right field for the price of one admission, but the proposition was not accepted and the clams escaped. They may be dug later.

After gazing over the wide expanse of saffron-hued waters, the baseball virtuosos thought perhaps the sea would recede sufficiently to permit of the second game. So they sat in the high places and waited. But the flood seemed to increase instead of diminish. Little streamlets trickled down from Coogan's Bluff (hill overlooking Polo Grounds) on the West in great volume than the capacity of the overworked sewer that drains the field into the Harlem River.

Besides, that stream was swollen, and as the river at high tide carries a greater elevation than the Polo Grounds, the outlook was not glowing. However, if Bos'n Arthur Bell and the ground keeper can dispossess the flood in time, two games will be played this afternoon, still leaving one postponed game to be settled at some future date.

The place resembled a duck pond more than a ball field. Water filled the paddock from fence to fence, and all communication was cut off from both club houses except by means of temporary causeways, built of planks. Right field was flooded, with the exception of a small green island within a few yards of first base, and the left garden resembled a private trout pond.

A portion of center field remained in the shape of a peninsula. A narrow strip of bog, about thirty feet wide, extended to the ropes, but the water on either side looked dark and foreboding. An efficient corps of men and boys, armed with spoons and sponges, will do their level best to bail out the place in time for today's festivities.
[New York Journal, August 25, 1897]

Cold

The spirit of pneumonia stalked up and down the grand stand at yesterday's game and touched one after another of the cranks with its congestive hand. The wind yowled and slatted among the half empty benches, turning red noses blue and freezing fingers to lead pencils. Everybody's spirits were down to zero and below. The only variation to dull monotony was an occasional snow slide from the roof of the pavilion or the sound of the man breaking ice in the players' water pail.
Every device know to the cabmen and the employees of the department of city worked for maintaining the warmth of the body was taken up by the spectators. They beat their arms together, they stamped "first in war, first in peace, first in the hearts of their countrymen," in unison; they blew on their hands and they went out and "had something." But it was mostly in vain. The coldness was from the heart as well as from the weather and victory alone was the remedy.
[Brooklyn Eagle, May 6, 1891]

It was not a game yesterday to make the spectators thrill with joy or much of anything except cold shivers, for an icy blast from somewhere near Toronto presumably, kept whistling through the grand stands and making noses blue and collars go up about the ears of the rooters. It was really too cold to root successfully, or even to keep the excitement at any kind of a pitch.
[Post Express (Rochester, NY), May 7, 1896]

The damp and raw wind that howled across the field placed overcoats at a premium and caused the players to do song and dance tricks in the field.
[Pittsburg Dispatch, April 27, 1889]

The base ball season of 1880 opened yesterday afternoon with a cold, leaden sky, and with a temperature that was about as uninviting as one could imagine.
The wind blew steadily down across the ball field and against the grand stand, so that the small assemblage of humanity were forced to seek comfort in convenient and get-at-able sheltered nooks; in fact, they resembled a flock of hens seeking shelter on the icy side of a barn on a rainy day.
...Outside of the passed balls and bases on called balls, the errors were all excusable. Numbed fingers and stiffened hands can not grapple a ball safely or surely, and it would be unreasonable to scold a

player for dropping a ball, when to keep warm, he had to wear his ulster.
[Providence (R. I.) Evening Press, April 20, 1880]

    The day was bright and clear, but the wind was cold and cutting, taking particular pains to worm itself in and around the clothing and anatomies of the job lots who huddled together on the east bleachers.
[Milwaukee Journal, August 18, 1890]

    The weather was execrable, the chilly, piercing winds of a couple of months ago returning, as it were, to make their farewell appearance for the season.
    Cold? Why, a ride of 100 miles in a refrigerator car would have been a tropical event in comparison. The weather was simply bitter, and as the wind hustled around cheek and jowl, or played hop-scotch through the hirsute appendage of some shivering crank, there was a look upon the sun that actually bespoke hilarity.
    It was a sad and dreary opening, and the game put up was as weary and weak-kneed an affair as human eye ever "sot" upon. The fact is that the weather was dead against good playing, and a man who ventured out expecting to see straight sport at such a time, ought to have been fined $50 instead of paying 50 cents admission.
[Milwaukee Journal, May 6, 1891]

    Things began to look squally in the first inning. A stinging, cold northwestern breeze swept over the diamond and the 2,800 spectators congregated in the sunny spots, and with chattering teeth and livid faces watched the game. The day was so cold that the ice did not melt when the sun was shining, and only about 400 cranks braved the rheumatism and kindred terrors to witness it.
[The Sun (New York), October 26, 1887]

    "Darn the fellow that wrote that rot (wrote) about the beautiful snow," remarked a forlorn-looking individual as he watched the game from one of the upper boxes at Athletic park yesterday afternoon.
    "Amen," responded a shivering crank sitting in the corner, while a stout gentleman to the left anathematized the weather in a string of blank verse that would have done credit to a Billingsgate fishwife.
    "Who would have expected it," remarked another, referring of course to the sudden atmospheric change. "Ah! who indeed," sobbed the gentleman who that balmy morn had shed his winter flannels.

[Milwaukee Journal, June 20, 1891]

The attendance was not so large as that of a week ago, but this was due, no doubt, to the threatening weather and the refrigerated wind that blew in from the ocean. Along with the wind came a bank of fog which settled down on the baseball grounds and deepened the gloom in the neighborhood of the Oakland bench. As the goose eggs came rolling in, one after another, this somber pall grew thicker and the cranks on the bleachers turned up their coat collars and remarked that it looked like there was going to be an early frost.

[Morning Call (San Francisco), November 6, 1893]

Yesterday was one of those days that penetrates a man's physical organism like a knife going through a pumpkin rind. There was not such a very howling mob at the game, but there were enough to shiver in the sticky dampness until the grand stand rattled like dead men's bones.

The elements were as undecided as a fat gentleman on roller skates. Sometimes Africus and Aeolus and those other zephyrs that end in -us would blow across the diamond in fitful gusts and again they would cease and give the drizzling rain a chance. It was a melancholy day for base-ball and the game was just like the day.

[Quincy (Ill.) Daily Journal, May 23, 1891]

The sufferings undergone by arctic explorers in endeavoring to locate the north pole and put a hitching ring on it are one long, sweet summer dream compared to the agony experienced by the 1,200 plank warmers who stamped and swore in the bleachers while the hideous game unrolled itself before them.

Nobody ever heard of an arctic explorer in a spring suit being compelled to sit down while the mercury sank out of sight and the wind blew a cold gale that would give a polar bear pneumonia and watch his favorite team put up ball that would be condemned in the Stock Yards; yet that is what the Chicago "rooters" had to stand yesterday. They stood it, too, and were joyous throughout.

Occasionally the wind would get so cold that a half-uttered yawp would freeze in the crier's throat, and at intervals everybody would arise and stamp they feet to keep from breaking off, but they stuck out the nine innings.

[Inter Ocean (Chicago), May 20, 1894]

Cold and windy as it was, 200 faithful fans journeyed out to

Exposition park yesterday and shivered through two hours and thirty minutes of benumbed baseball playing. The players felt the clammy touch of winter that was in the air, but seemed to be more comfortable than the spectators.
[Kansas City Journal, April 30, 1897]

In the neighborhood of 4,000 specimens of suffering humanity went out to witness yesterday's game between the Milwaukee and Minneapolis teams at Athletic park. These well-meaning people actually tried to look happy and comfortable, each vying with the other in attempting to inaugurate a full-fledged time of joy.

But their efforts were of an evanescent character that forbade the hope of long or successful duration, and if one, more timorous than his fellows, essayed a laugh of rotund proportions, it was long odds against his mouth recovering its normal condition. An afternoon spent in an icehouse would have smacked more kindly of a torrid temperature than did the chilling breath which swept athwart the faces and feelings of those who dared everything in the vain hope of seeing the locals get there.
[Milwaukee Journal, May 9, 1892]

Heat

Hot, muggy weather often took its toll on players. Most uniforms of this era were made of heavy flannel, which brought on occasional instances of heat exhaustion, at times severe enough to send them to the clubhouse for recovery. Prior to the advent of shady dugouts, sitting on a sun-exposed bench all afternoon didn't help things, either.

As a preventive, a pail of ice water was stationed near every players' bench, from which players ladled its contents to cool off. The old trick of stuffing sponges or cabbage leaves wetted with ice water under their caps was also popular with players to help beat the heat.

In times long past, "sunstruck" was the term used for heat prostration, and even blamed for the death of Andy McKean, the Pirates' former first baseman, so sayeth *The Evening Times* (Washington, D. C.) of July 9, 1897: "He was knocked out by the sun one day in Pittsburg and was not seen on the diamond again. He died in less than a month."

The weather was hot enough to boil sap out of a wooden man.

[Dryden, New York Journal, August 17, 1897]

    The game this afternoon was played under a sun that would bake pig iron.
[Inter Ocean (Chicago), June 3, 1892]

    The day was hot and the sun boiled and fretted in the sky like the open door of a furnace.
[Source misplaced]

    For five hours yesterday afternoon, three thousand people sweltered at Union Park. It was the most thoroughly disagreeable experience a local crowd has ever had, bar none. Twice did the Clevelands defeat the Baltimores, and in such a way as to not make any more agreeable the ruffled feelings of the people.
    It was a hot time, sure enough, but not the sort of hot times of which poets sing. Over on the bleachers the crowd broiled and sizzled, while on the grand stand there was a lot of more elegant but not more comfortable roasting. Even the ladies, usually so debonair at a ball game, looked wilted, and could not hide the fact that they, too, were on the griddle.
    Out in the field the players fried and cooked, and tried to play baseball according to the principles of Harry Wright, Ned Hanlon and other high priests of the game, when they would have been much happier hunting bears on Greenland's icy mountains, where the strident voice of the umpire troubles none.
[Baltimore American, July 22, 1898]

    It was distressingly hot weather, and taken together with the thrilling battle, kept the immense throng in a constant steaming and fretful mood. It can not be disputed that the equator seems at times to extend exactly through the center of the St. Louis baseball park with all its adjuncts of tropical distresses.
    There is ofttimes a vagrant breeze loafing around the grand stand, but the local enthusiasts notice it not when they are heavily engaged in witnessing the rush and the fiery ardor of battle that is in progress before them.
[Baltimore American, July 16, 1894]

    The heat was something appalling...There wasn't a breath of air. The flags hung limp and motionless, and those of the rooters who wore coats and collars took them off. Pitching ball in that blazing heat

was almost as pleasant as firing a steamship in the tropics. Big Mike Sullivan and his esteemed contemporary, Mr. Hastings, steamed like Turkish bath attendants.
[Dryden, New York Journal, September 11, 1897]

Along about 3 o'clock this afternoon (New York manager) James Mutrie was discovered limply leaning against the shade afforded by a timber pile near the New Polo Grounds.

Jim's face was a picture of conglomerated heat and misery. His collar looked like a string out of a paste-pot and great drops of perspiration were standing out all over him. His shirt-front was a wreck and a brand new silk coat wore a look as though it had interviewed a garden hose in the hands of a small and pranksome boy.

In reply to an anxiously-put query as to where he had been and what he had run against, the pennant-winning manager confided to the questioner that the weather was so infernally hot when he arrived at the grounds at noontime today, that he straightaway turned back downtown and had since then been hustling all over the city, securing insurance against fire on the new property.
[Evening World (New York), July 12, 1889]

When a body of men like the athletic group of finely built young fellows that the New Yorks and Pittsburgers are, to enter an open stretch of turf where the merciless shafts of Old Sol beat down in such relentless, broiling fashion as they did this afternoon and scamper about all unmindful of the enervating calorie, then does the occasional and not very close observer of the game begin to appreciate how hard a ball-player works.

A huge spread of white shirts, in various degrees of limpness, faced the woolen-encased athletes. Hats were lost sight of and collars and cuffs had things all their own melting way.

Hot! If Phoebus, the sun god, should drive his chariot right in through the northeast gate for vehicles and shoot his caloric bolts at such close quarters, it is hard to imagine that it could be a bit hotter. Thermometers up this way melted.
[Evening World (New York), August 8, 1891]

Fog

As the visitors came in to bat in the sixth, the fog came in with redoubled energy. Gore looked like a ghost in center and stood there seemingly in spirit meditation while Sunday banged a line hit right past

him.
[Source misplaced]

The heavy mist that hovered about the park all afternoon reminded some of the old-timers of the day that Eddie Burke sauntered into center field with a lighted lantern. It was in a game between Sioux City and Milwaukee. The fog was so thick that Burke was lost sight of in center field.
[Saint Paul Globe, May 5, 1898]

Jacksonville, Fla, March 25.—For a much needed change, the weather works turned out a nice sample of fog today, and blew it up the river in dripping banks. As variety is the spice of life, the Giants cannot complain of dull monotony in the meteorological line. They have enjoyed everything from frost bite to sunstroke on this expedition. All that is needed to complete the string of surprises is a fleet of ice boats sailing down the stream.
[Dryden, New York Journal, March 26, 1897]

A nice, big, full-grown and juicy yellow fog, thick enough to cut with a knife, was discovered in the vicinity of Athletic park yesterday afternoon. It was also a persistent fog, so persistent, in fact, that although a savage bull purp set his fangs into its quivering anatomy, he failed to scare a move out of it, while a billy goat in a neighboring lot, after working vigorously for a couple of hours, failed to butt it off the track.

The ladies who were present at the game thought the fog just too horrid for anything, because it was so dreadfully sticky—"worse than gum, you know," and as one confidentially remarked, "that top set of mine never did ___. Oh! my, don't you think it will rain before it fogs anymore, or will it fog first?"'

One old toper, after taking in two or three good mouthfuls of the substance, averred that he thought a chunk or two of that in a barrel of whisky would not only strengthen it, but improve the taste.

An astute individual decided that there was nothing very surprising about the condition of the atmosphere, and that the "Indians" (Sioux City team) had simply opened up a few bottles of their choicest brand, a full supply of which they always carry with them. This seemed quite feasible, for when at the end of the eighth inning, the fog had become so strong that it pushed a player off his base...

Somebody suggested putting bloodhounds on the track of our outfield in the last half of the eighth yesterday afternoon, so entirely lost

were they to the public gaze.
[Milwaukee Journal, June 3, 1891]

    Old ocean's vapory breath blew in from the deep in dull gray banks that rose and fell with the breeze, till the fielders looked like spectral bodies treading air. Here and there a juicy cloud hung fast in space and dripped on the just and unjust alike, with a cold, relentless grip.
    It bordered full-grown whiskers with a silvery lace drapery, and plugged up the air cells of the deep-lunged coachers till their voices sounded like the hoarse gurgle of an exhaust pipe in winter. A fog bell was hung on the wall as a warning to outfielders, and both clubs shipped a navigator to pilot the men into the bench when the teams changed sides in that exhilarating autumnal atmosphere.
[Morning Call (San Francisco), October 19, 1891]

Wind

    The progress of the game (pre-season, Yale vs Washington, at National Park) was arrested by the wind storm...Great clouds of dust swept over the grounds, blotting out the players from view and causing great commotion among the audience. The storm continued with varying intensity for upwards of half an hour. The grand stand vibrated, and the flagstaff made vigorous efforts to come down and join the game. When the rifts of sand would lift for a moment Hines could be seen with his head enveloped in a handkerchief. Carroll was apparently blown up against the left-field fence, but the solidity of Crane's calves enabled him to ride the gale at anchor.
    ...Umpire Cate spit the sand and dust out of his mouth from time to time and looked bored. When the sun finally shone out upon the ceasing of the simoon a more travel-stained and an up-all-night-and-go-home-in-the-morning looking crowd you would have to go far to see. Men of hitherto irreproachable character came out of the gloom with tiles as abandoned-looking as Jefferson was compelled to put up with in "Lend Me Five Shillings." Those who had received their Saturday's shave and cosmetic looked as if they had been playing mumblepeg and had had an intimate acquaintance with the ground in their efforts to pull up the peg.
[Sunday Herald (Washington, D. C.), April 25, 1886]

    Polo Grounds, June 18.—A strong easterly wind caught up the loose dust and dirt of the streets this afternoon and whirled it up and *over the high fence which surrounds the Polo Grounds, and then sent it down upon the devoted heads of the crowd upon the bleaching boards, and even sent it sifting in upon the grand stand occupants. And the same ill wind wafted sarsaparillas and lemonades down dusty throats and blew nickels into the pockets of the vendors of these fluids.*

But whatever the win did, it did not prevent the usual large crowd from assembling at the field long before the time set for the opening of the game.
[Evening World (New York), June 13, 1888]

Lightning

Jocko Halligan, while catching for the Buffalo Brotherhood club last year, was struck by lightning on the Cleveland grounds, and it didn't even make a dent in him. The other day, however, he was struck again and knocked out of the Cincinnati club.
[Omaha Daily Bee, August 23, 1891]

9. Humor in Baseball Maidens

Women have been faithful spectators of the national pastime since the very beginning. Whether attracted to the sport by curiosity, social whirl or genuine interest, they continued to show up at ball parks over the years in significant numbers. By the 1880s, when baseball became professional and stadiums were built, reporters often commented favorably on their colorful and conspicuous presence in the grandstands.

But these were male chauvinistic times in Victorian America, and gender discrimination unfortunately shown through when it came to baseball. Female attendees, for example, because of their disarming innocence and generally acknowledged ignorance of the rules of play, became the butt of demeaning "woman-at-a-ball-game" jokes, which became a staple of humor sections in newspapers.

A few business-minded ball club owners, on the other hand, saw women as potential dollar signs. Allow them free passage into the park, they figured, but charge their required male escorts full fare; more women plus more men equaled more revenue, not to mention more of that intangible, yet inestimable asset: good will. But would it work?

The idea was not new. In 1878, for example, unaccompanied ladies were admitted free of charge to all amateur games played on the Capitoline grounds, in Brooklyn, but it had never been tried at a professional level.

The theory was put to test in 1882, when the owner of the Providence Grays' baseball team, a member of the National League, initiated its first "Ladies' Day." The event was a smash hit and was soon followed in slow, but steady fashion by other League clubs over the next few years.

The Ladies' Day, introduced by the Providence Club on the occasion of their first match with the Bostons, turned out to be such a brilliant success in every way that the other League clubs are going to follow suit and have a ladies' day once a week.

The President announces that on such a date the club will have a ladies' day, on which ladies, accompanied by gentlemen, will be given

free admission to the ground, with reserved seats, their escorts paying their own admission fee and for their own seats.
[New York Clipper, May 20, 1882]

The Metropolitan Company's experiment (at the Polo Grounds) having a "ladies' day" every week resulted in a brilliant success. The crowd of spectators was the biggest since Decoration Day, and there were 500 ladies on the grand stand.
[The Sun (New York), June 16, 1883]

As an extra inducement to secure the attendance of ladies and thus popularize the game with them, Messrs. Moxley and Hollingshead will introduce a new feature here, which has proved very "taking" wherever attempted.
This is to have, at stated intervals, what is to be known as "ladies' day," on which days ladies are to be allowed all the privileges whatever for admission to the grounds and chairs in the upper tier of the grand stand. A general invitation will be issued for these days, and they will be pleased to see every chair in the tier occupied.
[National Republican (Washington, D.C.), January 26, 1884]

Many women became truly avid, screaming, foot-stomping, handkerchief-waving fans, who also astounded male counterparts by filling out their score cards properly, a no mean feat.

The result (loss of game to Baltimore) was so crushing to the ladies. Good fans they are, when the curtain rang down on the finale in the first half of the ninth when Billy Lush went out from Reitz to Doyle. The male portion of the vast audience had a recourse for their disappointment.
A man can always square himself with his feelings with language, either expletive or harmonious. He can gain more satisfaction to the inch by indulging in a good cussing than a woman can from a river of tears. The ladies cried yesterday; the men did the other thing.
[Baltimore American, date misplaced]

Matinee Girls and Diamond Heartthrobs

Among the usual crowd of feminine attendees at a ball game, not all came purely for entertainment. There was sure to be a few pretty young ladies who, sitting high in the grandstand with a pair of opera glasses, trained their eyes on every movement made by a

certain handsome member of the home team. Over time, what started as a casual fascination often grew into a full-blown infatuation. "Matinee girls," the press called these lovesick maidens who idolized players from afar.

No one knows how many of these smitten ladies were too shy or constrained by strait-laced social mores to make their feelings known, and resigned themselves to pine away in broken-hearted silence for an entire season.

But baseball reporters documented plenty who did not hide their romantic inclinations. They were overheard in the stands, openly declaring their diamond gladiator as "the dearest thing that ever happened." They were also known to send him perfumed mash notes, requesting something personal to remember him by—a signed photograph or lock of hair—anything, really, to keep their love light burning.

They were the same ones, too, who showered gifts on the objects of their affection. These events took place during games when play was halted temporarily as a basket of flowers or box of cigars was presented to the surprised, but extremely red-faced recipient.

The effects of this ball park romanticism also worked in reverse. Players were keenly aware of the bright eyes and sweet smiles of ladies in the crowd, and often exhibited better play when a number of them were present.

Sometimes, though, petty jealousies developed between players who competed for the turning of the same feminine head.

> *"Jocko" Fields has only one objection to a place in the outfield, and that is it takes him too far away from the grand stand, where his fair admirers are wont to congregate. He complains about Fred Carroll monopolizing all the bouquets and other tokens of esteem that are sometimes cast to the victorious gladiators, and requests the girls to hereafter attach his name to any memento designed for him individually, and if Carroll claims it, he will have to fight for it. The kid argues if a girl is worth admiring, she is worth dying for, and he is willing to shed a little blood if it will increase his popularity.*
> [Pittsburgh Press, May 2, 1888]

Fred Carroll is not receiving nearly so many letters from admiring fair ones now, asking for locks of his hair, pictures of his own handsome self and other mementoes, since his batting average fell off. Jocko Fields has benefitted considerably while the blonde hercules was taking a rest and never got tired of blowing about it. Brace up, Fred. There are other just as good fish in the sea.
[Pittsburgh Press, May 19, 1888]

W. H. Mercer, Pitcher.

There was never a lack of good-looking ball players during this era, whose mere presence on the field induced fluttering pulses and attacks of the vapors in the fair sex.

One in particular, receiving an abundance of press and wandering feminine gazes, was Win Mercer, pitcher of the Washingtons. This man, he of the raven locks and soulful eyes, was such a guaranteed chick magnet that he was purposefully paraded out on the mound on as many Ladies' Days as possible. After all, business was business.

It was a Win Mercer aggregation, as the nod and wave of pretty headgear in the grand stand evidenced every time the dreamy-looking Romeo hove in the vista of their optics. The amount and variety of the female adjectives of the invective kind hurled and hissed at Buck's "Brutes," as they called the Reds, for swatting "dear Mr. Mercer's" kinks and straight ones all over the field would have filled a dictionary.

No matter what Mercer did, it was O. K. and that Cincinnati knocked him sky west and crooked was an accident and "just too bad," according to the ocean of femininity that swept over the broad expanse of the new grand stand.
[Source misplaced]

"Handsome Win" Mercer—his sobriquet was no joke yesterday...the dark-eyed Romeo...The matinee girls gazed in ecstasy and their chaperoning mammas indulged them to the extent of admitting that "the young fellow was quite handsome and pitched the ball very well." The chappies, disconsolate in their eclipse, got in a "knock" by saying, "Mercer knows his business; he should do living pictures in a baseball form during the theatrical season."
[Morning Times (Washington, D.C.), August 26, 1896]

Win Mercer, young and handsome, is the favorite of the ladies who attend the local games. If an umpire is not disposed to call every ball Mercer pitches a strike, his pretty partisans hold indignation meetings all over the grand stand and figuratively jab the umpire's eyes out with their parasol ferrules.

And if some hard-hearted swatter of the opposing team lands on one of Win's curves and straightens it out for three bases or a home run, they weep and moan and refuse to be comforted. Win had a light attack of smallpox last winter, but has fully recovered. The ladies are assured that not a scar was left on his classic face.
[Morning Times (Washington, D. C.), March 18, 1896]

A box finished in ivory and tied with the yellowest ribbon, and bedecked with a bow tied as if by the daintiest of fingers, was presented Mercer in the third inning when he came to bat.

Just what the aristocratic carton contained was a mystery to the 9,000 curious fans. Nor would Win allay the anxiety by untying the pretty knot. One unregenerate rooter suggested that the box was stuffed with garters; another ventured to remark that it was a box of "kisses," and still another said it held a pair of curling irons.

What the gaily bedecked package enfolded in its four sides was twenty-five of the finest cigars, and a new ten-dollar bill, with which the handsome pitcher was to reimburse himself for the fine inflicted on him by Umpire Lynch at Brooklyn. And, furthermore, the gift was from a very pretty young lady.
[Morning Times (Washington, D.C.), May 27, 1896]

Many testaments chronicling this age-old phenomenon appeared in print, where writers found it fertile ground for much quippery.

There is a lady in Cincinnati of uncertain age who weighs 250 pounds, and who has become infatuated with John McPhee. The fair damsel makes life a burden to the great second baseman by writing him notes, odes to his eyebrows, and all that sort of thing. Last Valentine day she sent him an "epic," as she called it, containing ninety-six verses. It read like this:

*Oh, Bid McPhee,
I've thought of thee
With ecstasy
Since '83.*
[Baltimore American, July 10, 1889]

The latest story of fiction is entitled, "Rutherford, the Handsome Shortstop." Ruthie makes a triple when needed, and a lady in the grand stand falls in love with him. The villain turns out to be a pitcher, and he tries to soak Ruthie with a pitched ball.
[Baltimore American, June 20, 1890]

During the game, Schriver was called from the plate to accept a handsome bat tied with many colored ribbons, presented by a pretty young lady in the grand stand.
[Saint Paul Globe, August 18, 1896]

On the strength of the Apollo Belvedere charms, Lally, the new outfielder of the Browns, received in exchange for Hutchison, ought to prove a matinee drawing card on ladies' day. Lally has a figure that would fill the blasé soul of a Pompadour or a Cleopatra, and his pose at the bat is worthy of a calcium light (spotlight) accompaniment.
[New York Telegram, reprinted in the Saint Paul Globe, July 26, 1897]

Floral tributes are in disfavor with Detroit fans. The Journal says:
"The young lady who sent to the plate a bunch of posies for Lefty Davis early last week will please bestow her favors upon somebody who drives a dray hereafter. The young man in left didn't make a hit after (umpire) Sheridan handed him the bouquet until yesterday, nor did he stop a ball that was rolling along the ground. If (Detroit owner) Vanderbeck sees another nosegay sneaking up towards the gate, it will be taken from the bearer and tossed into the gutter.
[Saint Paul Globe, May 19, 1898]

The ladies of Quincy are hereby notified that Capt. Lauman's wife joined her husband in the city yesterday. No more throwing of roses or casting shy glances at the captain of the club.
[Quincy (Ill.) Daily Whig, June 1, 1889]

The fair sex is taking a deeper interest in baseball than of yore. The bevy of loveliness in the upper part of the grand stand at the Polo Grounds on a pleasant afternoon is almost enough to turn the heads of the players. Some people say that it's the reason Esterbrook forgot how to play.
[New York Tribune, May 15, 1887]

Yesterday being ladies' day at the Ohio street arena of manly diversions, a goodly number of what old man Harper, down in Prairie Creek, used to call the "female race," occupied the grandstand, notwithstanding the fierce bluff put up by Wappenhans's agency for J. Pluvius along about noon. Pink, blue, green, mauve, lavender, striped and brindled shirt waists made the place look like the scene of a boiler explosion in a florist's emporium and various twitters in the soft, sweet tones for which the American fair ones are noted the world over.
[Indianapolis Journal, May 17, 1899]

There was a highly fashionable audience out at the ball game yesterday. The grand stand looked lovely with a couple hundred of the fair daughters of Los Angeles. It was the first time that many had a chance to display their Easter bonnets.
Under each bonnet was a pretty face with a rosebud of a mouth out of which came such expressions as:
"Isn't Tredway just too sweet for anything?"
"Hasn't Park Wilson a classical face?"
"Captain Carroll's mustache is just too cute for anything."
"The umpire has a high regard for his good looks."
"I dote on 'Kid' Hulen."
"Jimmy Stafford is my choice."
[Los Angeles Herald, May 7, 1892]

(Pitcher) Terry's quiet, gentlemanly behavior on and off the field, combined with his good looks, has made him the pet of the fair patrons of the game. One enthusiastic fair one the other day, when Terry made an important three-base hit, exclaimed, "Oh, I think he's too splendid for anything." What it meant was only known to the fair young speaker.
[Brooklyn Eagle, June 1, 1884]

Next Mr. Payne lobbed a beautifully slow ball directly over the plate. "Ducky" dodged, twisted and flung himself all around to no purpose, for (umpire) Hank O'Day, in a cold, penetrating voice, told Mr. Holmes to go back to his lobster pots in left field.
"Wasn't it perfectly lovely," said a sweet young summer fashion plate. "I've guessed it now. They call him 'Ducky' because he dodges so beautifully. It was dreadfully rude to put him out for that."
[New York Journal, July 31, 1897]

Promptly at 2 o'clock, after a short preliminary limbering up, the Giants raced out on the field. Then there was another great fluttering of score-cards. "Who is that long fence rail object with a wire fence around his face?" asked the young woman in red of the young woman in blue.

"That? Oh, let me see; that is Jack Boyle. Doesn't he look awfully like an animated scarf pin?"

Then between caramels they turned their attention to O'Rourke's calves and Jack was forgotten.
[Cincinnati Enquirer, April 24, 1892]

A dream in chocolate brown, with an Easter bonnet of roses au naturel, pale pink streamers and untanned gloves, sat through the game yesterday afternoon in a box on the hurricane deck of the grand stand. The little one never took her eyes off Addison (Gumbert, Chicago pitcher), but sat as immovable as the Venus of Milo through the nine innings.

When Addison had blanked the last of the New York Leviathans, a bunch of American beauties shot out of the box and fell at Gumbert's feet. Addison picked up the dainties, pressed them to his lips, doffed his cap, and, mutely enough, two souls had exchanged congratulations on the result of the battle.
[Inter Ocean (Chicago), May 7, 1892]

10. Humor in Coaching

Line coaches, or "coachers," as they were originally called, made their first appearance on major league ball fields in 1886. Their function was grounded in real need and practicality.

Initially, coachers took the field as soon as their side went to bat, whether men were on base or not, and, from positions near first and third base, guided foot traffic around the bases, offered words of encouragement and kept a sharp eye on the ball to prevent runners from being victimized by the hidden-ball trick.

Their debut, however, was soon marked by controversy. Overzealous coachers, allowed complete freedom of movement, many times accompanied runners from third base to home so closely that they interfered with plays at the plate.

Next, their field manners took an alarming turn when coachers tried to rattle opposing players with a constant barrage of shouts and personal taunts, amplified by players on the bench and the bleacher crowd as well.

Targeted mainly were pitchers—especially rookies—in hopes they would lose control of the ball. Those with rabbit ears had little choice but to steel themselves or plug their ears with cotton, as Pittsburg's Frank Killen tried with mixed results. Consequently, coachers acquired unsavory reputations of being insulting, obnoxious and just downright rude.

The raucous theater grew even more bizarre. To create further distraction and confusion, coachers added to their vocal repertoire by engaging in crazy physical antics, such as jumping, running, dancing and waving their arms about, even performing handstands and other acrobatic stunts.

Curiously, the energy that started as a diversion on the field was taken up by the partisan gallery on the bleachers, who delighted in the circus-like atmosphere. The strong and loyal bond between the two parties was soon exploited by the home team. When needed, coachers, acting as cheerleaders, called on the bleachers to howl an ear-shattering chorus. The generated excitement rattled opponents or, when passed back to the players, resulted in more spirited play.

There was risk, however, in going too far with this purposeful orchestration. If the passion of the bleacher crowd was ginned up too much and used to intimidate a mutual enemy, such as the umpire, whose "wrong" decisions were hurting the home team, the fury could boil over and result in physical attacks on this unfortunate scapegoat.

Such explosive diamond scenes were more representative of the American Association than the National League, but in both leagues were made possible because, in this time, players, coaches, umpires, and spectators often indulged in communal chitchat on the diamond, unlike the near-sepulchral hush that prevails today.

Observers blamed the origin of this rowdy behavior on the St. Louis Browns, the powerhouse club of the American Association of the late 1880s. It was a legitimate charge, as this club was notorious for pioneering aggressive and bulldozing tactics. Most teams eventually adopted the disgraceful technique under the guise of a winning strategy, a notable exception being the Chicago team captained by Adrian Anson, who branded it as disrespectful and evil.

League officials struggled for years to contain the menace, which disgusted many ball park patrons. Strict rules were passed,  such as confining coaches to areas near the bases, allowing them on the field only when runners were present and prohibiting verbal contact except with runners. In 1896, baseball pundits, like former player John M. Ward, even called for abolishment of coaching, claiming that it was overrated and, worse, fueled violence on the field.

Nonetheless, the coachers' style of play continued on its turbulent course, unfazed by fines, ejections, or threats thereof. Most of the time, umpires, deeming the problem insurmountable, simply looked the other way.

But what regulations couldn't stop, time eventually did. Baseball was maturing. By the mid-1910s, the age of the clamorous coacher had faded away as an odd footnote to history, as baseball luminary Charles Comiskey philosophically noted in 1909:

How do most of the coachers go about their work today? Oh, they stroll up to the lines, fold their arms and stand around, waiting for the side to be retired.

One-Liner Humor

Latham is the ring leader of the kickers, and should have been born deaf and dumb

Perry Werden, whom a dozen umpires and a Gatling gun could not stop from talking

the Pittsburghs made enough noise on the coaching lines to drive a boiler factory into bankruptcy

Latham's chatter was like the music of the average street organ

he has a voice on him that should have been hired out to a tug boat

Speaking of Coachers

Not all of coachers were loudmouthed, tactless bullies. A case in point was quick-witted Arlie Latham, who had mastered a subtle and soft-spoken—but absolutely deadly—approach.

His "charm" was once revealed by a former teammate, Tom Loftus:

"Latham never stooped to anything coarse or loud to get the crowd started. He did his work just as legitimately as Francis Wilson would do his comedy stuff and it was more effective on that account. He never raved and yelled at the pitcher, but the minute one of his side cracked out a nice hit, Arlie was right on the job with that old oily talk of his.

"'Well, well, well, Mr. Pitcher'—always the mister—'that was a little hard luck for you. Oh, and look who's up now! But never mind; the trouble will all be over in a minute. We'll make it as easy for you as we can.'

"That line of talk is what gets a pitcher every time because he can't say anything back. Call him a lobster and a pitcher is back at you in a flash, giving as much as you can send; but get under his skin with the polite conversation and the pitcher hasn't got a chance. That was easy for Latham."

[Brooklyn Eagle, February 21, 1909]

It was no secret that the physical quality common to almost every successful coacher—far more than 20/20 vision, eagle-eyed alertness, and plain common baseball sense—was a voice strong enough to be heard in the next county. This attribute was memorialized by apt nicknames given to those who excelled at the loathsome art of vociferous needling.

Nevertheless, baseball writers found in these celebrated men with stentorian pipes a seemingly never-ending source of humor, as the following comments represent:

Of all base ball coachers' voice, that of Bug Holliday is the most excruciating. He starts off with an agonizing yelp, howls for a while like an auctioneer or circus sideshow crier, and finally winds up with a plaintive howl like a dog in pain. And the only one the "Bug" appears to rattle by his coaching is himself.
[Pittsburg Press, May 6, 1889]

Haddock of the Brooklyns is subjected to a large amount of good-natured roasting every time the team goes West. A Chicago correspondent says of him:
"Prince George Haddock coaches about as he would at a lawn tennis outing. The dear, sweet fellow may not be a coacher, but he is a la la poser. If the prince had his bangs with him on this trip, they were modestly smothered under a real vulgar base ball cap, so they were."
[Brooklyn Eagle, August 28, 1892]

"Heine Peitz, from past and present reports, is about the toughest proposition playing ball," observed a member of the team (Brooklyn Superbas).
"When he isn't catching, as occurred on the day Kennedy pitched in Cincinnati, he did the coaching. Before he left the players' bench, while the Reds were at bat, he filled his hands with pebbles and alternately shot the missiles at (pitcher) Roaring Bill and let out a bellow that nobody could understand. When Heine isn't making a catapult of himself, he transforms himself into an Indian, with a roar that is neither English nor German."
[Brooklyn Eagle, May 28, 1899]

Manager Irwin (New York) would like to lease or buy a high-pressure, triple expansion steam calliope for coaching purposes. Irwin goes out in uniform every day, but after two or three innings his pipes become choked with words and emotion and he has to subside. Voice troches do no good and onions fail to strengthen the vocal cords. He must either sign a calliope or a side show spieler.
[Dryden, New York Journal, May 18, 1896]

The Hoosiers did yelling enough for half a dozen ordinary teams. There must be something in Indiana air that gives a depth and resonance to Hoosier lungs. The voice owned and controlled by the big, loose-jointed Denny is like that of an ocean steamer lost in a fog. That of Jack Glasscock resembles the bellow of a Texas steer. The voice of Hines is not profound, but it makes up in insistence what it lacks in volume. "Now, we've got 'em," he would pipe to Glasscock in a shrill treble, "Let it come, Jack de Ripper!" Than Jack would rise on his toes with that peculiar jerky throw of his, and line it over to Hines with a roar and a growl that would shake the girders of the grand-stand.
[The World (New York), reprinted in the Indianapolis Journal, September 8, 1889]

That diabolical coach of the Baltimore team acted like an alarm clock with the whooping cough, and the noises he emitted ranged all the way from the cackle of a misguided hen to the chortle of a circus calliope.
[Brooklyn Eagle, May 18, 1893]

Tommie "Boiler Yard" Tucker and Baltimore's Clark will have to look to their laurels as shriekers and squawkers. In Stewart the Chicagos have a wonderful wind disturber. Stewart can take a good, long breath, use his hands as a funnel and let out yells that will shake grand stand seats loose from their fastenings. In a coaching hurrah, Mr. Stewart is a pippin.
[Cincinnati Enquirer, reprinted in the Brooklyn Eagle, May 4, 1895]

Jack Crooks went out near third base and began to coach. Jack has a voice that sounds like a locomotive emerging from a tunnel, but he got along all right yesterday until he aimed that voice at Killen. Then (umpire) Mr. Lynch said: "You go sit down." And Jack sat.
[Pittsburg Leader, reprinted in The Brooklyn Eagle, May 13, 1896]

When Stewart and Roat get on the coach lines, it is like a whole wagonload of fireworks going up at once.
[Evening Wisconsin (Milwaukee), reprinted in the Saint Paul Globe, May 15, 1896]

What a barker for a dime museum Peitz of the Reds would make. The fat catcher has a voice that sounds like a foghorn with the heaves and when he gets warmed up in the coaching box, spectators with delicate nerves want to go home.

[Chicago Journal, reprinted in the Pittsburgh Press, July 12, 1898]

    An exchange says of Tony Mullane's coaching:
    "Tony is a great pitcher, but when he 'chins' the man on first, he does it in an undertaker's tone, which reminds one of the well-worn invitation: 'Friends of the deceased may now step up and take their last look at the remains.'
    "There is nothing cheerful about Tony's coaching, and when he has Long John Reilly for a side partner, the cold chills creep all over the crowd. It is a solemn performance, and some day when they are at it, the opposing nine will feel so sorrowful that they will desert the field."
[Pittsburgh Press, August 2, 1888]

    Clark of the Baltimores must have put in the winter as an auctioneer, judging from his peculiar coaching. He keeps up a steady stream of words, each sentence being yelled in a monotone until the last word is reached, when his voice jumps about seven degrees. A little of it goes a long way, and it is doubtful if Mr. Clark's life would be worth much if he continued long in the City of Churches (Brooklyn).
[Brooklyn Eagle, May 17, 1893]

    The (Minneapolis) Millers are probably the closest approach to a band of half-starved jackals of anything in the league. They come up to the line and bark incessantly throughout the game. Wilmot is the worst offender. He seems to have no regard for decency or fairness. He probably never pondered over the word self-respect. Profanity flowed from his lips yesterday with startling frequency. He cursed one man in the grandstand, called another a liar, and hurled epithets at the (Kansas City) Blues.
[Kansas City Journal, April 27, 1897]

    All the same it is not good judgment to send Hassamer to the third base coaching box. Whether right or wrong in this particular case, there are a half a dozen men on the team who can turn round three times to Bill's once and give him loads of weight in a thinking handicap. He has just about as much judgment on base running as a Quaker about prize fighting, and there is no sense in allowing him to display his large stock of misinformation in that locality.
[Morning Times (Washington, D. C.), August 1, 1895]

"Dad" Clark's mouth has found a rival in the noticeable zig-zag slit that undulates across the face of one Tebeau, of Denver. When in action, it acts very much like the business end of a crater, for it is full of brimstone and other stuff that it vomits forth in large and solid masses. Tebeau is, in fact, one of that class of people who should be compelled to carry a door mat under his chin to wipe his tongue on every time before using.
[Milwaukee Journal, July 29, 1891]

"Show 'em how Paddy stole the rope with a bar of Ivory soap! Run up the hill, then down. It's easier to run down than up. Rasper, Jasper, Roosper, Joosper, where you goin', where'd ye come from, what ye here for, the object is to hit the ball!"

Such is the strain of bullfrog melody that pours forth from the sheet-iron throat of pitcher and fielder Dake, of the Rockford club. He is a coacher out of sight and were Mike Trost now with us, the honors would be equally divided.

Dake looks like a clown and when he unties that voice of his, you would think every circus on top of the green globe had broken loose. Dake is the right man to have in a coacher's box. Underwood, who pretended to coach at 3rd base, was completely drowned out and finally didn't say a word.
[Quincy (Ill.) Daily Journal, May 8, 1891]

William Lange, the Chicago outfielder, is the funniest coacher that gets on the base lines. He doesn't say a word. When he gets ready to coach, he simply opens his mouth and lets the wind blow down his throat. A roar escapes that would put the best lion in the business to shame.
[Brooklyn Eagle, July 7, 1894]

A young man named Schmidt (of Baltimore)…stands at first base and yells like a Comanche. His voice is a cross between a steam calliope and a side-show "screecher," and when he loses his job on the diamond field, he ought to find no difficulty whatever in getting a position as an announcer for some traveling show.

"Pop" Whittaker in his palmiest days could not hold a candle to him; if "Nate" Salisbury heard him he would turn green with envy, and Fred Burns would give ten years of his life to be able to yell as loudly as this youth Schmidt. In his efforts to urge his comrades on to victory, the coacher talks to himself, but he can be heard a quarter of a mile away.
[New York Times, May 3, 1893]

This anecdote dispels any doubt as to the effectiveness of coachers rattling pitchers, as crude and unfair as the tactic was:

A member of the Washington party, talking about the eleven runs that the Senators made off the Pittsburgs in one inning in Saturday's game, said yesterday:
"Those runs were the result of a little joshing and roasting from the coaching lines. Joyce did it. He stood in the coaching box and when he got through, Hawley didn't know whether he was pitching or in St. Louis. 'You're too purty to pitch,' sang out Joyce. 'Your place is up on the rialto with the bullies and the mashers. Why don't you wear your red necktie on the field? I hear that Connie Mack is going to buy you a blonde wig and take you out next season as a soubrette.'
"When Scrappy got through with Hawley, he didn't know the way to the plate. He hit one, then gave a base on balls, and then the gang began to hit. The whole Pittsburg crew quit."
[Cincinnati Enquirer, reprinted in the Brooklyn Eagle, June 7, 1896]

Not all coachers were proficient at their task, however; slackers existed. Here's proof:
Foutz showed remarkably poor judgment in allowing Anderson to coach at third base. Andy requires a tremendous amount of coaching on the bases himself, and to place him in a position to direct the movements of men is like putting a West Point cadet at the head of an army.
[Brooklyn Eagle, June 5, 1896]

About as useless an adjunct to a team as a scare crow in a hot house is Chiles, the official coacher of the Philadelphias. He runs up and down the coacher's box like a rooster on hot glass, incessantly scratching gravel and flapping his hands. His antics have no effect on the opposing pitcher and certainly do not cause the Phillies to move any faster on the bases. They unearth queer things in Quakerdom, but Chiles is the queerest thus far produced.
[Brooklyn Eagle, May 17, 1899]

My, How They Did Talk

Coaching-line grammar was never mistaken for the Queen's English, but the rough-and-gruff talk, quaint and entertaining even to this day, still got the job done.

Examples:

Gant, the Keystone (Philadelphia) coacher, was in his glory yesterday afternoon, and though he did not have much opportunity, he made the most of it. With a ducky runner on base, his double-basso voice might have been heard for three squares, rumbling out something like this:

"Get a move on, you, now! What you g'win to sleep on dat fust bag fur when dar's ripe water melyons awaitin' to be pulled at second! G'won, go on! He won't trow de ball. Slide! Now yer's going; keep on movin'! In yer goes! Now feet first and if he stands in yer way, gib him de spike! Now, do yer see dat third base? Jest imagine dar was a keg of beer waitin' yer appearance down dere. What yer afraid ob? Playin' fur a record, is yer? Now, dat's nice; keep him a-guessin'. He won't trow dat ball. Dat's da time yer nearly did it. Now, light out as dough de old debble was arfter you. Der you is, all safe and soun'! Now wait on a hit."
[Pittsburgh Press, August 8, 1888]

A specimen of Midget Miller's coaching at Recreation park Saturday, in a trombone voice to be heard two blocks:
"What are you doin' there now! Whoa! An old '77 hit, Jimmy! Get down there! Whoa! Smack her on the kisser, Pop! He'll smack her in the eye this time! Whoa! Get off your perch there! Whoa!"
[Pittsburgh Press, August 13, 1888]

The All-Stars

A few stand-out coachers received far more ink than others because of their proficiencies at the position.

Arlie Latham

As a jollier, nerve restorer, dyed-in-the-wool plugger for the game, Latham has them all faded. His face upon the diamond, his antics upon the lines and his sterling witticisms as the play progresses are features alone, nor will they ever be forgotten by the countless numbers who have heard him chaff an opposing pitcher and buoy up the hopes of a timid batsman with his "There! That's it! That's a beauty!" and, when they hit, his mellow burst of laughter and Dago monkey shines. Should they perchance fan out, there's always a word of encouragement for the retiring batter and a "boost" for the next man in the way he says "Hard

luck! Hard luck, eh? Well, here's a man that will hit it! Old Dan Brouthers, eh?"
[Columbus (Ohio) Dispatch, reprinted the Saint Paul Globe, May 16, 1897]

>Arlie Latham, the only original "dude" of the profession, is one of the great attractions of the St. Louis Browns. His coaching tactics are the most notable of his varied accomplishments as a diamond artist. His "Whoa there!" added to his witty tongue sauce, is peculiarly aggravating to opposing pitchers and catchers particularly. It is said that Deacon Jim White was so badly rattled because of Arlie's incessant chatter that he asked to be changed to first base from third.
[The Sun (New York), October 18, 1887]

>There is an originality about Latham's coaching, an innate humor, which creates considerable amusement for the crowd, and he is so sharp in repartee and so good-natured in his witticisms, that things are excused in him which in others would not be tolerated. In fact, Latham is the intelligent clown of the base ball circus, and hundreds go to a game to hear him coach who would not otherwise attend.
[Brooklyn Eagle, July 23, 1892]

Tommy Burns

>Tom Burns, the old Chicagoan, coached from the lines in a white tennis jacket and a confident air, while Beckley tried to convince spectators that his voice had as much to do as that of (umpire) Sheridan. The verdict was that Beckley's howl, compared to Sheridan's vocal efforts, were as the chirp of a canary to the roar of a lion. Sheridan's voice is very powerful, but his enunciation is poor. It is impossible to distinguish between his yell of three balls and one strike, and spectators are compelled to wait until the batsman goes to first or walks to the bench.
[Pittsburg Dispatch, June 2, 1892]

>The Brooklyn players cannot accustom their ears to Burns' style of coaching when men are on the bases. They say that Burns' style of coaching echoes away over in Bay Ridge, disturbs the babies on Jamaica point, shakes up the water in Red Gate and annoys the pitcher of the opposing team.
[Baltimore American, June 24, 1888]

Lieutenant Burns, of the Baltimores, is always the first man to be recognized by the women. As soon as he comes into the field, they exclaim: "There's the man who yells like a Georgia steer driver." His "Wow" to an adventurous base runner is a study—complex and resonant.
[Baltimore American, June 24, 1888]

Tommy Burns (of Brooklyn), the Howler, who is believed to carry a copper trumpet in his throat, and who uses it when he roars: "Get away up—way up! Whoa!" to the nimble base runner.
[Evening World (New York), April 18, 1895]

George "Foghorn" or "Calliope" Miller

Miller has a voice that the iron workers of Pittsburg may think beautiful.
[Pittsburg Press, June 26, 1888]

(Pittsburg's) "Calliope" Miller and "Safety Valve" Beckley are enough to rattle any well organized army, let alone nine base ball players, but when they have Umpire Sheridan's falsetto as an accompaniment, and the buzz of a neighboring saw mill as basso profundo, they come very near rivaling a German street band under the spell of a small boy sucking a lemon.
[Brooklyn Eagle, June 9, 1892]

The coaching of the Washingtons is music, compared to the hyena-like howling of Miller of the Pittsburgs.
[Boston Herald, reprinted in the Washington (D. C.) Critic, May 17, 1887]

At Eastern park Calliope Miller is a thing of the past, Noisy Miller is lost and forgotten, while Foghorn Miller awakens no memories in the hearts of the bleachers. The old nicknames have had their day and have perished.
It is now Bowwow Miller. While he was coaching yesterday, his deep bass voice sounded to one of the spectators very like the baying of a mastiff or a hound and he commenced to bark at Miller. The other cranks immediately caught on and every time Miller uttered a sound, he would be greeted with a chorus of bow wows from the bleaching boards which caused him to turn and laugh, although the joke was on himself. During the biggest part of the game he was addressed as Bowwow by

the crowd.
[Brooklyn Eagle, September 10, 1892]

George Miller—the human beagle, the only piano-legged man playing ball, the only professional whose flesh is bounding rubber—wouldn't acknowledge defeat until both teams had left him on the field.
"Never mind that, old man!" "Get at 'em now!" "Well, let's make some more runs!" and the like philosophy of hope fell from his lips constantly, as though there was a loaded phonograph cylinder in the broad, convex chest. If faith is the basis of Christianity, Mr. Miller should be a bishop instead of a baseball catcher.
[Morning Times (Washington, D.C.), June 8, 1896]

Boston now wants noisy coaching.
Says the Globe: "Boston could find use for a coacher like Miller. The coaching here is decidedly funereal. Men stand opposite first and third, and are about as useless as a couple of scarecrows. Why isn't there more life and go in this important department of the game?"
[Pittsburgh Press, June 13, 1888]

Tommy Tucker

Thomas Tucker planted himself on the coaching line and threw open what is usually called a mouth, but what in Mr. Tucker's case is merely a yawning abyss surrounded by a fringe of flesh. Thomas tore long, jagged furrows in the earth with his voice until the weather bureau, two miles away, ran up the black flag, and the cupola of the old State House was crowded with people gazing anxiously to the south. Then the umpire led Tucker away to the bench.
[Washburne, Inter Ocean (Chicago), August 7, 1891]

This verbose monologue captured the drama of an irksome coacher colliding with an irate umpire:

Tommy Tucker (of St. Louis) had a head-on collision with Umpire Warner at Union Park (Baltimore) yesterday. Tommy slammed into the toughest sort of proposition, and broke away from the conflict the worse for wear, and shocked as to temper.
Just before the Browns began to lead the Birds a merry chase yesterday, (Baltimore manager) Hanlon and (St. Louis manager) Hurst and Wagner, the umpire, had a friendly little tete-a-tete. It is the custom of the diamond for men of such importance to speak softly to each other

before the game, and, then, when things get hot, to rear up and come down with a crash on each other.

Yesterday was no exception to this rule. With evidences of extreme mutual respect, these three mighty men fraternized on the conditions surrounding the game, all three agreeing that the people wanted a dash of scrappiness, and that good warm coaching was as music to the ears of the savage rooter. When the coaching was thus given the stamp of approval, Hurst looked over his shoulder, and gave Tommy Tucker a prodigious wink, for Tommy, in truth, had been hanging on the words of wisdom of the mighty men.

So, it happened that Tommy trotted out to the game full of chesty ideas of his power as a coacher. He was burning with an ambition to let loose his clarion voice in defiance of McJames and the Baltimore team. Tommy broke out in spots all along, but he determined to burst aside all barriers in the eighth inning, and whoop her up in real old Tuckersonian fashion.

Then it was that the fun began. (Pitcher) McJames was not Tucker-proof, and the terrific howls and yells emitted by Tommy gave Jimmie's nerves such a shake that he opened the eighth inning by giving both Smith and Taylor free passes to first. With only two runs to the good, this was shocking to the faithful, and they thought daggers of Tucker, who was giving forth all the symptoms of Frankenstein's monster, after too freely delving with gin rickeys. With unanimity and enthusiasm the Orioles demanded the expulsion of Tuck, who, like a bogie man, was constantly jumping out of his box in a most ferocious way. Warner saw the justice of the protest, and gently hinted that Tucker should stay in the coacher's box.

Of course, Tuck did no such thing. The people wanted a lively game, and he was giving it to them so wat'll; but Tommy entirely overlooked the point that it was the local, and not the visiting twirler who was on the gridiron. The medico twirled, and Tommy yelped, and times were getting warm, when, urged by the local players, Warner issued an ultimatum to Tucker, who, after many inky looks and stage whispers, slowly strode over to the grand-stand, where, while the game was going on, he attempted to deliver a Spartacus address to the stand, over the head of Mr. Hanlon, but the stand didn't want any heroics.

They wanted to see McJames strike his stride. So, the eloquent Tomasio was jeered for his eloquence, and the more he talked, the more pestiferous he seemed. Even when the score is close, and the situation critical, the bleachers must have their fun, and so Tommy received a rough, though cordial invitation, to speak his little piece before the open stand. Tommy replied with alacrity, and stood before the hot boards, a *martyr looking for sympathy, but a murmur of "Oh! Rotten!" undulated through the ambient air, and once more Tucker's oratory fell beneath the hoar frost of cynics.*

Turning, disconsolate and a disappointed man, Tucker found himself face to face with an irate umpire. Then, how the fur did fly! Tucker picked up the broom used to sweep the plate, and advanced on Warner in a fury. He didn't mind being called down by the umpire, but to be thought an oratorical "ham"—well, some one must suffer, and why not the umpire? Again Tommy found himself in trouble, for he had run up against a buzz saw, revolving one thousand times a minute. Warner would put the whole Brown crew out of the game, and send Tim Hurst back to the mines, but that Tucker would cease making bum speeches before the stand, when he, the umpire, demanded the monopoly of public attention.

As inexorable as the laws of the Medes and Persians was Warner, who calmly surveyed and squelched the irate first baseman. During the shindy,* Jack Taylor must needs get in it, and Warner put both him and Tucker out of the game, but when it became evident that Hurst had a paucity of disciples, Warner relented and permitted the game to go on with "Scrappy" Jack in the middle of the diamond. So, it happened that Tucker and Hurst and Hanlon glowered at each other, forgetful old of their ante-game felicitations, and their well-meant desires to make it lively for the people.
[Baltimore American, August 21, 1898]
*noisy disturbance

Tommy Tucker accidentally got the ball over the right field fence in the 11-inning game at Boston on Monday, and the hit was such a hit with Tommy that he swelled to the coach line and opened up his face in basso profundo. Cartwright advised (umpire) Emslie to swaddle Tommy's face with a muzzle, and Joyce advised Tom to take an injection of chloroform. The crowd made further observations to the same effect, and the thunder-throated first baseman returned to the bench. Tommy's reputation as a coach line soloist was ruined by the Boston newspapers.
[Pittsburg Press, June 26, 1896]

Tucker...has a voice which should receive distinguished consideration from the operatic stage. It is a cross between a rasp saw and the wind which whistles for a blizzard.
[Baltimore American, August 25, 1889]

Tom Tucker's vociferous coaching caused him no little trouble along toward the eighth inning, and his dulcet notes pealed forth as if his throat were studded with nails. He was called down several times by Umpire Gaffney.
[Brooklyn Eagle, May 12, 1893]

In Their Defense

Despite their odious reputation, some coaches were crowd-pleasers, as O. P. Caylor pointed out in 1894:

Syntax, as a rule, cuts little figure in the professional baseball player's abilities. He may know all the tricks of his trade, but he is as barren of original remarks as a sand bank.

I am reminded of this fact forcibly by the frequent use on the coaching lines of that hackneyed expression after a batsman has a strike or two called on him: "Never mind that, old man. It only takes one to hit it!"

Besides being ungrammatical, the phrase is as common as the rooster crowing. Some coacher should vary the cry by shouting: "Don't get discouraged. You have another chance left." Or: "That's only two. Take your third trial." "Watch it close. You'll hit the ball next time it comes over," or a dozen different expressions meaning the same as "it only takes one to hit it."

It is astonishing to see what little originality there is among baseball coachers. Arlie Latham, however, is a bright exception. He is a man with a remarkable "gift of gab," and he never lacks for something to say apropos to the circumstance or the occasion. What is better, he seldom "repeats," and it is all the more wonderful that he does not because he is continually chattering from the time a game begins till it ends.

Latham is a natural wit, and whenever he is in the game, the audience (an audience, indeed, on such occasions) is constantly on the qui vive for Arlie's funny comments and remarks. I have seen "the clown," as he is sometimes called, make his own comrades laugh until the game was interrupted thereby.

Noisy coaching during the season has grown among the League games. The Tucker-Clarke-"Piggy" Ward method of making a noise by howling and shrieking from the coaching lines, in order to "rattle" the opposing pitcher, has been taken up by the older League man until in part the science of the game is obscured, owing to the frantic attempts of the players to confuse one another.

Captain Anson recently complained very bitterly to me about this growing nuisance. "It isn't respectable ball playing," he declared, "and neither will I adopt that method or let any of my players use it. If we can't win by legitimate means, then we don't want the game. So far as is necessary to direct my men in making bases, that far will I go in 'coaching,' but no further. The League will have to put a stop to the evil; it is growing to such a shameful extent.
[Roanoke (Va.) Times, September 9, 1894]

So did this editorial of 1894:

Let the National League, while adopting all reasonable rules to insure the orderly progress of games at the various grounds, go slow in knocking out the privileges of the coachers.

A game of baseball without the vociferous eloquence of a "Calliope" Miller, the properly restrained buncombe of a Latham, or the jubilant urgings of a Tom Tucker will be like a banquet dish without full savor. Suppress the robbers of the umpire, gentlemen, but let the coachers coach, that the sport may be kept fast and gingery.
[Evening World (New York), November 16, 1894]

TOMMY BURNS COACHING.

11. Humor in Pitching

The career of the famous base ball pitcher is not unlike the public life of an opera tenor. There is sudden glory. For a season the man is in the sunlight of success. His photograph is in the show window. His breakfast is described with pains by an interviewer. He is pointed at in the street. He receives perfumed notes. In the exercise of his calling, he is applauded before he gives justification. At the zenith of his fame a necktie is named after him.

But if he loses his cunning through nervousness or rheumatism, his name is Sejanus and the mob that once favored him is ready to tear him to pieces.
[Boston Journal, reprinted in the Evening Star (Washington, D.C.), July 23, 1892]

Today, the pitcher is arguably the most dominant force on the field, whose competence largely determines the team's destiny. It wasn't that way at the start of baseball.

The pitcher of 1860, for instance, when match play among amateur teams was organized and rules established, stood behind a line 45 feet from home plate and lobbed the ball to the batsman to initiate play. His delivery was restricted to an underhand flip with both feet planted on the ground and the arm swinging perpendicularly to it.

The only pitch was a slow, straight ball. In delivering it, he was required to keep his hand below the waist, and the slow pitch understandably led to high-scoring games. This delighted spectators and helped fuel the national craze for baseball.

But pitchers soon tired of playing a passive role. They began to challenge batters by putting speed and movement on the ball with a running, hop-skip-and-jump, and quick-snap release, and then mixed up fast and slow pitches to further confuse them.

This perceived edge of pitchers was countered in 1863, when new rules confined the act of delivery to the "pitcher's box," a six-by-three-feet demarcated space, which brought a halt to the running start.

Thus commenced a decades-long tinkering of rules, as baseball officials strove to equalize the matchup of skill between pitcher and batter. The impact fell initially on the pitcher: He was pushed back another fifteen feet from the home plate; the dimensions of the pitcher's box were tweaked several times before being replaced by a rectangular rubber slab, which, too, underwent resizing; and even the number of balls and strikes qualifying for a base on balls and strike out, respectively, were changed almost yearly for a while.

By chance, the balance of power swung back heavily in favor of pitchers in the mid-1860s, when Arthur Cummings, an amateur player of Brooklyn, mastered the ability to curve an underhand-thrown ball. Later improved upon by Bobby Matthews, a professional player of the Baltimores, the curve ball, devastating even at its birth, changed the art of pitching forever.

Pitchers continued to press rule-makers to allow elevation of the arm when delivering the ball, which was ultimately allowed, but only to the waist. Crafty pitchers took advantage of this law by hoisting their trousers to a point where the waist line was level with their chests, resulting in "the side-arm swing," and, not coincidentally, greater speed on the ball.

Emboldened even further, some pitchers flaunted the law by releasing the ball from an even higher point, illegal by definition, but countered by the spurious claim that the arm involuntarily rose as the ball was delivered.

Confusion and frequent arguments on the field over contested deliveries bedeviled baseball until 1884, when the National League, soon followed by the American Association, finally legalized the overhand throw, which ushered in the era of "swift pitching." Freed from all physical limitations, pitchers now armed themselves with a host of new and powerful overhand deliveries that formed the basis of the contemporary boast: *Age cannot wither nor custom stale the infinite variety of ways in which the pitcher gives batsmen the gurgling laugh.*

The names of these pioneering pitches, long obsolete, were legion. There were in- and out-drops; sharp, clean, drop, up, or down curves (the latter being a specialty of Edward "The Only" Nolan); in- and out-rises; in- and out-shoots; in- and out-curves, up-curves, raises, down-shoots, jump balls, etc., establishing a labeling mania that extended into the new century.

Though abandoned, a few swivel-armed pitchers of the late 1890s continued to employ the underhand throw, later to be dubbed "submarine delivery." Chief among them were Charles "Lady" Baldwin, Billy Rhines, and Joe "Iron Man" McGinnity, who mixed up under- and over-hand deliveries during games to confuse batters.

Lefties

The few left-handed pitchers employed in the early years of baseball game were generally looked upon by managers and players with suspicion, even dread. This was due to a stigma, common then, that they lacked long-term staying power and were thus destined for brief careers, estimated at three to four years. This baseless notion persisted into the late 1890s before their value to pitching staffs was finally recognized, making them a hot commodity.

"Time was when left-handed twirlers were a novelty. In fact, they were regarded as freaks, and bore the same relation to baseball that Jo-Jo, the dog-faced man, and the two-headed soubrette did to the museums," remarked Tom Brown to (sportswriter) Joe Campbell.
[Baltimore American, May 29, 1898]

The most common term applied by baseball writers to this particular mound stylist was *southpaw*, which first appeared in print around 1884, and has endured since. Others, less utilized, were: *south paddlers, south-siders, south-wheelers, south-winged pitchers, off-paws, off-siders* or any of a number of cute, one-of-a-kind inventions, such as *port pendulums, twirlers with the Antarctic* (or *port*) *pitching wing*.

Speaking of Pitchers & Pitching

Over the years, sportswriters created a wide vocabulary that applied specifically to pitchers and their vocation. Straight off, pitchers, for variety's sake, went by other names, such as *twirler* (the most popular), *moundsman, boxman*, and *slab artist*. In the 1880s, a pitcher *officiated* for a team, not pitched a game, and, in so doing, was either *on the marble, toed the rubber, rolled the sphere*, or *did the windup act*.

The term *change pitcher* was the forerunner of today's *relief pitcher*. An easy pitch to hit was dubbed a *balloon*, or *pudding pitch*.

When a pitcher lost his stuff, either being hit hard or losing control, he was *solved, collared, went away to windward*, or, much more commonly, "*went up in a balloon* (or *in the air*). A dead arm was referred to as a *bric-a-brac* or *glass* arm.

The term *whitewash* first appeared in print in 1868, followed thereafter by a synonym, *kalsomine.*

Warts and All

Baseball writers never lacked humor in highlighting a pitcher's skills, effectiveness and fate in colorful terms, as the following excerpts demonstrate:

Complimentary:

>*Foreman threw the ball with the easy grace of a farmer's boy throwing corn to the hogs*
>*the ball sped as if propelled by a barrel of powder*
>*McNabb had on a head of steam like a freshly tapped barrel of beer*
>*pitcher Gruber has got more speed than a young heir getting rid of his papa's fortune*
>*he sent the ball humming over the plate like chained lightning*
>*Terry's delivery approached the texture of silk in its fineness yesterday*
>*the gentle drop kissed the air as lightly as a summer zephyr*
>*Fifield was as steady as a chronometer and Carney was as erratic as a Texas steer*
>*Nichols kept hits about as well scattered as oysters in the ordinary church social soup*
>*Griffith was as steady as a wheel horse*
>*Getzein doubled him up like a small boy who has dallied too freely with green watermelons*
>*Dammann was as steady as an eight-day clock*
>*he made the visitors look like cigar signs*
>*Boyle had demonstrated that he hadn't enough arm to throw dice*
>*Foutz kept the hits scattered as telegraph poles on a railroad*
>*Klobedanz calmly threw the iron into the Orioles*
>*Meekin pitched like one possessed of a fifty-horse power steam engine*
>*the Saints found Hahn's curves as deceptive as a summer girl's engagement*
>*Sonier had more kinks and curves than the path of a crooked*

politician

    Coleman's arm was as easy as oil

    the ball sailed by Hulen like a bit of racy gossip at a women's sewing circle

    McGill was frequently belted for painful distances in the outfield

    the pitchers gave enough free passes to ruin a prosperous theater in one night

    Amos Rusie did it with his iron arm and whistling curves. The Pittsburghs couldn't have hit him with telegraph poles.

    his curves were like the pirouettes of a serpentine dancer

    with the languorous, yet entrancing wiles of an Oriental houri, Thomas fanned Count Campau

    old Cy Young was as steady as a stopped clock

    the pitch cut the plate like the bicycle fever going through a young ladies seminary

    Phyle was in phine phettle and phor a phull game kept them well in hand

    Hahn settled down like a toper who has taken the gold cure and kept the hits scattered like backwoods returns on election night

    "Silver" King was a whole club in himself and kept the Colonels score column at zero for eight innings

    the Giants swing at Cunningham's dew drops like farmer boys trying to bat hornets away from they ears after the nest had been robbed

    the Giants couldn't hit a cabbage with the side of a barn

    heavy hitters of the home team melted away before him like dew before the morning sun

    Hoffer's twirling was of the wondrous order, just as the enthusiasts are apt to dream of at night when they have read too many tales from Arabia

    Hutchinson proceeded to send a lot of sinuous things over the plate that wriggled away from the bats of the Saints, though endowed with eyes and other protective appliances in themselves

    John Clarkson has the pleasing trick of sending the ball whistling down the wind with the easy abandon of a drunken man convincing the people that he is sober, and has as many curves as a rifle target

    Hemming pitched a style of ball that looked as easy as a man on a load of hay, yet there proved to be mystery enough in those slow, tantalizing curves to make a skillful batter feel like a man who has been hit in the ear by a small boy in the presence of his family.

Less than complimentary:

George Cross was in the box and he had troubles enough to tell eight policemen

our fellows took as kindly to him (Stivetts) as horse flies to a galled shoulder

the pitcher had no more control than a stepmother over a job lot of children

Breitenstein's pitching was as ragged as a tramp's coat

Weyhing went to pieces like a beautiful bit of Dresden introduced to a thumbless domestic

Parrott's throwing arm is as loose as the wrapper of a cheap cigar

Lucid's efforts to fool the Browns were about as successful as the attempts of an ostrich to escape observation

he fell before the champions like a soap bubble before a gale

Morris pitched a slow, easy ball which looked as big as a fish basket

he was as wild as an inmate of a Bloomingdale padded cell

here begins (pitcher) Daub's tale of woe in one chapter

he couldn't pitch a fish ball into a pan

Boyle had demonstrated that he hadn't enough arm to throw dice

the Brooklyns straightened Jouett Meekin's curves until they were as flat as a copper penny

young Mr. Wright again essayed to twirl for the up-river aggregation and again demonstrated that his pitching qualities do not agree with his name

the pitcher wore his wonted smile, but was as wild as a Sioux ghost dancer

Foreman had a case of rattles that would have driven a backwoodsman to chronic alcoholism

the home team lit onto "Meek's" curves thicker 'n flies on a drop of molasses

as his strength was failing fast, Norton was swathed in a sweater and retired to the quietude of the bench

he was wilder than a lunatic with a hornet down his neck

Twitchell was in the box for Omaha and the Mountaineers hit him until they loosened the fillings of his teeth

the career of Pitcher German in the box was short-lived

then young Jimmy Martin, fresh from the wilds of Galesburg, Ill., took his turn in the box, and lo and behold the Wisconsin representatives knocked three runs out of him

all three pitchers were as wild as hawks

the pitcher was as easy to find as a short change artist at a circus front door

Denzer was fanning Deady into a listless lassitude even suggestive of his name

Carney is about as easy for the Saints as lying for a Duluth real estate agent

Mullane was as wild as a pirate's dream

Clarkson was again plunged into a sea of troubles that would have worried Hamlet himself

the visitors batted Roger around with a familiarity that signified the utmost contempt

the delivery of Mr. "Clubdance" (Klobedanz) was as easy as a peddler's peaches to a policeman

"Willie Bill" Hutchinson was hit so hard that he wished he was back in his mother's front yard

Pitcher Knepper started a series of bases on balls of varying degrees of wildness from umpire's choice to miles off

Mr. Fanning's delivery required no "open sesame" to pluck the jeweled swatlette from the enchanted cavern of drops, curves and in-shoots

Seymour could not place the ball between two telegraph poles more than once in six tries

Si Seymour, the man with a $3,000 arm and a ten-cent head

Hahn is a good pitcher, but he has evidently read it somewhere He poses as though he expected a calcium (light) to be turned on him from the right field bleacher at any minute.

That ended Daub. He yielded the ball to Stein and went off to nurse that tired feeling.

In speed and curves, Thornton has an assortment large enough to stock a department store, but he is as wild as a minister's son.

Lengthier remarks:

Jasper went in and in the middle of the sixth inning he found himself hanging limp and loose across the bleacher railing, with his funereal uniform sadly disarranged, his reputation missing and the bright, ruddy gore leaking from his breaking heart. Papa's children were so impolite as to pound the everlasting life out of him. His pitying friends untwined his lissome frame from the meshes of the wire screen in front of the sun seats, where Buck Ebright had flung him, and led him

out to short field, where he was allowed to finish the game.
[Omaha Daily Bee, June 2, 1894]

Kilroy was pitching for the Louisvilles and had been hit so hard that he wore a haunted, haggard look of one whom it would be unsafe to feed by hand. Instead of calling him to one side and telling him that he could put his vitreous arm into its plush-covered case and run away home, "General" Pfeffer sent him back into the box in the beginning of the seventh.
[Source misplaced]

Poor little Boxcar (Omaha pitcher Boxendale). The white immortelles will soon be sprinkled o'er his grave. He cannot certainly survive the vicious beating those clodhoppers gave him yesterday. He didn't last one inning, for after he had been basted for two singles, a three-bagger, three home runs and seven tallies, Bill got a pair of tongs and lifted him out of the box and threw him over the fence into the alley.
[Omaha Daily Bee, June 3, 1894]

Well, there's Johnston. Aside from the fact that he gave seven men bases on balls, and hit Menifee three times besides, and was slugged all round the lot for eighteen safe ones, Johnston pitched a pretty steady game.
[Saint Paul Globe, June 20, 1896]

Baby Baldwin deserves a long stretch of bench warming and entrance gate work, along with a big fine. The swelling in his head is commencing to hurt his pitching.
[Pittsburg Press, June 26, 1891]

Of what earthly use Fitzgerald is to the Grays it would be hard to determine. He can't pitch as well as (mascot) Baseball Tommy and the sooner he is fired, along with one or two others, the better it will be for the team. There are amateur pitchers right here in the state that can beat any twirler on the Providence team out of sight.
[Evening Telegram (Providence, R. I.), June 16, 1893]

McMahon pitched a style of ball that looked as easy as a man on a load of hay, yet there proved to be mystery enough in those slow, tantalizing curves to make a skillful batter feel like a man who has been hit in the ear by a small boy in the presence of his family. The bats of the Colts whizzed by on all sides of his curves, and occasionally struck one

corner of an exceptionally cracked one, but the majority were as safe as though they had been pitched to a blind man with green goggles on.
[Baltimore American, July 9, 1896]

Windmills and Grapevines

Each pitcher developed his own unique style of delivering the ball; many became show-stoppingly spectacular. Were film footage available of games played in this era, these dazzling gyrations would stand out as striking differences of how baseball was played then and now.

The prevailing belief at the time was that swinging the arms and twisting the torso during a windup imparted maximal velocity to the ball. This led to infinite variations of bending the body into a tightly coiled spring, then releasing its stored kinetic energy amidst the wild undulation and flailing of body parts, culminating in a tarantella-like finale. This dramatic act served another useful purpose: befuddling the batter.

Those pitchers who adopted contortionistic deliveries became sources of awe and fascination to many baseball writers—amusement, too, as attested to by these sketches:

There have been long-fought and dangerous disputes about the exact number of motions through which (Dupee) Shaw, of the (Washington) Nationals, puts himself before delivering the ball. One man claimed thirty-two, holding that he had counted them. An attempt to give all of them would be foolish. A few will be enough.

When he first lays his hands on the sphere, he looks at it. Then he rolls it around a few times. Then he sticks out one leg, pulls it back and shoves the other behind him. Now he makes three or four rapid steps in the box. While he does all this, he holds the ball in his left hand. After he has swapped it to his right, he wipes his left on his breeches, changes the ball to the left again and pumps the air with both arms.

Then he gets down to work and digs up the ground with his right foot. Then you think he is going with his right foot. Then you think he is going to pitch. But he isn't. He starts in and reverses the program and does it over again, three or four times, and just as the audience sits back in the seats with a sigh, the ball flies out like a streak. Nobody knows how it left his hand, but it did.
[St. Louis Post-Dispatch, reprinted in the Evening Star (Washington, D.C.), June 26, 1886]

The New York players tell wonderful tales of Murphy, one of the new Philadelphia pitchers. It seems that the youngster waves both arms like a windmill when delivering the ball, and from somewhere the sphere shoots over the plate before the batter gets over the mesmeric spell of the gyration. Another plan of Murphy's, it is alleged, is to double himself up in a bunch, with back turned to the plate, and "let 'er go" from this position. The batsman is too busy watching the pitcher to think about batting.
[Saint Paul Globe, May 20, 1898]

Stratton's (of Louisville) delivery has many peculiarities all its own. In delivering a swift ball, he lifts his left foot high in the air, jumps up on his right too like a ballet dancer, slings his arms over his head in an artistic curve and with a forward motion lets the ball drive. His is wild when pitching this way, but he has a slow, straight ball that is very deceptive.
[Brooklyn Eagle, July 22, 1892]

In the old days of freedom in the pitcher's position, he (Foutz, of Brooklyn) would wind his long legs and slim arms into a knot and then let go the ball with a delivery that appeared to dismember his whole body. Then he would slowly pull himself together and stand motionless like a sphinx fashioned in the shape of a pair of scissors. In fact "Scissors" was his nickname, and the favorite sobriquet applied to him by the bleacher boy throughout the League circuit.
[Morning Times (Washington, D. C.), March 7, 1897]

Duryea (of Columbus) still has his own incomparable delivery. He poses on one foot, and, executing a grand pas de seul, like a $1-a-month man opening a keg of nails, casts his mild blue eye toward (Manager) Comiskey with a sort of 'Willie-do-you-miss-me' look, and sends the ball hustling through the air of the hot summer afternoon with a swish like a comet an hour behind time.
[Pittsburgh Press, August 3, 1891]

This is the way in which a Louisville dispatch described Ewing's pitching in the last St. Louis game:
"Long John Ewing tried his old plan of tying himself in knots, kicking his heels over his head, and straightening out his elongated body with the startling suddenness of a jack in a box this afternoon, but it did no good.
"When the Browns got through with him, the lank twirler was so

bruised and mortified over the exhibition he has made of himself that he wanted to go right back into the southern league, where he belongs. The visitors took well to his alleged curves and they knocked the ball in every direction except where the fielders were waiting for them. Poor Ewing."
[Pittsburg Press, October 21, 1889]

    Jake Boyd has a very funny motion. In watching him, one forgets that its owner is pitching a baseball until it has gone by and the umpire has said "Strike," says a Boston paper.
    Boyd holds the ball in one hand and throws ball and hand carelessly round in a circle in front of him; then he describes a similar circle in the rear of his body, and while one wonders how he is ever going to get the knot untied, he lets it go right over the plate. His curves are his strong point, for his speed is inconsiderable and his head not much in evidence.
[Evening Times (Washington, D. C.), August 15, 1895]

    (Boston pitcher) Willis, late of Syracuse, went out on the slab. Mr. Willis gave the people the price of admission in amusement. He is an extremely elongated young man, with arms like flails. His delivery yesterday was as wild as a jingo war-cry, and he made the local batsmen do all sorts of "stunts" to dodge the terrible things which he served over the plate.
    At his start in the sixth inning, he began hitting men in rotation, varying it with serving up balls that had no intimacy with the plate, and it seemed that there would be no end to the Birds fluttering around the bases...Just at present the Baltimore team is not to be fooled with experimental pitchers, and they simply hammered Mr. Willis about until they grew tired.
[Baltimore American, April 21, 1898]

    Smiling Mickey Welch stands with one leg out in the beginning of the operation. This is withdrawn after awhile, and then Mickey plods up the earth with his foot. Next he changes the ball from one hand to another, wiping the disengaged member all over himself. Then he expectorates on either hand, shuffles around a moment, and in goes the ball. During all this time the smile, or grin, rather adorns his mug as usual.
[St. Louis Post-Dispatch, reprinted in The Sun (New York), June 27, 1886]

"He (Whitney, of Washington) is the tallest man on the team, and when he takes position in the box, he looks down over the batsman's head and slowly turns the ball in his hand as though he were sizing up his victim. His favorite position while pitching is facing the batter, and, planting his left foot well forward, he turns his body slightly so that his breast offers a fair mark for a line ball. His shoulders are thrown well back and his head bent slightly forward. His body assumes a backward angle of nearly fifteen degrees from the vertical, and then, with a sudden evolution, he lifts the left foot, curls himself into a wonderful figure, and the ball has sped across the plate. Perhaps his most familiar title is "Grasshopper Jim." He has a rolling gait that is noticeable in most long-legged men."
[Evening Star (Washington, D. C), April 7, 1888]

Hatfield began a queer motion preliminary to delivering the ball. He threw his arm clear around his waist from behind, and then, twirling his body as a swan does her neck, he unwound his arm and let her go. Apparently that motion had some hoodoo quality, for Boston failed to reach first.
[Evening World (New York), May 11, 1889]

When Whitney came to bat, he found something new waiting for him in the pitcher's box. It was Day, the new Quaker twirler. The young man tied himself into a lover's knot, and, with a wondrous move, shot himself loose and delivered the ball with such grotesque effectiveness that Whitney was struck dumb at the strange sight and was retired on strikes.
[Evening World (New York City, N. Y.), September 20, 1889]

Cuppy has a delivery, which is peculiarly his own. He lifts the ball high in the air for a few seconds, brings it down again with a snap that scares the batsman into submission, leans far back toward second base, points his left foot on a line with third and turns his face in the direction of first. Then he suddenly straightens out, turns half way around, and the ball shoots over the plate.
[Brooklyn Eagle, June 5, 1896]

The crowd had a lot of fun with Hawley in the seventh inning. The pitcher is very deliberate in his movements and makes three distinct swings with his arm before delivering the ball. When the bleachers get on to this wrinkle, they counted "One, two, three," in unison as he made his motions. Hawley had to laugh himself at the fun.

[Brooklyn Eagle, August 24, 1894]

(Boston pitcher) Jack Stivetts has adopted a new motion previous to delivering the ball. He doubles himself up into a bow knot with both hands tightly clinched over the ball as if about to deliver it with both hands.

[Brooklyn Eagle, April 29, 1895]

"The action of a player, while in the act of delivering the ball has much to do with the support given him by the fielders," says Tom Brown (center fielder, Washington). "Take Breitenstein of the St. Louis Browns for example. He has a free, easy, nervous style and is quick as a flash in gathering himself and speeding the ball to the batsmen. This lively action keeps his fielders on the mettle and they are constantly on the alert.

"On the other hand, there are pitchers who wind themselves up like a Waterbury watch and become so monotonous that they take not only the life, but the confidence out of the fielders. Many a pitcher's effectiveness is spoiled by the dreary waste of time he consumes in the box. They not only discourage their fielders, but put the batsmen whom they feed off their guard."

[Brooklyn Eagle, May 5, 1896]

Contortionist Boyd pitched for the visitors. He swashed his arm back until his elbow scratched his shoulder blade. Then he let loose an in-shoot that the Chicago batters rushed after with the despair of a short-armed man trying to get a second piece of chicken at a boarding house.

[Source misplaced]

There was supposed to be some pretty good pitching talent in yesterday's game. Columbus' pitcher was Boswell, the scholarly collegian whose curves were wont to rend the air of the New York Polo grounds with strike-outs and popular outcries. That was but a short year ago.

Yesterday bases on balls slipped from his bony fingers, and his slim legs shook with dread of impending disaster every time the ball left his hand. It was the first time he ever pitched here, and the small boys on the roofs took as much delight in his gyratory contortions as though a circus were in town with ten elephants and a troupe of tumblers.

Mr. Boswell—Andrew Boswell, he was known at college—is a few inches over six feet high, and but for the length of his legs, could weigh in as a cob rider at a rural fair. He must weigh 113 or 114 pounds, looking at him from the grand stand.

He has to pull his cap down over his eyes to make a shadow. Then he hides the ball in his two hands. Then he breaks the bunch and reaches one hand around behind him, the other to the other side. While the batsman is wondering whether he is a south-paw or a north-paw, Mr. Boswell's right mitt described the arc of a circle whose plane intersects first and third bases, and after whirling the ball for five or six seconds behind him, the ex-collegian loses his hold on the ball and it comes toward the grand stand. Sometimes it came over the plate yesterday, but not always, as seven bases on balls testify.

It is quite a mysterious delivery—to people in the grand stand. Those who are real close, say the St. Paul batsmen, for instance, could see it all, as the twenty-two hits made by them in yesterday's game will also testify.
[Saint Paul Globe, May 19, 1896]

Cy Young, lanky, angular and demure as ever, has invented a new motion in his delivery. He throws his arm around his head as though it were one of the wings of a semaphore. Then he brings it down with a short jerk like man grabbing for a coin that he knows has also been seen by another man. Suddenly jerking his arm upward and backward at the same time, he twists his right leg around his left leg and throws the ball. Any batter who undertakes to watch all those motions is reasonably certain to forget that for which he stands at the plate.
[New York Journal, June 18, 1897]

Old man Galvin...dealt out (St. Louis owner) Von der Ahe's men medicine that was bitter of gall and he had a whole medicine chest full of it, too. He brought an engine red right sleeve here with him from Pittsburg and up this sleeve he had grapevine twists, watchspring stragglers and a few "fly-up-the-creeks" that the Browns could not hit with a cellar door. Jack Glasscock frothed at the mouth, Perry Werden fainted twice and Cliff Carroll swore that he would return to his Bloomington farm and hoe his buckwheat rather than stand up like a fool and have old man Galvin sail the ball across the plate when it would make a man cockeyed to even try and hit it.
[Pittsburgh Press, April 17, 1892]

Added Attributes

The myriad habits of pitchers were subjected to comment by writers, good and bad, such as prowess in pitching and fielding,

breaking in a new ball and applying foreign substances to baseballs during the sport's early "Age of Innocence":

This man Vickery is not pretty. There are clay roads in Southern Illinois during the spring rains that are prettier than Mr. Vickery. But he can pitch a ball that will give a batter a haircut and a shave in three styles. He has a slow ball that he learned in Philadelphia, and a fast and wicked ball that he picked up in Milwaukee, and sometimes he throws both of them at once.
[Washburne, Inter Ocean (Chicago), August 21, 1891]

The reader who has never seen Ebright pitch a game of baseball will hardly be able to appreciate all that the fact means, but those who were there and saw the game drag its weary length along through all of the afternoon, and also saw the goodly sized audience gradually dwindle away until hardly a quorum remained to see the end, will trust and even pray that they may never be called upon to witness such a spectacle again.
[Morning Call (San Francisco), June 3, 1893]

The same paper gets this off about Pitcher Haddock:

"Prince George Haddock, a beautiful young man whose salary is said to be so large that the club's gate receipts are sometimes less than his daily income, was placed on exhibition by the Brooklyns. Mr. Haddock's attitudes, the cultured way he twirled his mustache and the dainty pose of his leg before he let go the ball were worth the price of admission alone. In addition he gave an exhibition of pitching that was all wool and a yard wide."
[Brooklyn Eagle, July 7, 1892]

Of the prominent and successful pitchers of the day, Robert L. Carruthers, of the Brooklyn league club, is probably the most graceful in his delivery. In pitching, he faces the batsman squarely, watching the bases closely the while. When called upon to throw to any one of the bases, he does so without any of the awkward jerks peculiar to so many other pitchers.
He has a habit of blowing into one hand while fixing himself for his pose. Then he takes the ball in his right hand and, with a quick half-swing of the body, shoots the sphere over the plate. He does not follow up the pitch with a run, except when on the lookout for a bunt. He usually breaks the momentum of his body with a sort of hop, and then

takes three or four dance-like steps backward, to resume his regular position. When the ball is returned to him, he snaps it up easily, pulls up the sleeve of his right arm—for he always wears long sleeves—and he is then ready to pitch again.

All these movements are pleasing to the eye, particularly as he is very light on his feet. As a fielder, he has no superior in the box. No ball is too hot for him to stop, for at least to attempt to stop, and as he puts the ball over the plate to be hit, he has many chances to display his ability. Bases on balls are scarce when he pitches and fielders have plenty to do. That's his policy, and a mighty good one it is, too, as a few base hits made off his pitching do not worry him in the least.
[Pittsburg Press, June 1, 1890]

For a man who had never faced a big league club before, Pitcher Waddell showed lots of nerve in picking out the champions for his maiden effort, says the Baltimore News. His performance was distinctly creditable, too. "Waddles," as the bleachers called him, has a peculiar underhand jerk and a speedy overhand delivery that held the Orioles down to eleven hits. His fielding of bunts is most peculiar.

With the crack of the bat, he hunches himself into a carpenter's "square," and, with the upper half of his body parallel to the ground, he goes toward the ball with his arms moving frantically, as if swimming. He cranes his neck, and when he reaches the ball and throws to first, such a reaction sets in that he usually falls flat upon the ground. In delivering the ball he makes wonderful facial contortions, but all that denotes earnestness. He watches first base closely, but is handicapped by being a left-hander.
[Kansas City Journal, September 18, 1897]

Hecker, who is the most scientific pitcher in the American Association, holds the ball idly in his hand for a moment, then suddenly turns around on one heel, and if a man is on first base, he frightens him back to the bag by several lightning motions, when the ball leaves his hand and speeds over the batter's square. Sometimes Hecker glances significantly at the umpire, then makes a hop, skip and a jump, winding his arm beautifully about his head, and throwing the ball swiftly but accurately just where he has signaled the catcher.
[The Sun (New York), July 20, 1886]

The Louisville correspondent of the Sporting News has this to say of "Strike-'em-out Fitz," of last year's Seattle team:

"Fitzgerald arrived Saturday. He is rather small in size, and

looks like a cowboy. He wears a felt hat, spring-bottom pants, and the timid man would think he had a pistol in his boots."
[Seattle Post-Intelligencer, June 15, 1891]

"Kid" Nicol, the lad from Barry, who has been pitching phenomenal ball for the Davenport team, spat on his twirling fingers, twisted the ball out of shape and made the Ravens strike at it like a drunk beating carpets. Nicol made his appearance but once on the Quincy grounds, but it was plain to be seen then that his calling was in the pitcher's box and not in the pulpit. While the phenom belonged not to the world's list of beauties, he has an arm like the walking-beam of a steamboat. He used it yesterday and to good effect...Nicol unwound his arm and the Ravens hit nothing but buffalo gnats.
[Quincy (Ill.) Daily Journal, June 2, 1891]

The Detroit correspondent of the Boston Herald writes concerning Wednesday's game between Detroit and Washington:
"'Flea' (Dupee) Shaw did his customary end man act* in today's game. He grimaced, pranced and sprung ancient gags with great absurdity, but all without avail...It has come out that Shaw 'works the clown racket' in order to distract batters, and he claims to have had considerable success in this respect."
[Washington (D. C.) Critic, June 24, 1887]
* **minstrel show term**

In the first place, the pitchers were off, way off. Johnson, poor fellow, tried his arm at it first. It took just 1 minute, 36 1/2 seconds to convince him that life is a dull, dreary waste of hopeless misery. He was summarily banged until his poor tired head rested itself on the mahogany players' bench in silent, yet bitter contemplation of the dire tragedy realistically enacted before his weary eyes. He had the satisfaction of seeing his illustrious successor, the Hon. Mr. Ossawatomic Brown, so completely pasted and miffed and whacked that he couldn't throw a deceptive ball to save his life, except in the case of Napoleon Bonaparte Bottenus, who fanned out with delightful frequency and precision.
[Post Express (Rochester, NY), May 27, 1896]

McVicker pitches like a straw-stacker in operation, but he gets there just the same. He stands on one foot and bobs up and down like a bashful man sitting on a sofa. Then he draws his arm up to his neck, at the same time elevating his leg to an angle of 27 degrees. A

simultaneous motion of arm and leg follows and the ball goes over the plate like a street car going down hill.
[Quincy (Ill.) Daily Journal, June 19, 1891]

    The particular shining light of the game was Ollie Birg (of Seattle), the new pitcher that Manager Dugdale secured from the Minneapolis team, after it got into a squabble with Peoria, over his services.
    He looks like some of Swinnerton's* famous pictures of baseball players. He is about five feet seven inches tall, and when attired in baseball togs that were intended for a heavyweight, has the appearance of a boy in his father's clothes. He may weigh 145 pounds, but the size of his legs does not back up the assertion to any great extent. When he walks, he makes one feel that he needs a pair of interfering boots.
    One spectator insinuated that he had been down on the beach copying the regulation siwash* walk. He ambles along in a most deceiving manner. Just when one becomes convinced that he is of the easy-going, calm, deliberate sort, he suddenly bobs up as an electric man. He can get over ground like a 2-year-old, and when it comes to covering first base, even John Clarkson was not quicker and more attentive to duty.
    When he gets ready to pitch, he jams his cap far down on his head and to one side. Then he looks at the batsman and tries to hypnotize him. Sometimes he wears an infielder's glove on his left hand, and then again he will throw it away and handle short hit balls just as well. There is nothing of the grand stand player about him. He is there for business and nothing escapes him.
    The way he wound the Tacoma boys up was a caution. Just when they thought they had him started down hill, he would give an additional swing to his right wing and pass them to the plate with such lightning-like rapidity, it was all off with the "Dooleys."
[Seattle Post-Intelligencer, May 23, 1898]
* **James Swinnerton (1875-1974), staff cartoonist of the San Francisco Examiner**
** **American Indian of the northern Pacific coast**

    "And, by the way, did you ever notice Mr. Haddock pitch on a ladies' day? Did you ever notice the mixture of savor faire and corned beef and cabbage in his air and attitude! Put wings on Haddock's heels and he would be an angel. But how he can pitch. He has more hot and hard curves in his fingers than anybody in the business."
[New York World, reprinted in the Pittsburg Dispatch, August 18, 1892]

"Pretzel" Getzein, who is with the Indianapolis nine this year, is a clear headed young man who can twist a ball almost out of shape. In a game in the west three years ago, he had such success in bowling down batters that the latter held a convention to see if they could not, by swapping ideas, arrive at the real cause of Getzein's wonderful command of the ball. After a long debate the disappointed batters went home. The only thing that they were unanimous about was that Getzein pitched a curve that looked like a pretzel; consequently Getzein and pretzel twists have been close companions ever since.
[Wichita (Kan.) Eagle, July 23, 1889]

> Pitch, pitch, pitch,
>   At a square, white slab each day,
> And would that my tongue dared utter—
>   The thoughts that I'd like to say.
> Oh, well for the haughty umpire,
>   Who talks about rules and fines,
> Oh, well for the doughty catcher,
>   With his winks and blinks and signs.
>
> For the game goes gaily on,
>   The pitcher must toss the ball—
> The batter may swipe it over the fence
>   The game go past recall.
>
> Pitch, pitch, pitch,
>   At a square, white slab each day,
> If I lose again, the manager says,
>   He'll "dock" my next month's pay.

[Pittsburgh Press, April 2, 1891]

Big Bill Phillips was in a particularly merry mood. He appeared on the slab in the first game with a long corncob pipe in his mouth and established a new record for pitchers, that of occupying the box and smoking at the same time. In the intervals he joshed the bleachers and joshed the umpire, but he always found time to attend pretty strictly to the pitching business, and kept the hits scattered until the last inning.
[Saint Paul Globe, September 24, 1897]

It was J. B. Seymour's turn to pitch, but the southpaw claimed to have a lame face, so Sullivan was sent forth as a sacrifice. All his *political friends were present, and the rooters, who presented Michael with a diamond locket on the occasion of his last visit here, smiled encouragingly at the big fellow.*

Salvos of applause greeted him while he warmed up, and then the unfortunate citizen walked forth to fill the hearts of his friends with pain and chagrin. That first inning should be industriously compiled as a grand testimonial to the team. Not that a record of that ghastly proceeding would reflect credit on the Bean Eaters, but it might serve as an illustration off how not to play ball, and thus shine by contrast. Sullivan was too full of politics and pent-up oratory to glitter in a baseball way. Gore, sudden changes in the cast, bases on balls, polka-dot errors and six tallies are a few of the incidents jumbled in together.
[New York Journal, September 18, 1897]

His south-paw was about as effective against their onslaughts as a summer sigh cuts ice in a Kansas typhoon. It was Carney's debut, and the more we looked at him wriggling around in the box and saw the ball scooting to the frontier from the Clevelands' bats, the more we thought of Scrappy Bill and wondered how (pitcher) Flynn could figure in a baseball deal unless as so much ballast for good measure. He might break window panes with his speed, but he will never stop a hitting team from burning up the grass of the infield with drives off his delivery.
[Morning Times (Washington, D. C., August 20, 1896]

Mr. Leon Viau, says the Inter-Ocean, couldn't have pitched a hod of bricks off a ladder last summer. He was so madly in love with his mustache and an unknown brand of chewing gum that baseball lost its test. But he has freshened up a good deal this year. He is a good deal wrapped up in himself and somewhat giddy at times, but as a pitcher he is becoming quite expert.
[Omaha Daily Bee, May 24, 1891]

Mr. Dunn, of Brooklyn, is as homely as a gob of mud thrown on a green-painted stable. He walks like a baboon on ice, and his uniform was made for some fellow twice his size. But he can pitch ball, and he had the Colts more than guessing yesterday.
[Chicago Record, reprinted in The Evening Times (Washington, D. C.), July 16, 1897]

Darby, the boy from the San Joaquin valley, was in the box for the White Sox (Omaha), and oh my! oh me! what a reticulation of curves and convolutions he did weave about the Blue Jays' (Indianapolis) necks.

He had enough steam on to run a saw mill, and at critical stages, the Indianans were but infants in his hands. For three long hours, he shot them over like bullets from a gun, and at the close was as fresh as one or two motor car conductors who might be named.
[Omaha Daily Bee, June 16, 1892]

Whitehill, the new man, was in the box for Omaha, and without exaggeration, he may be pronounced a bird. He is tall, slender and rosy, and when he goes to pitch a ball, has a fashion of reaching out with his left hand for the first baseman's hair in a way that would strike some people as funny, but when he lets go of the globe, no one has time for anything else but to watch its course. He has all kinds of curves and plenty of speed besides, and barring the second inning, he toyed with the big boilermakers like a cat with a mouse.
[Omaha Daily Bee, May 6, 1894]

Al Maul, the senatorial twirler, is said to have an invention of his own of breaking in a new ball. When the new white sphere is passed to him, he anoints it with a piece of pumice stone concealed in a handkerchief. This removes the gloss and roughens the smooth surface, thus giving the fingers a firm grip on the ball.
[Saint Paul Globe, May 14, 1896]

Pitcher Griffin annoys opposing nines by knocking the dirt from the heel spikes of his shoes with the ball. The cry is made that he spikes the ball and twenty times in a game he is called onto give the ball to the umpire for inspection. It is examined and invariably found unscratched, to the surprise of the annoyed ball players and the amusement of the crowd.
[Brooklyn Eagle, May 15, 1896]

Spectators have no idea of the figure which badinage among players cuts in the results of almost every game played. Pitchers like Dad Clarke, Cuppy, Killen and McMahon like to taunt their batsmen. Clarke is unusually sarcastic, and frequently goads the batsman till his victim loses cool judgment and becomes an easy mark to strategy.

"'Here comes Jimmy Fresh,' said Clarke in a recent game when a dangerous batsman stepped to the plate with men on bases and the score very nearly a tie. 'He thinks he's a batter. It's a mistake. I could drive him back to the coal mines if I had him on my list every day. His head is too big for what's in it. Hear it rattle when he reaches for a curved ball.' And as he talked he pitched, and the batter completely lost his self-control. The result was an easy out.

"The badinage which passes between pitchers and batsmen in a championship season would fill a volume, but if printed the book would be suppressed in the interest of morality. Ball players do not confine themselves to the language of the saloon in their efforts to chaff an opponent until he becomes 'nutty.'"
[Brooklyn Eagle, May 15, 1896]

For some unaccountable reason, the pitching of Prof. Stevens, which had hitherto been beyond the swipe of finite hand, became as readable as an open book. In other words, the Brewery boys "got on" and thumped and slugged until, from center to circumference, the sphere was reduced to a mass of pulp.
[Milwaukee Journal, May 27, 1892]

If the Kansas City players should live to be as old as "Pop" Anson, they will never dispel the vision of a tall, lithe young man, dressed in blue, who stood in the center of the diamond today and threw corkscrews at their bodies.

That young man was born into this vale of sorrow to be forever known as Isbell. The kinks and twists which he put into the ball bothered the Blues and caused them to reach out after poky benders that dodged past the ends of their bats to nestle cosily in the mitts of Heine Spies. Occasionally he limbered up and drove the balls into the Apostolic backstop with the speed of the Santa Fe's Chicago flyer.
[Saint Paul Globe, June 28, 1897]

There was story telling at Hot Springs the other day, according to the Cincinnati Enquirer.

Anson sighed and glanced reprovingly at Ryan. Then, after a moment's silence, Wobbly Wilmot spoke and said: "Tom was a queer character, but his eccentricities were not in it with those of Knowlton, who used to pitch for Detroit back in the old Association days. Knowlton was about the greenest leaguer that ever happened. He came to Toledo from the backwoods and he would stand for an hour watching the electric lights and street cars. He used always to chew slippery elm, and he invariably poured molasses into the hip pocket of his uniform. During the game, he would put two fingers into the pocket, get his fingers sticky, and make the ball turn inside out."
[Saint Paul Globe, April 4, 1897]

Breitenstein perspires very freely. He uses two handkerchiefs in every game he pitches. He has one spread out on the grass near third, drying, while he uses the other one. He changes every inning.
[Scranton Tribune, July 29, 1897]

Swaim is the most picturesque individual that has been seen in Chicago this season. He is built on the order of "the tall sycamore from the Wabash" and handles himself accordingly. He has a sort of spiral motion while in the box and is apt to strike terror to the hearts of timid batters.
[Chicago Times-Herald, reprinted in The Times (Washington, D.C.), May 30, 1898]

Good Days and Bad Days

Unpredictability in pitching performance, from great to lousy, has perplexed everybody in baseball since time immemorial, especially writers.

Thomas, the blonde giant that Vanderbeck picked up last summer in Alpena, or East Saginaw, or somewhere, was in the box. For three innings he was a good deal like pigs in clover, but after that he was as easy as the riddles in the Saturday editions of evening papers.

Base hits rattled off his pitching faster than the fusillades of Memorial day morning. From one foul flag to the other, and from home plate back to the patch of grass which grows apace despite the rough treatment of McBride's spikes, there was scarcely a square yard which was not the resting place of some swiftly batted, peace-destroying base hit.

Phyle, on the other hand, had the Tigers feeling around aimlessly, like huge cats from whose muzzles the whiskers had been cleanly shaven. Their elastic pupils expanded to the utmost limit in trying to detect the secret of the St. Cloud boy's pitching, but it was in vain, and when nine full innings had been hung up in Mrs. History's back yard, a total of seven safe hits was all that the nine Tigers could get together and count up.
[Saint Paul Globe, May 28, 1897]

Mark (Baldwin) was speedy, and controlled the ball so well that he could have knocked over a thousand cats in the Coney Island throwing gallery, and gathered in enough cigars to kill an army. The home plate looked as large as a platter to Baldy, and the ball, as it came

sailing over, buzzed like a rifle bullet.
[The Sun (New York), June 4, 1893]

They wore the varnish off their bats, hammering his deliveries all over the field. When they got through, the Cincinnati fielder looked like a lot of worn-out street car mules.
[Source misplaced]

Maul was batted so hard he looked like a man who had had a fight with some wild beast. He began his work by smiling sweetly at the crowd, giving several artistic flourishes with his right arm, and throwing in a ball that had a sign painted on it, which read: "You can't miss me."

Every one of the New Yorks read this sign, except Davis, who had a kink in his shoulder which interfered with his eyesight. Altogether nineteen glittering hits were picked out of his easy curves by the big bats of the local players. Such batting could win almost two ordinary games.
[The Sun (New York), June 20, 1893]

The day was dark and gloomy, and as the visitors began to score right off the reel, a pall of despair soon settled down upon the fans. A suspicious decision or two by the umpire added to the horror of the situation.

In the box there was a tall, thin young person, who shied the ball at the plate with his left hand. His name was Bruner. Ft. Scott, Kan., is his home. He had a peculiar delivery, which is described in the expressive parlance of baseball as "a dinky throw." It required six innings for him to locate the plate, during which time he issued four passes and hit four batsmen, three of whom were McBride.

...Every man he hit was left-handed, and the St. Paul players soon discovered his weakness and hippodromed their batting by standing at the plate to bat left-handed. Bruner's utter inability to field his position shows that he still needs some minor league training.
[Kansas City Journal, June 27, 1897]

Thornton was in the box for the Brewers, and he being known to the general public as a young man with a remarkably long head, it was expected that the enemy would fall like sheaves in autumn before his erratic and deceiving twirl.

But alas for human judgment. How applicable indeed was that old saying that "man proposes...," for in spite of every effort, Thornton and the whole galaxy of brilliant orbs from the city of beer fell as did Apollyon of old from the gates of heaven, the result at the end of the

ninth inning, being 7 to 4 in favor of St. Paul.
[Milwaukee Journal, July 5, 1890]

Hutchingson pitched for the Colts. He had speed and curves, but the ball was a runaway locomotive. He had no control over it. He would get two strikes on the batter and then have next ball smashed among the barley and the corn.
[Source misplaced]

>Their fingers were buttered,
>   They'd holes in their bats,
>The galleries groaned loudly,
>   The bleachers yelled "Rats."
>Cy Seymour grew rattled,
>   Rose in a balloon,
>And the chances are plenty
>   He won't come down soon.
[Source misplaced]

(Baltimore pitcher) Killen, a pigmy on Wednesday, had dieted himself on Nervine for three days, and yesterday strode on the diamond at Union Park, a Goliath. It was hard to believe that the weak-kneed, left-hander who made so miserable a failure of Wednesday, could have metamorphosed into the lion-hearted giant that dauntlessly faced the best of the League batters, and coolly sent them back to the water keg and bench often without the formality of treading the chalk line down to first. It was one of the paradoxical things of the great American game.
[Baltimore American, June 20, 1897]

(New York pitcher) Doheny's delivery was as wild as a chamois. Park Wilson would give him the sign for a certain style of ball, and then would wonder where in thunder it would come. But the boy has speed and good curves. He is also cool as a lemonade. He wasn't born and bred in northern Vermont for nothing. If his actions count, Doheny is so cold that his corpse would keep a month in summer without ice.
[New York Herald, reprinted in the Pittsburgh Press, September 18, 1895]

Jimmy (Callahan, of Chicago) was a Quaker when poor Harry Wright was manager of the team. He was a slim, loose-jointed bundle of angles, and while his pitching arm showed evidence of some ability, still Jimmy didn't look fast enough for the big League. Jimmy had a Weary

Willie habit of coaching the perspiration in leather chairs around hotel corridors, and was a big drawing card for flies as he sat slumped in a chair with the insects playing hop, skip and jump around him.

(Pitcher) Dr. McJames, of the Orioles, who is in a class by himself with a sleeping record of twenty-five hours out of twenty-four was a shifty proposition, a Captain Swift compared with Callahan. Harry Wright used to keep in fine physical condition off the exercise he got at chucking Sleepy Jimmy in the ribs. Once he went to sleep on the bench, woke up, inquired about the score, and then proceeded to tear off large chunks of the essence of Morpheus. And this is the same Callahan who is today one of the fastest and best-hitting pitchers in the League.
[Baltimore American, May 29, 1898]

Phillippe is the Minneapolis pitcher. He has been known heretofore as Phillippi. He might have adopted Actium, Thermopylae, or Bull Run for a name with equal grace, for it turns out that his family name is drawn, not from the frivolous French, and the puzzling pitcher of the Millers may be descended from the scions of a king's small brother. But whether his name was Fill-a-pie or Fee-leep, the local players did not seem to care a fillip.
[Saint Paul Globe, July 9, 1898]

Mr. Murphy, of the would-be champions, is a muscular, active young man, with good lungs and an amazing quantity of self-esteem. At the same time it cannot be denied that he has mistaken his avocation. He is not cut out for a baseball pitcher.

As the funny man in convention with a patent medicine fake in one-night stands, he would be a howling success. He could give the crowd an imitation of how he used to pitch and put them in good humor. He could shrug his shoulders as he does previous to delivering each ball, and the result would be large sales. He could prance out and show the people how he used to coach, and the spectators would no doubt think it was a Kiowa scalp dance, with aboriginal song.

There are certainly great possibilities in such a career for Mr. Murphy, and as his pitching days are drawing to a close, he would do well to cast around for an engagement. Sawing wood is very tiresome work, heaving coal is equally so, and working on a farm for $10 a month and 'keep' is neither pleasant nor profitable. It is, therefore, with the object of pointing out to Mr. Murphy some light and advantageous employment that even a speck of soot had touched him.

He pitched yesterday with all his might and main. He started in by shrugging one shoulder as he pitched the ball. That didn't work and he shrugged both shoulders and wagging his head as he pitched the ball. Nothing but disaster.

Finally, in desperation, he shrugged shoulders, wagged his head and did a highland fling step with the object of deceiving the batters. The Detroits hit the ball all the harder. Yet though all the cannonading, Murphy was as chipper as though he had shut the Detroits out without a hit."
[Detroit Free Press, reprinted in the Post Express (Rochester, NY), August 15, 1889]

On his first appearance in the Oakland team last summer, this paper dubbed Pitcher Ed O'Neil, "Easy" O'Neil, on account of his nonchalant air and easy-going ways, and the name will probably stick to him as long he remains in the business. Nothing bothers Easy. He is the Mark Tapley of baseball and life to him is one long, unbroken picnic with free beer and pretzels in spite of his bone spavin and the fact that he pitches winning ball and still loses more games than any other twirler in the league. But this is Easy's luck.
[Morning Call (San Francisco), May 23, 1891]

The Brooklyn pitcher (Kennedy)…appeared to have no baffling curves, but he swung his mighty right arm with the swing of a blacksmith fashioning iron at the anvil, and sent the ball over the plate, trusting to luck and speed to carry him through.
[John Foster, New York Journal, July 6, 1897]

Young (Wash. pitcher) Norton, who had risen from a sick bed Monday, was that confident of his health and strength that he assured Manager Schmelz he felt able to take his turn, but subsequent events proved that "Hotsafus" had overestimated his ability.

He was an easy mark for the swatters (of Chicago) from where the wild waves tell funny stories to Michigan's shores, and as his strength was failing fast, if it had not departed him entirely, he was swathed in a sweater and retired to the quietude of the bench.
[Morning Times (Washington, D. C.), September 2, 1896]

The whole trouble yesterday centered in the fact that Pitcher Foreman was out of form, and became an easy prey to the Milwaukee clusters. Do what he might, thwack-thwack came the willow wands upon the unresisting surface of the sphere, until it became wild and unmanageable, and flew and flopped around like a little puppy chasing its tail. Thicker and faster came the blows until everybody seemed bewildered, and fumbled and fuddled everything that came near them.

Then, on the other hand, the congressional batters could not fathom the muchness of Killen's delivery, which both terrorized and humbled them. There were no solids for them, and the swish-swash of their vain endeavor but seethed and sizzled through vacuity.
[Milwaukee Journal, September 11, 1891]

Brownie Foreman has cultivated a few of (pitcher) Dr. Pond's movements. He smokes a pipe, wears football hair under a golf cap, but has not mastered the English stride affected by the swell boys. Brownie has been giving so clever an imitation, however, that several eastern papers have referred to him as the young college pitcher.
[Pittsburg Press, June 10, 1896]

Terry pitched a masterful game. He had all sorts of speed and curves of the zip, zip, zip order. The way he steamed up when men were on bases was a sight for the gods. He kept the hits dripping through the innings and when men were on bases, unchained a few thunderbolts that scooted across the plate with a zig-zag twist that baffled the batsmen and kept the fans in a state of nervous prostration.
[Kansas City Journal, May 17, 1897]

...But there are other pitchers. This young man Isabell is one of them.

He comes here from North Branch, a community on the St. Paul & Duluth railroad, heretofore noted mostly for potatoes and wild and woolly pursuits of daring murderers. He is a stalwart fellow, big-boned and massive looking, with an arm that looks as though it would last fourteen innings as easily as one. He has been a student at Manchester college, and as such pitched consternation into the ranks of the other college teams here. He trained with the Saints a bit last year without any signal success.
[Saint Paul Globe, May 15, 1897]

Imagine a man as short and dark as a midwinter day, with the physiognomy of a Hungarian and the manners of a recently imported Irishman, and one has a fair idea of O'Brien, the newest Allegheny (Pittsburg) pitcher. He may be successful, but if he is, looks are very deceptive.
[Pittsburg Press, September 28, 1889]

William Phyle learned many things in the first inning. Chief

among these were the fact that seven singles and a two-bagger may be made to produce seven earned runs. He discovered later that it is a serious matter to try to win a game with such a handicap.
[St. Paul Globe, date misplaced]

The Dawdlers

Particularly annoying to ball park patrons were pitchers who slowed the progress of a game to a crawl with their deliberate, time-consuming work on the mound, which was as much an ingrained habit as intended to unsettle the batter. Needless to say, writers memorialized these infuriating interludes with typical acerbic commentary:

>*Thornton is as slow as an excursion boat up stream
Vickery's curves waddled up to the box on crutches*

>*No wonder Sioux City lost yesterday's game. They had a dead man in the box. His name was Meakin, and he came from Philadelphia—as a blind man would have known after seeing him move. Why, he was slower than the wrath of Jehovah, and before the game was half over, everybody was yawning in their seats. When he pitched down in Denver, they had to use a turn-table to switch him around in the box.*
[Omaha Daily Bee, July 1, 1891]

>*In these days of rapid transit a horse car is slow. But (Baltimore pitcher) Clarkson's delivery was slower than that. A boy going up to his father for a whaling is a lightning express to Clarkson pitching a ball. He clung to the sphere as firmly and inanely as a pup to a sassafras root.*
[Inter Ocean (Chicago), July 15, 1895]

Wild Bill Widner is the most aggravating and extreme pitcher in the Western association. Wild Bill takes his own time about delivering the ball. He generally poses a couple of minutes, looking at the people in the grand stand through the batter's eye.
>*Then he consumes another minute alternating his pitching hand from the ball to the bosom of his trousers; then he scoops up a little pulverized earth, powders the ball with it, gets into position again and then begins all over. This makes a batter furious, and that's what wily Wild Bill is engineering for.*
>*Finally, he begins to hitch his right leg, then he unravels his*

form, thrusts the ball up into the air, brings it down with a back action movement that causes all the little boys to fall off the back fence, brings it around with a swish like a cow's tail in fly time, and cuts her loose.
[Omaha Bee, reprinted in the Brooklyn Eagle, September 7, 1890]

Of all the slow pitchers, Malarkey of Washington is the slowest. He seems to have nothing but time. Before he sends in a ball, he seems to spend several moments in silent prayer. Mr. Malarkey would make a messenger boy explode with envy.
[The Sporting Life, reprinted in the Evening Star (Washington, D.C.), May 25, 1895]

Pitcher Mullarkey, of the Washingtons, might make a good corpse at a funeral, but he would never do for a pallbearer. He is entirely too poky to fill the duties of this mournful position. Not since the days of Larry McKeon, who was too slow in his movements to getup of his own road, has there been such a drone in the box at the Cincinnati Park as the young man who pitched seven innings of yesterday's game with the Senators.

What would otherwise have been a very interesting game was made tiresome and draggy by the deliberate work of Malarkey. This young man wasn't going to take any chances of making mistake by doing anything in a hurry. There was time enough between balls while Mullarkey was pitching to run around the grand stand. Mullarkey would first survey the batter from head to foot. Then he would fondle the ball between his hands for fully half a minute. Next he would look over his shoulder at the first baseman. Then he would rub his hand across his hip. Next a peep at the second baseman would follow. Then another rub at the hip. After he had taken a survey of the umpire, batter and all the spectators, he would finally straighten up and let the ball go.

He would go through this line rigmarole every time. He wore out the patience of the batters, spectators and the umpire, and every body was glad when Manager Schmelz took him out of the box and sent Anderson in to finish the game.
[Source misplaced]

(Washington pitcher) Boyd, the southpaw, who was so successful against Baltimore last year, had been reserved for this occasion. Judging from his work, he had been kept in the stable too long, and as a result, was stale. He had scarcely enough energy to pull himself together to deliver the ball. The effort was apparently so painful that it required fully a minute to collect his thoughts, straighten his

sleeves and shoot out his arm. Next to Cuppy, of the Clevelands, he beats anything for slowness ever seen on this diamond.
[Baltimore American, April 26, 1896]

Of all the mound sloths, however, the most vexing was Cleveland's Eugene Cuppy, who, despite his leisurely habits, achieved a remarkably successful major league career and along the way acquired an impressive list of monikers.

Cuppy is in a class by himself when it comes to slow pitching. He wastes a lot of time by a number of unnecessary gyrations in delivering the ball, causing a nervous strain on the spectators who like quick action. "The sun will do down before he pitches the next ball," said a disgusted rooter toward the close of the game. "McJames is slow, but he is chain lightning alongside of that fellow."
[Brooklyn Eagle, September 21, 1899]

O'Connor, Cleveland catcher, on Cuppy:

"(He) is the coolest man in the box I have ever caught. He will fumble and play with the ball for fully five minutes before finally delivering it. He is the most aggravating man in the world to a nervous batsman."
[Evening Times (Washington, D. C.), December 23, 1897]

(Cuppy's) slow, deliberate movements in the box seemed to disconcert the home batters...
...The deliberate Cuppy made all due preparations for a long siege in the box. He smoothed out all the dust within several feet of him, wound the ball around in his hand and then sent it toward the plate.
[Brooklyn Eagle, June 14, 1896]

(Cuppy, speaking of himself):
"I was accused of being slow in the box, and all that that. It is true I am a bit slow in delivery. Yet watch the time of my games...I am slow in delivering the ball, but I get into the box quickly, hustle from bench to the plate after innings and back again, pick up the ball and get on the slab in a hurry. In Chicago the other day, they called me a century plant and the 'human snail'; told how slow I was, how many motions I took in delivering the ball.
[St. Louis Republic, July 9, 1900]

>*Cuppy's deliberate style of pitching caused considerable delay...So slow was Cuppy's delivery that the bleacherites at one time actually counted 32 (seconds) before he sent the ball over the plate. Whether this is part of his stock of trade is known only to himself, but he succeeded in worrying the home batters by taking his own time.*
>*[Brooklyn Eagle, September 3, 1897]*

>*Pitcher Cuppy is so exasperatingly slow that the Cleveland management is to be petitioned by people who want to get their suppers warm to commence the games in which he pitches at 3 o'clock.*
>*[Morning Times (Washington, D.C.), July 8, 1895]*

>*Whenever that lobster-faced Cuppy pitches, the park management should be forced to provide patrons with rocking chairs and hammocks...He is slower than a freight elevator, or one of those bob-tailed horse cars...sneaking around this town.*
>*[Morning Times (Washington, D. C.), June 2, 1896]*

The School of Slow

The slow ball, even as today, was commonly thrown by pitchers to keep batters off-stride.

>*Mercer was as usual a puzzle for the Brooklyns, his slow drops creating havoc among the heavy hitters. He merely tossed up the ball and then stood laughing at the efforts of the batters to hit.*
>*[Brooklyn Eagle, reprinted in the Evening Times (Washington, D.C.), August 6, 1896]*

>*Mercer has a delivery very much like that of John Clarkson. His high slow ball is very coaxing and he is continually finding fault with umpires who fail to concede all he asks for. In fact, though as modest-looking as a backwoods maiden, this Washington man is said to be the most inveterate quiet kicker in the business. The way to trim Mercer is to go at him from the jump...as Baltimore always does.*
>*[Brooklyn Eagle, August 21, 1897]*

>*Cunningham's (of Louisville) slow ball was a Jonah to the Senators up to the eighth inning. He sneaked the ball across the plate like a snail and kept the local sluggers guessing.*
>*[Morning Times (Washington, D.C.), June 7, 1896]*

(St. Louis manager) Tim Hurst's left-handed twirler, Pete Daniels, has an odd delivery that suggests Breitenstein. Control has always been Pete's forte. His speed would never heighten the temperature of the zephyrs in the vicinity of home plate. But Pete can palm off his barrel-hoop curve and slow ball with enough success to win out a reasonable share of the game in which he performs.
[Baltimore American, June 2, 1898]

Tom Burns' latest importation from the Western League is a dapper chap, with hair as black as the wing of a jackdaw and an arm that can pilot a deceptive slow ball over the plate in an air of mystery. Phyle has a quick, nervous delivery, fields his position cleverly, and ought to be able to protect himself from the larcenies of the base-pilferers.
[Washington (D. C.) Post, reprinted in the Baltimore American, September 20, 1898]

Pitches That Can't Be Hit

Barnie's men (Brooklyn) could not solve the collection of curves and shoots dished up by the tantalizingly deliberate and calculating Cuppy, he of the rotund and insignificant appearance...To the ordinary spectator the ball went over the plate big enough to be hit a mile, but, although the visitors connected with remarkable frequency, the sphere persisted in going up in the air for an easy out or bounded along the infield into the waiting paws of the omnipresent Indians.
[Brooklyn Eagle, May 12, 1897]

Amole (of Baltimore), Hanlon's new pitcher, is proving a puzzle to opposing batsmen because of his speedy "cross fire" ball. He stands at the extreme left hand corner of the box, and so gets a ball over the plate at an angle unfamiliar to the batter. In the matter of holding a runner closely at first base, Amole is a "top notcher." It is difficult to tell when he makes the beginning of a motion to pitch to the batter and when to line the ball over to first. The movements are identical and the men who have faced Amole have soon found out that it isn't healthy to make too much of a lead toward second.
[Brooklyn Eagle, August 30, 1897]

Eccentrics on the Mound

Billy Hart, once a Brooklyn pitcher, practiced his peculiar

delivery, which The Eagle correspondent described while in Pittsburg last year. The delivery consists of going through all the motions of pitching with the right hand and throwing the ball with the left. It is deceiving to the eye and Hart appears to have excellent control, but it is a slow ball and would hardly prove effective in a regular game.
[Brooklyn Eagle, June 3, 1896]

Charley Jones started to pitch for Columbus. That is to say, he was drawing salary from Columbus. Most of his work redounded to the benefit of the St. Paul club, but that is one of the curious eccentricities of professional ball that cannot be overcome.

Mr. Jones is a nervous individual at times. He is very susceptible to remarks from the bleachers. He had a cute red jacket on yesterday, and its color enraged the coterie in the first base bleachers as though they had been turkey gobblers on a November diet.

The result was that Jones grew excited. He gave two bases on balls before he was frightened into a semblance of equipoise by Glenalvin's hit that went so fast Jones had to settle down for fear of being hit. When he struck out Isbell,

George Tebeau, who is almost as hopeful as the Prohibition party, thought there might be some hope of success yet, but Shugart lined out a good single, Frank muffed Gillen's fly, and this, with a pair of ragged throws on the infield, rushed four Apostles around the bases so fast that even Tebeau lost his confidence a little.
[Saint Paul Globe, September 16, 1898]

(Washington pitcher) Dad Clark:

Dad's face is not pretty nor handsome, nor is it even good looking. To be plain, in dealing with a plain subject, Dad is downright ugly. Neither is he a connoisseur in speaking the "Queen's Own." He talks the unvarnished United States such as is used as a means of communication by citizens of Harlem and residenters along the Bowery.

But Dad's vocabulary is quite sufficient for his purposes and he can use the whole of it to splendid advantage when engaged in a colloquy with an umpire. It is highly entertaining and edifying to hear him and Tim Hurst discuss the fine points of baseball during a close game and especially after Tim has termed a ball what in Dad's eye was a beauty strike.
[Morning Times (Washington, D. C.), April 16, 1896]

The Eternal Hunt for Good Pitchers

Two years ago, Pittsburg tried no less than sixteen or seventeen pitchers in a frantic endeavor to get a good one. One of them was brought to Washington park. He had been, according to reports, a phenomenon as an amateur, and the visitors thought he should hypnotize the Brooklyns.

But the shoe turned out to be on the other foot. In the first inning the home team made twelve runs off the young man by clean hitting. He had a most peculiar style of delivery, a sort of combination of Kid Gleason's arm swing and Long John Ewing's high kick, but it stood him in no stead.

After the opening inning, he went to right field where he promptly made two errors while attempting to stop base hits. Then he retired from the game, a sadder and wiser young man. His name does not matter, for it never appeared on a score card but once.
[Brooklyn Eagle, August 30, 1892]

Before leaving for home, Anson sent the following telegram to President Hart of the Chicago club: "Sign anything that says it can pitch."
[Brooklyn Eagle, June 20, 1893]

HARYWELL AND HIS HYPNOTIC DELIVERY

12. Humor in Game Account Formats

Masterworks in Metaphor

From time to time, clever writers with journalistic versatility used metaphoric themes to freshen up the daily grind of game accounts. This storytelling trick likened diamond action to that of other arenas of activity, its specification being left to the writer and its full implementation bounded only by his imagination.

Many motifs sufficed for this purpose, often based on current events. Let's look at a few:

Horse Racing

Comparing baseball to a horse race was the most popular theme, the idea first germinating in 1859:

Knickerbocker vs Empire

It was quite a race between De Bost, Wood and Davis, up to the 5th innings, when Wood "broke up on reaching the third quarter post." "Charley and Davis being 'neck and neck' on the 7th innings, however Charley "bolted," and was finally "distanced," Davis coming in the winner by one run…
[New York Clipper, August 27, 1859]

Others followed in much more detail:

In Chicago the other day, Anson made a hit. Here is the way a Chicago writer describes it:

"Anson made a home run. That was the features of features, and the crowd still roars at the thought of it. The chestnut colt made the run in the first. A man was on the bags and two out, and your uncle took a philosophical view of the matter as he tapped his big bat on the rubber and faced Mr. Young.

"The first ball up was a bender, and the big bat whipped around and met the sphere straight. It went like a line of light out between

Burkett and McAllen, and the head of the paddock got under way. Going down the first quarter, he attained the velocity of a messenger boy on a hurry call, and the second lap he was under full steam.

"In the third turn of the mud road and up the backstretch, his feet ran a dead heat with each other and he pulled down the stretch at a ten-minute gait and finished a nose ahead of his face, just before Burkett crawled under the fence out by the clubhouse and found the ball. Then the crowd went wild, and through the rest of the exciting contest, your uncle was a hero."
[Saint Paul Globe, July 19, 1896]

Charles Mathison, writing in the New York *Journal*, turned a Brooklyn-Boston game into a turf war:

The Eastern Park handicap was run yesterday afternoon on a fast track, and the favorite failed to win by several lengths. There were but two entries for this noted event and the Boston colt, sired by the celebrated "Three Times Winner," was an odds-on favorite over the Brooklyn runner, which carried weight for age, and was not regarded as in fit condition for a punishing race.

The talent plunged on the Boston cold and the Brooklyn racer was set down as beaten before the start.

To the consternation of all the experts, the long-legged Brooklyn horse set the pace from the drop of the flag, and had the Boston colt beaten before the stretch was reached. On nearing the winning post, the Hub jockey made a whipping finish, and tried to cut down the lead of Brooklyn, but it was without avail.

To deflect from the race track and get to the base ball diamond, the Brooklyns beat the Bostons very handily, and checked the winning streak of the Hub men. Had the Bostons won yesterday, it would have marked their eighteenth consecutive victory.
[New York Journal, June 23, 1897]

This equine account sounds more like a sulky race:

As things now are, and with yesterday's game to draw our inference from, it would seem as though we ought to take four straight heats (Milwaukee vs St. Paul).

In the opening heat, Vickery rode like a veteran, and never allowed the other to come near enough to worry him. At the word, go, he took the lead by a clear length, but opened the gap to four at the quarter. At the half mile, he was six lengths to the fore, going like an old stager, *and as he swept past the three-quarters, was ten lengths ahead of his field. Then he sat back in the saddle, coming down the stretch on a hand-canter.*

The St. Paul geldings made a desperate effort as they reached the straight to close the gap, and did, in fact, succeed by hard riding in reducing it by a third. That was their last expiring effort, however, and Vickery came under the wire, an easy winner by seven lengths.
[Milwaukee Journal, May 29, 1891]

Holy Scriptures

And lo! it came to pass that in the land of Baseballdom the most farcical treatment of all occurred when diamond play was transcribed by writers in the weighty, archaic language of the Bible. The finished work, unique as it was intended, was generally a one-off, as repetition, even with variation, was guaranteed to grow stale with readers in short order. Nothing was forever when it came to baseball writing style.

The idea of using the Bible as a metaphorical model was undoubtedly due to the little-known fact that baseball is mentioned within its covers. Yes, it is truly there, right in the opening line: "In the big inning…"

A classic example of risibly righteous writing was found in this New York-Brooklyn game account of 1895, which Brooklyn won, 12-11:

And it came to pass on the second day of the seventh month, the disordered troop from the land of Gotham came to Brooklyn and smote a certain star twirler hip and thigh. And the great Kennedy was sore thereat and became tired and sought consolation in solitude. But there arose a mighty Daniel, small in stature, but strong in curves, who turned the rabble to utter rout and won for himself the everlasting gratitude of the people. Yea, verily, he owned the earth.

And his right hand man was John, surnamed Grim, sober in naught but name. And when the Gothamites were in the midst of their victory and were shouting over the gain and glory that was within their grasp, John smote their champion heavily, turning defeat and disgrace into joy. Whereupon the people from the land of Gotham gathered up their wounded and dying and retreated to their stronghold, which lies a half day's journey across the big bridge that leads to shattered hopes.

And it came to pass at the going down of the sun, the followers of Daniel and John, surnamed Grim, raised their voices on high with joy and gratitude. And they dispersed, each to his tribe, and told their children and grand children yea to the third and fourth generation, of the great victory that had been won that day. And the children unto the third and fourth generation rejoiced and shouted, 'We are the people.' Verily, the tidings were spread broadcast, yea, to the very ends of the land of Columbia, and the people were loud in their rejoicings over the defeat of the Gothamites.

Now, when the sun had reached a point two hours before the time of setting, (umpire) Emslie, an unfavored man, of lengthy but store-purchased locks, rose up and shouted, 'Play.'

And the people who had gathered, yea, 4,500 strong, set up a mighty roar as Perkins Kennedy, who is called 'Roaring Bill' in the land that borders the banks of the river Ohio, appeared before the enemy. And the Gothamites began the attack. Yea, heavily did they smite him. And the first Gothamite was Murphy, and because of his stature, he is named Tot. He smote the ball upon the nose, and it went into the outer country and he was safe. Whereat Tiernan, the silent one, took his club, and the aim of Kennedy was wondrous bad, and the Gothamite reached his base on balls. So that the people from the other side of the bridge shouted with glee when the mighty Van Haltren toed the plate. But he was as naught in the hands of Corcoran, who stayed the bounding sphere and tossed it to Shoch, the substitute, whose place was at second. And Tiernan, the silent one, bit the dust.

But there arose a youth named Clark, from Scranton, on a far mountain, who had made covenant with the Gothamites. And he smote the sphere into the land of Griffin and the king thereof was sore pressed and fielded poorly so that Murphy scored his run. Wherefore, Kennedy became angry and caused Stafford, whom certain cranks call "Agnes," to foul out to Grim.

Again did Kennedy shoot with a faulty aim, whereat Wilson, the simple, and Farrell, he of the home of the Senators, walked to first, by which Van Haltren was forced to cross the plate. But German, he of curves and sardonic grin, was as naught in the hands of Kennedy, his hit causing the sore discomfiture of Farrell at second. Whereupon the host of Brooklyn began their onslaught on German, but their hearts melted and they were quickly repulsed. Griffin, the captain of the host, wafted the sphere at Fuller, and covered his head with his mantle.

Shindle, surnamed Deacon, from the land of the oysters that grow in the water of the Chesapeake, beat the air in his agony, but the ball passed unharmed. And La Chance wafted the ball to the breezes until it fell, yea, into the hands of Murphy.

And it came to pass that the Gothamites returned once more to the attack. And they were fierce and unrighteous and slew the great Kennedy, and it made the hearts of the Brooklyn followers sore. And Fuller, Murphy and Tiernan were allowed to pass unharmed to the very corners of the diamond, so that the multitude became anxious and offered complaint thereof.

And the leaders of the concourse yelled, "Take him out," but Kennedy heeded them not. Whereat Van Haltren took a great club and batted a single to left, which sent Fuller across the plate. And Murphy went in his footsteps on Clark's fly to Griffin. Stafford and Wilson hit safely, and Tiernan and Van Haltren were called home.

Farrell also smote and Stafford returned home. Whereupon Kennedy harkened to the votes of the concourse, and Daniel, he of small stature, attacked the foe. And it came to pass that the people were exceedingly glad and cheered lustily. And the great Grim discovered Farrell asleep at first and straightaway slew him. And German smote the ball, which sent Wilson across the rubber, and the number of the runs of the Gothamites was six. And it came to pass that Fuller was slain.

And now the people were sore distressed, because the Gothamites had long clubs and talked loud of routing the host of Brooklyn. But the followers of Daniel were of stout heart and limb and regained a part of their losses. It came to pass that after Anderson had been laid low by Fuller, Shoch, the substitute, hit to right for a base, and when Treadway had flied out to the silent one in right field, Corcoran dispatched the ball safely to left. Stafford did wrong in the eyes of the Gothamites and Grim secured his base, Shoch scoring. And when Daniel smote the ball for a single, the people cried with a loud voice. And Corcoran crossed the plate. And then the host of Brooklyn rested. Griffin forced Daub at second.

Now, it came to pass that the Gothamites grew valorous and added further successes in the third. Murphy's club failed him and he desisted. Tiernan, the silent one, stalked into the stronghold of La Chance because the stones which were cast at him were turned from their path. Van Haltren hit safely to left, after which Clark was fielded out by Daub. Stafford became a host in himself and smote to center, scoring Tiernan and Van Haltren. But the wily Stafford was reckless and was thrown out at second.

Now when the host of Brooklyn secured two runs in its half, the people did not shout because the Gothamites had too great an advantage. Therefore, the two runs secured on Shindle's base on balls, La Chance's two bagger to the outer wall, Anderson's out and Clark's misplay, were but as raindrops in the ocean.

And the Gothamites were joyous and rested on their arms in the fourth, because their blows had been great. But the host of Brooklyn rose in its might and broke down the strong arm of German. Corcoran, Daub and Griffin hit safely and Grim smote the ball exceedingly hard, that it was like to return not, yea, verily, a two-bagger. And there appeared as the Gotham champion, a man named Dad, surnamed Clarke. But he was of great conceit and self adulation. And the men behind him became as so many rattles, and errors by Fuller and Stafford sent in two more runs.

So that when the fifth began, the advantage of the Gothamites had been sorely reduced and they were harrowed by fears and their hearts failed them. They added one run in their half on two bases on balls, a force hit and a fly, but thereafter were as pigmies in the hands of Daniel. And the host of Brooklyn became courageous and secured another run in the sixth on hits by Shoch, Corcoran and Grim. And it came to pass in the eighth, that Anderson smote heavily at Farrell, who became sore pressed, and fumbled. And Shoch, the substitute, waited for four bad ones. Treadway smote at the breezes from the Bay of Jamaica. Corcoran hit to Stafford, and the runners went apace.

Then came the mighty John, surnamed Grim. And Treadway cried out in a loud voice: 'Soak it, my boy.' And Grim smote the ball in his might to center, and there was great joy thereat, for the runs which were scored were winners. And the host of Brooklyn rose as one man and lifted up their voices. And they rent their garments for joy and cast them into the air, yea, their turbans and their handkerchiefs and umbrellas did they wave. And their voices were raised in air, even from the grand stand to the lowly, among the bleacherites did they yell. And all was rejoicing and the mighty John was compelled to bow down before the multitude. And the Gothamites spoke not, but took themselves hence.
[Brooklyn Eagle, July 3, 1895]

As amusing as the previous account read, however, it was topped by this masterfully-woven gem that flowed from the pen of the nimble writer of San Francisco's *Morning Call*:

Now it came to pass that in the first month of his reign, Herr Most Vanderbeck (Los Angeles manager) waxed exceeding vain and proclaimed in a loud voice from the housetops at Los Angeles that he was the people. And the cigar store fans and them that dwelt in the purlieus fell down and worshipped their great man.

Howbeit a few wise men in the land of fleas and citrus products

(Los Angeles) communed among themselves, saying: "Whence cometh this youth who speaketh through his helmet?" But they held their peace, for dissension was not of their house.

And it came to pass that in the zenith of his glory, Vanderbeck rose up in his might against the stronghold of Hank, the Magnite, whose fame has spread in the land.

He gathered about him his valiant host, together with their batboys and baggage, and traveled a journey of two days to the northward. And lo and behold! They fell among sinners who smote them hip and thigh and took away their tallies in three days of battle. Thrice were they repulsed by the mighty hosts of Hank; and loud and deep were the lamentations thereat.

Now it came to pass that the young men who were athletic and agile of form gathered themselves together for another fray, and it was on the 29th day of the fifth month. And it was becoming fair.

On the plain which lieth over against the sea were to be Olympian games. And in the arena which is builded in with barbed battlements that teareth the toga of the sons of them that are short of shekels, were pitted nine of them that serve for Vanderbeck, and nine of greater merit, whose bread is won in bondage in the house of Hank, the Magnite.

And them that dwelt in the low places tarried on the bleachers.

And when the end was come, the disciples of Hank marveled greatly, saying one to another: 'What manner of men are these that have fallen upon us? Though we wrought valiantly, yet we are overcome by a score of 4 to 0.'

And they lifted up their voices and wept, saying: 'Verily, we are not in it.'

And all through the game the blame was laid upon the weaker host with a large brush from the pail of the numidian lion, which helpeth the whangdoodle roar for her first-born because it is not.

And they waxed fearful among themselves, for a plague was fallen upon them.

Now the multitude that was come to applaud the gladiators numbered 50 and 10 score, and they were the cranks and their descendants. And many pieces of silver were wagered on one side and on the other. And the maids and wives of them that were there came clad in purple and fine linen, breathing forth the soft perfume of myrrh, and of aloes, and of cinnamon, and of frankincense; and they were good in the sight of them that mash on the highways and on the byways and in public places.

And when the hour was come, it was meet that them that were

stripped for the fray should come forth, and do battle, inasmuch as the foe was in the arena.

Then came forth (California league president) Mone, he whose bubbling whiskers blaze even like unto an Italian sunset in vermillion pigments and oil, yet dominion and fear are with him and he maketh peace in the high places. And the multitude saw when he was yet afar off and knew him.

And it came to pass that when the time was come, Mone drew from his girdle a priceless Waterbury, set in sockets of fine gold, overlaid with sapphires and the topaz of Ethiopia.

At his word the loud tocsin sounded, and a youth who is wise even unto the next generation of them that cavort, spake unto them in a loud voice, saying: "Verily, I say unto ye, play ball."

And it was done, for his word was law, and his name it was (umpire) McDermott, a hireling whose road lieth in rocky places, even so that he crieth aloud in the anguish of his spirit: "Woe be unto me, for these people have a revolting and rebellious heart."

For he made a pit, and digged it, and is fallen into the pit which he made. His mischief shall return upon his own head, and his violent dealing shall come down upon his own pate.

And it came to pass that from this time forth half the servants wrought in the work on the plain while the other half sat on the bench where were the rulers, and held the bats and habergeons.

Now it was that Stafford—he that is short and thick, and red of face and stout of limb, like the cedars of Lebanon stripped in the fall—should wield the sling for them that were of the house of Vanderbeck. And Rogers, son of his father, with his face in jail, aided and abetted Stafford in the rear of the catapult.

And ever and anon the low-sat spit of the foul tip was heard above the roar and tumult of the arena. In all but six of them that serve for Hank did smite the ball, and three of them fanned out under the cunning curves of Stafford. He that cannot size up an inshoot is lost and the bat availeth him naught.

And it came to pass that it fell upon the disciples of Hank that they should be first at the trial of dexterity in wielding the willow and wafting the sphere. And it was in accord with the law as laid down on the league tablet.

When Peck Sharp, him that swatteth first, was come to the plate, the children of them that were in the city were on the bleaching boards and the eyes of the multitude were upon him.

A great hush fell as he girded up his loins and lifted a bat of gopher wood two cubits long, and stained with the dark brown spittle of the gladiator mixed with the dust of the earth. And with this weapon he smote the ball which is covered about with the hairless hide of an unclean beast.

Loud paeans of joy burst forth when he that guarded the third bag distressed himself with grievous bungles. And his name was Hulen.

Then came Blockers Hanley, a mighty player in years gone by, who dwelt in Bernal Heights. And Blockers was five and thirty years old when he began to bat. Then stood up Blockers and did that which was evil in the sight of the multitude. When the ball he smote was gone forth into the plain, a shot went up from the mouths of them that saw. And lo and behold, Sharp, he that was first, was pressed from his stronghold to give way to Blockers, who was of his kind. And it came to pass that before reaching second, an enemy smote him upon the back and he did perish at the bag which is second.

Now it came to pass that Blockers fled when there was naught to molest or make him afraid, and the enemy likewise smote him upon the back. Whereupon the hoary savant, who was of his kind, chided him, saying:

"'Verily, ye flee when no man pursueth. There was naught to justify thee in thy flight, for what shall it profit a man if he stealeth a bag with the eye of the enemy upon him? Verily, I say unto thee, in the wisdom of my years, thou art a chump.'

"When Reitz, he that was next, was come, he did wield the catapult with becoming skill. But when the ball had gone afield, it fell into the hands of Treadway, the Philistine, and great was the fall thereof.

"Now the wise men of the weaker host were Hoffman and Spies; and the youths that toiled with them were as reeds in the wind. And bases on balls prevailed and vexed them sore. Then they that were of the house of Vanderbeck did enter with zest into the pastime. Some did hit the wind with great force and others slid upon the face of the earth and rent their garments.

Now when Wright was come to the bat, the hand of his fellow men were turned against him; and he perished on the bag that was first. But Treadway, the Philistine, had the patience of Job and departed on his way with decorum.

It was then that the multitude marveled and rebuked Hoffman in a spirit of gentleness, but he answered them not. A soft answer trutheth away wrath, but grievous words stir up anger.

And it came to pass that when McCauley, who was third at the trial, did smite the ball. Peeples did that which was evil in the sight of Hank, the Magnite. Though his palms were placed to encompass the ball round about, it traveled into the plain. And when Hassamer, he that loveth the steam beer when it is sharp and reareth its foam in the can, smote the ball a mighty swat, it departed at great length and Treadway came in and rested from his labors.

And Hassamer girded up his loins and got himself hence to that sack which is second. His follower, Glenalvin, was sore afraid, being still lame with a Charley horse of many days, but he did swing the gopher wood with deadly force. And when the ball had departed unto the plain, Blockers became as one bereft of sense and sight; and behold! another tally was brought to the fold of Vanderbeck.

Again in the inning, which was fourth, the disciples of Vanderbeck did clout the ball with earnestness which begot two more tallies; and here the creation ceased.

And it came to pass that in the inning which was eighth, the house of Hank could have purged itself of the plague that was upon it. He that was called Blockers had nearly reached his journey's end, but the wise man, Spies, did beat the air.

Then came forth the savant, who spoke in a loud voice, saying:

"Incline thy ear, oh, my son, with mine sayings; wherefore swipest thou at wild pitches? for he that observeth the wind shall not swat." At these words the youth did wax exceeding wrath and he lifted up his voice that all might hear, saying:

"Go to, thou braggart! and remove the mote from out thine own batting eye. For a just and righteous compensation, I would smite thy face."

Then spake one who was not of the arena and whose home is in Tehama street, and he was a scoffer. He spake unto them, saying:

"Whence cometh this man brewing turmoil? He could not smite yon Grampian hill on which I tend my father's goat were he nigh unto it. Let him depart."

And he went his way.

And when the end was come, a great shout arose on the plain from the throats of the mighty host, for a plague was on the house of Hank. And though they rebelled, their voice was that of the dead.

And before the end was come, Hank, the Magnite, departed from the arena to commune with the money-changers at the outer gates of the amphitheater.

And it came to pass that his disciples lifted up their voices and wept, and they rent every one his mantle and sprinkled dust upon his head. But he that was wise unto the next generation spake unto them that were of the four tallies, saying:

"Rejoice not when thine enemy falter and let not thine own

hearts be glad when he is overthrown, for thou knows not at what hour he may come back at thee."

And there was peace.

On account of a hitch in the regular routine, the baseball reporter was unable to attend the game yesterday. The horse and fight editors were also engaged elsewhere, and, as a last resort, the religious reporter was detailed to take in the game. It is apparent at a glance that the good man made a sad mess of the job. However, he is not up in baseball and, therefore, could not be expected to turn out a thrilling tale. He has written up a narrative from which those well versed in the pastime may glean an idea or two, if posted in other walks.

From what could be learned from other sources, the game was a rapid affair, with lots of ginger and few startling features. Stafford was hit in a scattering way for eight swats, but not a Frisco man saw the plate in the full nine innings. The Los Angeles twirler was supported in excellent shape, but two fielding errors being recorded against his nine. As an illustration of how they performed, Pete Sweeney opened the ninth with a three-bagger, and then stood at the third corner, watching for a chance to deposit his tally while the next three men went out in order.

Hoffman held the hard sluggers down to five scattered hits, but with the air of these and a few carefully selected bungles, the visitors were enabled to register four tallies. A base on balls, two bungles and a double in the first produced two, and a couple of hits and an error in the fourth sent in another pair. Little Sweeney made a fine running catch in center, and completed a double play by a line throw to first. The usual Sunday crowd was there, but did not produce the usual noise.

Following is the score...
[Morning Call (San Francisco), May 30, 1892]

The great Dryden also lent his special talents to this shtick and came through with predictable audience-pleasing excellence:

Now it came to pass that on the twenty-second day of the fourth month, Amosenius, the son of Rusie, who dwelleth afar in the land of Indians, waxed sore afraid in exile, and wisdom increased with his years. Therefore, he lifted up his tongue, saying in a loud voice:

"This day will I arise and get me hence to the plains of Harlenium, where Bildad, the Bleacherite, roareth, and Andenius, the Magnate, mourneth for the pennant because it is not.

"For is it not graven on tablets in the temple of Adonis that I shall cop off four and twenty hundred scudi per? And I fain would clog my system with the doughnuts that the Giants do eat."

So saying, Amosenius, the son of Rusie, swart of face and stout of wing, did gird up his gunny sack with implements of war. He bestowed therein his sandals of kangaroo skin weighing ninety shekels of brass, a leather girt piece, two phials of precious charley horse ointment and many leaves of the tobacco plant, wrought into plugs and garnished with mosaics of tin from the marts of Jersey City.

And again and again, nay, even thrice, did Amosenius speak unto himself, saying in placid accents:

"Verily, I am a chump, no, not, nit. No more will I waste my substance in riotous pinochle, and only with the high fast ball shall the fans of Harmonium behold me engrossed."

At these words Andenius waxed exceedingly joyful, and caused them to be scattered broadcast among the scribes and Pharisees. And lo! the voice of the scoffer was hushed in the land.

Now when the twenty-seventh day of the fourth month as come, the multitude that assembled from the highways and byways of the city came to roost on the wind-swept bastions numbered 10,000 human beings, and the Philistine who did serve as umpire.

And the maids and the wives of them that were there tarried at home with the oil stoves.

And when the hour of four was struck, the disciples of Andenius said, one to the other:

"Behold, Amosenius, the prodigal, has returned to the plain. He will make monkeys of the hosts of the scoffer Wagnerius."

Verily, these words were the words of prophets, for though they wrought valiantly, yet were the invaders overcome by a score of 8 tallies to 3.

For it is written on the score card that the army of Wagnerius could not swat a marble mausoleum were it pitched unto them.

And lo and behold, as the tumult ceased and silence brooded over the plain of Harlenium, there did issue forth Colonel Cooganius, the Bluffite, who did observe the battle from his cave on the hillside.

And it as moot that this man should smite himself on the bosom and proclaim from the ramparts so that all might hear:

"Behold in me the Mascot that has come out of the wilderness to save."

And straightway the Bluffite did offer to the scribes some mixed pickles and besought them to smoke.

And so it came to pass that in the midst the battle, the umpire did take from one Giant ten pieces of silver and from another twenty pieces.

Whereat spake one who was not of the arena, saying:

"Whence cometh this man brewing turmoil? Let him depart and soak himself in the brook Harlenium, which is over against Astoria."

But they suffered him to remain, and he was an eyesore.

And when the end was come, the multitude fell into the arena to touch the hand of their redeemer, Amosenius, and kiss the hem of his toga.

The foregoing account was written by the man who reports sermons for the Monday morning paper. His effort shows traces of an early religious training, coupled with a smattering of baseball. However, the Giants have won a game, or rather, Rusie won it for them. The big boy is still first in the hearts of his countrymen and his triumph was complete.

[New York Journal, April 28, 1897]

Prize Fighting

This pugilistic-themed piece was unsigned, but it is very likely that Charles Dryden was responsible for its existence:

Baltimore, June 22.—Once more does white-robed peace spread her wings over the Monumental City, and tonight the erstwhile unhappy rooter pauses ever and anon to utter a gorgeous yell of glee as he separates the meek-eyed clam from the succulent chowder.

It was a battle royal between "Brother Joe" Corbett and "Si-"multaneous Seymour, to say nothing of one Bildad Joyce and Facial Expression McGraw, whose combined efforts added a new series of furrows to the corrugated brow now in the possession of Umpire Lynch.

First—Why it was a continuous, cinematographic, verascopic panorama of "he ain't out" and "tizzen't so" from start to finish, and the only wonder is that several athletic voices didn't have to be carried to the bench by their respective owners.

When (umpire) Lynch called time at 4 o'clock, the air was full of gentle zephyrs and hushed expectancy, and all of the principals in the bout were filled with a wild desire to win before the police could interfere.

For three rounds, the fight progressed without bloodshed on either side, although Bildad Joyce landed severely several times on Referee Lynch's lump of patience.

In the fourth round, the Corbett faction led carefully with their bats and hit Seymour with sufficient force to tap the tally claret to the extend of one run.

In the fifth round Corbett himself got in a swift uppercut on

Seymour that made old "Si's" ribs tingle.

This advantage was followed up by other jolts and jabs and finally Corbett leaned up against the ropes in smiling possession of another run.

In the sixth round everybody sparred for wind except Joyce, whose inexhaustible supply enabled him to continue in his life's work of saying things at the umpire and the world at large uninterestingly.

Mr. P. and K. Davis opened the seventh round with a left-hand swing that netted him two bases. Gleason landed on Corbett, but O'Brien jolted him on the southwestern corner of his face and the Kid slept at first.

From Warner's upper-cut a single ensued, and while Reitz was putting a pale brown bruise on Clark's ambitious efforts to beat out an infield hit to first, Davis slid over to his corner with the Giants' first tally in the fight. Immediately thereafter, Holmes attempted to chop, but Corbett parried swiftly and Holmes went out to left garden with a pain expression on that portion of his face that isn't occupied by his features.

In the eighth round the Corbett aggregation landed on Seymour's anatomical efforts with sufficient skill to produce bloodletting to the extent of one more run, but the Giants failed to get in even a short-arm jab above the belt.

In the ninth round the Corbett people posed and looked pretty for a veriscopic display. For the Giants, Davis landed lightly, but Corbett and O'Brien jolted him so severely that he of the Don Juan propensities had to sit on the bench and wait for the tally-ho. Gleason punched in McGraw's direction, and the latter responded by throwing the ball so briefly to O'Brien that Gleason was safe. Then Clark landed for three bases and Gleason scored. Corbett and O'Brien interfered so seriously with Holme's desire to reach first base that Referee Lynch called time and gave the fight to the Corbett people, while the faithful assembled by the ringside, glanced at the Brooklyn-Boston score and set up such a yell of triumph that old Chesapeake Bay rolled over in her bed and woke the oysters from their dreams of midsummer happiness.
(Baltimore won, 4-2)
[New York Journal, June 23, 1897]

Theatrical Productions

The second game, in which the Hoosiers crawled back to first place by grace of Buffalo distinguishing herself by being the only club in the league to win two games yesterday, was mostly pulled off in the fifth inning.

Two fumbles by Allen and a wild throw of Stewart to Motz were responsible for the Saints taking a lead of two in the first inning, to the intense satisfaction of the "I-told-you-so" contingent, which had developed in large quantities since the opening burlesque of the present nine-day entertainment, proved so dull and disappointing. If the after piece, which will go under the title of "Brewers vs. Hoosiers," proves as stale and dreary as the "K.-C.-at-the-Bat" affair which opened the show, the patrons will be justified by ordering the house closed for the season.

When Stewart came on to do his turn in the second, he opened with a lively knockabout act that resulted in three bases at one clip. Hickey followed as the other brother in the team, and scored Asa with a single, and scoring a hit with the appreciative audience by coming in on Scott's work with the slapstick, after Hartzell had rehearsed the justly celebrated bunt-and-die act.

Scott, in the third inning, sang eight verses, with but one break, of the pathetic song, "Oh, Where Is My Wandering Plate This P. M." with the result of advancing Houtz to the center of the stage and giving Geier a leading position at the right upper entrance. Further, Mr. Scott, the leading heavy, made so wild a throw to Allen, general utility, that his act, in conjunction with Second Heavy Kahoe acting a thinking part as the ball came his way from Hogriever, in the right wing, resulted in the song-and-dance team of Geier and Lally making a tremendous hit in their performance of "We Get Home Once Again."

In the third number of the olio, Kahoe was again the favorite, going through preliminary steps of the waltz, "Once Around the Diamond" while a few of the chorus were chasing a ball near the back drop. Scott's performance was essentially the same, as was Hogriever's, while Kahoe finished out his turn at the same time Shugart was giving his side-splitting rendition of the way a woman throws stones at a hen.

The fifth number in the olio was participated in by the entire Hoosier company, and was a most excellent exhibition of acrobatics, being distinguished notably by triple somersaults by Hartnell and Allen, doubles by McFarland and Hogriever, and a single by Stewart, all of which was skillfully combined in one of the best imitations of a merry-go-round ever seen on any stage, in which Hogriever, McFarland, Stewart, Allen and Scott participated.

The seventh number contained, among other interesting features, Scott's rendition of the ballad, "All Around the Mulberry Bush," in which he was ably assisted by Hogriever in his specialty, "Here Is Where I Knock 'Em for Two." The comedy in this number had been overshadowed by a little tragic bit by Isbell, Fisher and Houtz, but *fortunately their forceful presentation of "Let Me Feed My Face at Home Again," was not sufficient to change the general tenor of the entertainment.*

The same company will give two matinees today, beginning at 2 p. m.
[Indianapolis Journal, September 5, 1899]

The celebrated Dope family of acrobats gave a continuous performance at Exposition park yesterday afternoon, entitled, "How Not to Do It; or, A Tail Hold Is Better Than None."

The play began soon after 3 o'clock and lasted until the sun went down. Nine sun-bronzed and wind-tanned young and middle-aged men from St. Paul assisted the Dopes in their work of betraying the public confidence. For some time before the hour set for the performance to begin, dark and mysterious clouds skirted the skies, and the attendance was kept down at the park to a minimum.

"Brownie" Foreman Dope, who recently starred in a two-night stand piece called "The Mysterious Disappearance; or, What'll You Take," enacted the role of the leading gent, while the men from St. Paul pretty generally did the rest.

There were eight and one-half acts. Frank Blanford Dope was behind the rubber, and several times forgot his lines. The performance of the Dopes was a travesty on Charley Hoyt's "A Runaway Colt."

The stage setting was a baseball diamond with streaks of mud for base lines. In the first act Tim O'Rourke Dope is discovered waiting out four bad ones, after which Frank Connaughton Dope swings wildly at three benders. Mr. Heine Spies, who is suspected by the umpire of carrying a stick of dynamite concealed in his hip pocket, neglects to intercede a wild pitch of Isabell's, and O'Rourke paces to second. Thomas Gettinger Dope lands viciously on a slow drop, and the sphere goes to the stage flies, from whence it descends into Isabell's possession, and a subtle pass to second reveals the passing of O'Rourke. The technical term for the action is a double play.

A dark scene shift is made, and when the lights are turned on, McBride is found waiting for a pass to first. After considerable grumbling and stage thunder, the complimentary is issued, and he starts on his journey, but soon falls asleep and is deposed from his resting place at first through the concerted action of Foreman and Jack Carney Dope. Nicholson finds the actor's sesame to easy street—makes a hit. Glasscock duplicates the same feat, while George walks down. Then Shugart transforms the sphere into a double, and three runs come in. Parrott is relieved of further duty by Gettinger, and Hollingsworth is retired by Connaughton and Carney Dope.

The two succeeding acts are tame. There is too much Pankhurst and not enough "Little Egypt." The plot thickens in the fourth act. Hollingsworth hurries away from a bunt, Spies strikes out, but Blanford neglects to intercept the sphere, and when, later, Isabell sends it whirling into left field, two runs come in. Then the Dopes bend over their duties and gradually withdraw the outsiders from the scene of action. In the fifth act a forgotten line, a home run, and two singles, net three runs, while a cluster of three hits in the eighth add another.

The Dope family also scores in the eighth. A hit by a pitched ball, a double and a single was responsible for it. The score:...
[Kansas City Journal, June 28, 1897]

Instead of playing a game yesterday afternoon, the St. Paul and Des Moines teams gave an entertainment entitled, "The Possibilities of Base Ball." It was a comedy of nine acts, each composed of two scenes. The show was presented on the diamond and several acres of outlying territory. The curtain was rung up at 3:30, revealing eleven athletic young men, all in fantastic uniforms, except one.

The last-named kept his arms and voice going to keep from getting lonesome. One man had a long piece of seasoned ash, with which he hammered away at a piece of rubber at his feet, and the other nine stood around and smiled nine cynical smiles, as much as to say, "We are going to have fun with you,"

This young man was Patrucio Laurence Murphy, the heavy tragedian of the St. Paul team, who retired from behind the scenes through the connivance of one Connell and one McDermott.

The opening scene was entitled "It Is No Trick to Make Home Runs," and Hawes, Werrick, Reilly and Farmer each larruped one of Spalding's best out into the swamp, where chirps the bullfrog at eventide.

This lively opening put the crowd in good humor, and the applause was hearty and long continued. The second scene, "Two Can Play at That Game," was not well carried out, owing to the weakness of the Des Moines men assigned to that post. Connell was the only one of them to successfully perform the feat.

The second act opened with an attempt by Kennedy to pitch the ball over the grand stand, followed by a little exhibition of juggling by Patton and muffing by Maskrey. Reilly put a little life into the scene by banging the ball for four bags. The second scene was enlivened by the stealing of a base by daylight by "Ohne" Patton, Patrucio Murphy again appeared in the third. The scene was a successful presentation of the fact that two doubles, a single and a brace of errors are sometimes good for two runs, and the next scene showed how to make four runs on four singles.

The fourth, fifth and sixth acts were without special incident, the crowd began to yawn, and the critics were whispering that the comedy would prove at least an equivocal success. The opening scene of the seventh was also of a quiet nature, but interest began to revive in the last scene, which was entitled: "The Error Lurks in Every Bush." Murphy, Werrick, Tuckerman and Carroll gave a fine exhibition of muffing, juggling and fumbling, and the boy with the chalk tallied four for Des Moines.

The closing scene of the eighth was a continuation of the work of the seventh, Tuckerman and Carroll doing the juggling, and again the lightning calculator gave the Prohibitionists four. The closing act opened with a lively exhibition of fumbling and wild throwing by "Ohne" Patton. When he finished his artistic work, the score board stood St. Paul 23, Des Moines 16.

The last scene, entitled "Success and Failure Are But a Hair's Breadth Apart," began with Traffley as the central figure. The spry little catcher gave Reilly a fly and retired. From this point the play was a screaming success. Phelan hit safely, Reilly juggled Macullar's grounder, Kennedy drove the ball to right for a sack, Patton accepted a base, Maskrey and Connell made singles, and Cody gave Hawes a fly. Roach was hit by Mains, and Traffley reappeared with a section of oak, with which he slashed the ball to center for a couple of sacks. This brought in the twenty-second run for the Hawkeyes. Another would also have come in but for the trick of Reilly in pretending to be catching the ball, thus holding Roach at third. There were men on second and third, and the crowd stood up with its hat in one hand and its breath in the other. A hit meant defeat; an out meant victory. Dick Phelan had already made a hit in the inning. Would he make another? He hit the ball; it went to Mains, from him to Hawes.

The curtain was rung down and the comedy was over. The ground keeper brought the following over in a wheelbarrow at 10 o'clock last evening...(line score)
[St. Paul Daily Globe, September 16, 1889]

Cowboys and Indians

This account detailed a game between the Cleveland Indians and the Pawtucket (Mass.) nine in late summer, undoubtedly an exhibition game:

Yesterday the much-heralded Cleveland Indians, under command of Big Chief Patsy Tebeau, appeared at Crescent Park, arrayed in their war costumes, bedecked with plumes and feathers, after defeating the Bostons two games out of three, and liberally besmeared with war paint.

Before the game, Chief Tebeau called his braves to the bench and after all had assembled, they held a lengthy pow-wow, during which numerous sacrifices were offered up and incantations of all kinds took place.

Before dismissing his braves, the medicine man of the tribe told them that they must snow the white men under during the game or they could never look their squaws in the face after returning to their wigwams in the far-off country.

Then, amid the tooting of horns and tapping of drums, the red men performed a war dance preparatory to opening the battle. Before the game was called, Chief Tebeau stepped out and thus spake his mind to the Maroons:

"Pale faces of Pawtucket: We have traveled from our wigwams in a far-off land, over rivers, plains, valleys and mountains to meet you in a ball game on your own hunting grounds. My braves have feasted on the beasts of the mountains and the birds of the air and will make you feel the mighty arms of the red men before this game is over. We love you as our forefathers loved yours, and will do the same to you as was done to your ancestors in the olden times."

Then, turning to his warriors, he said: "Warriors, take your positions and begin the annihilation."

The game then started with the pale-faces at the bat. Sub-Chief Brown performed the evolutions in the pitcher's box and, to begin with, the Maroons clubbed his delivery for two runs in the first inning ...

The painted warriors came up in their half prepared to do as Chief Tebeau had said, but they had not reckoned on Toddy, the strongest of the pale-faces, to pitch against them. But this renowned white man was on the rubber for the Pawtuckets and proved himself to be more mighty than any of the Indians.

The latter clubbed at the ball, cut great chunks out of the atmosphere, did everything, in fact, but hit the sphere safely. Meanwhile they were retired and took the field and Great Chief Tebeau, who was spiked in Saturday's game with the Beaneaters, sat on the bench and raved.

In the third inning, the Pawtuckets came up strong again and scored two more runs...

The Clevelands kept coming in turn, but generally went out in one, two and three order, to show their appreciation of Todd's mighty arm. In the sixth the Maroons scored five runs...

In the eighth, the Indians scored their only run of the game...

The Pawtuckets were not satisfied with the lead they had already gained and scored two more runs in the ninth inning.

Thus the game ended, with the score 12 to 1 in favor of the pale-faces, the Indians barely escaping a shut out. The warriors did not rejoice after the game, but slunk to their improvised wigwams and tried to think what words Chief Tebeau would speak to them when he got them alone.

The score:...

[Pawtucket (Mass.) Tribune, August 30, 1897]

Poetry

There were a handful of baseball writers whose alter ego was that of poet, and quite capable of narrating a complete game in verse. *Regardez vous*:

The baseball reporter of the Herald, evidently in sympathy for the home team, had an "off day" of the rankest kind yesterday, and it was only at a late hour that he showed up with his copy. It will probably be a case of "inquirendo lunatico" for next Tuesday, if it doesn't take a fatal turn before then. Here is the screed:

> *It was an old-time "Leaguer,"*
>   *And he stoppeth one of three*
> *By thy bronzed cheek and battered hand,*
>   *Now, wherefore stoppest thou me?*
> *I'm on my way to see them play;*
>   *The Babes are winning fame;*
> *Jack Roach is in the pitcher's box,*
>   *There's ginger in the game."*
>
> *The Leaguer holds him with his eye,*
>   *"There was a game," quoth he.*
> *The baseball fan fought like a man*
>   *But the Leaguer had him—see?*
> *He holds him with his battered hand,*
>   *The baseball fan stood still;*
> *He stood and stared like one bereft—*

The Leaguer had his will.

"There was a game," the Leaguer said,
"That filled my soul with joy;
Where base hits came with runs and fame,
And two-base hits, my boy,
And home runs, too, though they were few,
And bunts and swatlets gay;
But that great trick, with ball and stick,
Was not played yesterday.

"The game they played on Saturday
Was of a different stripe.
The Dukes had on their batting clothes,
And merrily did they swipe
The in-shoots, curves and cunning drops,
And ball that had no faults,
From out the box their rapid knocks
Sent Phenom Louis Balsz.

"Then Tredway thought that he could pitch,
The Dukelets did but wait.
He couldn't send a single ball
Across the rubber plate.
Four times he sped the covered sphere,
'Four balls,' the umpire said.
Two tallies got without a swat,
Forced in by Southpaw Tred.

"And faithful Jimmy had a chance
To fill the box once more;
But still the men from San Jose
Piled up the runs galore.
Ah, me! It was a weary time;
The Angels could not win.
They'd get a man to first or third,
But could not bring him in.

"Base hits, base hits everywhere,
The horse-hide-cover batted;
Swatlets, swatlets everywhere—
But the Angels' swats were scattered.

> 'Tis said an orphan's curse would drag
>   A spirit from on high;
> But, oh! more horrible than that
>   Is the loss of one's batting eye.
>
> "Farewell, farewell! but this I tell
>   To thee, thou baseball rooter;
> He playeth well who swatteth well
>   Both out-curve and in-shooter.
> He playeth best who swatteth best
>   And fields all kinds of knocks;
> But the Angels need their batting duds
>   When Harper's in the box."
>
> The baseball crinkle heaved a sigh
>   As he thought of yesterday.
> A sadder but a madder man
>   He journeyed on his way.

Readers who desire to know the individual record of each player in yesterday's game will please consult the following official score: [*Los Angeles Herald*, July 3, 1892]

One of the poet laureates of professional baseball at this time was George V. Hobart, confrere of Dryden's on the New York *Journal* staff. Here is some bragging in iambic pentameter—or something like that—after the Giants downed the high-flying Orioles:

> Who chased the Birdies in their coop?
> Who made them candidates for soup?
> Who trimmed their big percentage sails?
> Who pulled the feathers from their tails?
>   The Giants.
>
> Who bravely won three out of four?
> Who brought dismay to Baltimore?
> Who clipped each little Birdie's wing?
> Who didn't do a blessed thing?
>   The Giants.
>
> Who won today's game like a breeze?
> Who ate up Hanlon's stars with ease?

Who played all 'round the sleeping champs?
And closed up all their batting lamps?
The Giants.

Who batted out the ball for keeps,
And gave the faithful few the weeps?
Who jumped on Hoffer's every curve
Until the Birdies lost their nerve?
The Giants.

Who played the game like crackerjacks?
Who hit with loud, resounding whacks?
Who beat the Birds at every turn?
Who had base hits and things to burn?
The Giants.

Who were not in the game at all?
Who played the dopeful style of ball?
Who went to pieces at the start?
Who had concussion of the heart?
The Champions (Baltimore).

Who fumbled, fussed and fumed around?
Who tore the cover off the ground?
But did no single thing of note,
Whose batting streak was on the shote?
The Champions.

Who left the Birdies in the lurch?
Who knocked them off their dizzy perch?
Who worked with grim persistency?
Who pitched with skill and brilliancy?
(New York pitcher) Sullivan.

Whose speed was extra superfine?
Who, in himself, was nearly nine?
Who kept the Birdies on the guess
And caused the multitude distress?
Sullivan.

Who couldn't pitch a little bit?
Whose efforts gave the crowd a fit?

Who had the stutters in his arm
And couldn't do a bit of harm?
(Baltimore pitcher) Hoffer.

Who shrieks aloud with gurgling glee?
Who smiles with fierce intensity?
Who swears this winning streak will last
And that he'll nail the pennant fast?
(New York captain) Joyce.

What tells tonight in "Champville" town
A tale that brings the tearlets down?
What brings to Gotham no regrets
And shows the skill of Joyce's pets?
The score.
[New York *Journal*, June 24, 1897]

Fourth Inning

Beckley lined a hot one westward,
Which wee Keeler could not touch;
Stafford flied out; Wilson nailed it
Hard, and Beckley ran so much.

That when clouds of dust subsided
He was resting safe on third;
Doheny hit to Nops,, and Jake died
At the plate without a word.

Van fouled to Doyle and ended
For the time a chance to score,
And by this time Joyce's voice was
Agitated and sore.
No runs.

Stenzel grabbed a neat two-bagger;
Then the Giants grew confused
And piled error onto error
While the multitude enthused.

Stenzel started stealing thirdward,

Wilson threw to Captain Joyce,
But he must have thought the Cap, stood
    Where the coacher throws his voice.

Stenzel scored on Wilson's wild throw;
    Reitz, a base on balls, and stole
Down to second; Wilson threw it
    Wild to short, who watched it roll.

Out in center; then Van Haltren
    Threw it wild for luck once more,
And young Mr. Heinrich Reitz did
    Not a blessed thing but score.

Robinson, the rotund catcher,
    Was presented with a base;
Nops flied out in center field, and
    Quinn's scratch single in this case.

Proved sufficient; Keeler landed
    On young Doheny's drop for three;
Adding two more to the tally
    Of the champs of high degree.

Jennings flied to Mr. Gleason,
    Kelley's shoulder stopped the hide;
Whereupon he stole, but Keeler
    Fell down at the plate and died.
Four runs.

Fifth Inning

After this most sad disaster,
    All the Giants seemed to sleep,
And while sleeping seemed to dream
    Dope was plentiful and cheap.

Tiernan flied out to Quinn, and
    Joyce struck out, 'mid cheek and yell;
Davis flied to right, ah! sadder
    Grows the story that I tell.
No runs.

Out in simple rhythmic order
Went the Birdlets, one by one;
Adding to the game no interest,
Adding not a tiny run.
No runs.
[New York *Journal*, April 30, 1897]

Honorable mention for poetic expertise went to an Indianapolis bard:

'Twas yesterday and the sun was hot,
And shone with fierceness on the spot
Where men played ball around the lot.
And various runs and things were got
By Hoosiers batting manfully.

The band of scrappers from St. Paul
Were slammed so hard against the wall,
That one lone tally was their all,
Just one lone tally, thin and small—
Eight goose eggs showing painfully.

McFarland's hit for a single span,
Was juggled by the right field man,
While Mac lit out and ran and ran,
And landed on the three-time pan,
While rooters hooted hootfully.

Big Asa Stewart joined the fight,
And slammed the ball far out to right,
(Ye gods! His running was a sight!)
He nailed three bases in his flight,
McFarland scoring easily.

Up sprang one Hickey, lithe and slim,
And landed on the sphere with vim,
And sent it down to Ball. For him,
'Twas hot, or else his eyes were dim,
And Stewart came home pantingly.

A single fell to Mike Kahoe,

And Fisher's soul was filled with woe,
His reason tottered 'neath the blow
The while he saw the Hoosiers go
    Like Iser rolling rapidly.

Next Newton came up for a spin
And met the ball, but Fisher's fin
And fielding by Lord Glenalvin,
Brought Newt to grief, though there came in
    One Hickey, springing speedily.

Now in the sixth came up St. Geier,
His eye alight with battle fire,
Says he, "I'll pull us from the mire,
Or else I'll know the reason whire,"
    And straightaway smote two-baggedly.

St. Burke essayed the ball to place,
But Hickey yanked him from the race
While Geier gained another base;
Then Lally fluttered out to Ace,
    The shut-out dying painlessly.
    [The Indianapolis Journal, July 27, 1899]

Come all ye fair maidens and list to my lay,
As I tell how the Hoosiers were again in the fray.
How they made poor Comiskey, of the spotted socks, pray,
And ask why in thunder his gang couldn't play;
    Sing, down, down, derry down.

The thing was so easy, it seems like a sin,
The way the bold Indians took Commy's men in;
But we need the percentage, the pennant to win,
And in battle each warrior must save his own skin.
    Sing, oh, my, such a hot!

The up-river geezers was first at the bat,
And before they let go, they had taken two flat;
And the bold hammer-swingers was feeling quite fat,
While the rest of us wondered just where we was at.
    Sing, oh, such a headache!

You see, Geier gets him a base upon balls,
And Burke, like a hero in sacrifice falls;
And Brennan then four more for Lally he calls,
And Decker's soak brings 'em both home to their stalls.
Sing, oh, gee, what's the use?

Brave Motz then comes out with his bat in his hand,
And faces the pitcher, so great and so grand;
He's the boy with the nerve, he's the boy with the sand,
For he poked out a single right where he did stand.
Sing, oh, ain't he all right?

Four balls and a first base McFarland did win,
And after him follows our own Dibby Flynn;
And all of the people, they start in to grin,
For Dibby his single sends Motz romping in.
Sing, oh, well, I don't know!

But next comes up Burke, who's a fine Irish lad;
And the single he hit was the best that he had;
Then he gets third on Hickey, who fumbled so bad,
And come in a-running, and then he was sad.
Sing, oh, let's all go home!

But Motz and Hogriever gets bases on "four,"
And McFarland's two-bagger then settles the score;
He brings them both in, while the rooters did roar,
And Comiskey's gazabos ain't no good no more.
Sing, oh, ain't we the cheese?
[Indianapolis *Journal*, July 28, 1899]

War

Here is an early example of a generic nature:

It was a terrific, though one-sided battle between the new steel cruisers, Boston and Chicago, in which the crew of the latter was victorious. Rear Admiral Anson's tars raked the Boston's decks from stem to stern, shutting out the pirates by a score of 9 to 0, and when the smoke of the battle had cleared away, it was learned that seven of the winning points were won on their merits. Clarkson, gunner's mate of the Boston, was hit 14 times by the enemy, including three home runs, while

long John Tener, captain of the Chicago's battery, was hit but seven times.
[Chicago Times, reprinted in the Pittsburgh Press, 1889]

A real war, however, was guaranteed to infect baseball writers with metaphor fever, such as the onset of the Spanish-American War, in May, 1898—and especially the great naval victory, the Battle of Manila Bay:

Jimmy Manning's rough riders (Kansas City), fresh from the plains of Missouri, slaughtered the Stallings tribe (Detroit) at Bennett park today. The locals fought bravely for awhile, but were repulsed with terrible loss. The rough riders charged fiercely upon General Irwin, who commanded Detroit's only battery, riddling him with shot and projectiles. When he was carried from the glory field of battle, it was found that he had exactly twenty-two wounds, four being inflicted by the heavy artillery of the rough riders.

It was the finest battle waged at Bennett park this year. Irwin received a veritable baptism of fire, the rough riders swatting his delivery for twenty-two hits for a total of twenty-nine bases...The fusillade was terrific in the seventh. Shot and shrapnel flew all over the field. ...Hulen let Campau's grounder go through him like a shell from the (cruiser) Brooklyn through a Spanish fleet...Glenalvin let Tebeau's grounder go through between his legs with the facility of the (cruiser) Baltimore passing Corregidor batteries.
[Kansas City Journal, July 14, 1898]

It is unlucky, according to the Sampsonian philosophy, to be in a fight and not of it, as was the case of the (battleships) Massachusetts and New York, as it is to be of a fight and not in it, as was the case with Jim Corbett when he met Fitzsimmons. But the cruiser Detroit, of Rear Admiral Van Derbeck's fleet, Capt. George Stallings, commanding, can double discount either of these varieties of misfortune.

The unfortunates attempted a blockade at Lexington park yesterday afternoon, but when the fight came, the Detroit was neither in it nor of it. The foreigners' armament, too, was far superior. They bore down on the (pitcher) Denzer with a four-pounder, three three-pounders and several rapid-fire single barrels, while the St. Paul fleet had only light-weight weapons.

Still, they were in their own doghouse, to change the metaphor from sea dogs to land dogs.
[Saint Paul Globe, July 2, 1898]

Klondike Gold Rush

The subjugated Senators discovered the bitter of the assertion yesterday when they went to the stamping ground of Barnie's men to complete the work of devastation so ably carried on by the Giants. The Senators met with obstacles more insurmountable than the Chilkoot Pass, and they retreated in consternation. The pitching of young Dunn was what barred the passage of the visitors towards the Klondike of victory.
[New York Journal, September 5, 1897]

13. Humor in Off-the-Wall Writing

Whether on the verge of an acute mental breakdown or temporarily overcome with the power and grandeur of their own words, some baseball writers cut loose with bursts of near-psychotic chatter. As crazy as it was, though, it still read funny.

Styles varied. On the one hand you had smart alecks who invented new or meaningless words or terms to either show off their writing prowess or heighten dramatic effect.

And then there were the "scholarly" ones. They dropped names from ancient Greek and Roman literature, or the Bible, or added superlative endings to base words that didn't grammatically qualify for them in the first place, or seasoned text with long out-of-date references that obscured its modern meaning altogether.

Others churned out narrative in a stream-of-consciousness manner that often defied comprehension. And, lastly, some over-the-edge writing reflected the emotional highs and lows felt in the wake of a significant game win or loss.

When Minds Wandered Too Far Off Base

Hands, down, the winner in this distinguished category was a writer for the Quincy (Ill.) *Herald*, who, temporarily deranged by a crushing defeat (15-2), took baseball slang beyond the pale and, in so doing, made the tirade darn near unreadable, Nonetheless, it made a reader wonder: Could baseball writing get any better than this?

> *Donnerwetter und sapristi!*
> *The dad-wiggled goony-goon is after us!*
> *Drat the measly, pestiferous luck anyhow!*
> *The glass-armed toy soldiers of Quincy were fed to the pigs yesterday by the cadaverous Indian grave-robbers from Omaha. The flabby, one-lunged Reubens who represent the Gem City in the reckless* 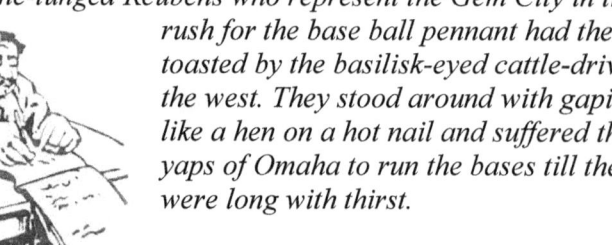 *rush for the base ball pennant had their shins toasted by the basilisk-eyed cattle-drivers from the west. They stood around with gaping eyeballs like a hen on a hot nail and suffered the grizzly yaps of Omaha to run the bases till their necks were long with thirst.*

Hickey had more errors than Coin's Financial School* and led the rheumatic procession to the morgue. The Quincys were full of straw and scrap iron. They couldn't hit a brick wagon with a pick-axe and they ran bases like pall-bearers at a funeral. If three base hits were growing on the back of every man's neck like a wen, they couldn't reach 'em with a feather duster.

It looked as if the Amalgamated union of South American Hoodoos was in session for work on the thirty-third degree. The geezers stood about and whistled for help and were so weak they couldn't lift a glass of beer if it had been all foam. The Omahogs made pigeons of them, pinned them to the wall like bats punctured with bow and arrow. Everything was yellow, rocky and whang-basted like a stigtossel full of doodle-gammon.

The game was whiskered and frost bitten. The Omahogs were bad enough but the Brown Sox had their fins sewed up until they couldn't hold a crazy quilt unless it was tied around their necks.

Roast the scar-eyed crocodiles anyhow. Here is the whole dad-binged business and how it was done:
[Quincy (Ill.) Daily Herald, May 25, 1895]
[*Pamphlet, published in 1894, that popularized the Free Silver Movement.]

From the selfsame author comes this companion piece, composed while still under the effects of a mind-altering drug:

There is a jibbering skate in Rockford with a polka dot for a head, who has been temporarily elevated to the emoluments and throne of a base ball umpire, but it is an undisturbed, physical fact that he cannot tell a strike from a lock-out. Sometimes the home plate looks to him the size of a cheese sandwich, but when a Rockford pitcher is in the box, it is as big as a bale of hay. Sometimes his eyes are like twin stars and then again they see like narrow slits in a bean bag.

This petty tyrant of the field is named Burns, and he used to work at silver-plating until he took to Nicol-plating. The manager of the red-legged runts of Rockford succeeded in placing this obstacle to human progress in the office of umpire and then flattered himself that he owned his picturesque carcass. And so indeed it seems he does.

He has been making Christmas gifts of every point in the game to Rockford, and yesterday he handed the victory to sawed-off Nicol on a glass dish with parsley trimmings. It was a brutal revival of the creed and practices of Dick Turpin. The honor and virtue of the national game was ravished, plucked and made a theme of idle jest. Corruption and

conspiracy stalk through the Western Association like a hired hand through a brewery. The whole foundation, cap-stone and smear of the Republic is tottering into drooling and dreary ruin.
Skat the blad-dadded snork anyhow.
[Quincy (Ill.) Daily Herald, June 12, 1895]

A graduate with an advanced degree from the School of Dysfunctional Baseball Journalism penned this mythic beauty:

Great jumping Jupiter and flaming balls of fire! To be jamboreed, razooed, golly-washed, buffeted and stingareed by nine little St. Paul Saints until the faces of the cranks are as swollen from crying as the cheeks of a small boy stung by bumblebees; to be stamped into the yielding, mushy loam of Exposition park and buried under a score of 23 runs 'against'; to be slapped, jerked, twitched, pulled and pushed until the whole spiritual, spinal, moral, mental and physical nature is everlastingly flabbergasted. It is enough to drive the dog star from his kennel. Nay, more; it is woe sufficient to cause a grand opera prima donna to retire to a convent.
[Kansas City Times, reprinted in the Saint Paul Globe, April 27, 1897]

This column sub-header, expressing heartache over a lopsided loss, might well have been uttered by a wailing banshee reincarnated as a Brooklyn sportswriter—or a failed entry in a creative writing contest:

> *O, Ye Muse, That Dwelleth in*
> *the Slough of Despond and*
> *Feedeth on the Fricasseed*
> *Wails of Thrice Doomed Souls,*
> *Fly Hither and Give Thy Aid in*
> *Framing the Words of Anguish*
> *That Must be Herewith Writ—*
> *Small Wonder That the*
> *Heavens Weep and Gloom*
> *Pervades the Town—The Score,*
> *O! Ye Tears, Was 11 to 3.*
> *[Brooklyn Eagle, May 14, 1893]*

Here is another diseased work seasoned with erudite Gallic salt:

The Kansas City Times thus speaks of one of Manager Manning's pitchers:

"Young McFarland is pleasant to look upon. With cheeks like Siberian crabs, he is at once a delight and a pain. He has a blasé and sangfroid and pâté de foie gras manner of acting in poker's only rival as the national pastime; it is nice to see him throw the ball. He puts his daintily gloved left hand upon his off hip, raises it to the ball in his nigh hand, taps the ground uneasily with his left foot, smiles at the theater party in the grand stand, and then his left foot suddenly erupts and shatters the atmosphere. He wiggles uneasily like a tramp with camel's hair underwear on in August, screws his trolley around until he faces 'Connie' Connaughton, casts his mild blue eyes back with a sort of lonesome, is-there-a-light-in-the-window-for-me look and with a grand pas seul, like a $4-a-month man opening a keg of nails, he shies the ball toward the plate."
[Saint Paul Globe, April 30, 1897]

This rambling outpouring of free-association blather reads like a sequel to *The Jabberwocky*:

Now, about the only man I know who has not been killed every now and then is this tall Texan, that Anak from the Navasota swamps, Garvin, of Chicago.

He is a wonderful man, is Garvin. He looks like a curvester, a kinkster, a cunning, twirling thief, with a crafty phiz* and a hybrid repertoire. In appearance he is cross between Uriah Heep and Oily Gamin. He is tall, thin, flabby, sinuous, consumptive-looking, clammy guylet.

But he can pitch. Why his tender kinks, coils, twists, undulates, seethes and hisses like an angry rattlesnake. It comes along slowly until it gets almost to the plate. Then it cumulates, breaks, and instantly achieves new speed and power, for all the world like a big, lumbering wave comes along at seacoast resorts.

Majestically, powerfully, but slowly, then breaking. It seethes, rushes, ducks, dodges and wiggles, like a myriad of living, hateful, noxious things. His curve writhes like a long-lashed whip in the hands of an Eskimo dog driver.

"Sometimes I have watched this Garvin pitch and wondered that his ball does not explode like a shrapnel shell. His curves are like himself, sallow, writhy, snaky-looking things, entertaining to look at but Hades to hit.

Hitting him hard is impossible. His weakness is on the dump.

Drop them down and he will have trouble getting them. Brooklyn worked for eight innings to kill him, in vain. In the ninth they began to bunt. Nine runs came in a minute. But to hit Garvin, to meet it square on the nose, to La Joie or Wagner him, he is the hardest."
[St. Louis Republic, June 10, 1900]
[* physiognomy]

The same pitcher, Garvin, was again appraised in similar wordy tones of another equally addled author:

Back and forward swung a long, sinewy arm, a human catapult, today, out on the field where Chicago gives battle to all league invaders. Behind the directing the leathern shot that was hurled toward helpless batsmen was a pair of eyes as unerring as any that have ever guided a pistol bullet. Only the long, steady sweep was seen, and then something hissed by in an angry manner and landed against the soft leather of a mitt with a dead thump.

Nine warriors under Major General Ned Hanlon (Brooklyn manager) attempted to change the course of this ugly twisting ball. Many a sigh was sent up by these invading braves as backs were broken and sored in vain attempts to connect with the missiles from the swinging catapult that was mowing them down. They wished and longed for something a trifle wider than the clubs they brought with them, and well they might.

Humiliated by a shut out the day before, the Brooklyns thirsted for revenge and "they got it," so a fan said, 'in the neck.' For eight long innings they tried in vain to start from home to home again. Then in the ninth, when Chicago was in the verge of scoring another shut out, a hit, a base on balls and an error gave Brooklyn a tally. Before the shoots of Garvin, the present champions of the National League seemed as puny as a baby in the path of a modern locomotive. They were almost helpless. They got nothing more than five singles.
[Brooklyn Eagle, July 1, 1900]

What happened when writers hatched from the same blighted egg of schizophrenic journalism told the story of a ball game in outlandish narrative? Feast your eyes on the answer, a recounting of Quincy's sixth-inning uprising against Omaha, which hung on to win, 18-17.

At the commencement of the sixth, the bulletin board showed nine runs for the Rourkes (captain, Quincy) and five for the Andy

Sommers mob (captain, Omaha). In their half of this memorable inning, the Omahas added three more to their total, which made it 12 to 5. But what did the Quinces do in their half?

Mertes came up first. Mertes is imported, and has a big blue turkey buzzard tattooed on his chest. He has a voice full of old door mats and an unabated forehead. He wiped his nose on his sleeve and grasped his club and looked. He hit and the ball ripped its way through the ozone out over right field. Boxy was there and muffed the ball with remorseless eclat.

And Mangan comes up.

Mangan is built like a sand hill farm, well laid out, and he stands at an angle of 45 degrees sou'east. He took the precaution when very young to run a barbed wire through his legs, and in drains, ditches and subways his frame is well supplied. He sags a trifle in the chest, but otherwise is up to the best standard of Quincy citizenship. He hit the ball a resonant whang and two bags were his'n, the imported youth skating home.

Krehmeyer next toes the pan. He used to live in Omaha, and is courageous enough to face a cast iron lion. He is very beautiful, and from the looks of his clothes, his laundress has an easy time of it. While quite young, Charlie got hold of an old tin lantern and ate the top of it. He fell very sick and they thought he would die, but he recovered and his parents still refuse to forgive him.

To show how well he was yesterday, he placed his tree against one of the Deacon's rainbow curves and straightened it out like a chalk line. It hit the fence and netted a couple of pillows and another run.

Mango came in. Right here Andy Sommers altitudinized the sphere and Paddy Boyle swallowed it when it came down. That made one out, but what did the Quinces care?

Jack Johnson, a cousin of Jasper's, was at the bat. I don't exactly know how to describe Jack's style, but it is eminently suited to the Deacon's best bent balls. He has a voluptuous form, is scarcely 40 years of age, entirely respectable and plain enough to be appreciated by the most fastidious.

He had his hammer with him, and pounded out a single. Then Mike Johnson arrived. He is no relation to Jack, but looks enough like him to be his sister. Mike isn't much of a hitter when there are no pipes around. He pushed a little, hollow-eyed, thin-chested grounder down to Munyon, and Munyon, knowing the girls were in the grandstand, tried to stop it after turning three handsprings and one double somersault.

Of course his effort was a dire and dismal failure. Mike reached first, Krehmeyer scored and Jack Johnson went to third.

Bertchold was the next man to force himself upon the public. He is very graceful in his sleep, and weighs something like 140 pounds, without his feet.

He smashed the Deacon for a bag. Then Paddy Boyle endeavored to tear the lights out of Broderick's grounder, but after wrestling with it collar and elbow rules for over a minute, he gave it up. In the meantime, Jack and Mike swarmed over the plate.

Captain Mac was now in a terrible humor, and he acted just like Patsey Tebeau used to when he had hydrophobia. He ate up all the grass in front of the west bleachers, together with a couple of sections of the intervening fence.

But the Quinces never winced. They simply shrugged their ears and went on chopping wood.

McGreavey now stepped up to the pan like a naiad queen, well soaped, approaching the bath tub. McGreavey has a long-waisted face, and means well. He hit a hard one out to old man Seary, and Emmett made a lunch of it.

That was two out, with Mertes, the imported, at the bat. This time he cracked out a nice one, and Paddy Boyle's second miscue spared Mangan's fair young life, Krehmeyer, the beautiful, tears off his second two-sacker, Mertes and Mango both tallying.

Then Sommers elevated one to Boyle, which he fearlessly tackled, held and the nightmare was over.
[Omaha Daily Bee, July 6, 1894]

    A writer in the New Orleans Times-Democrat has, in his leisure moments, culled some gems from some of the reports of baseball during the season and presents them as follows:

"Lockjaw sent a messenger to Kingdom Come that threatened to scrape the stars out of the sky. It fell into the trap of O'Rourke, who froze to it, while the crowd on the bleaching boards shivered the air. Radspinner pushed a lawn-mower over to center that left a blue streak behind it in its eagerness to do the Eli act. Goblets lifted a regular blue-bottle buzzer that fell into Sandy's bread-winners, but there wasn't enough fly paper there and it didn't stick.

"Fitzjones got an undercut, and banging the ball on the nose, took second, while the sphere went sailing, the angels only knew where, and though not on speaking terms with the white-robed throng, O'Rafferty got a clue and took the wandering leather into camp when it dropped from the clouds with the perfumed breath of Paradise still on its whiskers. Hague's curves were deadlier than curvature of the spine, hissing over the plate, hot as a kitchen stove, and after the usual swipes,

Bladdergast was sentenced to the bench for assaulting the wide outdoors.
[Pacific Commercial Advertiser (Honolulu), September 13, 1889]

Other Examples of Poetic Genius

It looked very much yesterday as though the crew sailing under the skull and cross-bones flag on the waters of the Ohio and Allegheny would lose their prey. The senatorial merchantmen has clapped on all canvas and seemed about to escape. A loaded shot across the bows brought the victims to, and they were soon forced to walk the plank. The Pirates sent another craft to Davy Jones, or in other words, Pittsburg defeated Washington yesterday.
[Evening Star (Washington, D.C.), August 20, 1895]

Cornelius is a young man Watkins dug up out of one of the Indian mounds up on Superior's billowy shore. He looks something like a soup bone and has a face on him that resembles a yard of red flannel hung out on the clothesline to dry. He would make a good ornament for the new city hall. The gyasticutises (sic) wouldn't be in it with him. Just before pitching a ball, he makes a kick with his off foot at his chin, shuts his eyes and lets her go.
[Omaha Daily Bee, June 20, 1891]

On the occasion of the Maysville (Ky.) team of taking three straight from despised arch-rival, Ashland, came these giddy words of jubilation:

Now, Bre'r Miller (Ashland player/captain), will you be good?
Dam up Niagara Falls with tissue paper; bottle up the Atlantic Ocean in a whisky flask; paste "to let" on the moon; catch a flash of lightning between your thumb and finger; build a fence around a winter supply of summer weather; harness a thunderbolt to a sulky; waft all the clouds out of the sky with a lady's fan; saddle and ride a hurricane; fasten a dish rag to the tail of a comet; pack up all the stars in a beer keg; knock a tornado out of time with your fist; put Hades to cool in a springhouse; put the sky in your pocket; unbuckle the belly band of eternity; but never, never allow yourself to fancy for a moment that you poor little wonders stand a ghost of a show against our aggregation of hard hitters.
[Daily Public Ledger (Maysville, Ky.), June 1, 1895]

The Scrapbook of More Zippy Baseball Whimsy

Reader, relish the redolent resplendence of these fantastical passages:

Who is the New York Sun's Pittsburg base ball correspondent? He is an original, beyond doubt. Here is something worthy of Caylor in the palmy days of his Gazette reporting.

It is the report of the New York-Pittsburg game of September 18, when the fight was very close up to the eighth inning, at which time the score stood at 1 to 1 and then New York rallied in their eighth inning and came in victors by 5 to 1, Pittsburg having led by 1 to 0 up to the seventh inning.

The Sun's correspondent, in describing the contest, says:

"(Pitcher) Mr. Galvin, Buffalo's fairy, started in today to place his trademark high up in the starry scroll of fame, but somehow or other the old sport lost his grip and fell from the ladder in a mangled heap. The late Jerry Jerome one time told a story that he saw Mr. Cody, otherwise known as Buffalo Bill, give a rattlesnake the first bite in an argument without gloves. So with (manager) Mutrie's aggregation, they gave the famished Pittsburgs the first nibble at the cake, and then when fond hearts were buoyant with hope and expectancy they just bagged it and bolted the balance of the goodies.

"It was one of the shameless exhibitions of gluttony ever seen in Pittsburg, and none of the base ball enthusiasts in this city will ever wear themselves down to skeleton proportions with grief if the black robed terrors never come this way again. It was against all rule of common decency or propriety to treat Galvin so. There are many men in the New York team like O'Rourke, who have been playing ball with Jeems (Mutrie) ever since the days when the spray from the turbulent waters of the flood washed over the gangway of the ark.

"They went at the old hero from the city that sprung rivers on an expectant public, and marked their triumphant pathway with bright red gore. The home team had no excuses to offer or apologies to make. It was too clear a case. They just threw themselves at the mercy of the court and took chances on the tenderer feelings of the ruling power.

"Up to the seventh inning all the Pittsburgers could do was to chew gum and holler. It was like a race between thoroughbreds. The home team made the pace. They led to the quarter and by the half. Mutrie had to keep his teeth shut to hold his heart inside its proper boundaries, and (team owner) Mr. Day looked as nervous and fidgety as

a newly married man. On they came, with New York taking the dust, but as they swung into the stretch the Pittsburgs were seen to be in distress. The New Yorks had located on the soft spot and it was all over, but they rode it out, and finished in a walk, with lots and lots to spare."
[Brooklyn Eagle, October 21, 1888]

In the closing game of the recent series between Chicago and Detroit, the fourth inning is graphically described by the Chicago Herald's reporter.
He says:
"The fourth inning came with Ryan at the bat. A weak cheer arose from a Chicago man who sat in the memorable nest of cranks. The center fielder was quick to act. He plugged the ball for a base hit. Then Sullivan fouled out to Brouthers. But Farrell was mighty. He was large. He fell upon the ball with a bang that started every crank in the three stands to their feet. The ball soared high in the air. At its maximum altitude it looked no larger than the bowl of a clay pipe. Away and away it glided, as though it were being propelled by some power within its black cover. Over infield and outfield, over a whitewashed fence, over the heads of a hundred spectators who sat on the roof of a shed and through the branches of a big elm tree in a reputable citizen's dooryard went that battered ball.

"Another home run and two more large and succulent runs were won by Chicago. The Detroits were now but one run ahead. The great rally of the Illinoisans in the face of terrific hitting by their opponents and the severe rulings of an umpire would have won the admiration of any crowd but the one sweating in those three rickety stands in Detroit that day. But there was no cheering, save that which came from the lone Chicagoan. The cranks were in a state of coma; they were dared; they would not have bet a fried egg against a crop of cotton that the Chicagos would not win after all. But the Detroits again took a strong lead in the fourth, and after the Chicagos had been retired in this inning the score stood 7 to 4 in favor of the home team."
[Wichita Eagle, August 5, 1888]

Up to this time the Chicagos had been unable to do anything with the grinning red-faced Morris. But in the third inning they began to feed off him. It was a cold lunch in the drizzling, sticky rain, but the spectators seemed to enjoy the banquet. Ghoulish-looking Hutchinson sank his fangs on the ball for a base. Ryan was not so hungry, and sat down.

Van Haltren, however, was ravenous. He was swinish. He stuck his fork in the ball, which looked larger than a manhole, and then swiped it with his knife. The spherical-looking pudding went up into the air with a noise that sounded like the cough of a horse in a church stable, and after soaring in a diagonal direction, dropped among the hoop skirts and tomato crates in a vacant lot in Harrison street. Two runs came over the plate.

It need only one more to tie the score. Morris took a reef in his trousers and wiped the rain out of his eyes. Then he gave Duffy his base on balls. Anson plucked the wishbone out of the ball for a base, sending Duffy to third. Pfeffer, who was also hungry, was given a pudding, which he dropped with a soft, mellow noise away out in center field. Duffy crossed the plate and the score was a tie.

The crowd yelled uproariously. Anson was now on second. Farrell popped up an easy fly to Smith. Old Anson trotted out of the base line to make a demonstration in order to disconcert the effervescent and carbonated "Pop." He jumped in front of the shortstop, waved his red arms and opened his face. Smith simply squeezed the ball and before the 'old man' knew what he was about he was folded in a neat double play from short to second."
[Pittsburg Dispatch, May 12, 1889]

In the recent 1 to 0 game, in which the Chicagos defeated the Washington, there was some great playing by the old man, for The Chicago Globe narrates the winning of the contest this fashion:

"Uncle (Anson) took his bat, determined to drive home hard, but all he could do was to force Ryan out at the plate, getting to first himself. Then it was that Uncle's massive brain began to whirr, and a brilliant scheme rolled off the spinning wheels. Before Abbey had even started to pitch the ball, Uncle walked off first and strolled down the line with all the dignity of a tomcat walking the woodshed roof on a moonlight eve.

"Of course Abbey threw to second, while the Senators laughed a loud, coarse ha ha at the idea of catching poor Uncle asleep. But Uncle cavorted up and down the line like a yearling calf charging a book agent, and before the Senatorial gang could catch the old man, Dahlen skated over the plate and the one run of the day was tallied. It was a neat trick, smoother than a quart of glycerine, and clearly showed the supremacy of mind over matter and the superiority of a real head to a jug of mud like the brain of (captain) Danny Richardson.

"The last phrase spoils the paragraph, however, for it is a slur on a player who little deserves it. Danny Richardson is all right. The only trouble is that one man does not make a full team."
[Brooklyn Eagle, August 30, 1892]

"Old Pete" Browning, the famous Louisville gladiator, appeared with Columbus. He only made one hit and two errors. Pete's lamps are very bum and a Roentgen ray would undoubtedly discern pachyderms, trinidads, plate glass, cobble stones and everything else in his throwing arm. The first ball pitched to Pete caused him to stop and blink like an owl. He couldn't see it any more than a rabbit.
[Kansas City World, reprinted in the Saint Paul Globe, May 17, 1896]

Fate, in the shape of a slight-built young man bearing the somewhat of a Deadwood Dick Library cognomen of Wilfred Carsey, loomed up like a fly in a mug of milk against the Senators yesterday afternoon, and as a consequence the Toga Wearers are not so chipper as they were."
[Morning Times (Washington, D.C.), September 12, 1896]

Thomas, who was putting them over for Detroit, lobbed up 'a beauty'—as "Lath" (Arlie Latham) would say—and Crooks swiped it. By the long hairs in the plaster, you ought to have seen that ball go. Say, it never finished rolling until Jack got to third. But he never stopped, and steering sou'wes' by a half sou' just crossed the outer bar in time to make the dock as the ball started back into Big Mike Trost's hands. Did he slide? Well, say! He made that white suit with the red letters on it look like a grave digger's pajamas. Then how they howled! Say, boy, there'll never be another like that game. We beat 'em to a fare-you-well, 7 to 3.
[Columbus (Ohio) Daily Dispatch, reprinted in the Saint Paul Globe, April 26, 1897]

(Pitcher) Friend had promised Manning (Kansas City manager) that he would win the game for him, and he sent the ball to the plate, singing that old familiar tune, "Just Tell Them That You Saw Me." The farmers from Minneapolis missed it every time they tried to guess which shell the pea was under. Friend served hot tamales when they expected ice cream, and then mulled their cider with an icicle.
[Kansas City Times, reprinted in the Saint Paul Globe, June 25, 1897]

Exciting? Well, just ask the 2,000 cranks who dragged themselves home to a late dinner last night with the flounces all torn off of their nervous systems and their lungs stretched across their manly bosoms like so many porous plasters.
AskHerbert Whitehill, the boy with the carmine cheeks and a

hump on his back, who, in the eleventh inning, with the score tied with a hangman's knot, and Paddy Boyle on third base, couldn't have carried the ball out of the diamond if he had had it in a hod.

Ask Joseph Emmett Seery, the man who used to make mud pies with Israel Putnam's little sisters, and who, upon the same vital occasion, hit the ball with the savage ferocity of a man about to sink his teeth in a hot tamale.

Then get a shotgun and approach Papa Rourke, the man whose shoes are full of feet, and who has to tie his neck in a knot before he can pull his shirt on. Ask him if it was exciting when he fell like a shovelful of mush over Mr. Somers when he overran third in the eleventh.

Ask Patrick Henry Boil, the boy with the rusty hair and a sunburnt smile, if it was exciting, and in the same breath inquire of him why, every time a ball is knocked down to him, he steps on one leg or the other and tries to catch it on the point of his elbows.

Then gently go up to Wood, the gentleman with the décolleté cheek bones, after you have got him firmly tied to a fence post, and ask him why he dances the ghost dance every time a grounder glides out his way, and grabs the hair off the ball after it has gotten by him.

Then you will probably understand just what an afternoon we had of it.
[Omaha Daily Bee, May 13, 1894]

This picturesque greeting to Tebeau was handed out by a St. Louis writer, and it is not surprising that the Clevelands won that day:

"When Patrick Rosemary de Tebeau, Sieur de Cleveland and Comte de Kerrie Patche, rose from his snowy white couch yesterday and looked forth upon early morning lief in the Rue de Biddle, he was mentally a very sore man. The vacant betomato-canned lots and battening goats had no soothing effect upon him, and the very sight of the bare-legged scions of adjacent families playing "ketch" upon the street fairly drove him into frenzies of passion.

"'Them kids,' said the Lord of Cleveland, 'them little runty kids can play better ball than them guys of mine.' And he swore by his halidom that the night would view him a conqueror or a corpse.

"No more would he bend his proud knee in homage to the hated tribe of Miller (?Pittsburgh). No more would he hearken to the umpire. The unconquerable spirit of the ancient French noblesse arose within him; he was once the Tebeau of old, the fierce, bounding gorilla, the terror of umpires and bete noir of young, nervous, unseasoned pitchers."
[Morning Herald (Baltimore), April 30, 1895]

Burdock (pitcher, Sioux City) was there determined to have the fight, and rebuscent Harrahan (ss/captain, Sioux City) was with him. Oh, dear! oh, dear! how buoyant and hilarious that great man was. He had victory on his pale lapis lazuli eye. There was triumph in his lofty tread. Like Banquo's ghost, he would not down. He was a daisy. He had jocular quips and tantalizing bits of repartee for the groaning populace in the grandstand, and when the tying run scooted across the plate, he executed a few steps that would have shamed the greatest song-and-dance man who ever skipped over a stage.
[Omaha Daily Bee. April 28, 1890]

"Big Fat Jakey" Strauss was on hand as big as a skinned horse. He has had a new ash pan put in his mouth, and whenever he opened it, the people recoiled as before some yawning abyss. Jack Farrah made himself very numerous, too, and when this prize beauty got up on the coaching lines, he spouted like an old-fashioned volcano. If you have ever been admitted into the mysterious workings of this fellow's face, you can form some vague idea of how he loped up to the umpire in the ninth inning, hooked his upper lip on his collar button and poured a torrent of passionate oratory into his off auricular. If you ever watched a boa constrictor endeavoring to cough up a cow it had swallowed in an unguarded moment, you may be able to imagine Bill Willie Letcher telling Colonel McKelvey that he was a fit subject for the garbage wagon.
[Omaha Daily Bee, May 9, 1894]

Enshrined among the memories of dolce far niente 'neath the cerulean vault which poets have sung for ages is a face—swarthy, sinister, determined. It may have belonged to one of the banditti who swarmed over Italy's soil, but the chances are it was owned by a macaroni maker.

The simple ideas that were inspired in primitive times by the contemplation of the spectacle of Count Campau pushing a banana cart through the streets of Genoa have been transformed, if not completely overthrown, by his coaching performances on the ball field in these modern times.

In this day and age the fans have scarcely ever heard there existed such a man as the Count, and only recall the name as figuring in some old poem, pervaded with a mythological perfume, and they didn't know what to make of him. But the old men in the audience remembered well the venerable banana vendor, and as he pirouetted about over the budding dandelions in his fiendish Italian glee, their minds were led back to a ancient times, and open-eyed they gazed upon him as one resurrected and infused with new body and new life.

Is it any wonder, then, we lost the game, when compelled to buck against such a mould and antiquated curio as the Count?

So much for history.

[Omaha Daily Bee, April 28, 1892]

This how the Boston Post celebrates Wednesday's victory over the Chicago sluggers:

"When beans meet pork (Boston v. Chicago), then comes the glorious summer of our discontent," sang the poetic man who sat over by first base yesterday afternoon, at the Roxbury forum, and shied airy persiflage and peanut shells at Uncle Adrian Colt Rearer Anson (player/manager). And the old man bowed his silver locks and wept.

"Pork had met beans—Chicago had tackled Boston, and the George Washington of base ball had been slaughtered in the shambles with his eight disciples. The champions had spiked him in the ribs, trampled ruthlessly open his front shirt, and then put him down cellar and shut the trap door over him. And, worst of all, Michael Jeunesse Kelly and Hugh Duffy, of all men, had been instrumental in his defeat. It was a hard, cruel blow for the Swedish giant, and the poor old gentleman felt it."

[Brooklyn Eagle, June 10, 1892]

When the smoke of battle lifted from Exposition park field yesterday, the cheers of a happy multitude could be heard rising, swelling and echoing even to the outskirts of the village. A tremendous battle had just been fought and the warm blood of the recent dead was still steaming in the trenches. Victory rested with neither side and gaunt-eyed defeat stared at the scene in undisturbed amazement.

The tide of battle had been with the Turks. Edhem Pasha Alleniski (Detroit captain Allen) seemed about to triumph over General Jack Smolenski Carneyo (Kansas City captain, Carney). There was joy in the harms of Detroit and the band was playing before the largest seraglio. In the gloaming and the ninth inning the Grecians, who had been steadily pressing the Turks backward across the Thessalian frontier, tied the score and scattered dismay in the ranks of the enemy.

Then Prime Minister Haskell (umpire), in behalf of the powers of darkness, declared an armistice (13-13 tie), while the multitude applauded.

There was sorrow in the heart of Edam P. Alleniski when, with his Wahoo warriors, he trooped from the field of carnage. He chided his hired help, for he was wroth.

Above the din and roar of many voices sounded the name of one long absent from public print—Crown Prince Constantine Bevis, (Kansas City pitcher) surnamed the "Kid." He it was who had saved the day and earned the encomiums of the populace.

A vagrant whirlwind would have created less excitement than the finish of yesterday's game. Out of a bad beginning came a royal ending.
[Kansas City Journal, May 23, 1897]

In the language of a horseman who came over from Lexington to root for "Old Kaintuck," the game went thus wise:

"Looeyville went away from the post like a stake horse befo' the Cincinnati hoss got into motion. She set a hot clip around the fus' turn, but died out an' were fetched befo' the half was reached. Cincinnati jus' run an even race, lettin' out a kink whenever Looeyville got near. In the stretch Cincinnati run easy an' bridle free. The Looeyville hoss tried for a nose finish, an' while it looked like she was a-pressing the Cincinnati mount, she was never in it. While the form book shows only a length, it might jes' as well be ten. Looeyville was a good hoss, but Cincinnati's better."
[Kansas City Journal, May 23, 1897]

For once here's a game that will go down on record as one in which there's nothing to tell. It was one, two, three and out. That is, for the visitors. Faces at third base for them were as scarce as Spanish doubloons in a crap game. Only once did they land on the missile—at that. Gray was more surprised than Daniels, for he didn't know he hit it—and, when the ball ploughed its way through the summer breezes over in the peach orchard, he ambled around the bases as if he were treading upon forbidden territory. No one else got anywhere near home plate save when they stood up there and allowed themselves to be crucified.

Hit him?

They couldn't have hit Pete Daniels with a bundle of bats, let alone one stingy stick.

It was Daniels at the break—Daniels at the quarters—Daniels at the half; in the stretch, it was Daniels by 20 lengths, and under the wire he came away with his mouth wide open and his head swinging.

Oh! what a beating he gave hard-loser Watty.

Thumped him to death.

Picked him up and set him down.

*Jumped on him.
Rolled over him.
And—
That's all."*

We got our start in the fifth. Two men were out and Eddie O'Meara waited for a good one—and went to first. Here Daniels lit up against a low one, driving it skipping and sobbing out along the ground to left. Butler bumped one over Stewart's head. Hulen put another in the same place. Mertes sent his contribution sizzling out across the sand to center. Did they hit it? Umph, umph! They laid up agin' it. Je' pushed it. For three runs.

In the seventh, Crooks lambasted 'Brownie' Foreman's big brother for three bags and Daniels brought him home with a merry bump out to right. "Hoggie" was playing tag with himself during this interim.

It wouldn't do to let them off so easily, and in the final chapter we went at 'em again. Again, with two outs, O'Meara reached down in the grab-bag and brought up a base on balls. Two diamond-studded fumbles by Eustace—wonder how he pronounces that name?—and Hulen's single out over Stewart's head score Eddie.

*A sum total of 5.
To 1.
That they didn't know they had until after the seventh inning was over.
Viva Pete!
There's a man that can free Cuba.*
[Columbus (Ohio.) Dispatch, reprinted in the Saint Paul Globe, May 15, 1897]

There was a flavor of allspice about today's contest, which carried one back to the days when (Pittsburg owner) J. Palmer O'Neill's follie comiques played so many week stands from home and died fighting day after day. When that lad with the conflagration locks stepped into the box, he grew coldly proud after he had fooled the Reds' boss home-knocker into striking out. It was a long time before he coaxed another into belting the air with his club, and ere that occurred, Ehret had trouble enough to fleck his flame-tinted hair with gray. Latham, McPhee and Browning cracked out singles in succession, sending one earned run over the rubber. A liner into left sent two more home. Vaughn reached third, and scored when Smith sent a corker to left. There is no telling just where the slaughter would have ended had not "Germany" attempted to travel to third after Dwyer's safe spark to right.

Donovan fired the ball straight to Farrell and Smith was caught. "Four runs will never win this game" was the declaration of "Calliope" Miller a bit later after he and Beckley had started things off with hits. He was right. Had the Reds stopped at that limit the Keystone Italians would be canning another scalp for their winter preserves. Smith, however, forced Beckley out, but on Mack's fly to Holliday, Miller skirmished home. The "Gladiator" put in right had made two fine running catches when "Lath" took the crowd into his confidence and said: "Billy Earle has got Pete under control today."

The old warrior stood like an astronomer looking for more canals in Mars. There was life in every inning. Van Haltren dragged down a line fly from Hoover's bat in the third that turned a home run into an out. The Smith family was strictly in it. The Cincinnati member stretched one hit into a double by a vest button scrape of a dozen feet. He scored when Ehret became wild after Dwyer's rap. The latter was sent in by Holliday.

...The last half of the eighth was exciting. The first dews of evening had fallen. Farrell was hit with the ball. With two out, Beckley cracked out a liner to center that Holliday failed to see and Jake reached second. The Pittsburg band awoke the echoes of Lick Run when Elmer Smith dropped a ballot among the sun gods for a home walk. Mack's grounder was thrown low by McPhee and things looked squally when Bierbauer's liner got away from Browning, with two men on bases, Egret came to bat. A hit meant a tied score but he sent a high fly which Holliday took on the run. The game was then called on account of darkness.
[Pittsburg Dispatch, October 14, 1892]

Jakey Strauss hit the sphere a welt that filled the air with gemmed colors—sapphire, emerald, topaz and amethyst glanced athwart the sky—and when the Deacon finally picked up the ball way out among the buffalo grass near Jeff Bedford's sign, Swart was shaking hands with Manager Buck at the bench, and Jakey was tearing down from third like a big St. Bernard with a tin can tied to his tail.
[Omaha Daily Bee, July 3, 1891]

The mourners were few but boisterous, and before the last nail was driven into the coffin of old '92, those who had turned out to the last, saw making noise enough to drive a mass meeting of howling dervishes into the woods. There was a little 156-pounder in the box who was doing the pitching for the Reds. He wore a nondescript sort of uniform, and he twisted himself into the living figure "7" before he let

the ball drive. That deceptive motion was puzzling enough to fool an ordinary batsman, and added to that he had the speed of the whirlwind. There was no demonstration when the chunky mortal began his task, but as the game wore on and not a semblance of a hit was charged against him, the crowd unbuckled and every put out was signalized by cheers.
[Pittsburg Dispatch, October 16, 1892]

It appears that the waggish spirit of Lawrence Washburne haunted the sporting desk of the Chicago *Inter Ocean* newspaper long after his untimely death in 1891, judging by the outpouring of game accounts composed in the same extravagant style.

Titillate your baseball palate with these lulus:

Take them out and drown them! Pour the water especially deep on Bill Everitt, who failed at the decisive moment, and made a bow-legged, trans-Atlantic chimpanzee of himself, and would have made monkeys of the whole team had not nature long since saved him the trouble.

Two out of three to Louisville! And after those thirty-six runs of Tuesday! Oh, the shame, the horror, the agony of it—the unutterable, inexpressible worthlessness of the whole proceeding.

Win it? Why, that game ought to have been stowed away so tight that Apollyon couldn't have pried it out with a bungstarter. There was no more cause, barring the antics of that misguided, zoological garden, Thornton, in left field. There was no more excuse for losing that game than there was for Grover Cleveland's being President. Wow and wowah, but it was outrageous.
[Inter Ocean (Chicago), July 1, 1897]

There was a succession of noises that sounded like a red-headed water girl dropping a tray of dishes down an elevator shaft and then all was still. Pfeffer walked in from second in a dazed sort of a way and told Menefee to pitch the game out, while Kilroy tried to hide behind a bat on the bench, but it was everlastingly too late to save the game.
[Inter Ocean (Chicago), May 14, 1894]

Tears blind the writer's eyes and his pen staggers across the page, for he loveth the Chicago team better than Frankfurter sausage, and the game of Tuesday has left so few heartstrings to tear this screed of sorrow must necessarily be short—short as the sorrow of the Spiders (Cleveland) over the woe they have caused.

It was worse than the seven-year itch with a complication of

Chinese warts on the face. It was heartrending, outrageous, disgraceful, soul-harrowing, putrid, awful enough to scare a blind building into nervous prostration, and people were compelled to see it.

A large man in the grand stand, who has followed the fortunes of the Colts through swamp and upland, and who has the extreme honor of being acquainted with Jimmy Ryan, waited until the eighth inning, when he solemnly spat three times upon the floor and departed.

It was more than even his massive strength could bear, and as he trickled mournfully down the stairs, while the hits were still running the legs off Decker, he was heard to swear softly in the language of tears at fate and Tebeau, and even at Anson.
[Inter Ocean (Chicago), July 2, 1896]

Willie Bill Hutchison (pitcher) can again look you in the eye.

For many months Willie Bill has been sneaking away from the ball field through dark alleys and by circuitous routes to his home on the North Side. He has been shunned of men and ostracized by women. He has been made the butt of ridicule and the target of derision. He has been frowned down upon and made small of. His name has been mentioned only with execrations and anathemas as conjunctives.

Out of the little Iowa town whence Willie hails, and where his name has, in years agone, been used to advertise the wee burg, the name of Hutchison has been stricken from the tiny fly-leaf directory. Every yellow dog in the village has been christened "Hutch," and the name has become a synonym for all that is weakly, fainthearted, and feeble.

Yesterday afternoon, ten minutes after the game between the Colts and Von der Ahe's St. Louis Browns, a stalwart, proud-bearing form strutted out of the main gate of the park. Orations were delivered in front of the big grange store and a pack mule was started off inland thirteen miles away to bear a message to Willie's folks, telling them he has again come to life.

Two sickly little infield hits, one of them strained into a hit out of consideration for Dahlen, and a two-baser were all that the Browns could find Hutchison for yesterday. His heart has come back to him and he pitched in his old-time form.
[Inter Ocean (Chicago), August 1, 1894]

Readers, here is the longest sentence ever written by a baseball reporter—guaranteed! Enjoy every word of this rambling tour de force, which consumes a minute and a half of otherwise perfectly good time:

After a wearisome, one-sided, whopper-jawed conglomeration of inanities, stupidities, erratic deliveries and incoherent team work more or less distributed among the players of both nines, the debris was shoveled up at the end of about 210 minutes, which had been occupied in the exercises aforementioned, interspersed with arguments with (Umpire) General Phil Sheridan, specimens of ball-play badly in need of the laundry, and merry-go-rounds on the bases, punctuated by monotonous calls of "four" in sequential regularity, at the sound of which the heads of the patriotic fans, rooters, devotees and mere dilettanti constituting the moderate attendance would sink in weariness, only to rise again with the faces on the fronts of the aforesaid heads wearing an expression in which hope and despair were curiously intermingled with an expression of chastened joy left over from the day before, when the Tigers had been done for three straight, and by narrow margins at that, though it was evident from the very beginning, yesterday, when young Willie Dammann gave an example of real Cincinnati work by passing in one inning no less than three of the fierce and fiery-tempered gentlemen clad in uniforms which looked like the result of a hard winter on the frightener of the predaceous and intellectual sable-clad birds known to scientists as corvus Americanus, that unless something was done to stem the tide of dismal disaster, and were done in a whooping hurry, too, there would be no chance for a repetition of the glorious records of the three preceding days, which had been so filled with sunshine and joy, notwithstanding the fact that Cronin, head artillery man for Van Derrick's aggregation of malcontents, did all that in him lay to make it a series of four by whooping it up to the tune of ten bases on balls, some of which jammed men in from third across the home plate to the delectation of the wearied, yawning and hungry crowd, and to the discomfiture of a tiresome person whom the suffering neighbors christened "Jack the Screamer," who howled clangorously in the grand stand for the enemy in a vain attempt to get himself looked at, and a bunch of three high-priced mistakes by Cronin's backing was also an aid, and it was found the Tigers had gotten unto themselves thirteen runs and the Hoosiers only six, which was not enough by half, as any small boy with a rudimentary knowledge of mathematics could plainly demonstrate. [Indianapolis Journal, June 28, 1899]

14. Humor in Being Hit by a Pitch

In the early, freewheeling years of baseball, rules of play were always in a state of flux, as rule makers strove to make the game as fair as possible and to punish cheating. It was a constant battle fraught with obstacles.

A good part of the problem lay in a ready pool of opportunistic, morally-challenged schemers whose sole purpose in life, it seemed, was to remain one step ahead of baseball law. With uncanny accuracy, these quick-thinking men sought to take advantage of playing situations not covered by rules—or found loopholes in new ones—and exploited them, both instances necessitating yet more corrective entries in the ever-expanding rule book.

In 1882, for instance, regulations outlawed the sudden calling of "time" by a player while the ball and runner were still in motion on the field, thus preventing the runner from taking an extra base. Likewise, base runners deliberately running into fielders holding the ball were summarily dealt with by being called out.

Imagine the gall of rule makers, however, when, in 1887, they moved to protect players from notorious brushback artists on the mound, notably Tony Mullane, of Cincinnati, and Tim Keefe, of New York, who intimidated batters by purposely trying to hit them. This dangerous brush-back habit was checked by awarding batters first base upon being hit (or any part of their uniform) with a pitched ball.

It didn't take long for devious players to find ways to game the system, even at the risk of serious personal injury. Among the first to subvert the rule were stars of Comiskey's famous four-time winners (1886-1889) of the American Association, the St. Louis Browns, led by the cunning outfielder, Curtis Welch. Unlike others who deliberately and clumsily stuck their arms into the path of the ball, Welch honed his skills into a subtle and virtuoso performance that was once praised by baseball columnist O. P. Caylor:

> *He would stand, leaning well over the plate, as if ready to bunt the ball and then, as if trying to get his arms out of the way of the ball,*

would let it graze his wrist or the sleeve of his shirt. He had this practice "down so fine" that his calculations seldom missed it by the smallest fraction of an inch and nothing more serious than a slight external bruise, and seldom that, ever came from this practice. But many a close game was won for the Browns by the trick.
[Saint Paul Globe, September 13, 1896]

The con was immediately copied by other players who turned the very rule intended to protect them into an instrument for winning:

"The old Baltimore team was the greatest bunch of ball players ever gathered together. Every point to win a game was taken.

"Once McGraw got a base on the queerest trick ever known. A pitched ball hit his shirt. He at once pinched his arm and claimed his base. The umpire was skeptical, but McGraw showed his arm, which was red, of course, from the pinching, and was given the bag. This won the game, for it resulted in the prettiest batting rally ever seen.

"Yes, of course, a good many times I succeeded in getting hit, and the pain and throbbing were all a bluff. We were after games, and we got them.

"...When I determined to get hit in order to 'walk,' I just braced myself, tightening my muscles, and the ball would bound off like rubber. It's easy. Oh, yes, it takes nerve, but you can't play ball without nerve, and the old Baltimore team had plenty of that article, always on hand." [Salt Lake Herald, May 5, 1907]

In Other Words

Baseball writers had little trouble coming up with colorful words to describe the act of being struck by a pitch. The verbs "soaked" (which had dual meanings—to have hit a ball hard or to be fined) and "plunked" were the most commonly used, but the noun form, "rib tickler," was cuter.

More detailed descriptions, which follow, somehow had the effect of amplifying the amount of pain suffered—or taking some of it away:

Mr. Whited inadvertently lost control of the ball and

inadvertently made an indentation in Mr. Motz's anatomy, not far distant from the solar plexus.
[Kansas City Journal, July 16, 1897]

Moran again received the hurtling sphere in the diaphragm, and with both hands clasping the sore spot, ran to first.
[Omaha Daily Bee, April 30, 1890]

The first ball that left Mr. Devlin's hand caught the middleweight champion amidships, and flinging aside his stick, he trotted to first amid the portentous "Ahs!" of the army of cranks in the stand.
[Omaha Daily Bee, April 2, 1890]

Meekin began the first game by foolishly shooting a ten-pound projectile into the side elevation of Douglass's solar plexus.
[New York Journal, May 30, 1897]

Dalrymple got between the ball and the catcher before it began to curve, and he trotted to first with a couple of loosened ribs.
[Omaha Daily Bee, June 28, 1891]

Mulligan stopped an inshoot with his kneecap.
[New York Journal, May 19, 1896]

Bill Clark has a rib that is not on speaking terms with the remainder of his anatomy.
[New York Journal, May 29, 1897]

"Never touched him," exclaimed Cartwright facetiously, as the ball landed kerplunk in the small of Wilson's back and nearly pushed a hole through him.
[Source misplaced]

Hart, who did the pitching for the locals, had received instructions to defeat, kill or cripple his opponents, and as it took but a short time to convince him that the former was impossible, he started firing the sphere into the anatomies of the Brewers. This proved too expensive to the liking of the management, as none of his shots proved mortal, so that after he had filled three bases in the third with limping veterans, he was retired to the bench and Dewald was substituted in his place.

[Milwaukee Journal, June 15, 1891]

  Almost the first ball pitched struck Doyle a terrific rap on the head. The blow resounded all over the grounds, and everybody expected to see plucky Jack drop like a stricken ox, but he wasn't in the dropping business just then, as he had a pressing engagement to keep at first bag. Not only did the blow not faze him, but it put in several ounces more of ginger, and he slid down to second, and then, just to keep the thing going, got around to third without leave from anybody from Boston.
[Baltimore American, April 23, 1896]

  Then in the seventh round, Bill Clark got hit on the thumbs, where he had them furled around his bat. The impact of the ball on these fat brown thumbs sounded like slamming a wet towel against the wall, but (umpire) Emslie declared for a foul and stuck to it. A Committee on Thumbs, consisting of Scrappy Bill, Gleason and Warner, felt of Bill's mushy digits and induced him to show them to the umpire as a guarantee of good faith. But the ruling stood.
[Dryden, New York Journal, September 2, 1897]

  George Rettger opened the pitching for Milwaukee with an in-shoot. The scientists say that there is not such a thing as an in-curve, but there certainly is, for this shot into O'Rourke's back and knocked him clear to first base.
[Source misplaced]

  Hamilton gazed into the cerulean depth of Terry's eyes. He guessed a slow ball was coming along and let it hit the plug of tobacco in his hip pocket; Hallman yielded his anatomy as a sacrifice on the altar of victory.
[Inter Ocean (Chicago), July 17, 1895]

  Knaus went in to the box for Cleveland at the kick-off. He was tolerably effective, was Mr. Knauss, but he was as wildly inaccurate as a Democratic election judge. He hit Mr. Dahlen on the lobe of the left ear, and Mr. Clifford Carroll a welt that made his intercostal nerves swell up like sausages.
[Washburne, Inter Ocean (Chicago), May 9, 1891]

15. Humor in Baseball Etiquette

This is a short chapter, composed of two newspaper articles that spoofed baseball's playing rules. The "helpful" advice was freely offered to players by well-meaning and conscientious baseball writers, which, no doubt, was the culmination of deep contemplative thought and not at all composed in a moment of abject boredom or temporary writers' block.

The following "field manual of manners" was assembled by George Hobart, of the New York *Journal*:

After much research into the musty tomes of the past, and after careful consultation with all authorities, a book of baseball etiquette has been arranged and compiled by a gentleman who does not wish to have his name mentioned for sanitary reason, says G. V. Hobart. From advance sheets of the valuable work, the following extracts, dealing with the players on the field, are taken:

Rule 24.—Managers, field captains and players should refrain from an endeavor to alter the geographical formation of an umpire's face while the game is in progress. Such players may, however, entice the umpire behind the grand stand after the game and present him with a series of swift kicks. This is considered very good form, and denotes refinement on the part of the kickers.

Rule 25.—It is a social offense utterly unpardonable for any player to exclaim: "Excuse me, gentlemen, I will get it!" while running furiously after a fly ball. Custom and the best authorities have sanctioned the use of the term "I got it! I got it!" Any deviation from this rule is likely to invoke harsh criticism.

Rule 26.—When two men are out and a high ball is batted to the outfield, it is considered extremely good form for all except the player in whose territory the ball will ultimately fall, to drop their gloves and tumble over each other in their anxiety to reach a sitting position on the bench. This rule has received the sanction of the Baltimore club, and, as they are the leaders of the league 400, it permeates.

Rule 27.—The use of the prefix "Mr." in addressing the umpire is very much minor-league and entirely unprofessional. If a player desires to attract the umpire's attention and cannot do so by hitting him with a rock, that player should hurry to the club house and get an ax. An ax hurriedly applied generally brings forth the desired result.

Rule 28.—The pitcher should not carry two pounds of coal tar in his bloomers' pocket with which to decorate a new ball. One pound is sufficient.

Rule 29.—It is considered very ill-bred for a base runner to remove with his spikes portions of the bag custodian's face while sliding in to a base. If a souvenir of the occasion is desired, chip the pieces off some other portion of the opposing player's anatomy.

Rule 30.—When some unthinking person on the bleachers advances the statement that a player is in an advanced state of decomposition, that particular player should treat the originator of such a remark with contumely. If he hasn't any contumely, he should get a club and stand by the gate as the crowd files out.

Rule 31.—When a batsman's slats are misplaced by a swiftly-moving, but misguided in-shoot, he should turn quickly and bow profoundly in the direction of the grand stand. This will allay all suspicion that he struck himself with a pitched ball.

Rule 32.—When two fielders, chasing a high fly, make an earnest endeavor to stand upon the same spot of ground at the same time and become telescoped, it is not considered bad form if they ask, when they regain consciousness, for their front teeth, or their eyebrows, or any other portion of their features which may have been mislaid during the excitement.

There are many other valuable hints in the book, but it isn't wise to push a good thing with too much celerity.
[Kansas City Journal, April 18, 1897]

The next farcical guide to proper ball field decorum came from the fertile mind of Charles Dryden, and given that he and Hobart were office mates at the time, it is possible that Dryden was the author of the preceding material. Whatever the case, though, its recurring theme of equating low-class manners with bush league towns probably contained much truth.

Here is a new code of ethics, said to have been promulgated by the National League, the object being to elevate the game to the social status of golf, tiddlee-winks and lawn tennis, and import that recherché tone which has long been lacking.

Rule 1.—Field captain and thirty-third degree kickers must refrain from altering the natural expression of an umpire's features in the presence of the populace. To convey an air of correct St. Louis, Mo., the Mafia should entice said umpire into the dressing room after the game, pull a bat bag over his head and imprint a series of swift kicks. For authority on this point, see the case of Latham et al. vs. Sheridan on Thursday, April 23, 1896.

Rule 2.—Mixed-ale language reflecting on the habits and character of annual pass-holders who intimate by word of mouth that the performance of a player is in an advanced state of decomposition can be taken as conclusive evidence that the offender is hopelessly Walla Walla, Wash. It is much better to tell the critic in placid accents that he is bughouse, whatever that may be.

Rule 3.—Winning pitchers, unless they wish to be branded as irredeemably Omaha, Nebr., should avoid grooming a bright new ball on the slack breadths of their bloomers before submitting it to the batsman. Such procedure is not only heartless, but exceedingly Battle Creek, Mich., as well. Unlicensed endeavor to put good men out of the business cannot be tolerated. The ball is best practically invisible to some of them, particularly the most pronounced New York, N. Y.

Rule 4.—No League player can be too Baltimore, Md. For instance, when a batsman with an average of .372 dodges into a wild pitch or perverted inshoot that loosens his slats, he must not walk around in a gradually decreasing circle with his pallid face upturned to the grand stand, unless the game is taking place at Wilmington, Del. In this case, he is not amenable to the new code.

Rule 5.—White-garbed catchers or first basemen, if gifted with the instincts of true Brooklyn, N. Y., will abstain from depositing vast quantities of distilled tobacco in the palm of the large mitt and smiting the same with the furied fist of the other hand. Such conduct, while no doubt improving the efficacy of the performer, is now considered too Dubuque, Ia., for the big League.

Rule 6.—Another offense unpardonably Upper Sandusky, O., in itself is that of a fat-footed athlete tearing up the soil while sprinting several inches in advance of his hair and howling; "I got it! I got it!" To declare instead "I have it!" denotes the highest Boston, Mass., attainable. This rule should meet the approval of all grammar fiends.

Rule 7.—When the head-end collisions result from enraptured fielders bent on retrieving the same fly ball, the victims should not display the least sign of Mobile, Ala., nor seek to inflict further injury. The most Washington, D. C., course is for the young men to assist each other in plucking distorted teeth from the grass so as not to delay the game.

Rule 8.—For runners to willfully hamstring a bagman, or for the custodian of the bag to chip souvenirs from the faces of prostrate base-stealers with his sharp shoe plates, is now regarded as utterly El Paso,

Tex., according to the latest handbook on true baseball politeness. Besides, the shedding of blood lowers the pastime to the level of inter-collegiate football.

Rule 9.—It is also bad form, or the height of South Bend, Ind., for a player of national repute, in the act of cooling his pipes at the water pail, to hold the dipper in such a position that the overflow from his jowls dribbles back again into said pail. This breach is and should be tolerated only in horses and Oakland, Cal.

Rule 10.—Any player, when bowing to the plaudits of the peanut-eaters after landing a home run or for other meritorious exploit, should not at the same time employ the thumb and forefinger of either hand in lieu of a handkerchief. While this odd conceit enables the palpitating athlete to appear entirely at ease, at the same time it betokens extreme Shamokin, Pa.

Rule 11.—Visiting teams cannot be too guarded in the matter of table etiquette while away from home. Curving hard-boiled eggs around the dining rooms of leading hotels no doubt keeps the throwing arm in splendid condition, but at the same time it does look distressingly Beloit, Wis.

Rule 12.—Lose without frenzied exhibitions of Kankakee, Ill., and in case of victory, avoid undue symptoms of Cheyenne, Wyo.
[New York Journal, April 28, 1896]

16. Humor in Umpires

The umpire was a member of the original cast that opened baseball. In those early, halcyon days of the great amateur era, he was treated by players and fans with utmost courtesy and respect. It was an idyllic existence, albeit short-lived, as James Wood, captain of the Chicago White Stockings in the early 1870s, remembered it:

In the early part of my baseball career—from 1859 to 1869—an umpire was highly honored. After each game the players would give three cheers for each other and then, as a grand finale, they would bellow forth with three more—and sometimes nine—for the umpire.

Arbitrators in the early days were chosen from among the crowd. In most cases, at least up to 1865, the umpire often was one of the distinguished men in the city. The clubs vied with each other in trying to secure the most prominent personages.

The old time umpires always were accorded the utmost courtesy by the players. They were given easy chairs placed near to the home plate, provided with fans on hot days and their absolute comfort was uppermost in the minds of the players. After each of our games in the early '60s, sandwiches, beer, cakes, and other refreshments were served by the home team. The umpires always received the choicest bits of food and the largest glass of beer—in case he cared for such beverage. If he didn't, he needed but to express his desires in the thirst-quenching line before the game started—and he got it.
[El Paso Herald, August 15, 1916]

But that was not to say that umpiring back then was always a bed of roses, to which this tongue-in-cheek recollection attested:

My son, if sinners entice thee, consent thou not. In other words, if any two tined man with a diseased brain requests you to umpire a base ball game, when there is a probability that there will be a large male audience, you look him calmly and steadily in the eye and in a staccato tone of voice remark, Rats!

The man who stands between a large mob of free thinkers and a flannel mounted cannon of the human variety that spouts a five-ounce ball in his direction, as often as once in two minutes, is inflicted with a job that possesses about as many pleasant features as an ordinary hand-painted morgue. There is always a disgraceful competition between the crowd in the grand stand and the man who circulates the ball to see who will have the exalted honor of removing a lung from the umpire or rearranging his spinal column with a long flesh-colored club.

The umpire is the only man in this light-hearted variety of amusement who can't take his base when hit by the ball. He is expected to allow a sweet two-year old smile to ripple over his face whenever the leather-covered missile slips off the bat and knocks a hole in him, and when it pounds his jaw around so that he can gnaw the oroide (metal alloy) off his rear collar button, an air of gloom settles down on the audience if he don't let off a wad of hearty laughter and announce that it was a good joke.

When a strong, able-bodied man went his way into the vacuum between the grand stand and the home plate, he wants to forget that he still lives. This removes all possibility of his being disappointed when the generous horde in his rear come down off the roost and dance on him.

It was in the year 1852 that I stood for the last time between the grand stand and home plate and attempted to teach the assembled multitude the rules of the game. It was a bright day in June. The air was full of sunshine and flies, and life spread out before me a beautiful panorama on which fortune had traced her most lovely etchings. I saw naught but happiness, and I was congratulating myself that I had been ushered into this world under the light of a lucky star, when I was requested by a long-distance friend to assume the duty of playing a game of ball for the Base Eaters and Ball Swallowers, clubs from rival factory villages.

It was the first position of the kind that had ever been tendered me and I thought it would give me an opportunity to demonstrate to the people that I knew my business, and informing my friend that the salary was no object, so long as I got the position, I agreed to umpire the game.

When the clubs got ready to play, there were between 500 and 600 people squatting on the fence, busily engaged in daubing the surrounding landscape with tobacco juice and peanut shucks. Of course they knew a great deal more about the game than I did. Audiences are always better posted on base ball than the man who umpires. I didn't know this till that bright day in June, but it has always been handcuffed to my memory since that day.

Along about 2 o'clock in the afternoon, I told the boys to go ahead and play, as it got dark that time of the year about 9 o'clock, and I didn't want to see the game stopped on account of darkness. By 7:30 three innings had been played and the score stood 412 to 411 in favor of the Base Eaters. The game at this point was exciting. The Ball Swallowers were at bat and there was a man on each base.

The pitcher threw a mikado twist and the ball got lost on the interior of the batsman. I told him to take his base, that he had been hit by the ball. He said he knew it and started down to first base and man on third started to come home. I told him to go back and stand on his base until another man with an appetite for death had been set up in front of the pitcher. He said he wouldn't. He had been forced off the base by the man who took first because he was hit and accidentally escaped a coroner's inquest. I told him that he couldn't make a chump out of me and to go back to his base, as there was plenty of room for two men to stand on it.

Some gentlemen in the audience suggested that I poison myself and another advised me to take chloroform. The Ball Swallowers' friends were mad because I wouldn't let the man in. If I had, the score would have been a tie and three men on bases. But I didn't propose to show any partiality, and when the man who had come home told me to throw myself in the sewer, I concluded the time had come for me to demonstrate to the people that I knew my business, and picking up a well-developed club I started in his direction.

I have no distinct recollection of what followed, further than that there was a kind of a rushing sound from the direction of the spectators. I must have fallen into a deep ravine about that time, for the next recollection I had was opening my eyes one warm July morning and finding my mother sitting by my bedside, fanning me and weeping piteously.

I asked her if she was running that fanning by water power. Bending tenderly over me, she said, between her sobs: "Be still, my boy, for we can't tell whether your legs will grow on or not, and the doctor says he will never be able to get your brains back into your head unless you keep perfectly still for another month. We've set your shoulder all right and have got you a glass eye exactly like your real one, and nobody will ever be able to tell the difference. The doctor says if you lie perfectly quiet. you will probably be able to walk without crutches in about a year, providing no signs of internal injury make their appearance."

This information quieted my nerves, and I inquired how the game came out. They said it was decided off, as the fifth inning hadn't been finished when the moon rose.

Since that day I have always umpired base ball from the grand stand, and I find it much pleasanter, and there isn't so much wreckage lying around. Nothing affords me more pleasure now than to sit on a hard board in the grand stand and devote my time yelling, "Kill him!" "Cut his feet off!" "Aw, go pound sand," and other rhetorical gems at the umpire. In doing this I am perfectly safe from bodily harm, as I stand in with the mob. Take my advice, my boy, and never attempt to instruct a large and interested audience how a game of ball is being played.
Yours with a low bawl,
Tom Holmes
[St. Paul Daily Globe, August 1, 1886]

Rules stated that only the team captain was allowed to argue an umpire's decision in those days, but flares of temper were rarely recorded by the press; cool heads and gentlemanly manners ruled foremost.

Also concurrent, and running into the early 1880s, it was customary for players to shout "Judgment!" when demanding a decision from the umpire for a fair or foul ball, or ruling on a close play on the bases. The latter was rendered in the words "out" or "not out."

Umpiring in the 1870s & 1880s

Throughout most of the 1870s, no regular staff of umpires existed. A man was selected on the field and received in pay whatever sum the home club saw fit. This awkward arrangement, though, was corrected in 1876, when an umpire's pay was fixed at $5 a game.

In 1879, a staff of umpires was introduced, consisting of twenty men located in the different cities comprising the National League. As a means to control umpires, club owners, in 1881, declared them as league officials and, as such, subjected them to discipline if they did not uphold strict enforcement of the playing rules. The same clubs also paid their salaries, not the League.

In 1883, the model for the modern-day umpire system was introduced when the National League and the newly-formed American Association each appointed a regular staff of four umpires at a stipend of $1,000 per season.

But this time in baseball was marred by a dark pall that descended on the national pastime: gambling. Ever since the beginning of the sport, as with prize fights and horse races, betting

on ball games was one of its main draws. Odds of winning, for example, were commonly cited in game accounts of the 1860s and open betting in the stands during a game was a common sight.

The gambling fever that had arisen during the amateur baseball period boomed in the early 1870s. Baseball "pool rooms" (betting parlors) sprung up in every large city and were even permitted on the baseball grounds, where high-stakes gamblers won—and lost—substantial sums of money.

The corrupting influence of gambling came to a head in 1877, when four members of the Louisville team were caught throwing games and consequently banished from baseball forever. The public distrust sowed by the scandal, however, caused interest to wane and game attendance plummeted, virtually bringing professional baseball to its knees.

However, through extreme tightening measures and the hard work of a few high-placed baseball personages—plus the passage of time—faith and confidence was restored once again in the national game, but it had been a close call.

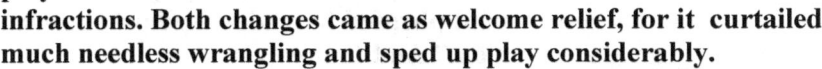

Back on the field, beefs over trivial decisions were a time-wasting nuisance for umpires, who had no recourse except to patiently wait them out. That changed in 1882, when umpires were permitted to levy fines on problematic players, followed in 1889 when they were allowed to expel players from the field for various rule infractions. Both changes came as welcome relief, for it curtailed much needless wrangling and sped up play considerably.

Until the practice was stopped for all good reasons in the mid-1880s, umpires customarily traveled with the same team, stayed at the same hotels, shared the same dressing rooms, and developed personal associations with the same players.

The Umpires' Fall From Grace

The reputation of the poor, guileless umpire was irreparably and irretrievably destroyed during the rampant gambling craze of the 1870s. It happened through no fault of his own, but merely from executing the job he had been paid to do.

In short, the umpire became the convenient scapegoat for anybody who ever lost a bet on a team because the official had made a "wrong" call that caused its loss. It wasn't always fair, but this was how many fans interpreted his actions. Growing resentment followed, creating a wedge that forever separated the umpire from the rest of baseballdom—players, managers, team owners, spectators and, seemingly, the rest of American humankind.

From that point forward, the umpire became pure anathema, a pariah, a loathsome appendage attached to the body of baseball as a hereditary, yet undesirable vestige, much like a chronically inflamed appendix.

The umpire's downfall was aided immeasurably by the sporting press, which joined the witch hunt almost in a body. Baseball writers found it more convenient—and safer, career-wise—to blame a loss on an umpire's perceived ineptitude than that of the home team, which was more often the case.

As in many other arguments, the truth lay somewhere in between. The single umpire on the field made many incorrect calls because it was physically impossible for him to be close enough to call all plays with accuracy, not to mention the illegal ones pulled once his back was turned. After much wrangling and experimentation, this no-win situation was remedied in part in 1890 by the adoption of the two-umpire system.

It was rare for writers to praise umpires, even on the rarer occasion of a dispute-free game. That's when writers paid them a weak, left-handed compliment phrased in trade-standard fashion: "Umpire ___ gave satisfaction." And that was it.

Growing Pains

The decade of the 1890s was the most dangerous time in baseball history to be an umpire. Hardly a week passed when an umpire was not physically set upon by a fist-swinging player or angry mob, much to the disgust of patrons of the game.

The extent and frequency of the rowdiness make for incredulous reading today, and scenes of an umpire being escorted off the field after a game, surrounded by a cordon of policemen or home team players wielding bats, were not exaggerated or manufactured.

Life insurance companies now rate the baseball umpire in the "extremely hazardous" class, along with men who work in dynamite factories.

[Seattle Post-Intelligencer, December 15, 1890]

Most umpires endured these frightening moments with impassive fortitude, but a few chose to take matters into their own hands—literally. The most prominent of their number was Timothy Hurst, a diminutive, but hard-nosed Irishman with a quick wit and short temper. A trained and adept pugilist, he didn't take guff from anybody. Once his dander was up, he often challenged an overly aggressive player to a "meeting" behind the grandstand after the game, an invitation wisely passed on by knowing players. Or Tim simply punched him in the face on the spot and saved himself the trouble.

Throughout the 1890s, the "umpire question," as the player-umpire conflict was understatedly termed, worsened, despite preventive measures adopted by team owners each winter. While all owners unanimously supported their enforcement, it was a different matter once the season started. That's when their true hypocrisy shone through, as Ren Mulford noted:

"The moguls are to blame for the trouble over the umpire question. They get together, look wise, pass rules about enforcing discipline on the field, and then, when the first luckless umpire puts their own regulations in force, they rise and demand that Uncle Nick serve to them the head of the knight of the indicator on a silver-plated charger. There are two or three magnates who are doing their best to turn the great national game into a national farce."
[Saint Paul Globe, June 22, 1897]

Finally, in 1898, as the umpire problem reached crisis proportions, Cincinnati owner John T. Brush promulgated a draconian rule bearing his name that empowered umpires to fine and eject players for obscene language and/or threatening actions, which did much to cut down on confrontations.

Umpires were appointed each winter by National League President Nicholas Young from a pool of applicants, most of whom were sponsored by current or former players and managers, as well as team owners themselves.

Selection, though, was a crapshoot in the end, as no reliable indicator existed that even hinted at the chances of a candidate's ultimate success. During the season Young often had to defend his charges against team owners who beefed endlessly about their alleged incompetence.

The selection of the umpires is one of the most trying duties "Uncle Nick" has to perform. It frequently occurs that the very men who recommend the appointment of certain umpires are the first to protest him and urge his removal. There are now on file at league headquarters over fifty applications for appointment to the staff.
[Pittsburg Chronicle-Telegraph, reprinted in the Evening Star (Washington, D. C), July 6, 1895]

Most umpires were former professional ball players. It was natural for them to do so once their careers ended, as many had no other real job skill to fall back on. Opinions varied in baseball circles whether their past experience made them better umpires. No final consensus was reached, however, which rendered the argument moot, just as it did with the notion that college graduates made better ball players.

Profiles in Umpire Courage

The life of the Texas league umpire is not a pleasant one, and if that much-abused individual escapes with only a fusillade of beer glasses, he considers himself lucky.
A gentleman of Louisville, who has a friend in the Lone Star state, received a letter from him yesterday. That friend made the unprecedented record of umpiring down there two seasons, and now he is a candidate for a position on the association staff. He wrote to his friend in this city after this fashion:

"I will put in my application for a situation as association umpire in a few days. I have officiated in that capacity in the Texas league for two seasons, and that should insure me a position with any organization on earth. It is unnecessary for me to say that I possess a cast-iron nerve, and can withstand a charge of Winchester rifles and gatling guns. So far I have lost but two limbs, but that will not interfere with my work. I have been a little more successful of late, owing to a little scheme of my own. I had sewed on the back of my uniform a placard which read as follows: 'Gentlemen, don't shoot; he is doing his best.'

"That worked very well, and since then, I have been shot at but five times and run out of but two towns. Several more of the unfortunates wanted to do likewise, but I had a patent on it, and refused to give them the right. They then struck upon another scheme, and wherever a railroad track ran near the ball grounds, they chartered an engine and kept it under a full head of steam and stationed just outside the park. When a railroad was not convenient and the owners refused to build one for the purpose, they substituted ponies.

"A very laughable thing happened in Fort Worth last season, when I was run to the hotel and escaped through the scuttle on the roof. Hoping that my application will be given due consideration, I remain yours, etc."
[Pittsburg Press, April 22, 1890]

This tale of a former umpire, which appears to be true, is that of unrequited revenge and long-suppressed rancor, and is appropriately labeled: "The Umpire Strikes Back."

Monday afternoon, a man of massive mold ambled ponderously up to Recreation Park about 3 p. m. He descended to the remotest depths of his pockets and fished out two ten dollar bills and a golden fiver. These he invested in a season ticket and then passed triumphantly into the grand stand. He took a seat in the front row, and right behind the umpire. A smile of content wreathed his face, but the delight that shone in his eyes was quite demonic.

"Here's where I get even," he said confidentially to his friend as his eye fell on the patient and long-suffering umpire. And all through the game he poured out his vials of wrath upon that individual. Whenever the audience manifested disapproval as audiences always do, he was wildest in denunciation. Once he even yelled "Rats!" He paid little attention to the game, but showered maledictions on the head of the umpire. He enjoyed it immensely and even rounded up by howling *because the game was called with Detroit seven in the lead.*

When asked the occasion of his hilarious joy, he confidentially remarked: "You see, I've been down on the diamond there taking the medicine and I just wanted to see how it seemed to give it. It's great fun, I tell you, and the umpire is made for that purpose. Umpires ought to be killed every game!"

The malicious individual was George W. Burnham, ex-League umpire. He had tasted the umpire's cup of bitterness on many a hard-fought diamond.
[Sporting Life, reprinted in the Washington (D. C.) Critic, May 17, 1886]

Umpire Haskell: A Man of Mixed Reviews

There was a feature about the game yesterday which should not be overlooked. The feature was a certain person named Haskell. This man Haskell is an umpire—that is, judging from his work yesterday, he is an umpire, although, of course, umpires are much like women—they force you to admire them one day, and then force you to wonder at what a fool you were the next day; but all things aside, Haskell's work yesterday was of a high-class order. It was not the character of his work particularly, however, that made Mr. Haskell a feature—or rather "the" feature of yesterday's game. It was Mr. Haskell himself.

There was once a man who said: "I have troubles of my own, but I can't tell them. I'm no opera singer." That's Haskell. He's a revelation on the bleachers. It has all those sweet cadences which mark that wonderful instrument that follows in the tail-end of a circus parade. It would cause horses to run away, but the small boy dwells upon its every intonation with ecstasy.

It is a wonderful thing, this voice of Haskell's. He lets go of his words reluctantly, and in their lingering sweetness, there is a strange cadence. It is like Wagner. You are constantly searching for the motif. He gargles his words. He thoroughly masticates them and then he throws in just enough of the nasal shrillness to give them spice, and they come forth in the same condition a steak is in when it is converted into hamburger.

His voice is not all, however. Haskell's body is in the game. He is a posy among posers. He spreads himself out and gathers himself together as does no other man. There is the humor of the end man in his make-up, coupled with all the seriousness of the middle man. He is interesting. He is a good thing. His judgment does not depend upon his calico voice or upon his contrary-to-Delsarto poses, however, and if his

judgment continues as good as it was yesterday, the only eggs he will see this season will be those he calls for to appease his appetite.
[Saint Paul Globe, April 25, 1897]

Umpire Haskell is undoubtedly a man of great mental endowment but he is still unable to tell a strike from a Welsh rarebit when the wind is in the south. It is also hoped his judgment on ducks is better than it is on fouls, else he would be a poor man to send to market after poultry.
[Quincy (Ill.) Daily Herald, May 23, 1895]

Coming Out Parties: The Umpire's Debut

An umpire's first game was occasion for close scrutiny by all eyes in the park, especially those of baseball writers, who were often the most critical of all.

Umpire McDonald made his debut before both teams, and was greeted about as cordially as a tenderfoot in a western town.
[Source misplaced]

McFarland, the new umpire, has a voice like a calf entreating more hay, and falls down on himself when he tries to run across the diamond.
[Baltimore American, August 12, 1896]

Umpire Macullar made his first bow to a Brooklyn audience yesterday in a barber shop coat and a well-oiled voice. He is small in stature, but big in authority, and, from all appearances, is averse to having his rulings disputed.
[Brooklyn Eagle, May 24, 1892]

...venting his temper out on Umpire Mahoney (of the American Association), the new official who was recently engaged from the New England league. Mahoney is a familiar figure here, for he umpired last year in the Atlantic Association. He is a little man with statuesque methods and a large voice, who kindly explains things to the pitcher and the batsmen by means of object lessons in the form of diagrams that he draws all over his anatomy with his hands to show where, in his humble but final opinion, the ball crossed the plate.
[Evening Star (Washington, D. C.), July 31, 1891]

De France, the latest acquisition to the Southern League staff, gets behind the pitchers to umpire. His novelty does not take well, as foul tips, when exceedingly fine, are often called strikes. De France is exceedingly corpulent, and would be a fine specimen for a dime museum to pose as a fat man. When umpiring behind the bat, he is exceedingly unfortunate in being hit by fouls and wild pitches, hence his position back of pitcher.
[Sunday Herald (Washington, D.C.), August 30, 1885]

Umpire Powers made his first appearance, and he created more than a favorable impression. He preserved the best of order and the players soon learned that he was a man who would permit no back talk. Daily tried it once, but Powers shut him up with, "I said it was out and I will permit no argument."

Powers is a tall, well-built fellow, with a bronzed face and dark moustache. He has a deep double bass voice which resembles the roar of a railroad train coming out of a tunnel. He gives his decisions promptly and has a quiet way about him which impresses the crowd.
[Washington (D. C.) Critic, July 26, 1888]

The debut of the new league umpire, Conahan, at Philadelphia, yesterday, is described by the (Philadelphia) Inquirer in this wise:

"Twenty-three hundred deposited their bits of Bryanish coin and sat them down in the Colonel's pet edifice and the adjoining 'bleachers' to see and listen. The speedy and unerring construction of victory rewarded their vision, the shrill, piping notes of a human voice, nay, rather the silvery tone of some celestial musician, fell upon their ear, and they were spellbound. 'Twas the new umpire, Conahan, unearthed by Nick Young in the wilds of Jersey; and who henceforth will have the temerity to ask: 'Can any good thing come out of Nazareth?'

"Conahan's a 'peach.' In the line of making himself heard, he can give the Angel Gabriel cards and spades and a beating. While his judgment was not severely tested yesterday, still what he had to do was done all right. He's a nice, accommodating lad, too. He runs around and picks up the catchers' masks for them and, with deferential bow, delivers himself: 'Illustrious sir, allow me.' He'll get over that, though."
[Evening Star (Washington, D.C.), August 15, 1896]

Another cause of grief was the latest acquisition to the umpire staff from the minor league cemeteries, where a choice lot of stiffs seem to be kept in pickle ready for President Young's grappling irons whenever Washington, for any reason, gets too gay and needs discipline.

This last lot is named Hunt and he comes from nowhere in particular.[Source misplaced]

Yesterday was Mr. Umpire Corcoran's first appearance on the Quincy grounds. Mr. Corcoran has been dubbed by the boys as "Corky." The gentleman looks more like an Indiana school-master than a base ball umpire. He is straight of stature, walks like a young minister whose pants fit too tight and has a complexion like pickled beets.
[Quincy (Ill.) Daily Journal, June 19, 1891]

One of Nick Young's new umpires, a gentleman named Long, refereed the game. Ryan said that he had a red head and a black heart; Wilmot declared that he was the worst that ever came over the pike. The grand stand referred to him in terms of gross opprobrium and likened him to everything from an Egyptian crocodile to an uncaged monometallist. He called strikes that skimmed the ground and sailed just under the sky, and he called balls that cut the plate squarely in the center. His decisions on the bases were better, but the crowd could not be pacified, and regaled him bitterly from start to finish.
[Inter Ocean (Chicago), May 15, 1895]

It is a lonesome day when the Eastern Association does not spring a new umpire on a long-suffering public. Of all the job lots of alleged referees that were ever "read of in books or dreamt of in dreams" the aggregation that has swung around the circle this year is comparably the worst.
The latest addition is Grace Pearce, now on earth for the seventh time, and it was he who officiated at Culver Park yesterday. If the Eastern Association has got down to such umpires as Pearce thus early in the season, what in the name of all that is good and great will it bring out in the latter part of August! The thought of the possible appointees is enough to provoke the horrors. President White ought to take a day off and look up a couple of men who are at least half-way competent.
[Rochester Democrat and Chronicle, July 3, 1891]

Redheffer's Ragged Roll-out

When rookie National League umpire Charles Powers Redheffer stepped onto the field at National Park, Washington, D. C. in 1895, to call his first game, little did he anticipate the vicious roasting he was about to receive from a local writer, who chronicled

the worst day of the young umpire's life in these words:

> *It's a lucky thing that the Washington fans have a month in which to rest their shattered nerves after yesterday's excitement. They went through every emotion that a combined ball game, prize fight and murder could furnish. Despair and exultation, fiendish rage, hate and joy raced in ghostly procession up and down the spinal columns, till nothing but the death of an umpire could have adequately brought comfort.*
>
> *It was all along the line of the latest acquisition to the judicial staff of the league. When the game was called, a nice, quiet-looking youngster with a lady-like mustache trotted out and chirped "play." Every thing went well for one inning. He gave a diagram with every ball called and a nice little lecture of admonition and advice to the pitcher.*
>
> *In the second he perpetrated one of the worst decisions ever launched on this long-suffering community. Hallman ran more than ten feet out of the line to avoid being tagged by Crooks. He was declared safe, and in the twinkling of an eye, 3,000 maniacs were thirsting for the umpire's blood, and for a quarter of an hour, the stands were ruled by a howling mob.*
>
> *Everybody wanted to know who he was and how he got there. Someone said that it was something that Nick Young's cat brought in; others that he had just escaped from St. Elizabeth. He proved to be the owner of the euphonious name of Redheffer, and to hail from Camden, N. J., and is without a doubt the first and only one of the species ever born in captivity. His training for an umpire has evidently been received on Duke Bill Thompson's race track at Gloucester, and he was snatched from his native jungle and let loose on the ball field to satisfy a yearning which has possessed him for years, to show the league how the thing ought to be done.*
>
> *...He sweat blood for about two innings, and a riot was imminent the whole time. Suddenly the trim figure of (league umpire) Miah Murray was seen on the players' bench, and, with a cry of joy, President Young yanked him into the game, and the crowd received him like Sheridan at a second Cedar Creek.*
>
> *Miah went behind the bat and peace spread her white wings over the stricken field, and when Mr. Redheffer actually gave Maul safe on a close call, the bleachers really gave him the glad hand, and things settled down to a quiet, gentleman's sort of game.*
>
> *(Addendum to article):*
>
> *It seems that Redheffer has been trying to break into the League for years, and asked for just one chance to show what he could do.*

Murray happened in town to get instructions before going West, and saved a riot. Mr. Young was about the happiest man on the ground when the tide turned.
[Morning Times (Washington, D. C.), July 4, 1895]

Two weeks later, salt was rubbed in Redheffer's wound when a "concerned" fan submitted the following poem, inquiring after his fate:

Oh! where has he gone to?
Oh! where has he went?
Oh! where has Redheffer,
The umpire, been sent?

Has he left the baseball business?
Has he gone, beyond a doubt?
Has he made his last decision?
Has he put the last man out?

Will he see the District ball games?
Will he keep the official score?
And I, trembling, looked at "Nicholas,"*
As he whispered, "Never more."

Let us hope that this be true,
Let us hope his work is done;
Let us hope, and be it granted,
That he's on his last home run.
[The Morning Times (Washington, D. C.), July 18, 1895]

* **Nick Young, President of the National League and appointer of umpires.**

The Clothes That Made an Umpire

Before league rules prescribed a uniform uniform for umpires, the attire they chose to put on public display during a ball game was left to their discretion—or indiscretion, as it sometimes turned out, which was often made sport of by ever-vigilant reporters.

The Louisville Commercial says:

"Mr. Thomas Burns, esq., late of Chicago and Pittsburg clubs, attired in a natty blue coat, a checked shirt, striped trousers and a Tuxedo scarf, in which shone with great brilliancy a diamond pin, made his debut as a league umpire.

"He went at his business in a very lady-like fashion, his soft, mellow decisions not being heard twenty feet away. He was so modest and retiring that at times the spectators forgot he was in the game. All in all, Mr. Burns is the most lady-like umpire that has ever visited Eclipse park."
[Brooklyn Eagle, August 31, 1892]

Umpire Gaffney has discarded his green pants and cap, and on Decoration day he appeared in a new suit of dark brown material.
[Pittsburg Press, June 2, 1888]

Umpire Holland appeared in a new gray uniform-suit and cap yesterday. He looked like a letter-carrier who had been stripped of his buttons.
[Morning Herald (Baltimore), April 19, 1889]

Herman Doescher, one of the new umpires of the American Association, bears a striking resemblance to Big Jim Davis, of the Kansas City team, and with his pretty uniform of light-gray flannel, is the perfect type of an umpire.
[Baltimore American, June 9, 1888]

One of the greatest surprises yesterday was the appearance of Umpire Goldsmith...When he appeared in the game, he was clad in black pants, white shirt, jacket and cap, with red stockings.
[Baltimore American, September 1, 1889]

The uniforms of the umpires come as near being the homeliest thing ever invented that could be desired. Lane looks like a sea-diver with his mask on.
[Evening Telegraph (Providence, R. I.), May 19, 1883]

Umpire Stage made a good impression on the Philadelphia public, as he is sure to do wherever he goes. He wore a large chest protector fastened by straps crossed behind his back. The rear view was like the front of a member of the Twenty-third regiment on dress parade. The front view gave one the impression of one of Dante's angels with the wings in the wrong place.
[Brooklyn Eagle, May 8, 1894]

There were about 4,000 in the park when Umpire Lynch called the boys to action. It just seemed as if a day only had intervened between Lynch's last appearance and his appearance yesterday. He looked just as positive and emphatic as ever. The only difference was his new padded vest, which gives him in some respects the appearance of a cropper pigeon.
[Pittsburg Dispatch, April 25, 1889]

An unexpected thing happened as Umpire Keefe walked up the field from the Brooklyn's dressing quarters (at Polo Grounds). The crowd actually applauded him, and in his natty blue uniform, Sir Timothy looked for all the world like a champion bandmaster or king of a shooting fest, minus the medals, as he paraded to the plate, doffing his cap and bowing right and left. It was a triumphal march, a tribute to the Keefe of long ago, when he was king of the pitchers.
[Brooklyn Eagle, August 18, 1895]

The Voice Heard 'Round the Park

Each umpire, in his own way, developed an individual and customized style of umpiring, complete with idiosyncrasies. Like fingerprints, no two were exactly alike. Basic to all, however, was a loud voice, which was essential as players needed to know a decision instantly on the field during rapidly evolving play.

This hard-to-miss trait naturally attracted the attention of baseball reporters and became a fount of much good-natured ribbing. As with the voice of coachers, its essence was captured in as many simile-formatted comparisons as there were writers in the trade. Witness these:

The new Association umpire, Mahoney, like Orator Puff, has two voices. "Strike one" is rapidly uttered in high C, pure chest tone. "Ball two" comes out slowly in a melodious baritone. Mahoney seems to be a first-class man.
[Pittsburgh Press, August 4, 1891]

Umpire McFarland has a peculiar drawl in announcing decisions. After a particularly long-drawn-out vocal effort in the fifth inning of a game at Chicago the other day, a shrill voice in the stand piped out: "With a voice just like Charley's Aunt."
[Morning Times (Washington, D.C.), August 12, 1896]

McFarland, the new umpire, has a voice like a calf entreating more hay.
[Baltimore American, August 12, 1896]

The umpiring of Powers, a new man, gave general satisfaction. He is a big man, with a voice resembling the whistle of an East river ferry-boat, but he has promptitude and backbone, both of which he displays in a degree that commanded respect.
[Baltimore American, July 29, 1888]

Bob Emslie's pipes have a clarion ring this season. Davenport said Bob's voice sounded like he had been feeding it on lemons and old hand files.
[Morning Times (Washington, D.C.), June 2, 1896]

Umpire Sheridan

Next to Tim Hurst, one of the most picturesque and unforgettable umpires of this era was Jack Sheridan. He captivated—and amused—fans with his distinctive voice, which writers likened to a long list of things known to be very loud.

Mr. Sheridan umpired an excellent game. He was with us before, voice and all, although only a few of the regulars remember him. Sheridan was on Nick Young's staff a couple of years ago, but the players made it too hot for him and he resigned. A year in the minor league, coupled with the more stringent rules, gave Mr. Sheridan added courage.
He returns with a voice that sounds like a cross between the roar of a tornado and the wail of one of Dante's lost souls. Those who have been used to the chirrup of Timothy Hurst and the "s-t-r-e-e-k" of Lynch were thrown into an agony of apprehension when Sheridan shrieked his "baw'un" and "stri-tree, yerrout" with enough volume to be heard by the mob on deadhead row back of the right field fence. The rooster man wasn't heard after Sheridan got in his fine work.
[Brooklyn Eagle, June 2, 1896]

"Orreadee, play bauell (All ready, play ball!)" said Mr. Sheridan.
[Brooklyn Eagle, June 3, 1896]

> Umpire Sheridan has a voice that draws rain. It sounds like the echo of a roar of thunder.
> [Pittsburg Dispatch, May 15, 1892]

> Umpire Sheridan has been endeavoring to cut the sharp edges off his voice while he has been sojourning in other parts. He has met with poor success, however, and a plentiful supply of cold chisels will be required to take out the nails in his larynx.
> [Exchange, reprinted in the Pittsburg Dispatch, June 10, 1892]

> Then Sheridan was there, too. He is the umpire with a voice he caught and swallowed as it welled up from the grave of a side-show barker who died from the effects of a bad cold in his throat. He displayed the same ability to make "Two strikes" sound like "Barn's on fire" as he did during his last visit.
> [Chicago Record, reprinted in the Pittsburg Press, June 27, 1896]

> Sheridan's voice is still intact, after the winter's blasts, if the comments of a Louisville paper may be depended upon. The Post of that city says the "S-t-t-t-r-r-r-i-i-k-e," "w-w-a-a-n," "t-w-o," in long drawn, bellowing accents, served to confuse most of those not accustomed to Sheridan's voice.
> [Kansas City Daily Journal, May 18, 1897]

> ...heard the magnificent voice of Umpire Sheridan, as in tones like the delivery of a load of anthracite coal down a cast-iron chute, he announced the first ball pitched by Scott to be "one strake."
> [Source misplaced]

> Umpire Sheridan has a voice that resembles the noise made in a boiler factory. He seems to tear his decisions out by the roots, and, striking the atmosphere, they are shattered into a thousand pieces, and roll off like receding thunder.
> [Evening Times (Washington, D.C.), June 10, 1897]

> If, as the report says, Umpire Sheridan swallows a raw egg before each game to mellow the tones of his musical voice, there is reason to believe that some farmers feed their hens on dynamite.
> [Evening Star (Washington, D.C.), May 21, 1892]

> Sheridan's voice could give a megaphone cards and spades and a beating. It is the most horribly discordant air disturber ever emitted

from a human factory.
[Morning Times (Washington, D.C.), July 31, 1896]

Umpire Sheridan has the oddest voice yet heard here. He cannot make the crowd understand what he mean as he says "Three!" and "Strike!" in almost the same way. The only chance the mob has to understand what Sheridan says is by watching the motions of the catcher and batter. If the catcher kicks, it's a ball; if the batsman howls, it's a strike.
[Chicago News, reprinted in the Brooklyn Eagle, May 22, 1896]

Umpire Sheridan's voice would hardly win him a scholarship in the new conservatory of music. It starts to vibrate with a suddenness that is deadening, gains volume as it cuts its way through the atmosphere, hurls itself with sickening force against the ears of the populace and dies away in a wondrous gurgle far down in the fastnesses of a compound, triple-expansion, double-back-action, perpetual motion larynx. It would make an elevated railroad conductor green with envy.
[Brooklyn Eagle, May 31, 1892]

There is no danger of a postponed game on account of rain while Sheridan is stationed in Washington. His voice will turn the path of any storm coming this way.
[The Times (Washington, D. C.), June 11, 1897]

His (Sheridan's) enunciation is like a primitive eruption of Vesuvius, or an argument between a boiler rivet and a steel-head hammer.
[Morning Times (Washington, D. C.), August 4, 1896]

Umpire Sheridan made his debut before a Washington crowd, and right well did he entertain them with his foghorn voice. One of the grand-stand rooters remarked that Phil Sheridan might have been easily "twenty miles away" and yet have shouted his orders with that voice so as to be heard by his troops.
[Evening Star (Washington, D.C.), August 4, 1896]

Bad Press

The poison that flowed from baseball reporters' pens over the years, blaming umpires generally for all of life's ills and specifically the loss of yesterday's game, was legion. The following

comments, with infinite variations, typified their convictions of the imagined and tacit conspiratorial collusion indulged in daily by most umpires:

The Omaha management should play no more games with this blockhead in the position of umpire. He is thoroughly incompetent and should be fired bodily before his ignorant work culminates in some dire calamity.
The Bee touched Mr. Leech mildly in yesterday's issue, simply from the fact that it was the writer's opinion that he was rattled by the din kept up by the spectators and that his mistakes were of the head and not of the heart. It is but fair to give every man a chance. Leech has had his. Sic him.
[Omaha Daily Bee, June 1, 1890]

This is the way a Cleveland paper sizes up an umpire: "Billy Stage is a popular young man, a champion sprinter and he has nice, curly hair—too bad he can't umpire."
[Brooklyn Eagle, July 6, 1895]

The fans at Detroit love (umpire) Snyder as dearly as the Kansas City rooters worship Clark, and are already addressing him with such endearing terms as "rotten," "yellow," "robber," "thief," and other expressions that would not look well in print.
[Saint Paul Globe, June 25, 1896]

(Umpire) Clark is the worst that ever happened—barring the Johnstown flood. That was pretty bad for one day; Clark is pretty bad—and he lasts longer.
[Saint Paul Globe, June 26, 1896]

Umpire McFarlan, a little man fresh from heaven knows where, attempted to see that justice was done. St. Louis took several violent and protracted exceptions to his rulings, but the umpire has a jaw which strongly resembles that of the late lamented Napoleon I, and protests affected him no more than lake breezes.
[Inter Ocean (Chicago), August 7, 1896]

Umpire Charley Morton is about as much use in his official position as coal at the equator.
[Rochester (N. Y.) Post Express, July 3, 1896]

Kansas City baseball fans are perfectly well convinced that Ban Johnson is a regular Dr. Jekyll and Mr. Hyde. As Dr. Jekyll, he is the urbane president of the Western League, striving to do justice to all the teams; but as Mr. Hyde, he is evidently the manager of a home for blind and decrepit ex-ball players, the inmates of which, from some sinister motive, he is continually sending to Kansas City in the guise of umpires.

Kansas City has hardly recovered from an attack of a fellow named Sommers, whose only correct decision was when he decided that he was not cut out for an umpire, when here comes along a freak by the name of Clarke, in comparison with whom the memory of Sommers is a sweet reflection to be lovingly dwelt upon.

If the Creator had provided Mr. Clarke with two eyes, out of which he could see, and given him a real backbone instead of the piece of India rubber which does duty for that useful portion of his anatomy, he might make a very good umpire with several years' experience, otherwise—nit.
[Kansas City Journal, reprinted in the Indianapolis Journal, June 15, 1896]

There have been some very bad umpires and some very unruly scenes upon the Polo grounds, but never anything to equal the first four innings of yesterday's conflict. Mr. Burnham robbed first one team and then the other with delicious nonchalance and praiseworthy impartiality.
[(New York) World, reprinted in the Pittsburg Press, August 8, 1895]

Umpires, it seems, so far as Omaha is concerned, are a very demoralizing element in baseball that can't be well gotten rid of, although the Black Sox would have fared better in any number of instances this season if a wooden man had been hired for the position.
[Omaha Daily Bee, June 11, 1890]

They (spectators) also saw one of the wonders of the age, a curiosity that knocks Barnum's What-Is-It into a cocked hat, and lays over the Bearded Lady like a horse blanket over a mule's back.

It was Mr. Lucas, the umpire.

He is a regular—a regular rosette—and was discovered by Your Uncle David while cleaning out cisterns in Bucyrus, O., and was hired on the spot to come out here to Omaha and show the masses just how measly a game of base ball could be umpired.
[Omaha Daily Bee, May 13, 1894]

Young, slender Mr. Carpenter took on his delicate shoulders the

load of calling balls and strikes for the second game. He's the most fragile piece of work that ever trod Union Park diamond, being a dainty confection of an umpire who wears tennis shoes and long hair.
[Baltimore American, September 18, 1897]

Between Umpire Hoover, the little man whom the crowd wanted to murder at Adelside Park Saturday, and one of the two butter-fingers members of the Providence team, yesterday's game on the grounds at Rocky Point went to swell the percentage of the gang from Troyanville, and the Grays stand one round lower on the pennant ladder.

Mr. Hoover should immediately give up the job the league has bestowed upon him, in order to save himself the mortification of being kicked out of it. He is utterly incompetent, and his presence on the field is unmitigated aggravation to players and public alike. He is not only laughably poor on judging balls the strikes in reference to the plate, but he doesn't seem to be able to recognize a strike when the man swings his bat at the ball.

Once he yelled "foul" on a batter who hit at the ball but missed it by six inches, as the protest of both benches and grand stand rose in an indignant chorus, he changed the decision and said "strike." For base players, he had a better eye, but his opinions were pretty shady, even at that. It is impossible for a pitcher to successfully use anything but the straightest balls with Hoover as the umpire, and thus handicapped a man of Jim Sullivan's strategy can do but little against hitters, compared to what he would achieve otherwise.
[Evening Telegraph (Providence, R. I.), August 15, 1892]

"Sandy" McDermott's umpiring was about as good as a water-soaked bunch of firecrackers on the Fourth of July. Catcher Speer, who used to be as mild-tempered as a breeze softened to fit a shorn lamb, said a few words to the umpire yesterday in a turbulent tone of voice. Five dollars.
[Kansas City Journal, May 14, 1897]

When he (Umpire McDonald) decided that Seymour had made a balk, he was the center of an animated debate which can only be likened to a night session of Congress in the dying hours of that legislative body.
[New York Journal, July 6, 1897)

Manager Powers, in speaking about umpires yesterday, said: "My idea about umpires is that a club should have a new umpire every day, and kill him after the game."

[The Sun (New York), reprinted in the Post Express (Rochester, N. Y.), June 17, 1889]

(Umpire) Hartley escaped from the New York Asylum for the Blind and became an umpire.
[Baltimore American, July, 1894]

Mr. Weidman, called by courtesy an umpire, made decisions which he regretted and tried to smooth over. As a smoother, he is as diplomatic as a street Arab at a meeting of the Society for the Promotion of Esthetic Speech. He called things by such far distant names that several broods of chickens in the neighborhood hatched prematurely from the shock.

Weidman is too good a man for an umpire. He should be in the blacksmithing business, or some place where his keen discretion and acute judgment might find their proper reward. His talents, at present, are wasted upon an unappreciating desert of popular opinion.
[Chicago Inter-Ocean, reprinted in the Saint Paul Globe, June 2, 1896]

Double-Barreled Bile

Getting under the skin of an Omaha baseball writer was not only Guenther, the umpire, but the Western Association president responsible for his hiring, prompting the reporter to let fly with remarks of a highly personal and slanderous nature:

The secret of today's defeat, without explanation or apology, was Guenther's hideous umpiring. I know it is the same old horse chestnut, but what are you going to do about it?

He had both teams standing on their heads before a dozen balls had been pitched, and the crowd cried murder at divers and sundry stages of the game.

Guenther is a fathead, and has probably made his last appearance before the great American public in the guise of a minion of the diamond.

The English language contains over 280,000 words, and yet it is wholly inadequate to convey the vaguest conception of what this man doesn't know about a ball game.

The dazzling coruscations of his execrable work will manifest themselves, however, as the history of the strife proceeds.
[Omaha Daily Bee, June 14, 1892]

He was on hand again yesterday afternoon as big as a horse.

Who? Why, Guenther, the megatherium nincompoop of modern times.

Again, he metamorphosed what would have evidently been a matchless game of ball into a howling farce. A few more such exhibitions and base ball will be ready for interment in Omaha.

After Monday's egregious burlesque, the local management swore by all that was on earth, in the air and under the sea, that Guenther should never umpire another game at Sportsman's park, though the heavens fall. (Omaha) President Stout and Manager Rowe both went so far as to say that he should not even enter the grounds, no matter what the consequences were.

But he was there just the same, as large as life and twice as natural, and the masquerade of the two previous days was repeated.

Jimmy Williams, the premier maggot (magnate) of the Western league, telegraphed that Mr. Guenther must be allowed to umpire the game or it would go to Indianapolis 9 to 0.

It is high time that President Williams tied a bar of railroad iron about his neck and jumped into the Scioto (river passing through Columbus, Ohio).

He is nearly as bad as Guenther. The Western league requires the most delicate nursing to maintain life, and a few more idiotic moves like the Corcoran and Guenther deal and up goes the sponge.

The people are getting nauseated. What President Scott should have done was to have wired Williams to go on, and if Indianapolis refused to play, give them the finger for their guarantee, and laid off until some club happened along that would play. If none came, disband, divide the profits and go home.

[Omaha Daily Bee, June 15, 1892]

The Home Umpire

Falling into particular disfavor with the press under certain circumstances was the so-called "home umpire," the arbiter whose decisions on close calls tended to favor the home team. While this ensured the umpire's relaxed and uneventful return to his hotel on well-lit boulevards after the game instead of nocturnal routes through back alleys, it never set well with reporters on the road when his team was on the losing end of these biased decisions. Here's what was said about them:

Umpire Warner added today to the showing which he made

Saturday of his marked proclivities for favoring home teams. He was evidently fully mindful of the religious suggestion that he who hesitates is lost, for he began the opening inning to stack the cards so that the Saints could not get a show in the game no matter which end of the deck was dealt from.
[Saint Paul Globe, August 4, 1897]

"*The Senators made a splendid start…and would have won out had not (Umpire) Mr. Hunt played tenth position for the Pirates and given them decisions at critical times that were palpably erroneous. Time and space are too valuable to give in detail the instances of his bad work. Suffice it to say that fans and players entered vigorous and pronounced protests.*"
[Evening Times (Wash DC), August 18, 1899]

"*There was no possible chance for the local men to score a victory, as they were not only outplayed by the Chicago team, but umpire Powers was clearly with the visitors, and even had the contest been a close one, the lank individual who is paid by the League to do impartial work, would have protected the interests of the Anson aggregation. So far as can be remembered, the Indianapolis players have never won a game in which Powers umpired. It is a notorious fact that he has always been against the Hoosiers. Why, no one seems to know, but for the protection of himself and his patrons, (team owner) President Brush should make it a point to find out if the local team has any rights that Mr. Powers is bound to respect.*"
[Indianapolis Journal, August 29, 1889]

The obvious advantages accruing to a home umpire were satirized in this story, which contained more truth than many would admit:

A tall, well-built young man, with features as fair as those of Romeo, and with a suit of clothes that fitted like the kalsomine (spotlight) on the ceiling, strode into a newspaper office. He had tickets in his pocket over all railroad lines, looked well fed, and carried in his hand a silver-headed cane.

"*Who are you?*" *asked the editor of the paper.*

"*I am a gentleman of leisure just now. During the season, I have been a base ball umpire,*" *replied the stranger.*

"*I cannot believe it,*" *said the editor. "Where are your bruises, your battered head, your broken arms, your bruised limbs and your coat of mail?"*

"I have none of them," replied the umpire. "I have been living on fatted calf all summer. This walking stick was presented to me by the grand stand at one of the places where I worked."

"That cannot be," replied the editor, "or if it can, pray tell me how have I seen you painted in all papers as a thing despised, abused, much railed at, thumped around the goal and back again, as it were, for so are all the pictures I have seen of you."

"There may be such, but I am none of them," was the reply.

"How then are all my brothers of the press mistaken?" said the editor.

"I chanced to umpire only in such games as where the home team won," was the reply, "and thereby have a reputation and a shape, the former sweetly scented as the fumes of Araby, the latter fair and plump as when I first saw light of day. No visiting team takes printing presses with it, and grand stands do not mock at rulings where the home team wins."
[St. Paul Daily Globe, October 23, 1887]

Not all reporters were umpire-bashers. The venerable baseball writer and historian, Henry Chadwick, for instance, came to the defense of the embattled arbiter on many occasions, often accusing umpire-beaters as sore losers, who themselves had bet and lost money on the game. It was a far stretch, but was probably true to some degree in baseball's very early days.

It is really sickening to read, in country papers, of the gross abuse showered upon umpires by betting reporters when "our club gets beat." When "our club wins," then the umpiring is first class, when otherwise, it is something like this from the Buffalo Commercial Advertiser:

"Of all the outrageous exhibitions of umpiring we have, none will compare with that by the fossilized catcher, Powers, yesterday. He is no more fit to be an umpire than he is to occupy a position in a first class club, and that is something he will never have a chance to fill."

"The reporter who wrote the above paragraph evidently bet on the losing side."
[Chadwick, Brooklyn Eagle, July 18, 1881]

"Umpires who fail to give decisions to suit the grand stands are particularly open to journalistic censure. So long as this abuse goes on, good umpiring will be next to impossible...Young and inexperienced

writers for the press are peculiarly prone to fall into this error of setting up their own individual judgment or that of the bystanders in their immediate vicinity as superior to that of the official arbiter...The work of an umpire in baseball is difficult enough at best, without newspapers adding to it by encouraging the partisans of clubs to hiss or berate whenever he fails to give a decision to their liking."
[Chadwick, Brooklyn Eagle, June 29, 1884]

17. Humor in Uniforms

In the pre-professional period of baseball, up to 1870, the smartly-dressed amateur player took the field in the *haute couture* of the day: white flannel shirt with a shield-like front, closed with large pearl buttons and bearing the team's initial in Old English type; blue, woolen trousers; black, ankle-high leather shoes; wide leather belt; and a fancy cap of varying designs, often fitted with a jockey's visor.

Players soon discovered, though, that trousers interfered with running, which led to them being gathered about the ankles, producing a bloomer effect, distinctly feminine. Masculine embarrassment was short-lived when trousers were replaced with knee-breeches, or knickerbockers, plus knee-high colored stockings. This combination, which became a standard feature of uniforms thereafter, was first introduced to baseball in 1868 by the Cincinnati Red Stockings.

At first, uniforms (called "costumes" back then) were custom-made for teams by local tailors, later by major sporting goods houses, such as Spalding and Reach. While they conferred identity, exclusivity and a certain degree of class to a team, thereby boosting pride, and competitive spirit among its players, they were a most unreliable measure of ability. Throughout the 1860s, for example, the Troy Haymakers, a strong amateur team of Lansingburgh, New York was once described as: "a grotesque lot of farmer boys, who did not rise to the dignity of having real baseball uniforms, but played in their ordinary attire and without socks or shoes."

From that point forward, the styles of baseball uniforms changed more rapidly over the years than rules of the game. Uniforms of the 1870s generally featured a laced-front, full-collar shirt carrying the team's name, and various forms of a tie.

In 1877, professional players were assessed $30 for their uniforms, a practice that was also in vogue with amateur clubs.

In 1872, the Forest City (amateur) club of Cleveland, wore a uniform that cost $55 to the player. The material used was all of the best

and the players wore black silk stockings. The shoes alone without plates cost $10. In addition to this, the club furnished each player a gray traveling suit at an additional cost of $25 per man.
[Pittsburgh Press, April 24, 1888]

Until 1882, teams were permitted to wear uniforms of any color, but in that season a rule was adopted in the National League to prevent any two of them from wearing the same one. It was decreed that the colors for the various teams should be: Chicago, white; Boston, red; Providence, light blue; Cleveland, navy blue; Troy, green; Buffalo, gray; Worcester, brown; and Detroit, old gold.

The period of the 1880s and 1890s was the scene of wild and extraordinary experimentation with uniform design. In many instances the results proved catastrophic when the designer, usually the team manager, possessed not one ounce of artistic talent, to say nothing of what constituted a pleasing sartorial effect. Thus, players were forced to dress up in mismatched colors that shamed the rainbow, made ladies shudder in horror, and astonished the most hardened bleacher denizen, as if the crazy-quilt effect had been inspired by a tent full of circus clowns.

Wardrobe Malfunctions

To understand just how much these "special" uniforms profaned the field of baseball play, just read what baseball writers had to say about them:

The Baltimores came on the field attired in red shirts, looking like old-time fire boys.
[Brooklyn Eagle, October 15, 1873]

The Providence team wore their new uniforms. Farrell, Start and Denny wore blouse shirts, which are striped up and down, making the boys look like zebras. When Start came to the bat, there was a grand shout of laughter from the crowd. Joe looked like a great big overgrown school boy. His jacket was red and black, and his knickerbockers with the broad white belt, appeared to come well up under his arms.

...Farrell kept on his old gray knit jacket until the game was about half over, when he became so warm that he had to doff the cardigan. Then the laugh was turned on him, for he bloomed out in a blouse of bright yellow and black, and as he danced about, looked like a huge yellow-jacket wasp. Seriously speaking, the new uniforms are not

to be compared with the attractive gray and blue of the past four seasons.
[Providence (R. I.) Sunday Star, April 8, 1882]

When the two nines came upon the field, their "song and dance" uniforms were greeted with sarcastic applause and laughter. The Troy pitcher and catcher wore bright green and brown blouses, having through some misunderstanding, put on those, which are to be worn by substitutes only.
[Providence (R. I.) Sunday Star, May 2, 1882]

The new uniforms of the New Yorks look like the suits worn on Wards Island*.
[Providence (R. I.) Evening Telegraph, May 2, 1882]
* Insane asylum

The uniform of the Washington Club is black pants, drab jackets, and stockings with similar trimmings. They were afraid to put them on, going to the game, for fear the people would think they were going to a funeral.
[Baltimore American, April 14, 1887]

Some of the uniforms in use in the American association next season will be as gorgeous as a brand-new three-sheet circus poster, says the Sporting Life.
[St. Paul Daily Globe, March 25, 1888]

The Ravens (Quincy) appeared in their new suits yesterday. Welt, the tailor that made them, was as generous with his cloth as he could well be without bankrupting himself. We must say those suits fit like a horse blanket on a skeleton and some of the players' nether limbs resemble the twin screws on a steamboat.
[Quincy (Ill.) Daily Journal, June 19, 1891]

(Pitcher) Galvin has kicked on the new orange-colored uniforms of the Pittsburg team, and says that he would not think of donning one without first insuring his life. He threatened to slide to bases so often this summer that he will scrape the color out of the cloth, but the managers are not bothering much about this calamity. These uniforms are said to cost over $42 apiece. Galvin would look like a good, large orange, indeed.
[Evening Star (Washington, D.C.), April 20, 1889]

A barber sign isn't a circumstance in loudness to the costumes worn by the Smoky City fellows (Pittsburg). If their bodies were incased in the same material as covers their heads and legs, they would much resemble the variegated potato bug which the farmer plucks in July time. Bright yellow and black stripes cover the extremities of these ball players and white flannel robes their bodies. The Giants, in all-black tights, looked far better.
[Evening World (New York), May 17, 1889]

The oriole uniform of the Baltimore Club does not catch on in other cities, and lots of fun is poked at the players. One of the Brooklyn papers had the following to say after the first game in Brooklyn:

"High winds, a high-winded throng of 5,000 and the struck-by-lightning costumes of the Orioles were the prominent features of the Baltimore-Brooklyn game at Washington Park. The first was of such a persistent and vigorous nature that it converted the game into a triangular contest, the cyclonic zephyrs having it all their own way with the ball; the second lent their united aid to the breezes in rattling the players, and the third filled up any gaps in the razzle-dazzle business, the truly wonderful make-up of the Baltimoreans' new clothes being sufficient to add the finishing touch to the intermittent dashes of insanity that characterized the tussle. Precisely who is responsible for the costuming of the Baltimore men has not leaked out yet, but some of the players regard Manager Barnie with reproachful mien and whisper that he is the one who victimized them.

"The costume is a lot of black and old-gold scraps, thrown together in longitudinal fashion, the whole, or rather the players, being surmounted by a custard-pie cap, really cute, but funny. The trousers are cut in the latest Bedouin style, and at time it is impossible to tell whether the extremities of the Baltimoreans are clad in knee-top skirts or hidden in the conventional knickerbockers.

"It is asserted that the costume was designed by a far-seeing individual, with a view to dazzling all opponents; but already it is acting as a boomerang, young Cunningham having taken to tutti-frutti and others showing inclinations to wander off to different irregular channels. Mr. "Tatty" Tucker declares that he feels like a black-legged zebra painted yellow and going to seed; and diminutive Mack, the imitator, solemnly asserts that he holds on to his little yellow belt in order to make sure that he is not losing any portion of himself."
[Baltimore American, May 5, 1889]

The Cleveland Press says of the Indianapolis team: "The Hoosiers, as they appeared upon the field Wednesday, are a tough-looking gang. Their uniforms are without doubt the most execrable that perverted genius ever devised, and give to their wearers the appearance of game roosters with their tail feathers pulled out."
[Pittsburgh Press, May 19, 1889]

Cleveland has followed the funereal idea and has clothed the Spiders in black suits, with black stockings and caps and white belts. They were booked to wear them yesterday, and as they lost, were in the right sort of garments to do their mourning. Crape rosettes and an undertaker for manager will complete the outfit.
[Cincinnati Times-Star, reprinted in the Post Express (Rochester, NY), July 30, 1889]

A change of raiment must have brought a change of luck to the visitors. They appeared clothed in spotless white even to caps and stockings, great white woolen stockings with ribs down the sides like weather strips on a barn, and caps much too large.
It was a sudden change from the somber black of the day before, and at first gave rise to the impression that the players, while dressing, had been chased out of the clubhouse in their underclothes, or that a team of bakers had come out to play a match game.
[Morning Call (San Francisco), May 9, 1892]

The St. Louis players wore caps that fairly dazzled the crowd. They were of brown and white striped flannel, and in the distance looked like so many bird cages.
[The Sun (New York), June 4, 1893]

(New York Journal writer) John W. Foster tartly observes:
"If there is one thing that (Washington manager) Arthur Irwin cannot do is to select colors for a base ball uniform. We know those stockings he selected are going to get Arthur in trouble, and the future will prove it.
"What was he thinking about when he ordered hooped (striped) stockings? Did he imagine he was rigging out a team of female song and dance artists? Just imagine Sam Thompson's feelings when he gazes down on his long-drawn shanks and contemplates the ensemble. A cross-section of a piece of old-fashioned jelly cake would be a thing of beauty in comparison.
"Then there's Kid Cross. Maybe he won't present a sort of

phantasmagoria effect, when he skins up for third and the sun's rays fall aslant of those red and black stripes."
[Evening Star (Washington, D. C.), April 21, 1894]

The Phillies look quite chipper in their traveling uniforms of light gray, with black belt and cap to match. The effect is marred, however, with ugly-looking stockings of red and black, which make their legs look like elongated barber poles on a dark night.
[Brooklyn Eagle, April 25, 1894]

Polo Grounds, Apr. 10.—When the Senators trooped into the field this afternoon, the few spectators who were present at the time exclaimed: "Well, look at the Salvation Army band!"
They were quite excusable, too, for of all the quaint uniforms the palm must be awarded to the Washingtons. It is a cross between a bathing suit and a Salvation Army make-up. They wear a startling combination of red and black—black blouses and knickerbockers and red sleeves and stockings. The blouses are belted with scarlet webbing, and atop of each Washingtonian caput is a black-and-red-striped cap that would do excellent service for a tonsorial palace.
[Evening World (New York), May 10, 1894]

The St. Louis uniform makes a horrible blot on the green of the diamond. The suit is of dark blue, trimmed profusely with bright crimson, and carries a tag bearing the title in letters a foot or so long across the shirt front. All that is left of the old Browns is the dingy stockings, some of which look as though handed down for two or three generations.
[Evening World (New York), May 30, 1894]

No such uniforms as those worn by the Colts have been exhibited at Eastern park this year. Those which adorned the St. Louis Browns were fierce. The costumes of Billy Joyce's Senators were piratical, but the Chicagos are simply ghoulish. Steel gray knickerbockers, blouses and caps are bad enough with a strong sun, but with stockings of a dirty white, the effect is startling. It must have taken the designer a week of nightmares to evolve the combination. Jackets of white, reaching below the hips, complete the conception.
[Brooklyn Eagle, June 1, 1894]
Boston, like Joseph of old, believes in a raiment of many colors—red caps, gray pants and shirt, blue stockings and belts. Why not have yellow shoes and a green collar to complete the outlandish rig?

[Baltimore Telegram, reprinted in the Brooklyn Eagle, August 19, 1895]

The Chicago papers were a little inclined to poke fun at the Grand Rapids uniforms. One said they were as gay as the wallpaper skirts so fashionable this season, and the Inter Ocean said "They are as pretty as a pink and green snowball."
[Saint Paul Globe, May 17, 1896]

Bottle green trousers, red stockings, white shirts and blue caps is the song-and-dance make-up the Bostons will wear on the Southern practice trip. Why not add a red vest to this cake-walk toggery?
[Saint Paul Globe, February 14, 1897]

The Boston club will have a novelty in the uniform line the coming season. The shirts will be decorated by a mammoth blue circular patch, upon which the word "Boston" will appear in white. The Beaneaters will look like an assortment of signal flags.
[Evening Star (Washington, D.C.), March 6, 1897]

Manager Schmelz called his Senators to order yesterday morning at National Park, and after a few remarks befitting the occasion, he turned them over to Capt. Tom Brown, who told them to proceed to business.

The players presented a rather motley appearance. There were little men, long men, and short men, and the different uniforms they wore would have furnished material for half a dozen crazy quilts. The left-over suits from last season covered a majority of the athletic forms, but the colors in the caps, sweaters and stockings were as variegated at the leaves of autumn.

Charley Reilly, the new third baseman, was more gorgeous than all in his make-up of a white suit, red sweater, black cap and St. Patrick's day stockings. Manager Schmelz also, 'twixt the bicycle, baseball, and spring fever, looked very debonair in knickerbockers with jacket and cap to match.
[The Times (Washington, D.C.), March 23, 1897]

The Bostonians of the diamond are gotten up this year as if they were cast to do a chorus in Jesse Bartlett Davis' "Serenade." Their traveling uniforms are of a mardi gras make-up, and 'twixt the gray of the caps, the white of their shirts, the steel color of the Knickerbockers and the deep blue socks, they are the most picturesque fellows that ever came down the pike since Gus Schmelz rang the bell on the Senators'

clown clothes of 1894.
[The Times (Washington, D. C.), April 30, 1897]

It is all sheer nonsense to expect players to appear neatly on the ball field with but one change a week. Every club should have two suits for home use, and the men would not look as if they had been exploring the bottom of a mill pond or a pig sty. The public supports the game liberally and is entitled to the best of everything in return.
[Boston Herald, reprinted in the Saint Paul Globe, June 22, 1897]

The Philadelphia Inquirer takes this shot at the (Louisville) Colonels' make-up:
"The Bourbons's traveling make-up is positively the most ultra thing that has developed in base ball garniture since the season in which the players were dressed according to the positions in which they played in the field. Their trousers are unusually long, and suggest the kind McCann furnishes at bathing hours. The stockings, with their horizontal patriotic stripes, convey the idea of teaberry candy sticks of generous proportions, while the caps might be utilized for anything from sleeping in to playing golf."
[Saint Paul Globe, June 5, 1898]

Out-of-this World Ensembles

The Nadjy Uniform

Perhaps the most controversial uniform to appear on the baseball stage during this period took place on July 28, 1888, when the New York Giants emerged from the clubhouse wearing a *stunning suit of coal-black, tight-fitting jersey trunks and shirts, over which the word "New York" is worked in heavy, white letters*. The nobby uniform acquired the name "Nadjy," taken for some reason, presumably, from a comic opera by that name concurrently playing at the Casino theater in the city.
The uniform was unmercifully attacked by many baseball personalities, including writers, who facetiously labeled it as "undertaker" or "mourning" garb. Some wits suggested that New York's title of "the Giants" should be changed to the "Happy Hottentots," on account of the jet-black uniforms.

The Giants appeared on the field clad in their old black jersey suits, which, by the way, in spite of their age, looked far better than the costumes of the Phillies, in which the red and white had so run together that a sort of shrimp pink effect was produced.*[Evening World (New York), July 22, 1889]*

The black "Nadjys" are a success. Out of the most mournful-looking fabric which it is possible for the human mind to conceive Keefe & Becannon have manufactured a mascot that has lifted the Giants up another rung on the ladder of fame.

When the boys came out on the field this afternoon, they looked like nine Hamlets, or better still, like a squad of those dark ghosts which rowed the dying King Arthur over the mystic sea from Camelot. They were Hamlets without Hamlet's menial warp. They were ghost in everything but avoirdupois. They moved like spirits over the green face of nature, but every one of them would have made a penny weighing-machine shriek with agony.

But stay—there was one among them who looked like an airy, fairy Lillian in disguise. Did anybody ever see John Ewing in a Nadjy uniform? If not ,it is well worth a journey out into the wild, woolly West to see him sporting round, far from his native heath, in all the abandon of a skirt dancer without the skirts. From the sausage-like fullness of Crane's fatted calves to the graceful contour of John's Nadjy loins is a range of adipose tissue that fills the gamut of human physique. The only bitter drop of John's cup was the fact that his best girl was not here to cheer him on to victory or death. He did the best he could without her, however, and from the way he pitched it is evident that her bright smile haunts him still.
[The World (N. Y.), July 22, 1890]

Despite its detractors, the uniform was immediately copied—for a while, at least—by the Cincinnati and Louisville clubs. While still in use, the Giants periodically substituted the Nadjy for its color opposite, white with black lettering, a routine that carried over into 1889 when the black uniform was abandoned forever.

Larking Around

On rare occasion uniforms became convenient instruments of amusement. On opening day, for instance, in May of 1888, the entire Chicago team marched onto the field in formation, wearing "tight-fitting shirts and pants of white jersey with black trimmings, and full-dress swallow-tail coats with buttonhole bouquets in the

lapels." The Prince Albert coats were removed once the players reached their bench, and the farce was repeated several more times that year before coming to an end.

The Chicagos made their first appearance on Saturday (in Philadelphia), claw hammer coats and all, and did their little march across the field...The steel-pen garments must be Chicago's "hoodoo," for they have not done very much since they added them to their wardrobe.
[New York Clipper, June 9, 1888]

Likewise, in July, 1892, the Boston team, feeling impish, showed up for play on the South End grounds wearing false beards and "calico and gingham suits of the loudest pattern and color," all of which proved that light moments in baseball truly existed, albeit rarely.

18. Humor in Fans

Baseball fans were called "cranks" back then and its origin is pretty much clouded in mystery. That the term arose in the 1870s was the belief of Thomas W. Lawson, who said so in a book he wrote in 1888, entitled "Kranks":

"The 'Krank' is a heterogeneous compound of flesh, bone and base ball, mostly base ball. He came into existence in the early seventies. He came to stay. The Krank is purely American. He is found in no other country. The Krank has a shell into which he crawls in the month of November. He does not emerge from it until April. While in this shell his only article of food is stray newspaper articles on 'deals.' During the season from April to November, he subsists on air, and waxes strong. His first characteristic is 'knowing it all' the second, 'telling is all.' Times have changed the 'Krank' to a 'Fan,' but is a change in name only."
[Salt Lake Tribune, May 18, 1907]

Be that as it may, the mindset of the average baseball fan has always been as capricious and unpredictable as spring weather, an observation that has been noted on many occasions by writers:

There is probably no more fickle crowd than that which attends base ball games. It likes to make idols of the ball players seemingly for the purpose of tearing them to pieces the next minute.
[Brooklyn Eagle, July 25, 1890]

If prose failed to convey the average baseball fan's abnormal preoccupation with ball scores, verse stepped in to stress the point:

He fears no nation's overthrow,
    Nor cares what kings hold sway;
His ardent soul burns but to know
    Who won the game today.
[Source misplaced]

His eyes were wild, his teeth were set,
  As down the street he ran.
The crowd made way, as on he went,
  For this excited man.
Was fire, murder, sudden death,
  The tidings that he bore?
Oh, no; he is a baseball crank,
  Who wants to know the score.
[Shoe and Leather Reporter, reprinted in the Ludington (Mich.) Record, June, 7, 1888]

Through the ages, the one basic function demanded of all true cranks—and sworn to with the solemnity and permanence of a blood oath—was to make as much noise as possible while rooting the home team to victory.

Strong-lunged voices in Rooters' Row were aided in decibel-shattering volume by any number of noise-making instruments, such as fish horns (type of bugle), reed whistles, cymbals, kazoos, gongs, cowbells, clapper boards, megaphones, and various homemade contraptions.

The Fourth of July brought out the loudest racket-makers of all: "fire-crackers and cannon torpedos," which were, believe it or not, tossed onto the field and deliberately aimed at specific players or the umpire. This potentially hazardous practice, however, paled to that displayed in the wild and woolly Western League, notably Kansas City and Denver, where spectators nonchalantly fired off revolvers into the air to honor key plays and/or victories.

Disapproval of umpires' decisions or dirty play engaged in by opponents drew out the fans' worst behavior of all. In these emergency calls for action, the stands were often the launching pad of airborne missiles ranging from symbols of mild protest—seat cushions, eggs, and quids of tobacco—to heavier statements composed of rocks, bricks, and beer glasses, all meant to inflict harm. As shocking as this is to modern readers, know that such incidents were not unusual on baseball's early, lawless frontier.

*Pittsburg has the name of being the toughest base ball town on earth. Baltimore is famous for its beer-bottle volleys from the bleachers—in the Smoky City (Pittsburg), the Chimmie (Jimmy) Faddens stop nothing short of old iron and coupling pins...Pittsburg rooters don't exactly use gatling guns and Winchesters to help their club along, but they always carry a goodly supply of scrap iron and coal nuggets to fire at any visiting player who has the audacity to attempt a put out.*
[Morning Times (Washington, D.C.), May 7, 1896]

Like many ball players of the era, baseball crowds also developed superstitious habits. In 1889, for example, Giants' fans got it in their heads that the seventh inning was a lucky one and the belief soon spread around the leagues. Its rationale was presumptive, though, being based on a few recent seventh-inning rallies that were thought to be ordained by a higher power. So, to invoke benevolent spirits, rooters as a group, with utter blind faith, obeyed the command, "All up for luck."

Surprisingly, the tradition not only survived, but grew in popularity. In 1892, a new wrinkle appeared that formed the prototype of today's "seventh inning stretch":

The peculiar unanimity with which a large crowd obeys the orders of one man is shown between the innings by the occupants of the bleacherites. As soon as a side is retired, someone gets up in his place and shouts "Everybody stretch!"

With one accord the several thousand men and boys get up, straighten out their cramped limbs, stamp once or twice and shake themselves. Then the same party yells "Everybody down!" and the thing is done with the regularity of a disciplined army.
[Brooklyn Eagle, May 25, 1892]

Through six innings the down-hearted cranks saw great, healthy goose-eggs marked down to Quincy's credit. You would have thought there had been a funeral in the near vicinity and that the mourners were all present with their sorrowing friends. Save the applause in compliment to a brilliant play or a ray of sunshine through the clouds of defeat, the enthusiasm was very, very limited until the "lucky seventh" came. That inning of yesterday's game will long be remembered.

It was one of those where an enthusiast yells until he gets hoarse, then roars until he loses his yelling powers entirely, and winds up by wearing out a brand new pair of shoes trying to kick the boards out of the grand stand floor. There was many a fine tenor and bass voice ruined yesterday and many of them, when the Ravens had scored four runs, sounded like a man with a wooden leg having a fit on the roof. [Quincy (Ill.) Daily Journal, May 17, 1891]

Finally, in 1895, the practice was confined to the seventh inning, thus fulfilling its last requirement, but minus the familiar accompanying tune that topped off the ritual in 1908:

"Now for the lucky seventh, all stretch," said somebody as the home team came in for its half (of the seventh). Everybody arose and stretched, while several rooters turned around three times for luck. [Brooklyn Eagle, May 1, 1895]

Sizing Up The Audience

Most baseball writers, in remarking on a ball park crowd, usually viewed its human makeup as a whole, as if seen through a wide-angle lens. As a result, comments tended to be superficial and impersonal.

Just as the announcement of Boston's loss was made, Kelley leaned on one of Breitenstein's twisters for a corking two-base hit down the third base line. The scene that followed entirely beggars description.

Leading judges, warm from the bench, where weighty questions were being decided, jumped in the air like schoolboys, capering about and throwing their hats up, carried away by the same wave of enthusiastic joy as swayed the most humble bleacherite. Politicians forgot all about schisms, visiting merchants thought all other joys as nothing. Sire and son, master and servant old and young, man and woman—all forgot everything else but that, after the most gallant fighting baseball annals, the Baltimore team had rounded into first place by peerless ball-playing and courage.

There have been other scenes of excitement just as great at Union Park, but that of yesterday is so fresh in the minds of the people that the faint echoes of the other jollifications seem insignificant compared to the tumult of more recent feelings. The over seven thousand people that took part in this great scene left, alive to the fact that a fellow-feeling makes all mankind wondrous kind. The wave of

excitement was intoxicating in its effect, and players and Manager Hanlon where showered with congratulations.
[Baltimore American, August 28, 1897]

For the benefit of the real fan, the man who knows how many freckles are on the back of every player's neck and can tell you the runs, hits and errors made when the picked nine from Columbus's ships defeated the Cat island champions, in 1492.
[Indianapolis Journal, July 1, 1899]

The majority of those who are worthy and proud of the title of "ball cranks" witness the games from the roughly-constructed and completely exposed arrangement known as the "bleaching boards." Perched on seats that seem to be composed principally of aggressive and viciously-barbed splinters, and unprotected from either sunshine or storm, are the men and boys who keep alive the spirit of base-ball; the base-ball leaves of the community; the people who will uncomplainingly eat cold dinner six times a week so long as the home team does its best.
These enthusiasts are deserving of more consideration than has yet been given them. The boards on which they sit should be planed, and over their heads should be stretched a stout canvas awning. When that has been done, their cup of happiness will be full to overflowing and only the umpire will be left for them to kick at.
[Editorial, Evening Star (Washington, D.C.), February 10, 1894]

Few of those sitting on the bleaching words had umbrellas, and the way those unprotected and summer-clad individuals crowded into and under the grand stand reminded one of a flock of frightened sheep.
[Source misplaced]

The grand stand was loaded to the muzzle with ball-loving humanity, from the pert and pretty miss who makes hen tracks on an ivory tablet and calls it "keeping tally," to the crusty old man who possessed himself of two seats and a bag of peanuts at the same time. The bleachers were filled with coatless cranks and the vendors of lemoned liquors and malty froth did a lively business among them.
[Evening World (New York), May 25, 1889]

There is something about a good game of ball that will make a man forget all his troubles, condone with his bitterest enemy, and if his favorite team is winning, the blackest cloud of an unknown future will at once be transformed into a harbinger of brightness. The joy of an opium

fiend is not to be compared with that of a base ball crank, when under the spell of enthusiasm and excitement aroused by an interesting contest, says the Brockton Times.
[Evening Times (Washington, D.C., September 6, 1897]

The story of what happened today may be briefly told. First came the awful struggle at the gates for tickets, then the straining, pushing and fighting for admission, then the scramble for places from which the diamond was visible, until every seat had an occupant, every inch of standing room was pre-empted and men and boys clung, spider-like, to fences, flagstaffs, telegraph poles or any other point of vantage. The Boston "rooters" with their brass band formed so small a part of the vast throng that they sank into comparative insignificance, but the band played on and the "rooters" rooted and shouted all the same.
...During the volley of base hits in the (nine-run) seventh, the crowd was a study. As the first two or three were made, the vast throng (25,375) looked serious, than as hits began to pour out like water from a trough, a smile and then a hearty laugh broke forth, and some could have enjoyed the discomfiture of the Champions more than did their admirers in the vast audience.
Of the many hearty and spontaneous bursts of applause, none were more ringing than that which greeted Hamilton (center fielder, Boston), when, in the fourth inning, after being trampled upon and severely stunned by Jennings at second, he made a grand run for home on Lowe's single, collided with Baltimore's fleshy backstop (Robinson), and, falling heavily, pluckily crawled toward the base, almost fainting as he touched it.
Again, at the end of the game, ten thousand people gathered about the visitors, shook them by the hand, shouted cheerful pleasantries at them, told them what good fellows and fine players they were and finally sent them away with such a shout of approbation as made a fitting climax for the greatest base ball spectacle Baltimore has ever seen. (Boston won rubber game in match for pennant, 19-10)
[Saint Paul Globe, September 28, 1897]

The baseball crank is ordinarily a mild-mannered person of cheerful disposition and a tendency to smile and look pleasant without reference to the quantity of richness of the milk that has been spilled. This is especially true of New York cranks.

Disheartening and overwhelming defeat for the home team invariably calls forth comments of a sympathetic character, while decisions of the umpire, by which the home team is deprived of victory, are noticed by a simple uplifting of the eyebrows. The docile nature of the metropolitan enthusiasts has, however, undergone a change, all the result of the rain storm of yesterday.

For a month past the cranks have been preparing for the happy day when the strong New Yorks would again meet the champion Bostons and take a trifle of the conceit out of the men from the Hub.
[The Sun (New York), April 28, 1893]

Cranks are divided into three separate and distinct classes, denoting as many different stages of baseball insanity. These are the tacks, nails, and spikes, and this classification from a hardware point of view is a fair estimate of their depth of penetration where many of the finer points involved in a game of ball are at issue.
[Morning Call (San Francisco), October 17, 1891]

In fact, there were times when the crowd grew drowsy, and now and then a head nodded, suddenly assuming a most erect and dignified position when a muscular gentleman rang a still more muscular dinner bell to express his great joy.
[New York Journal, July 31, 1897]

Sane patrons are inclined to complain of the war whoops emitted by the more rabid rooters in their efforts to rattle visiting pitchers, and in the racket is becoming a nuisance in the grand stand. Opposing twirlers are entitled to as much consideration, by fair-minded people, as the local talent. Besides, the unearthly shrieks are a positive annoyance to the ladies with nervous systems, and the voice of the umpires simply lost in the uproar. If these men must yell, let them carry empty barrels into which they can stick their heads while letting off steam.
[New York Journal, August 24, 1897]

The rooters were there in all three divisions, and they kept the interest up. Over on the bleachers of Burkeville* sat rows upon rows of wildly tumultuous little boys, skewered like reed birds ready for the grill. In the bedizened boxes were the gem-studded shriekers, adding queer volume to the tumult of sound. And far back in the paddock lolled the languidly enthused, who view the gyrations of their favorite athlete through the portholes of hired hack.

It was the typical crowd of an opening day, early on hand and reluctant to leave, and rooting for the home team from the time the gong sounded. Thus the hours flitted by—hours fraught with alternate outbursts of woe and ecstasy, the deep-lunged baying and airy persiflage of gifted coachers, swats, swipes and futile swings, punctured ever and anon by the muffled plunk of foul tips as they sank to rest in the mushy mitt of the backstop. Great indeed is the national pastime.
[New York Journal, April 22, 1896]
*Left field bleaches behind popular outfielder Eddie Burke

The Indianapolis bleachers are enemies of Umpire Curry. In a recent game he was called a "robber" and a "skin" upon the slightest provocation, and did not get hot until a bleacher called him an "old skeleton," and invited him "to come off the nest." Then he tried to locate the offender, but finally gave it up amidst the laughter of the crowd.
[Pittsburg Press, August 5, 1889]

Cranks of Especial Note

A number of non-sporting celebrities of this era adopted certain teams as their "own," and became ardent supporters.

In New York, for instance, the Giants were cheered to victory in the 1880s and 1890s by a select coterie consisting of well-known comedian Digby Bell; stage performer De Wolf Hopper, who became famous for his recitation of "Casey at the Bat"; and the corpulent Judge Cullom.

All three were holders of the coveted "silver pass," issued to them as a token of friendship by the National League President. It was good for admission to any league game at any league park. One day in 1896, however, the new and unpopular Giants' owner, Andrew Freedman, refused to honor Hopper's pass because of a petty personal slight. In retaliation, the men switched allegiances, first to Baltimore and ultimately to Brooklyn in 1899, which was well-timed as the Trolley Dodgers won the pennant that year.

De Wolf Hopper, Francis Wilson, Digby Bell, George C. Boniface, Jr., and Thomas Powers are found at the Polo Grounds on every baseball afternoon except Saturday. They hug the front rows with persistency, and try to outyell all competitors with schoolboy energy.
[New York Tribune, May 15, 1887]

Baltimore v. Philadelphia:

  Times were made lively by a combination of Digby Bell's Fifty Rooters and Primrose and West's Minstrels. There was music in the air all the while. Sweet choruses from a big box in the upper stand filled in the times between the sharper tones of the bat banging the ball. When the ball was not being hit over the lot, sweet melodies floated from the Fifty Rooters, and the music was certainly the finest ever heard at a ball park. "Music hath charms to soothe the savage beast," and while "The Only Girl in This World for Me" floated over the grounds, there wasn't a man of them who could even look wicked at the umpire, and after the minstrel band had dissolved the air by discussing "Dixie," Steve Brodie was heard soothingly murmuring to himself in center field. It was a happy day for the umpire, who authorizes this paper to say that he will pay the admission every day if the rooting singers will only attend the balance of the season.

  So sure was Baltimore winning after that first inning that the music of the Bell Company and the favor of the minstrel band was like gushing waters to the heated hopes of the spectators, and they thought it the finest thing they had ever experienced to have their tranquil moods told of in such delicious fashion.

  There was Gus Thomas, leading tenor, at the head of it, while Digby Bell, with a voice unidentified, was mixed up in it somewhere, and there were thirty theatrical ladies and more actors adding their might. The music was labeled for Baltimore, and the musical rooters declare it won the game, for it charmed Esper and rattled Lucid.

  They have been out to four games now, and the home team has won each time, so their notes have been gay and pitched up at a high key. Should they run against wet weather sometime, they have something especially dismal prepared.

  So, with joyous song and sweet refrain, they inspired the Champions to do their best and hit the ball. Twelve mascots, dressed in flaring blue and gold, sat on hard pine boards in front of the Baltimore players, and they were armed with brass music. It was the minstrel band, and they were there as the first musical mascots of the season.
[Baltimore American, September 24, 1895]

  Down in the front row over the Brooklyn players' bench sat a New York rooter of 300 pounds or more in avoirdupois, who yelled himself hoarse while the Giants were in the lead. He was none other than the renowned Judge Cullom, who went so far as to bet Tom Kinslow $100 to a bag of peanuts that he could beat the Brooklyn ball tosser in a 100 yard dash. After Ward's men took the lead, his demands to have the Giants make a hit were heart rending.

[Brooklyn Eagle, July 30, 1892]

> *Hats and canes were thrown to the winds, and Judge Collum sat down on a tray of beer in his excitement.*

[The Sun (New York), August 1, 1894]

> *About the most surprised individual on the grounds was Judge Cullom, who has his own seat chained up (at Brooklyn's Eastern park) and carries the key in his vest pocket.*
>
> *There was an "I told you so" expression about his fat and smiling countenance during the early part of the game, which led him to several indiscretions, notably among them being a disposition to guy the Brooklyn players every time they came to the bench. Again he offered odds anywhere from $100 to $1,000 to $1 with a wine supper thrown in that the New Yorks would win in a walk, and strange to say there were no takers.*
>
> *When the Brooklyns made their wonderful rally and finally won, the judge sat as quiet as if he were in the electrical chair and it is safe to say that Carlyle Harris was more cheerful than he, despite the fact that the judge occupied his own padlocked receptacle for his three hundred or more pounds of concentrated crankiness. After the game he dragged himself laboriously out of the grounds, and concealed his own private key and his individuality in the crowd. He was the most disgusted New York rooter of them all.*

[Brooklyn Eagle, May 10, 1893]

Boston's counterpart to the New York triumvirate of fans was a wealthy and reclusive enthusiast by the name of "General" Arthur E. "Hi Hi" Dixwell, who occupied a private box at the park, luxuriously furnished. His unusual title, implying a military origin, was a misnomer; the "Hi Hi" part was not. On the former hangs the following tale:

> *Dixwell at one time was a minority stockholder in the Boston club; and when the Boston management declined one season to sell season tickets, Dixwell was very indignant. He set up what he called a "gen'ral petition." The old man bothered everybody so much about this petition that they got to calling him "Old General Petition." This finally dwindled down to "General," and Mr. Dixwell has since been known as General Arthur Dixwell.*

[Wichita Daily Eagle, June 13, 1891]

Of the second part, the following explains:

He (Dixwell) occupied a front seat in the stands, kept a careful score and studied the game with a seriousness that was appalling. He maintained a deep silence during almost all the game, but when a really great play was made, he emitted two sharp staccato barks: 'Hi Hi!' and then dropped into silence again.
[Washington (D. C.) Herald, October 1, 1911]

It was the unstinting habit of Dixwell to lavish gifts upon the team, among them a customary box of cigars after every victory. He often followed the team on the road, which is where his constant yelping was deemed a nuisance and got him into trouble.
In 1891, for instance, the president of the Baltimore club ordered him silent, and the following year, Charles Byrne, owner of the Brooklyns, warned Dixwell before a game to shut up or risk expulsion. Nothing came easy in the old days.

Cranks Up-Close and Personal

There were also writers who loved to zero in on certain individuals in the stands whose oddball appearance or antics simply cried out for comment.

The Brooklyn baseball crank has characteristics all his own. He loves to sit on the back of his opera chair, composed of an oak plank, about an inch wide, and stamp with his feet on the seat. The only reasonable theory for this unusual custom, if the reader will kindly pardon the digression, is that the Brooklyn crank pays his fifty cents with a primary desire to keep "on edge" during the game. Please omit cabbage heads and carrots of mature years.
Then, too, the Brooklyn crank loves to talk through an improvised megaphone, formed by rolling up a poster, and the sallies of wit that float over the diamond may be crude, but a baseball crowd is like that at a minstrel show—'twill laugh at anything. Levity is vastly more conspicuous at Brooklyn games than base hits.
The leading megaphone orator of the day directed his remarks at the Brooklyn mascot yesterday afternoon, and today that ebon-hued young man may be hiding in some haystack, trembling for his safety. It was at the fifth stage of the contest that he thundered across the campus, "Say, if we don't win today, we'll kill the mascot."
The son of an African king, who carries bat bags and buckets of

water in his honest endeavor to pull the Brooklyns through to victory, turned two shades paler and looked ready to bolt for the grand stand. Finally he summoned courage to stick it out, and for a few moments in the ninth inning, it looked as though luck was coming his way. But, after mocking the players and the mascot with her smiles, Dame Fortune daintily lifted her skirts, said, "Ta, ta, s'mother's day, boys," and disappeared in the direction of Sheepshead Bay.
[New York Journal, July 7, 1897]

    There was a man from Sioux City in the grand stand on Friday—a traveling man apparently, for he wore a splendid blue scarf with diamond attachments, a leopard vest, and pulled his trowsers up when he sat down to prevent them bagging at the knees. His clothes fitted him to a nicety, and he sat bolt upright with a score book in his hand when the game began.
    In the second inning...dropped an easy fly and let in two runs. The Sioux City man's fist flew out like a shot, his necktie walked around under his ear, his leopard vest almost changed its spots, and he rained imprecations on G. W. for half of a minute at the rate of thirty to the second. Then Joe Miller knocked out a two-bagger, and the Sioux City man collapsed entirely. The transformation was scarcely less striking than the metamorphosis of the very good Dr. Jekyll into the very bad Mr. Hyde.
[St. Paul Daily Globe, September 29, 1889]

    There is to be a game of ball tomorrow. "A weal live game of ball?" says one. "Impossible. Why we haven't had such a thing in three weeks."
    Nevertheless, dear people, it is a fact, and if you only stand on the sidewalk along the line of march, tomorrow afternoon, you will see the swells of crankdom, literally falling over one another in their anxiety to get there.
    Oh, what a rolling, rollicky mass of humanity it is, which with cosmopolite indifference good-naturally jostle and bandy each other on the ways to the ground. Then how easy to call the turn on each individual.
    There's the board of trade man over in the corner of the car. How do we know it? Just listen and you will learn. Futures? Oh, ha, you have him already. He talks about the game, you see, in the vernacular of the shop.
    Look at that sedate-looking gentleman on the third seat. That's a deacon, who passed the plate this morning in a high-toned down-town

church. Note the twitch to his lip and twinkle in his eye. God bless the old boy, his heart is in the right place, the world is better for his living.

There next to him—that dark-browed man, I mean—is the villain. 'Tis he who will make a holy show of himself presently, should the home club lose, by talking of conspiracies, put up jobs and damnable plottings. There, too, is the hilarious cuss, and the idiot who "told yer so." Well, well, they'll all be there tomorrow, go and see them for yourself.
[Milwaukee Journal, August 16, 1890]

Louisville has evidently unearthed a base ball crank who will take rank with Brooklyn's William C. DeWitt, Boston's General Hi Hi Dixwell and New York's Judge Cullom. The (Louisville) Commercial describes him as follows:

"Seated in the grand stand at Eclipse park yesterday afternoon was a thin, cadaverous individual who never once took his eyes off the massive form of Sanders, the Varsity twirler of the Colonels, who was out in the sun with the perspiration rolling off his Hamlet countenance like rain off a roof.

"The strange onlooker was not a fan, but no fan ever pulled harder for victory than did the intellectual-looking man. At times a faint tinge of blood would mount to his pallid cheeks. He looked like a college professor all over. The hey day of his youth had evidently been spent far from the ball field. The musty atmosphere of the ancient classics seemed to cling to him and pervade the stand.

"When the battle seemed to be turned against the Colonels, he raised his gold-rimmed eyeglasses to the sky and softly repeated a supplication to the gods in the purest Greek for victory. This prayer was heard and in the fag end of the contest, when the game looked irretrievably lost to the Colonels through errors, lo and behold! Pfeffer's men fell on smiling Trafalgar McMahon's curves like an avalanche and slugged out victory.

"Then the joy of the pale-faced stranger knew no bounds. He could hardly remain in his seat while the Colonels were putting the finishing touches on the contest by retiring three Orioles at first. As soon as Ward, the last man, was retired by Merritt, the happy collegian rushed to the rail of the grand stand; he frantically called to Sanders and after attracting his attention, he cried in ecstasy, "Magnificent, magnificent!" and then subsided and resuming his staid, somber look, he fell in with the crowd and wended his way slowly through the turnstile."
[Brooklyn Eagle, August 26, 1892]

William F. Tydings, the big colored man who made the Union Park welkin ring in 1894 with his stentorian "Ginger up—how many?" is back in town, and says he will be at his old stand this season with something new. Tydings says he has spent the winter at St. Augustine, Fla. He looks prosperous, and says he is Maryland champion of the cake-walkers. He was with the Philadelphias last season, where he sold sandwiches, as he does here, and rooted for the Quakers until the Champions came, when his bugle mouth was sealed.
[Baltimore American, April 10, 1896]

There was one young man, we heard some one call him Murphy, who is probably the most modest, retiring individual in seventeen states. The audience divided its time between the game and Bro. Murphy's mouth. Bro. Murphy's mouth is the most generous piece of furniture that we have any knowledge of at the present writing. He has a rich, dark brown voice that goes with the mouth at the same price.

We have no idea where he keeps that voice at night and on Sunday. He has brought it with him in the last two games of base ball, and given the people an opportunity to get acquainted with it. On Saturday last he brought it to us and introduced it. As we withdrew our attention from all earthly things and banished all other cares and afflictions from our mind, we gazed down into the depths of that young man's anatomy, studied the marvelous internal mechanism of his digestive organs and realized more than ever before, how wonderful are the works of the Creator. That young man's voice will haunt us for many long, weary days. Its robust notes still fill our ears, and if we live for a century to come, we shall ever hold that voice in humble reverence.

The young man is not in keeping with his voice. He is of slight and effeminate build. His girlish face with modesty pictured upon it would not suggest the muscular tones of the steam calliope, or the wild, weird screech of the African glasticutus (sic). And yet this blushing, backward boy can give them both pointers. Our rural neighbors may not have much of a ball team, and they may be behind the balance of the world in everything save mud, but we defy any place on this mundane planet to produce a "rooter" who can make more noise of a seriously objectionable character than can this remarkable young person who answers to the name of Murphy.

Murphy was a leader of the Logan choir at the game on Saturday. His seal brown voice could be heard above all the rest. Out of the general pandemonium, the notes of Murphy's bazoo arose and swelled like the squall of the Thomas cat in a feline carousel in the silent

watches of the night. He may be here next week and our people will have an opportunity to hear him. They won't have to visit the ball park to listen to his mellow notes. He can be heard to the summit of Mt. Pleasant.
[The Ohio Democrat (Logan, O.), June 23, 1896]

    There is one instance of a banker of sedate mien, with white mutton chop whiskers and a smug exterior, who, when spoken to on the question of baseball, smiles, shrugs his shoulders and refuses to be drawn into a discussion. Yet at dinner at night he is wildly jubilant or immoderately depressed, according to the results of the day's game. He has not missed a game this year, except on Tuesdays and Fridays, when he is compelled to be present at board meetings. He is only one of literally hundreds of men who are known to the frequenters of the ball grounds, and who are wound up in the national game to a degree of absorption that even the devotees of racing could not rival.
[The Sun (New York), reprinted in the Orleans County Monitor (Barton, Vt.), July 16, 1894]

    Cincinnati has a brand new rooter this year in the person of a white-whiskered man, who must have celebrated his 70th birthday some time ago. The old man wears a straw hat and a handkerchief, besides the other garments required in civilized communities. He carries a dilapidated umbrella and always sits in one corner of the bleachers. Upon the slightest provocation he gets up and shouts and the bleacherites make the chorus strong.
[Saint Paul Globe, May 7, 1897]

    It was fondly hoped that when the long-haired nuisance who was wont to make a sideshow of himself last year from the top gallery in the grandstand had been squelched, the patrons of the game would be permitted to enjoy themselves. But fate has decreed otherwise. At yesterday's game, there was a full-grown man with a base ball vocabulary consisting of one word, and he was garrulous at that.
[Kansas City Times, reprinted in the Saint Paul Globe, June 27, 1898]

    Our fellows simply won on superior play, aided by the advent of the fish peddler mascot on the right field bleachers. He used to sit in the grand stand with his whistle, bell and horn, but the enthusiastic gentleman had squandered so much money for newspapers in which he expected to find favorable notices with portraits of himself and his paraphernalia that he was obliged to retrench.

Grand stand patrons who root with the hands and tongues only are delighted with the change. However, the man with the bells and other implements of torture helped the game along by applauding every effort of the home team, and the less rabid fans followed his lead.
[Dryden, New York Journal, September 15, 1897]

He was alone in his glory, like the lone fisherman in Evangeline. He was a stranger from the alfalfa district, but he had the whole kindergarten bleachers to himself. He only occupied one solitary seat, however, on the extreme end, but he was observed by everybody.

The stranger wore a biled* shirt and was protected from the sun's rays by an umbrella. In one pocket was noticed a copy of the Herald with an account of the thirteen-inning game. He also came armed with a tin horn, a bottle of "sojer water" and a voice that would do duty for a calliope in a circus parade.

Well, the stranger had more fun to the square yard than everybody else at the ball game. He was a fan from way back and the way he rooted for Los Angeles just double-discounted either John Brink or Digby Bell in their palmiest days. In fact, the rooter and his bugle blasts on a 10-cent fish horn made more than one person laugh.

The stranger unloaded a bushel of witty remarks during the game, and Manager Van Derrick should lose no time in getting the man from the rural district on his pay roll. He is a whole show in himself, and he managed to keep the grand-stand in good nature throughout the entire contest.

Virtue is its own reward.
[Los Angeles Herald, August 7, 1892]
* Boiled

One of the regular occupants of a seat on the grand stand is a young man with heavy features. The lower part of his face is so heavy that it sags down, leaving his mouth always open. He wears a high collar and a stiff hat and carries a small tree for a cane.

If a player gets his base on called balls, the man with the cane applauds. If the player hits a foul ball, the cane thumps the floor; when the umpire says "three balls," or "two strikes," the cane thumps the floor.

No matter what happens, or fails to happen, the bangity-thump-bang of the fat dude's cane resounds through the grand stand. He applauds when a player gets out, applauds when he is safe, applauds a catch and applauds a muff, and he spits on the floor when the New Yorks make a run.

[St. Paul Daily Globe, July 3, 1887]

The Brooklyn *Eagle* Portfolio of Ball Field Weirdos

On the subject of remarkable ball park characters, baseball historians owe a debt of gratitude to the writer of the Brooklyn *Eagle* in the early 1890s, who kept just as sharp an eye on the human composition of the stands as action on the field.

His graphic, in-depth sketches captured their dress, mannerisms, and actions in a delightfully whimsical way. Along the way, we see just how much—and how little—the habits and foibles of those attending a game of ball has changed over a century's worth of time.

Quod vide:

At Tuesday's game (in Brooklyn) a friend who was old enough to know better, or else his gray hair and whiskers belied his age, gave vent to his enthusiasm when Anson struck out by blowing a whistle on the top of a silver-headed cane. The noise he made was a cross between Sheridan's voice and the saw mill racket over the way. He only blew twice and the grand standers in his neighborhood immediately changed their seats.

This same man said to (Brooklyn captain/player) Griffin, "You're doing well, Mike!" Griffin, in his quiet, easy way, with just the faintest tinge of sarcasm, replied, "Yes; I think I am on the improve!"

A veritable grass-eater (Irishman) from way back, accompanied by a friend who evidently didn't know a home run from the umpire's mask, afforded much amusement to those who were fortunate enough to be within hearing distance at one of the games recently.

O'Brien was his pet, and the way he showered praises on Darby would have made the rest of the team green with envy could they have heard him. The grass-eater had been explaining Darby's bunting abilities, and incidentally enlightening his friend as to what a bunt was, but seemed to make little headway. A runner was on second and O'Brien went to bat.

"Now, thin, Da-a-arby, boont it!" was the advice given. "Strike one!" said the umpire. "Boont it, Da-a-arby," pleaded the grass-eater. "Strike two!" was heard, as Darby nearly turned a somersault in his frantic endeavor to send the ball down to the center field fence.

A couple of foul tips followed. The old man was uneasy, and in a heart-rending voice said, "Boont it, Da-a-arby; phy the divil doant oo' boont it?"

"Strike three!" came in harrowing tones, as Darby walked back to the bench.

"Is that what ye call a boont, Moike?" said the friend. The old man subsided; his heart was broken.
[Brooklyn Eagle, June 16, 1892]

A small boy with an eye to the main chance (grand stand) pocketed $1.25 worth of rubber, hemp and sheepskin which came sailing over the rail fence at the bleaching boards during the sixth inning. The coming star, ball and all, made a dash for the stands, but Fritz, who does the "gate," nabbed him and compelled the boy to disgorge. There was quite an uproar for the time being, but it soon subsided.
[Brooklyn Eagle, June 2, 1892]

The man who pays 25 cents for a seat on the bleacheries and has a $2 umbrella smashed by a foul tip is the same person who walks home to save car fare and spends 10 cents for a whisky sour.
[Brooklyn Eagle, June 3, 1892]

Among the regular attendants at the ball game is a jolly, pleasant-faced little man who divides his time between the proof room, ball grounds and half a dozen or more masonic bodies. He invariably makes a bee line for the row of seats directly over the Brooklyn players' bench.

If too late, he will sit patiently in the row behind, until somebody moves, and then with a skip and jump, he is in his favorite position. Our masonic friend is well acquainted with symbols, but he does not know the first rudiments of scoring. He cares little about that, however, but dotes on a close game, with Brooklyn having just a shade the better of it.
[Brooklyn Eagle, June 7, 1892]

A view of the grand stand brought to the surface some of the peculiar specimens of the genus crank. Seated at the left hand side of the stand was a consumptive-looking person, who was wrapped up in a heavy shawl, which covered every available portion of his anatomy except his face. This was turned straight toward the diamond throughout the entire game and his interest never flagged, although an occasional fit of coughing caused him some distress. Beside him huddled a little woman, evidently his wife, who divided her time between the game and arranging the shawl, which fell off when the young man jumped up and danced around when a member of the Brooklyn team made a brilliant play.

A few seats removed from this couple was the robust young man who roots for the opposing team "just because he goes by contraries." This fellow applauded every fine play made by the Philadelphians, and correspondingly jeered at anything off-color on the part of the Brooklyns. Then, when the game was over, he got up and howled louder than all the rest over the home team's victory. This is the young man that bets on a 100 to 1 shot at the races because the favorite might fall down and break his neck in the stretch.

Way down in front was a fine-looking old man, gray haired and happy, with a handsome little fellow, presumably his grandson, beside him. There were many knotty points for him to solve, which he did with the assistance of the small boy, whose tongue was ever ready to set his companion right on the subject of base hits, strike outs and foul tips.

An ancient-looking couple, fresh from the backwoods of Canarsie, who were under the care of their city cousins, stared at the antics of the players as if they were at a theater. Although they did not understand a single thing about the game, they cheered when others did, while the old man jumped up despite his rheumatism, and watched the course of the ball from the time it left the bat until it reposed in the paws of some graceful outfielder. Then he sat down with twitching muscles and remarked confidently to his better half that it was "mighty slick the way them fellows handled that there piece of chained lightning."

Perhaps the most numerous was the gay young man with his best girl. The accepted idea of a youthful couple of this description is that they are as much alone in a crowd as if they were at home in her parent's best parlor and they act accordingly. While everybody else is absorbed in the battle of the giants, his arm steals surreptitiously along the back of her chair, and as she leans back his hand in some peculiar manner known only to themselves, gently grasps her. Then his head inclines toward her ear and, for the time being, the game may go on as it pleases for all they care. Unless the ubiquitous small boy is elsewhere, their blissful thoughts are allowed to go on uninterrupted, but if he is close by, they are doomed. Suddenly, as the young man is about to say his most sugared say, a small voice behind them yells: "Play ball!" They know that this is directed to them and they turn all their thoughts to the game.

Perhaps the liveliest party at the game was the "Mad Bargain" company, which is making a short stay in New York. While in Philadelphia last week, the Brooklyn team was the guest of the company, and the ball players returned the compliment. There were fully a dozen in the party and they did all they could to encourage the home team to win.

Over behind first base was the man who always likes to sit where he can see how the pitcher twirls the ball and he entertained those within a dozen rows of him with his ideas on what the umpire should have called a strike or a ball. His judgment is indisputable and he has facts and figures to prove his assertions. These are accordingly acknowledged as the only authorized rulings by his hearers.

On the upper tier sat the young woman who does not know the umpire from a hit to right field and the young man who knows it all, and is there not only to enlighten her, but also all those within hearing distance. This is the couple that is surprised because the seats in their immediate vicinity are religiously shunned by interested spectators.

The "Well, well, well!" man was interesting, but, by some unfortunate miscalculation, the man who crows like a rooster was not there. He had evidently been overlooked when the invitations were sent out, and as he does not always have the wherewithal to gain admission, his voice was not raised in exultation over the victory. The evident attempt on the part of the club to ignore such an important personage is an affront on the Sixth ward, of which the rooster man is a prominent resident.

Perhaps the most conspicuous person at the game was the man who thought he was at the old Washington ball grounds. When Dave Foutz came to the bat in the seventh inning, this individual got up on his hind feet and yelled encouragingly:

"Now, Dave, put 'er over the Fourth avenue fence."

It is needless to say that Mr. Foutz failed to follow this advice.
[Brooklyn Eagle, May 6, 1893]

Along toward the third inning a tall, young man with a cracked cornet wandered in from some unknown quarter and began to toot encouraging blasts for both sides indiscriminately.

When Schoch caught a ball, he was greeted with a reveille, and when Ehret struck out Stovey, the cornetist sounded taps. When Foutz anchored on third in the sixth, his arrival was greeted with a single blast that must have shaken every nerve in Ehret's body and caused his red hair to burn more fiercely.

Then Secretary Ebbets threw a bag of peanuts into the mouth of the instrument and Brooklyn made four runs.
[Brooklyn Eagle, June 3, 1893]

Cranks who sit on the end of the grand stand nearest the bleaching boards cannot fail to have noticed, sitting in nearly the same spot day after day, a short, quiet-appearing young man with dark curly hair and eyeglasses which give him an intellectual appearance, who keeps a full score of the game according to his lights on the subject.

There are only two things really remarkable about him. One is his unique method of scoring the direction of base hits. Each and every hieroglyphic of this kind resembles a miniature gallows with some poor unfortunate hanging on either side or the other. His second peculiarity is illustrated in this fashion: Whenever a Brooklyn man makes a big it or a fine play, he turns to his friend and says: "Say, buy peanuts, will you? Here comes the boy."
[Brooklyn Eagle, June 18, 1893]

    Those who sit over behind first base will notice an interesting picture which may be seen almost every day on one of the housetops beyond the left field fence. Shortly before the umpire calls play, a man carrying a chair, an umbrella and a palm leaf fan appears through the scuttle, places the chair firmly near the edge of the roof, plants himself down, raises the umbrella and is ready to watch the proceedings undisturbed. He looks for all the world like the lone fisherman in a well-known opera and takes things with Christian-like resignation, notwithstanding the fact that he is beating the Brooklyn club out of the price of admission.

    There are fully one hundred spectators who watch the ball game daily in this way. Not only are neighboring roofs covered with cranks who root just as conscientiously for the home team as if they paid for the privilege, but windows, fire escapes and other available places contiguous to the ball grounds are crowded with deadheads. Even the engineers, firemen, brakemen and conductors on trains of the Canarsie road stand on the roofs of their cars and watch the sport. The waiting specials on the Kings county L (elevated) also have their full compliment, despite the distance.

    Among the daily visitors on the grand stand is a tall young man, with a downy something on his upper lip which might be taken for cigar ashes but for his otherwise spruce make-up. What he does not know about base ball may be seen in the league guide, but in his own estimation there is no episode on the ball field which he cannot fully explain. While Burns was on third in the fourth inning the other day, Richardson flied out to Dowd. The youth arose in all his splendor and yelled ecstatically: "Good boy, Danny. That was a beautiful three bagger." And he wondered why everybody else maintained a discrete silence.

    These warm days are uncomfortable for the bleaching board occupants. Were it not for the balmy breezes that blow from Jamaica

bay, the uncovered stand would be too hot for occupancy. Some long-headed cranks bring umbrellas and find them useful.
[Brooklyn Eagle, June 10, 1894]

The field seats were solidly packed. Curiously enough, every man and boy on the field seats wore a black derby hat. There was not a single tall hat, felt hat, bonnet or straw hat to relieve the even monotony of the solid phalanx. Looked at sidewise, or from above, the field seats had much the effect of a great pile of cannon balls.
[Brooklyn Eagle, April 24, 1892]

(Opening day):
There were to be seen, of course, a few who had taken the precaution to do all of their nerve-soothing in a bunch in advance, and judging from their antics some of them must have anticipated a very nervous affair, indeed. This does not mean that they were obnoxious, for a more orderly gathering of the size was never seen and the fifty coppers that lined the inner side of the field had absolutely nothing to do but stand up and take all the guying the good-natured crowd could hand their way.
...But there were several funny men. One of these, a little the worse for wear, sat in the grand stand and periodically stood up and shouted and waved his hat until he lost both voice and hat. Then he stood up and gasped until his legs failed him. Behind him sat a sad-looking individual with a dinner bell and an effeminate voice, the two making a highly picturesque combination. The nearby crowd had doubtless been happy with either had t'other of the dear charmers been away. As it was, however, they made some fun.
[Brooklyn Eagle, April 16, 1899]

The action of the spectators, as inning after inning came and went and the string of goose eggs lengthened, was amusing to the cool-headed veterans who sat in the front row. One despairing crank wanted the game called and resumed today with the same player in each position.
Along toward the ninth inning, a diminutive Scotchman with a prodigious growth of whiskers and a heavy cord holding him to his spectacles invited his friend to go down and liquidate. They got as far as the top step and turned to watch the last man out. They waited another inning and still another, their eyes riveted on the changing scene. When the thirteenth inning had ended and Stein had crossed the plate with the winning run, they were still there, the drink and everything, but the game

forgotten.

    All sorts of experiments were tried by the cranks to bring luck to the home team. To the right of the reporters' box sat a stout young man with a boy companion. The boy had a shock of red hair that grew rusty from overexcitement. When the thirteenth inning began, the boy started to change his seat for luck. Quick as thought the young man grabbed him by the scruff of the neck and held him down by main force. Today he is telling all his friends that his action won the game.

    The bleacherites did everything possible to mascot the home team. Hats were turned, fingers were crossed and faces were twisted in all shapes in the effort to coax Dame Fortune into bringing home the necessary run. The man with the umbrella held the point downward. Other equally impressive ceremonies were gone through to hoodoo the visitors.

    J. Earle Wagner, the Washington magnate, sat in a front row and went through some interesting performances. He changed his seat a half dozen times and became so excited that he could not keep still. He dashed up the incline of the grand stand and stood at the top for a few minutes only to return and repeat the performance. Then he borrowed a cigar and lit it, but was unable to enjoy the weed. (Washington won, 1-0)
[Brooklyn Eagle, June 27, 1895]

    For quality, the attendance yesterday could not be equaled...It was a good-natured assemblage of Brooklynites, with just enough New York rooters sprinkled about to prevent the shouting for the home team from becoming monotonous. The Gotham enthusiast is a strange being with a disposition not unlike that of a mule. He will call the Giants dubs and other things calculated to make other people believe that they are beneath notice, but when it comes to saying something nice about the Brooklyn team, that New Yorker would rather lose a limb.

    There were a number of specimens at Eastern park yesterday, and the way they shouted for Washington was a caution. They were in their element and the best the Brooklyn folks could do was to say nothing. This refers to the grand stand. On the bleachers and in the pavilion the Gothamites, if there were any, had to do the thinking, as the occupants of those two choice locations will brook no foreign interference. If they want to call the home team rotten they'll do it, but the Brooklyns will have to play poorly before any such thing happens.

    They didn't have long to wait yesterday, because in the very first inning the home team played what the bleacherites call for the grand stand and they demurred. La Chance threw the ball into the outfield in an effort to make a star double play and the groan that went up must have made the big first baseman's hair stand on end. But the suffering occasioned by this misplay wasn't a marker to that caused by Captain Griffin's muff of Abbey's fly. The idol was shattered into at least 17,000 pieces.

Hisses actually mingled with the yells of horror that went up, the first that ever greeted a misplay on the part of the captain. Similar misplays during the remainder of the game and inability to bat Mercer's tantalizingly slow delivery were the cause of defeat. Bases on balls, in the gift of which Gumbert and Harper were unnecessarily generous, contributed to the downfall.
[Brooklyn Eagle, April 30, 1896]

Those who have seen an old man with grizzled beard and horn-rimmed spectacles gazing with undivided attention at the diamond, from a seat well out of the reach of foul tips, will recognize Under Sheriff Hugh McLaughlin, more familiarly known as Bud McLaughlin. He usually sits with his feet firmly planted on the edge of the seat in front of him, while a fuma protrudes, unlit and unnoticed, from his lips. He invariably carries a body guard in the person of his nephew, who performs the same office on the night of a battle at the Coney Island casino.
[Brooklyn Eagle, May 27, 1893]

The recent cold weather that made the limbs and fingers of the bridegrooms (Brooklyn) tingle at Eastern park brought into relief the features of a hitherto undiscovered style of bleachery-haunting crank, who, despite his best efforts, was unable to secure for himself immunity from the natural effects of indulgence of his propensity on others. He sat mid-way up from the bottom row on the hard, cold boards and he had secured his position half an hour before the teams began to practice.

He was dressed in his last summer's clothes, brown derby hat and all, and his gaunt, bony figure and cadaverous countenance apparently offered little opposition to the breeze. Curiously enough, his mustaches were long and silky, otherwise the enterprising zephyr which hustled by might have gone unrewarded.

My attention was attracted to the phenomenon by a series of low, ill-bred chuckles and spasmodic contortions resulting from an effort to restrain more boisterous mirth on the part of several portly, overcoated fellows in my rear whom I set down at once as medical men. Presently the laughter grew and spread until it came in a hilarious chorus from behind and on both sides of me. The provocation for this singular unanimity which seemed to swallowed up all disputes about the game and every other topic came to me along with the reigning infection when my glance rested on the crank

That individual was engaged in one of the most remarkable performances of which modern civilization has any authentic record. He was chewing tobacco, puffing a cigar, ballasting his whiskers against the heavy wind and while shaking like an aspen was keeping what would be a perfectly correct score in Choctaw, meanwhile applauding all the good plays with feet, hands and lungs. It was, however, not the diversity of this specimen's accomplishments that made him the cynosure of all eyes, but the artistic style in which he shivered.

Tremors started at the toes of his big, loose-fitting shoes and ran in eloquent ripples up the length of his anatomy, getting in particularly fine work on the small ribs and along the vertebral column, until, reaching the caput, the up and down motion was diversified by a side twist of the jaw with castanet performance of the teeth and a spasmodic contortion of the abdomen. Each successive shake seemed more violent than the preceding one and the breeze was freshening and the laughter growing all the while.

The crank finally took his eyes off the game long enough to buy a glass of beer. He tried to drink but spilled it down the back of his neck instead. Then he bought peanuts, but his aim was so unsteady that in only one case in thirteen by count was he able to get the kernel where it would do the most good. "Gracious!" he said finally, "there must be something the matter with me."

At the imminent risk of getting into fights with a dozen men who through his motions were backed by hostile intent, the arch-shiverer passed down the tiers of seats and out of the gate, and as the laughter subsided, I heard one of the fat men say: "Well, I've seen little yaller dogs shake, but I'll bet that fellow can shiver a mile a minute ahead of any canine that ever grabbed a bone."
[Brooklyn Eagle, May 17, 1891]

The Brooklyn *Eagle* All-Stars

Among this writer's vast collection of misfits on public display in the stands, there were a select few who deserved even closer inspection and commentary. They were the ones who tickled the fancy of spectators and writers alike for their odd, one-of-a-kind methods of impromptu rooting that turned into comic routines, not by design, but by accident. Essential to their success was, as with umpires and coaches, a strong voice that soared over the background clangor of the stands.

But their fifteen minutes of fame usually came to inglorious ends. What was amusing and entertaining at first became stale and tiresome with repetition, and the erstwhile entertainers of the bleaching boards ultimately became yesterday's news.

Baseball writers elevated a number of the more picturesque performers to celebrity status, whose mere mention by name lent a welcome and familiar touch to readers of the sports page. In this folklorish manner we welcome readers to a few larger-than-life characters, thanks to this writer's obsessive fascination with this rare and colorful species of spectator.

The Rooster Man

"The rooster man's a jolly fellow,
He's up to every play.
'Tis fun to hear his noisy bellow—
Uhr, aroo, ouray!"

This unforgettable individual was first noticed by a New York reporter in August, 1886, when his loud crowing pierced the air at the Staten Island grounds and earned for him the original nom de plume (no pun intended): "the Brooklyn chicken." He soon took his act to the Polo Grounds, where he was declared a good-luck charm. From that time forward, the human rooster shuttled between the Brooklyn and New York ball parks, effectively pestering and entertaining those in his immediate vicinity, all at the same time.

The human rooster appeared on the bleaching boards in a white blazer, a demitasse hat and a new assortment of alleged imitations of barnyard fowl.
[Brooklyn Eagle, June 5, 1894]

His true identity was finally "unfeathered" in 1892:

Everybody from Bay Ridge to the city hall knows Thomas C. Murray, better known as Tomsey Murray, the rooster man. Tomsey is quite an important personage in the Sixth ward (Brooklyn), having had a social club named after him, an honor which is vainly sought by half the population of Alderman Wafer's bailiwick. Tomsey was a frequent visitor at Washington park in the halcyon days of 1889, when the admission fee was not too great for Tomsey's purse.

Then he crowed the Brooklyn team into the championship, despite the fact that umpires and policemen tried to suppress him. The 50 cent tariff of the past two years was too much for Tomsey's ideas of equity and he stayed severely away, leaving the team without his needful assistance. When the magnates proposed a 25 cent admission, Tomsey gave his sanction to the scheme and it was decided on.

Now, Ward's men have no firmer adherent than this same Tomsey, who visits Eastern park daily, without the incumbrance of a coat and vest, but with his suspenders showing prominently, a la summer girl. He brings his voice with him and uses it to good effect when a good play is made by the home team. Tomsey is well known and admired by the bleachers, not for his looks, however, but for his crowing abilities, which are envied by all those who know him.
[Brooklyn Eagle, August 3, 1892]

Tomsey's unorthodox style of rooting ceased in the greater New York area in 1897, when he flew the coop and came to roost in Pittsburg, where he was last seen performing his unusual act.

The Well, Well, Well Man

Also competing for pain-in-the-neck honors was this spectator, who responded to plays with a unique comment of his own invention, "well, well, well," which, rendered in a deep, rumbling and sonorous tone, reverberated uncomfortably around the bleaching boards. Deemed a nuisance by ball park officials, he was often asked to leave the premises of Eastern Park in Brooklyn; those at the Polo Grounds took it one step further in 1895 by permanently barring him entrance. Flaunting authority, however, he continued to sneak in and make his stentorian presence known.

In an article on baseball "fans" in the August American Magazine, Hugh S. Fullerton writes as follows about two famous old baseball fans:

"'Well, well, well,' was another character who was named because of his cry, which followed just after a big outburst of applause on the part of the crowd. The moment the applause subsided, his 'Well, well, well' would boom over the field and never failed to start the cheering again.
[Perrysburg (Ohio) Journal, June 13, 1913]

A man with a large brick-red mustache, a wild eye, and a

generally disheveled air has made a practice of going to the Polo grounds and shouting in a frenzied way for opposing teams. With him, it is anything to beat the New Yorks, and every successful play of opposing players is greeted with the screech: "Well, well, well! Did you see that?"

This conduct has rather jarred on the feelings of the New York rooters, who regard the man with the voice in the nature of a hoodoo, and yesterday they plotted against his personal comfort. The man referred to has a weakness for beverages of one sort and another, and yesterday he was presented with an attractive lubrication, in which was concealed certain mixtures not generally conducive to physical serenity. The Jonah gulped down the decoction, and then took his favorite position on the bleachers, while the schemers watched him closely, expecting every minute to see him grow pale and anxious-looking.

To their astonishment and dismay, he maintained his usual composure and screeched louder than ever before. At the close of the game, he walked upon the field, and, grasping (Philadelphia manager) Harry Wright by the hand, said regretfully:

"Harry, I worked hard for you, but it was no go, but we'll beat 'em the next time you come."

Then the rooters who arranged the scheme went out under the elevated railway tracks and kicked each other.
[The Sun (New York), July 5, 1891]

The "Well, well, well!" man had at last disclosed his identity. He is tall and thin, wears a Mephistophelian beard and bets on the Brooklyn team. The deputy sheriff may find him on that end of the grand stand nearest the bleacherites.
[Brooklyn Eagle, May 31, 1892]

Many people were no doubt surprised to learn of this man's extraordinary background:

The "Well! Well! Well!" man, who accompanied the New Yorks on their trip is creating a big impression out West. The Cincinnati Times-Star says of him:

"There is only one 'Well! Well! Well!' The peculiar war cry which gave to him this pseudonym is inimitable. Hundreds have tried and failed as completely as if they had attempted to imitate the roar of the angry surf.

"During the season old 'Well! Well! Well!' grew into a conspicuous figure at the Polo grounds. From almost every square yard

of the stand he has sent forth his singular war whoop. It has swelled up and rolled out over the field from the grand stand, from the uncovered seats in right field, from the left field bleachers, from the quarter stretch, from the club house and from the steps at the entrance from Eighth avenue.

"The New York players have acquired a superstitious belief that he brings them good luck, inasmuch as since the club gave him a roaming, rooting commission at the Polo grounds, the team has been doing good work and playing successful ball. The knowledge of the Giants' belief in his mascot powers has caused old 'Well! Well! Well!'s soul to swell with pride, has fired his already uproarious soul with new ambition and has added, if possible, to the voluminous thunder of his slogan.

"'Well! Well! Well!' in private life is Frank B. Wood, and his biographer says:

"The romance in Wood's life dates back quarter of a century. He has been ball player, school teacher, soldier and magnate. He was not 15 years old when he enlisted as a Union soldier in the fall of 1862. He served out his time, returned to Lansingburg and taught school the following winter.

"In August, 1863, he re-enlisted for three years in the Twenty-first Griswold Light Guard, New York volunteer cavalry, and it may be that the sound of his voice as he charged on the enemy saved the Union from disruption. Who knows? In December of 1864, he was captured by the enemy and thrown into Libbey prison, where he was confined till the following February.

"In September, 1865, he was honorably mustered out of service. Four weeks later he came to New York and went into business and has been a resident of this city and vicinity ever since.

"To Frank B. Wood the noted Haymakers owe their fame and their name. He took an interest in a base ball club at his old home, which was known as the Unions of Lansingburg. In the winter of 1867-8, Wood was a delegate to the base ball convention held in New York which organized the National association."
[Brooklyn Eagle, September 18, 1893]

The last, but lesser light in the category of ball park pests was the "Oh, so easy!" man, who never achieved the envious level of notoriety made by others, but he tried:

A crank in the bleachers persisted in shouting "Oh! so easy," in a tantalizing way as each of the visitors was retired. And they were easy. [Brooklyn Eagle, June 2, 1897]

19. Humor in Making a Hit

One of the more charming features of baseball journalism of this era lay in the language used by various writers to describe the drama and suspense surrounding the classic confrontation of batter versus pitcher—the pitch, the crack of the ball against bat, and the instant activation of all players on the field. It drew the best out of their creative minds.

In the case of long or important hits, writers deliberately slowed the pace of the action to a barely perceptible crawl while describing a pivotal moment, when the next pitch could determine the ultimate fate of the ball game. The precise moment of impact of ball against bat was freeze-framed, and then the subsequent flight or path of the ball described in minute detail.

It was the art of telling a story within a story, the *sine qua non* of the trade. Old-time writers were good at this.

The Act of Hitting the Ball and its Aftermath

It wasn't the actual hit that made the hit a hit, but <u>how</u> the hit was hit that made the hit a hit, to wit:

> *two strikes were called on Van Haltren and then he railroaded a liner over Connor's head*
>
> *the ball shot from their bats as though greased by lightning*
>
> *he lathered the ball just inside the first base line with the speed of a rifle ball*
>
> *the ball looked like a Park Row butter cake*
>
> *he struck at the ball like a man driving a stake for a circus tent*
>
> *Hanlon used a club that looked as though it had been cut from a hearse*
>
> *Ewing came to bat with the gay and festive demeanor of an heir apparent*
>
> *Burns hit a hot one that singed Cross' trousers as it passed the pitcher's box*
>
> *Robbie put his avoirdupois against the leather for a three-*

bagger into right

Ward whacked one which singed the grass from the plate to second

there was smoke in the wake of the final hit of the game, a liner from Little Casey's bat

Brodie lunged at the ball with enough force to start a trolley car

William smote the ball and the report was like unto the breaking of day on July 4

McGill put a fire-eater over second base

Billie Gray smashed the ball with a crack that sounds like a scaffold falling in a new building

Dillard broke up the Southern league by batting all the balls into the Gulf of Mexico

Andrews sent one to Morrissey hot enough to roast a turkey

the year that Preston batted over .300, he broke all the mirrors in Des Moines, looking at himself

the Giants opened the first with the rush of a frenzied stock speculator

the Millers started at Denzer like hungry weasels after Easter eggs

they went at the luckless Colonels like a thousand of bricks

Whitney's liner cut its way through Bastian's hands

the base hits rattled like hail on a tin roof

Turner and Stenzel hit balls that are still journeying, and other members of the team got the ball so far away on drives than an inning or so would elapse before relays of urchins could return them

he pounded a single that scorched uniforms all the way from the pitcher's box to center field

singles, doubles, triples and home runs were just as numerous as flies on a sunny day

the general fusillade yielded a total of five runs, and Baltimore's stock was in the ascendant

then that dreadful man Smith swooped upon the ball and sent it wailing like a banshee into right for a pair of sacks

the ball hit the fence hard enough to jar the knots out

the men from Minneapolis straightened out his curves with the ease of a shell-operator fleecing greenies at a county fair

St. Paul had another inning then, and stock went up like the miner who dropped a cigar stump in a powder keg

Hollingsworth hit an incandescent one to Hulen

Glasscock mauled him (pitcher) around the field like a love-sick maiden caressing a sofa pillow he could almost see the smoke coming off the ball, which was being rapidly incinerated by the friction of the circumambient atmosphere

Anson walloped the ball until it was covered with ridges

Scrappy Bill, the big chief (captain), hit a grass scorcher to right field which left a wave of flame in its wake

there was a collision like the rap of a bed slat against a sugar barrel

Parker tipped one to Foreman that was so slow the trade mark could almost be read

the Falls City man caught the ball on the point of the jaw, and like an aerolite, it went sibilating into space

the Quakers played their positions mechanically and walked up to the plate like charity patients falling in line for medicine

they were about as handy with the stick as a woman is with a rock

he made one lunge at the ball, missed it and spun around like a five-cent top

he swiped at the ball as if he were a man feeling for a banister on a dark night

Ball opened with a hit, a pinky punk fly which dropped just behind the infield

he couldn't hit the earth if he fell off a house

Gore put his leather-pusher against the ball and shoved it clear over the right field fence

Longer compositions also worked:

Cross struck out, and a little rift of silver could be seen in the murky clouds. Clements dissipated that slim shaft of hope when he belted the pellet in left and made Burke scramble lively to stop it from rolling out into the Reading Railroad tracks.

Their hits were not of the screaming kind, but were those dumpy, tantalizing taps that make monkeys of the infielders and drive them to drink or other means of desperation.

He picked out a ball close to him and with a dull thud lost that horse-hided yarn forever. When last seen, it was dropping with never a backward look over the dismantled masts which once proudly bore a pictured Rome (old stage set on St. George grounds on Staten Island).

Stocksdale, the man from Baltimore country, with the brawny arm and the keen eye of the squirrel-hunter, took the club and went to the plate on business bent.

Spies opened the eighth with a live one that had electric sparks on it as it passed the pitcher. Cross made a jab at it, but thought of his fingers and did not touch it. Shannon tried to get it, but he, too, only succeeded in breaking its force, and it remained for Stewart to pick it up, but by that time, it had lost its value, as well as its heat, for Spies was so close to first base that a Gatling gun could not have gotten the ball there in time to cut him off.

Burns sent a liner over the pitcher's box which would have carried away Umpire Clarke's topmast had he not gotten the low bridge sign in time.

King fired one that cut the plate and there came a sound as if of hail pattering on the shingles of the grand stand. It was a honey cooler and it did not stop rolling until it paused at the feet of Hanlon.

Nyce played an errorless game and batted— not with the dash and recklessness of the fiend incarnate—but with the precision of a trip hammer and the regularity of an eight-day clock.

Sir David Orr, corpulent and as good-natured as ever, looms up with the Columbus team like a Pennsylvania barn in a heavy fog [Post Express (Rochester, N. Y.), June 15, 1889]

Selbach started the music with a corking two-bagger against the left field fence. Anson nearly stretched himself in two, reaching for an out-curve, but his effort was only rewarded by a silly-looking grounder which Richardson, in a careless, off-hand way, chucked to first.

Sweeney might have done likewise, but he tried to stretch the two-bagger out to a triple, and as he was ploughing up the soil around third base with his features, the ball arrived from the field and Ebright put him out. [Morning Call (San Francisco), June 17, 1893]

A great cheer went up from three-fourths of the

5,800 cranks when Dan Brouthers strolled lazily to the rubber with a bat that resembled a small tree. One ball came over and Daniel swiped at it as if he meant to break a window way down at Canarsie.*

...Then Marcus hurled in another, and the big fellow slugged it for a red-hot foul that went straight for Judge Cullom, who was sitting with some New York rooters on the extreme left end of the grand stand. The Judge saw it coming and dodged, but the ball struck him where the belt buckle ought to be, and there was a crash that shook the grand stand and made the Brooklyn supporters roar with delight. The Judge had been capsized, but he was up in a jiffy and bowed his acknowledgments to the big crowd.
[Brooklyn Eagle, date misplaced]
* Residential/commercial neighborhood of Brooklyn

The score was twice tied before the calcium (spotlight) was turned upon G. Davis. There were two hands out, two on the bases, two runs needed to win and two strikes on Davis. No wonder the hearts of the cranks stood still as they gazed at the broad back of Davis.

"Will he hit it?" the pale-faced rooters whispered, not daring to move their eyelids lest the worst should come. Slowly and with extreme caution, the gladiator (Davis) placed the handle of the bat between his knees, moistened the palms of his hands, dipped them in the dust of the arena and then wiped the grime off on his new, white bloomers.

Ewing's infield stood on tip toe to guard the plate as Damming unhooked a curve. G. Davis swung his bludgeon. It made connection. The ball dropped safely in right field, and with a mighty roar bedlam broke loose. The problems in twos had been solved in a truly artistic manner, thanks to G. Davis.

The ovation lasted all the way to the clubhouse. Men and boys who never met Davis personally called him by his first name and went into ecstasies of delight if he deigned to smile. When he finally gained the shelter of the clubhouse, the crowd stood and gazed with awe at the building. Old Well Well clung to the palings and bayed and barked like a coon dog at the foot of a cottonwood tree. The demonstration was one to warm the heart of any man.

But supposing Davis had struck out; what would the cranks say? This is it:

"Oh, what a dub!"

But that last round was well calculated to stir the blood of the

most phlegmatic rooter. It was a pretty windup, made all the more pleasing to the eye by the fact that the Giants had won.
[Dryden, New York Journal, September 2, 1897]

Speaking of Dryden (above), one of his successful writing techniques was lingering at length over a single time at bat. Here is a trilogy of sketches, all starring his favorite foil, New York Giants' first baseman, Bill Clark:

Should the Giants fail to land the Temple Cup—and their chances are now sadly emaciated—the disaster may be attributed to hypnotism, an unheard-of factor, surely, in baseball. Farmer Dunn's hold over summer weather also figures in the finish, but it was the subtle science of a Svengali that hoodooed Scrappy Bill and his athletes.

...It is not generally known that Bill Clark, the big brown boy who covers first base, is subject to hypnotic influence, but he is. The fact has been demonstrated twice in the last two days, and the evil eye undoubtedly cost the locals two games of ball.

In the first contest of the double-header on Thursday, Bill fell under the malign influence of (Pittsburg pitcher) Pink Hawley, who has the Svengali eye, though he does not boast of it. Hawley has even been known to hypnotize himself with the aid of a mirror.

It will be remembered that in the contest Pittsburg won, Bill came to bat in the ninth inning with one man out and George Davis on third. Clark has always been an emergency hitter, and would no doubt have scored Davis but for the influence of Hawley. The pitcher walked up to Bill, looked him in the eye and said:

"You are going to pop it up in the air."

Bill laughed, but Hawley's warning was no idle jest. The ball shot straight up and (Pittsburg catcher) Merritt caught it within ten feet of the plate. Clark was worried, but he felt easier yesterday, because Hawley was not in the game.

However, he sat on the bench and his subtle influence dominated Bill again in the eighth inning. Gettig was on second, with one man out, when Clark came to bat, and the cranks felt encouraged. But Merritt whispered through his mask:

"Look up, Bill."

Bill thoughtfully looked up.

"That's where you're going to hit it," said Merritt in a low tone. "Hawley said so, and he's watching you from the bench."

Sure enough, Clark lifted a tall foul fly, which Merritt captured

a few feet from the plate. As these two plays actually occurred, the Giants may be said to possess a baseball Trilby,* who doesn't sing, however.
[New York Journal, September 11, 1897]
*After Trilby (O'Ferrall), heroine of George du Maurier's novel of the same name, who is hypnotized by Svengali into becoming a talented singer.

Short Stories of Long Hits

George Gore came to bat and put his forty-six ounces of wagon-tongue ash against the fifth ball pitched, and sent it on a line to left field. For eighty yards the ball screamed through the air on a line, and then, being apparently lifted by some unseen force, it took a slant upward, and, sailing over the head of Twitchell, it went on the bound through the very gate where a year ago, gayly dressed ballet girls were wont to prance (Staten Island grounds).
[Source misplaced]

The Professor was the first Lamb to bat in the second. He was evidently out to square himself, for the first ball that left young Clausen's hand he caught square between the visual organs, and when it pulled up among the artichokes out along the center field fence, the college graduate was blowing his bellows on second.
[Omaha Daily Bee, June 30, 1891]

Then there was pandemonium. Van Haltren cut a swath in the air with his bat, and the ball was on the way. It went up and along, and was headed for the other bank of the Harlem River. When it dropped, Ward was nearly home and Van was at third. McCarthy flung it back with the desperation of a dervish to Long, who had a bad attack of the "wattles," and threw it way over Nash's head. That suited Van, who scampered home, close in the track of Ward, and everybody cheered.
[Evening World (New York), May 5, 1894]

Unfortunately for the well-being of cranks' paradise, Ryn, of the silent tongue, was the next to bat. He immediately squared away, catching the ball a horrible biff in the mug, as it tried to steal its way across the plate. There was a flutter of flying limbs, a soulful, sobful sigh along the bleachers, and the score was tied.
[Milwaukee Journal, May 27, 1891]

That sixth inning is one that is not seen every day. With two men out and Cooley resting his tired feet at the second bag, and Malachi Quinn posing on the first bag by virtue of an umpire's donation, a youth named Hawley came to the bat.

Now, Hawley is a nice boy, and all that, but since first his childish hands gripped the horsehide, he had never been known to hit a ball hard enough to create a sound wave. His batting average has limped along on crutches and has scarcely mustered strength enough to peep over the .100 mark. But Hawley did the trick for St. Louis yesterday.

Ryan swung his bat dreamily and landed the ball away out where the landaus and victorias were anchored.
[Washburne, Inter Ocean (Chicago), June 5, 1890]

Here was (Grand Rapids pitcher) Eiteljorg's chance to save the game, three on bases, two outs, and a hard rain coming.

(St. Paul pitcher) Phyle put the ball over. Eiteljorg thought it was aimed straight at his head, and he stepped back. It cut the plate like the bicycle fever going through a young ladies' seminary.

"One strike," remarked the umpire.

Phyle sent the ball down again. Eiteljorg was not going to make any mistake this time. He swung his bat from his shoulder and nearly hit the ball, when he decided that he would let it go by. It went right by.

"Strike two," the umpire said.

Once again the ball came through the air, and again Eiteljorg dodged. This time, it was not a strike, and twice more did the umpire fail to say strike when the ball passed unhit.

Matters were reaching a critical stage. It was even up now between Phyle and Eiteljorg—how one does love to dally with that name—and the question was whether Phyle would put the ball across in front of the nomad's collar or rip a corner off the base with a wide curve lower. Phyle tried the latter.

Fatal mistake, as was said of the girl who stepped off the bridge because there was only one man in the world for her.

Eiteljorg had curves of his own. He solved the problems of rise, direction and other complications with the ingenuity of a small boy accounting for his hair getting wet on a dry day. Judicious application of a stout stick to the exterior surface of the ball was the solution resorted to.

The leather immediately changed its line of march from westward to eastward, and renewed activity was noticeable in the affairs of Burns and George. Jim was after it first, but George, being faster on

his feet, was first to the ball. When it was returning to the inner circle, Eiteljorg was on second base and three young yellow jackets had scurried across the plate.
[Saint Paul Globe, May 17, 1896]

    Then Charley Farrell walked up to face the music, and McMahon eyed him carefully as he shook his heavy bat defiantly. First there was a strike, then a ball, followed by another strike.
    The crowd was silent as still another ball was called. Then all of a sudden, as if Bedlam had been let loose, the people leaped into the air with a terrific scream of joy.
    Farrell had nailed the ball on the doorplate, and it sailed far over Joe Kelley's head in left centre field. On and on it tore through the glistening sunbeams until it gradually settled in its mad flight and finally rolled along on the cinder path near the carriage gate.
    It was easily a home run drive, but Farrell only went as far as third, for Stafford meanwhile had rushed across the plate with the winning run. At this there was one of the greatest bursts of enthusiasm seen at the Polo grounds in many a day. But it was confined to the crowd, for the champions looked as if they could cry as they walked silently to their bench for a short rest.
[The Sun (New York), September 28, 1895]

    Mr. Inks made his bow. He made two wild-eyed jabs at Darnbrough's twisters, and stooping, rubbed a little mud on his hands, stood up like a real man, and then there was a crack like a pistol.
    It was his bat colliding with the ball!
    Away it went, nipping the clover buds as it fled through the grass, way out to left field among the carriages, and every last man on the bases galloped home, Inks himself reaching third!
[Omaha Daily Bee, May 9, 1890]

    If the Colonels (Oakland) had won the game with Frisco yesterday, that would have made two in succession; then it would probably have snowed some today. Still the Colonels have no cause to grieve. They made a gallant fight for victory, and only yielded to the superior force of one measly, little lop-sided single, known and designated in baseball parlance as a timely hit.
    Long before this unfortunate timely hit occurred, Colonel T. Robinson had the contest stowed away in his game bag with both the straps on the flap buckled down tight. It almost broke his heart to disgorge at the eleventh hour, but such are the fortunes of war and

baseball.

It will now be necessary, gentle reader, to go back a few chapters, as they say in the novel, on account of that base hit. Had the hit been omitted, P. P. "White Wings" Cahill would have gotten off with a slight reprimand, but now he must be jumped on. A careful summing up of the evidence shows that P. P., etc., is the guilty party who lost the game for his side, and the subjoined testimony is offered in rebuttal to the timely hit.

The hit took place in the eighth inning, at which time the score stood 5 to 2 in favor of Oakland. A few minutes before the hit, the Colonel wore a smile that sundered his face, while Harris was under the grand stand, kicking himself. After the hit, the magnates changed places.

This untimely timely hit, about which so much has been said and written, tied the score into a hard knot, which was set adrift by Harris' men in the next inning. In the third, Frisco men stood on the bags when Cartwright toed the rubber. Not a run had been scored, and people watched the big fat boy with breathless anxiety. There were two men out and two strikes had been called on the batsman when he suddenly landed his bat up against a tender spot on the ball.

Half mad with rage and pain, the ball lit out for left field, with both hands frantically rubbing the injured place. Cahill, who was quietly cropping the herbage in the field, left his feed when he saw the ball coming, and started to meet it. Then he changed his mind and backed away, then rushed in again and stuck up one hand with a National-League-phenomenal-fielder movement.

The ball plunked into his calloused palm and then slid out again, and while Cahill was recovering from his surprise, two of the runners scored. This is where Cahill's guilt is established beyond the shadow of doubt. Had he used the commonplace minor league catch, those two runs would have been shut out, and the fearful ravages of that timely hit would not have been felt. With this one exception, Cahill led a blameless outdoor life for a couple of hours.
[Morning Call (San Francisco), June 14, 1891]

A Home Run by Any Other Name

Few events occurring during a ball game inspired writers to dig deep into their creative resources than to recount the granddaddy of all base hits, a home run:

Connor, who had been batting in the worst of luck, asserted himself and planted his bat against the ball with such force that the mangled sphere picked up its spirits and took a quick trip over the right field fence.

He lifted his bat up against the ball with such force that the sphere was knocked out of the lot, climbing the right field fence on its way to freedom.

Ed Crane made the longest hit of the series, the ball going over the left field fence, crossing the street and landing on the porch of a red brick house, where two little girls were sitting.

In the fifth inning, he mused unto himself: "I, too, will land thee, (pitcher) Orth, into the bleacher," and straightaway swished the leather into the land of happy souls.

The broad-shouldered king of batsmen of the old Southern League now faced Dwyer. The Hobart College pitcher tied himself in a knot and shot a ball as big as a rain barrel over the plate. Maul caught it with his club with a vicious bang and sent it in a dead line over the Congress street wall and among the cottonwood trees.

A Chicago reporter thus describes a home run hit by Crane:
"Crane's drive for four bases in the eighth inning was the kind taxidermists enjoy. The ball went on a dead line over the north wall, tore through the soughing branches of a cottonwood tree, galloped hurriedly up the steps of a brick house, and then, with joyous laughter, burst through one of the front windows. It was not seen again."
[Post Express (Rochester, NY), July 2, 1889]

Kansas City Katz was the third of the rolling mill hands to try his hand on Shorty Boxendale's convolutionary attainments. He found them easy. After hitting the May winds an awful belt, just to try his strength, he bent back for business. Boxey let the ball go and Colonel Katz caught it on the end of his tree and it went whizzing out over Wood's fair young head, out over the tall fence, with its wire screening, over the hoss-car tracks and the houses beyond, until a mere speck in the oriental distance. It was found this morning by a fisherman out in Cutoff lake, floating about on the billowy surface, flattened out for all the world like a big pumpkin pie.
[Omaha Daily Bee, May 4, 1894]

Turner, with a triple and a single to his credit, took his big bat *and the first good ball that came sailing up to the plate was his. He brought his bat against the horsehide-covered sphere with a resounding whack. Straight at the right field fence went the ball, while Catcher Dugdale, mask in hand, gazed at it in speechless amazement. Pray as much as "Dug" might, he could not change the angle at which the ball was traveling.*

It cleared the fence and kept on going. Two runs crossed the plate ahead of Turner, who trotted around with a self-satisfied smile lurking around the ends of his magnificent mustachio. It was a beautiful hit.
[Seattle Post-Intelligencer, June 4, 1898]

Uncle Abner here bobbed up again, and rubbing a little pulverized terra firma upon his hands to make them stick, he smashed out another single, and the bases were full and so was the audience—with disgust.

Robert Pettit took his position at the pan. Twice he struck at high balls and did not reach them, but the third was on a level with his bottom vest button. He slammed his bat at it, putting all the power of his nice round shoulders and two sinewy arms into the slam.

The noise that followed was tremendous. It was so loud that it produced an echo way off against the bluffs across the Missouri river, two miles away. People looked around, expecting to see the fragments of something flying in the air, but instead they saw a concrete mass of hog hide, yarn, rubber and other ingredients leap away from the plate like a maddened thing of life and go soaring off, and off, over the fence, over the trees, over the house tops, off toward Cut-off lake.

They also saw a fielder, called Mickey Phalen for short, run to the right field fence and look for a gate, and then turn away with a look of disappointment plastered over his classic phiz an inch thick.

A man found the ball this morning, two miles this side of Missouri Valley. It was soft and flabby and flat as a pancake on the near side, resembling very closely a piece of strawberry shortcake! Manager Leonard will have it stuffed and sent to the Smithsonian Institute. SEP

So, amidst a storm of courteous cheers, the four men came home and the day was irrecoverably lost!
[Omaha Daily Bee, June 8, 1890]

But when Big Mike stepped up, aerial, vapory, changing rose-colored lights began to dance over the park, and everybody said to themselves that something was going to happen.

And something did happen.

The profound quiet was broken by the ball striking his bat. It sounded for all the world like that big fire cracker that fellow put under the World-Herald scorer on the Fourth. Everybody looked up in the air for the pieces, but there were none in sight. The pulpy mass had been driven over the left field fence.

Oh, dear me! How the people did cry and clap their hands and stamp their little feet as Bobby came marching home.
[Omaha Daily Bee, July 7, 1892]

While the hitting was profuse, it was not of the robust kind. It seldom is at Piedmont. Several crops of hay have already this season been cut from the Piedmont outfield and placed on the market, and now another golden harvest awaits the reaper's sickle. The golden heads of grain nod and sway in the gentle breezes, bending heavy with their weight, and seem to beckon the husbandman, but when the ball goes skating across the open and strikes into the waving seas, it just cuts a few little capers and then kaflumixes.

Levy's home run was over the fence, but Peeples' was about the shortest home run hit on record. The ball just went a little way over Ebright's head and got lost in the uncut hay, while Peeples continued around the circuit.
[Morning Call (San Francisco), July 27, 1893]

Davis met the first ball pitched squarely on the point of the chin, and put it out of the business forever. The ball struck on top of the left field fence, bounded up, quivered in midair a second, and then toppled over into the waiting clutches of a small boy.
[Dryden, New York Journal, September 17, 1897]

Jim Burns was first to bat, the same Jim that the Minneapolis papers said was a back number. James deciphered one of the quaint and curious lines described by Mr. Fifield's pitching, and the ball left the home plate in search of new and less sweltering climates.

High in the air it sailed. Knoll thought it was easy and lingered in the lot, about thirty yards back of second base. That was not the place he should have picked out. The ball had a through ticket, with no stops for way stations, and by the time Mr. Knoll had presented his credentials, the sphere was rolling down the well-packed sand almost directly toward the farthest corner of the fence.

Well, you know how Jim Burns can run. He would not be in it for a minute with Joe Patchen, and there's a possible chance that Tommy Coneff could beat him, but that ball, why, that ball was hardly

within sight of the diamond when Jim danced an Irish jig on the home plate.
[Saint Paul Globe, May 14, 1896]

McVey was the next man up. As he posed at the plate, rosy clouds glowed overhead and in the east the horizon burned in gold. Mr. Corish took a long aim and cut her loose.

Biff.

That was Georgie's war club meeting the tortuous sphere. A phosphorescent streak was descried in the air as the hoghide soared out into the east. A blue-clad man was seen tearing frantically toward the fence. He reaches it, holds up his hands imploringly, then drops them like pieces of rope. Then he lingered and gazed and dreamed. The scene was so soothing, the tranquility so holy.

Georgie had knocked the ball across Seventeenth street, and both runners came in. The tumult that followed was actually scandalous.
[Omaha Daily Bee, May 9, 1894]

The Deacon was the first man up in the second. He approached the plate as if loath to disturb the quiet of the dreamy Sabbath afternoon. Then for a moment he sadly watched Mr. Conway wrap his fingers about the ball. The solitude seemed so intense he fain would have lingered there and gazed.

Far away was the world, with all its darkening sorrows and corroding cares, and he couldn't see why Mr. Conway would insist on polluting the scene by tossing the ball over the plate when he was there.

Twice he tried to push it away from him, but failed, but the third time was the charm.

Talk about Mozart's "Twelfth Mass," the symphonies of Beethoven, Wagner, Strauss and the Troubadours—but the song of the home run hit is the most bewitching of all.

All bitterness of spirit vanished when Canavan swung his bat. The ball started due north, and was marked "rush" over Schoch's head. It travelled into the deserted haunts of the sun gods. Canavan jogged around the heavy path like a messenger boy with nothing but time, and his progress was marked by the deafening cheers of the crowd.
[Source misplaced]

When King Elmer fished the sphere out of the lagoon, way out in the northwest precinct, the Deacon was standing at the oatmeal trough, cooling her fevered brow with is moistened handkerchief.

[Omaha Daily Bee, July 6, 1891]

Away out in the left field (Capitol Park, Wash DC), an enterprising Washington merchant had erected a big board proclaiming that, during the 1897 season, DeMontreville won three hats and ties for banging the ball against its sable outlines.

That was last year. Gene did not win a hat and tie yesterday, but Anderson had his eye on the rewards offered when he stepped to the plate in the ninth inning of the first game. The score was 7 to 7, and there wasn't a Washingtonian in the grounds that would have taken an even-money offer that his team would win.

Hughes had not been easy for the Senators since the "fatal first," and Anderson was not thought to be the man for the emergency. Biding his time, the Brooklyn cast-off caught one to his liking.

There was a sharp crack, and far out into the left garden sailed the ball. Holmes was after it like a shot, but up and away sailed the sphere until it dropped behind the hat-and-tie board for the second round of its expedition. With seeming new life imparted, it caromed off the fence and bounded further and further on, ever eluding the panting "Ducky", while Anderson was circling the bases to the noise of a thousand plaudits. It is well known in Baltimore that Holmes injured shoulder prevented his throwing.

Therefore, when, at last, he came up with the ball, the best he could do was to "jerk" it to Kelley, who passed it on to DeMontreville. Like a shot, Gene fired it to Robinson, but a second before Anderson had crossed the plate, and another Oriole game had gone wrong.

[Baltimore American, June 15, 1898]

Two hands were out and McVey at the bat. There was gore in his gleaming orbs, and everybody felt that he was about to burst one of Colonel Lookabaugh's furniture-van curves wide open.

The colonel was evidently inclined to the same belief, and he bent his supple form for a mighty effort.

Mac was watching him, however, and he lifted his tree menacingly.

Whiz! came the ball.

Then there was a ringing crack, like the report of a torpedo, and a thin cerulean streak was descried glancing through the air. A moment later a loud crash was heard coming from somewhere down in the heart of the city. It was the ball bringing up against the linseed oil works. Realizing this, the crowd broke loose in rapturous applause. What a world of fun there is in a cracking good hit at the right time, anyway.

[Omaha Daily Bee, June 4, 1894]

>Tom (Turner) did not look dangerous when he faced (Seattle pitcher) Birg and allowed a nice one to pass near the end of his long, graceful mustache. Then he put a little sand on his hands, squared his shoulders and caught the next ball on the seam.
>It went straight at the right field fence and kept going while the crowd and players watched it in breathless interest. When it dropped somewhere in the evergreens up on the side hill, Birg looked sad and the boy with the chalk put down two scores. It was the first home run of the season and how the crowd did yell.

[Seattle Post-Intelligencer, May 31, 1898]

>And now came Roger the bold. He got a peep at the pellet and slam-banged it full in the eye and over the right field fence. It sailed in rataplan fashion. It was a home run, and Connor didn't have to get any sort of a gait on to complete the circuit of canvas hillocks.

[Evening World (New York), date misplaced]

>And then! Cummings strode, like Casey, to the plate. The coacher hushed his cry. The crowd was hushed and still. Pitcher Ray escorted a ball up the central aisle.
>Bang! Mr. Cummings' bat collided with that ball head on. Up sailed the white sphere. It caught the gleam of the setting sun. It became a speck, an atom, a mote. It sailed joyously over the left field fence. A home run with three men on bases. That hit belongs in the heroics of baseball.
>...An invalid in Alameda was disturbed by the noise that crowd made. That noise going south collided with a noise coming north from Los Angeles and caused rain on the Mojave desert where rain had never before been known at this season. No convention ever set up such a shout.

[Los Angeles Herald, November 4, 1896]

A writer in Omaha had a lot of fun recounting the stories of hometown Kelly's two home runs, one of which was a grand slam:

>In the seventh, Kelly hired a small boy to expectorate on his hands, then he braced himself at the plate, lifted his tree aloft, bent his back and—biff!
>The air seemed full of flying bits of yarn, leather and rubber, and all that was left of one of Al Reach's very best went sailing, sailing,

not exactly over the dark blue sea, but 'way out over Nichols' head to the remotest corner of the yard. Before the battered and pulpy mass could be fished up from out of an archipelago of pigweed and dog fennel, Kel was shaking hands with uncle at the oatmeal can!
[Omaha Daily Bee, June 5, 1892]

    The bags were full and Kelly at the bat. Dad clenched his teeth and concentrated all the Worcestershire in his angular frame into his good glass arm. It was a momentous moment. Not a whisper disturbed the quiet of the dreamy afternoon. The solitude was intense. Far away was the world with all its darkening sorrows and corroding cares.
    "One strike!" sounded McQuaid's baritone lungs.
    Dad's face would have made a good stamp for children's cookies in holiday time.
    "Two strikes!"
    He grinned in fiendish glee.
    Crack! King Kel had met an Oswego curve and it sounded like the explosion of a giant torpedo. It was one of those royal smashes you see but once in a season. A homer with three men on the bags.
    The crowd howled in their agonizing joy, and their unearthly mocking tones sounded to Dad—so he said at the close of the game—as if they had emanated from a legion of maniacal throats.
(Source misplaced)

    Sandow was next on the list. He had not been getting into the hit column with the frequency of his predecessor, but he had salted one down in the former inning, and he was sure he had another coming, even if the crowd was not.
    With an easy confidence, he waited while one or two bad ones were gathered to their fathers, and then he picked out a nice one. It was coming right over the plate, and would undoubtedly have crossed that object in the exact middle, had its progress not been interrupted by the contact with Sandow's heavy stick.
    There was a violent collision, the result of which was that the ball retired from the scene at a rapid rate and was soon rolling in the middle of Fuller street. It looked for a time as though Sandow would get a hat (free hat, if sign hit), but the ball went farther up the fence, so it was a sure home run and the score was tied.
[Saint Paul Globe, May 23, 1896]

    The fans went to the park prepared to adopt the St. Louis style of "roasting" the home team by "rooting" for the visitors. But their hopes were raised and their loyalty aroused to a flaming pitch in the first inning by "Pat" McVicker singling out a high-thrown ball and driving it over the right field fence to the north of the sign with the unpronounceable hieroglyphics.

It was one of the longest hits ever made on the grounds. The ball was one of the swiftest of the medley of inshoots and outshoots propelled from "Jot" Goar's thick right arm, and when it collided with the bat, there was a cheerful resonant swat. And then the ball rose gently and gracefully in the air and winged its flight for the hemisphere beyond the walls.

Its course was gradually upward, and strength seemed to come to it as it passed high over the heads of the wondering fielders. On and on flew the ball. It passed above the fence, dipped downward and forty feet beyond, touched the roof of the long stable, rebounded into the air and rolled and tossed toward the ridge, faltered, regained its momentum, and with a mighty effort, scaled the ridge and passed from the vision of the thousand or more screaming, shouting fans. McVicker had almost reached third base before the sphere made its exit.
[Kansas City Journal, May 30, 1897]

Harry Stovey hasn't been well this spring, and commenting on an incident in the Chicago series, (sportswriter) Leonard Washburne said:

"Harry Stovey dragged his six feet up to the plate like a man with one foot in the grave. 'Poor Harry is very ill,' said Tim Murnane (baseball writer) in the press box as a sympathetic tear stole down his cheek. Just then Poor Harry moaned fitfully and wrapped his bat four times around the ball. There was a woman washing steps in front of a house near Throop street, on Congress. She dodged just in time. Poor Harry crawled around the bases and back to the bench."
[Omaha Daily Bee, May 24, 1891]

Cartwright, with his 240 pounds of beef, landed one of Westervelt's sweetest, and, suffering sailor, the pellet flew through the ambient as if it was sure to climb up and kiss a few of the fleecy clouds that were darting through the air. It fell into the 25-cent bleachers, and all "Carty" had to do was to walk around the bases. It was a gorgeous home run.
[Evening World (New York), May 4, 1894]

Then Tommy Kearns (outfielder, Omaha), the Canuck, came up, smiling.

"One strike!" cried the umpire.
"What?" yelled Thomas.
"Two strikes!" from the umpire.

Then Kearns squared himself, and there was an ominous look about the back of his head as viewed from the scorer's box. The next ball that came his way, he met full in the face. It was a base hit. That is, it was a base hit when it began life, but when it got a little older, its growth increased. It left the Canadian's club with a dull roar and seemed intent on exploring the corners of the earth; in fact, it didn't stop until it rolled against the center field fence, and Kearns made the circuit.

The people stood up and cheered and cheered again, and Dave Rowe (first baseman, Denver) looked just like General Jackson after a man had pulled General Jackson's nose.
[Omaha Daily Bee, June 21, 1890]

There were more than 5,000 people at Recreation Park yesterday afternoon who forgot all about that historic gentleman, George Washington, and the demonstration in honor of his triumph. Pete Conway was the hero of the Recreation Park crowd and for a time his glory obscured all that could possibly surround the head of a Washington, an Alexander or a Napoleon.

Pete knocked the ball clean out of the lot and the probability is it is not found yet. Never since Mr. Sullivan, of Chicago fame, performed a same feat at the opening game last year has a home run been made, and the rarity, combined with the fact that it tied the score, caused a demonstration of cheering, yelling, jumping, stamping and knocking seldom if ever seen on the home grounds.

And Pete's home runs was a corker. He seemed to know that he had the dead wood on Beattin. They had never met since their separation in Detroit last year. Past memoirs were thrown aside and only open hostilities went yesterday.

Pete placed himself in front of Beattin with a grain that beckoned devilment and after refusing two or three decoy balls, he pulled himself together and with a "biff, bang" nailed the ball fair on the nose and it went sailing into the air with the grace of a bird. "Twitches" evidently knew its destiny because he stood calmly and gazed upward to the flying sphere. Over the fence it went, midway between the center field and left field corners.

It was a long hit and no mistake. Conway's performance entitles him to a silk hat offered by Gusky's firm. The latter offers a silk hat to every Pittsburg player who makes a home run.
[Pittsburg Dispatch, May 1, 1889]

20. Humor in a Baseball Writer's "Confession"

It was exceedingly poor form for baseball writers to talk about personal feelings in the text of a game account, such as griping about their job, for instance—unless, of course, they were kidding. In this vein, behold the following literary composition, one of sublime lyrical beauty, a perfect blend of subtle, erudite humor, feigned melancholy and poignancy. Any thought of it as a possible farewell statement by this Bay Area wag quickly vanished with the readers' first grin, and he went on to report games over the next several years from the same loopy but hilarious perspective.

Few folks on the outside ever can or ever will know the exquisite mental torture endured by that unfortunate member of society whose business compels him to remain seated until the game is over or suffer a relapse in his salary.

To him alone is denied the priceless boon of making a graceful but hasty exit over the backs of chairs to the open air in whichever inning his better judgment tells him it is time to go. He cannot seek the cramped seclusion of his hall bedroom, where bases on balls and hit-by-the-pitcher never enter, except in troubled dreams.

Neither can he hide himself away to the somnolent shades of the adjacent park, where the discordant blat of the coacher, softened by the harmony distance lends, lulls his aching soul into sweet oblivion. To him the swinging doors of the hot sausage grotto are closed until after the paper has gone to press, and the harsh refrain of the milk cart carols the dawn of a newborn day.

Week after week, month after month, adown the schedule's weary length, he sits behind a wire screen in sunshine, wind and fog, envied by penury's legion mob because he gets a front seat at each and every game for nothing. Little they know of his inward workings; of the endless conflict between three meals per diem and surcease from carking care, and which is always decided from day to day in favor of victuals.

They know not of the moments when he lapses into a reverie of the happy past, long before he aspired to doubtful journalism and carfare to and from the grounds, only to be yanked back to the dull routine of his job by the vicious swat of a hot ground ball and the imperative duty of thinking for the public, prints some scintillating baseball bon mots that have never been thunk before.

Then, after a neat but not gaudy dinner in an obscure joint unknown to fame, he is once more thrown in the convulsive paroxysms of labored composition. These are the moments that make his tired ache, as it were, and extends the hairless area he is cultivating at the apex of his dome of thought. Quaint qualifying adjectives and felicitous similes that appear from time to time do not flow with that spontaneity which characterizes the acceptance of an invitation to have something with a man who has credit or the price. They might occur in one or two games, but not ad infinitum that anybody knows of.

If these inside facts were generally known, those who take an interest in baseball as she is played here, would go to the park and think for themselves, provided they could hold up under the strain. This would confer a great favor, besides saving much valuable space that could be turned to good account for advertising purposes or the expose of shady municipal transactions.
[Morning Call (San Francisco), October 5, 1891]

21. Recap

Reader, our journey through the early years of baseball journalism draws to a close. Looking back at this brief, but extraordinary phenomenon that once stood traditional baseball reporting on its head begs several questions: How did it arise and prosper, why did it die out and what was learned from it?

Birth and Development

This offbeat, "the-game-as-it-was-writ-funny" movement arose during the explosive growth of the national pastime in the late 1880s. Central to its origin was a core of baseball writers who, perhaps stimulated by the energy surrounding the sport, came up with a new and novel way to elevate the description of the usual drudgery of play-by-play action of a ball game to a higher plane of enjoyment, namely, to inform and amuse at the same time. Basic to its creation and success, of course, was the ability to write in this manner, which was more an inherent, unteachable talent that not all writers possessed, thus limiting the numbers who could participate in its expansion.

Needless to say, its emergence in the early 1890s was met with overwhelming and enthusiastic favorability by baseball fans, and the word disseminated quickly. This was facilitated by a telegraphic transmission mechanism that interconnected newspaper offices nationally called "exchanges," which conveyed articles of wide-ranging subject matter appearing in other publications.

To handle the flow, newsrooms often employed "exchange editors," whose sole task was to sort through the daily deluge of messages and route them to appropriate departments for possible re-publication, including sporting desks. By this handy means of communication, it was common practice for sporting editors to pass on noteworthy, cleverly composed game accounts, accompanied by comments of bemused wonderment and awe, to counterparts on other papers as a matter of interest, thus publicizing this "crazy-funny" writing.

Some idea of the success of this method can be found in the case of baseball writer Leonard Washburne of the (Chicago) *Inter Ocean* (see Chapter 5), who first cut loose with his electric prose in

1890. It brought him almost instant national recognition and praise, which was documented in a memoriam following his death in 1891 when the following excerpts from other newspapers was printed:

Rockford (Illinois) Evening Republican: ...The work done in base-ball reports during the past season gave him a high reputation throughout the country.

Indianapolis News: ...(his writing) was the most original and entertaining, and during the past season his writings have been more extensively copied than those of any other writer.
[Inter Ocean (Chicago), October 19, 1891]

"Nothing in the line of base ball reporting has ever excited the wide interest which Washburn's work did for its original humor and graphic descriptions."
[Mitchell (S. D.) Daily Republican, October 10, 1891]

Lastly, a late homage:

"It was he who invented much of the original and bizarre expressions that are used in the stories and reports of baseball. His work on the Inter Ocean attracted universal attention and made that paper unusually popular in the sporting world."
[Kansas City Star, reprinted in the Wichita Daily Eagle April 12, 1903]

Baseball writers of this era were always on the lookout for any fresh journalistic gimmickry that might polish their reputation and sell more newspapers. Thus, in this way, Washburne's celebrity also acted as an inspiration to other writers; some even mimicked his creative genius as best they could. It is interesting to note that in the post-Washburne period at the *Inter Ocean*, game write-ups continued with the same wildly eccentric flair for the next six years, as if to honor the master and maintain the tradition he had established.
Clearly, the movement brought success to both baseball writer and his employer, the newspaper. It is impossible to assess the nationwide extent of this style of reporting during its glory days of the 1890s, owing to the relative paucity of old newspaper archives available today for research. However, the fact that its discovery for variable lengths of time in thirty-eight newspapers across the

country during this decade attests to its far-reaching use, proving, at least in baseball, humor sells.

Fading Out

But, all things, however good, stale with time. It is a fact of life. One can only assume that the luster wore off and, by the new century, with Charles Dryden as its sole standard-bearer, it was discarded as old-fashioned. Baseball had outgrown its need.

Retro Journalism?

Could baseball writing like this be resurrected today with any hope of success? Or are fans to forever suffer the same fate as classical music lovers, who replay masterpieces of the past because a second coming of a Mozart or Beethoven is never to be?

It's an intriguing thought. With modern American society's penchant for revisiting past clothing fashions and interior decor, even remaking old movies, for example, perhaps baseball fans would greatly appreciate it, but would any writer with a wicked bent be daring enough to give it a go?

The talent is there—it always has been for well over a century now. All that is needed is to pierce the protective shell of journalistic norms, harness the imagination and release the creative juices within, for it is carved into a bleacher board somewhere: Baseball humor waits for no one.

It is heady stuff to think of projecting the vivid, image-provoking language of old into a modern-day context. Those who appreciate it wait impatiently and expectantly for the day when they open the sports page and read catchy lines, even in defeat, such as: *"Gordon romped down to second like a singed cat"* or *"Arrieta had a drop of a professional lyncher"*? or, better yet, *"Errors are as common to Villar as pig tracks in an Arkansas swamp."*

It is food for the baseball soul. No question.

About the Author

A Washington State native by birth, Gerard S. Petrone is an 80-year-old retired physician who lives in San Diego with his wife Pam, two spoiled Welsh Corgis, and a cage full of very loud parakeets. His interest in baseball dates to his childhood when he enjoyed brief glory in the summer of 1952 as a terror on the mound in the Under-14 League in Tacoma. In recent years, Petrone has confined his baseball research exclusively to the 19th Century, irresistibly drawn to the period by its zany lawlessness, rough-and-tumble ways, and host of unforgettable characters.

www.ingramcontent.com/pod-product-compliance
Lightning Source LLC
Chambersburg PA
CBHW070733170426
43200CB00007B/516